# Spring MVC Blueprints

Design and implement real-world web-based applications
using the Spring Framework 4.x specification based on
technical documentation

**Sherwin John Calleja Tragura**

BIRMINGHAM - MUMBAI

# Spring MVC Blueprints

Copyright © 2016 Packt Publishing

First published: July 2016

Production reference: 1250716

Published by Packt Publishing Ltd.

Livery Place

35 Livery Street

Birmingham B3 2PB, UK.

ISBN 978-1-78588-827-4

www.packtpub.com

# Credits

**Author**

Sherwin John Calleja Tragura

**Reviewer**

Samer ABDELKAFI

**Commissioning Editor**

Priya Singh

**Acquisition Editor**

Smeet Thakkar

**Content Development Editor**

Zeeyan Pinheiro

**Technical Editors**

Abhishek Kotian

Vivek Pala

**Copy Editor**

Safis Editing

**Project Coordinator**

Suzanne Coutinho

**Proofreader**

Safis Editing

**Indexer**

Rekha Nair

**Production Coordinator**

Aparna Bhagat

**Cover Work**

Aparna Bhagat

# About the Author

**Sherwin John Calleja Tragura** started his career as a student assistant and a mathematics tutor during his college years at the University of the Philippines Los Baños, Laguna, Philippines. With meager resources, he graduated as a Department of Science and Technology (DOST) R.A. 7687 scholar under the bachelor of computer science degree. Immediately after graduation, he took up the offer to teach CMSC 150 (numerical and symbolic computation) at the Institute of Computer Science and completed his masters degree in computer science simultaneously. He became part of the International Rice Research Institute (IRRI) software team, which gave him the opportunity to use Struts, Spring, and RCP frameworks in many of its software projects.

Based on his experience at IRRI, he was given the opportunity to work as a Java analyst in various companies in Manila, such as ABSI, PHILAM- AIG, and Ayala Systems and Technology Inc. (ASTI). These companies have strengthened his skillset through training in Java and Java Enterprise platforms and some popular tools such as EMC Documentum and Alfresco Document and Records Management System. He got his first career certification in the EMC Documentum Proven Associate course (E20-120).

After a few years, he decided to become an independent consultant and trainer, providing services mostly on Java-based projects, Alfresco, and Apache OFBiz requirement. He started his venture as a Java-JEE Bootcamp with 77Global and is currently the trainer at Software Laboratory Inc. (SLI), Alibata Business and Technology Services Inc., and Nityo Infotech, Philippines. He also conducts training and talks around the Philippines such as in Cebu City and Tacloban City.

Sherwin has contributed as a technical reviewer on various books by Packt Publishing, these include: *Delphi Cookbook*, *Alfresco 3 Records Management*, *Alfresco Share*, and *Mastering Hibernate*. He owes everything to Packt Publishing with the unforgettable experiences on technical editing tasks, which have been an essential part of his career.

As an Oracle Certified Associate and Java SE 7 Programmer (1Z0-803), author will continue his mandate as a technical trainer, developer, architect, and designer to help the industry improve its standards on information technology. He will always be the epitome of honor, excellence, and service when it comes to software development and business intelligence.

*This book is dedicated to my father, Cesar Tragura, who passed away on July 8, 2016 while I was adding the finishing touch to this book. I am greatly saddened about your sudden passing, but I know, after all, that you are happy for my first book, and you will always be happy for me and my brother. Thank you for all the memories. Goodbye.*

# About the Reviewer

**Samer ABDELKAFI** has over 10 years of experience as a software architect and engineer.

He has contributed to numerous and diverse projects (web applications, data integration, batch, security solutions, web services, and many more) in different sectors, such as banking, insurance, education, public services, and utility billing.

In his free time, he enjoys blogging and sharing his experience on his site (`https://samer abdelkafi.wordpress.com`).

# www.PacktPub.com

For support files and downloads related to your book, please visit www.PacktPub.com.

## eBooks, discount offers, and more

Did you know that Packt offers eBook versions of every book published, with PDF and ePub files available? You can upgrade to the eBook version at www.PacktPub.com and as a print book customer, you are entitled to a discount on the eBook copy. Get in touch with us at customercare@packtpub.com for more details.

At www.PacktPub.com, you can also read a collection of free technical articles, sign up for a range of free newsletters and receive exclusive discounts and offers on Packt books and eBooks.

https://www2.packtpub.com/books/subscription/packtlib

Do you need instant solutions to your IT questions? PacktLib is Packt's online digital book library. Here, you can search, access, and read Packt's entire library of books.

## Why subscribe?

- Fully searchable across every book published by Packt
- Copy and paste, print, and bookmark content
- On demand and accessible via a web browser

## Free access for Packt account holders

Get notified! Find out when new books are published by following @PacktEnterprise on Twitter or the Packt Enterprise Facebook page.

# Table of Contents

# Preface

Many books have been written about Spring Framework that discuss its design patterns and principles, core components, and coding standards and styles, as well as the configuration details of its container, all of which provide a good start to creating a web application. Some literature focuses more on the new features of every release and provides a marketing model for how Spring can help boost the software industry. There are a few that serve as a cookbook of Spring definitions and components for advanced users. Rarely are books written that provide readers with all the core concepts of the Spring specification in collaboration with the most common and popular software libraries, plugins, or frameworks needed to create software with optimal, if not fast, performance, efficient and effective workflows, clever data presentation and business intelligence, standardized graphical user interfaces, and testable, robust, and simple architecture.

This book offers 10 chapters that aim to provide a full guide to maximizing the features of Spring in order to provide technical solutions to some needs from different areas of discipline. It consists of basic concepts about how to start implementing and deploying Spring applications. It provides some new workarounds to Spring users and poses open-ended questions to advanced developers to continue doing research on the Spring 4.x specification.

Writing this book was time consuming since each chapter has its own dedicated software blueprint to be implemented in order to exhibit all the concepts elaborated in the chapters. Not only the results, but also the technical issues and bugs have been taken into consideration to check whether all functional specifications can fit into one project with the correct API library versions available. Due to time constraints, not all software blueprints are as good as finished products yet, but they are fully executable specimens for the book, covering all the details of the Spring 4.x framework.

## What this book covers

Chapter 1, *Creating a Personal Web Portal (PWP)*, highlights the Inverse of Control (IoC) and Dependency Injection (DI) design patterns of the Spring 4.x MVC architecture. All classes and interfaces of Spring 4.x specification, which create the types of controllers, models, and views, including their validators and property editors, are explained by implementing a Personal Web Portal (PWP) prototype that uses only @ModelAttribute and @SessionAttributes to transport and store data through Spring's common page navigations and redirections. Spring MVC applications, Maven deployment and core coding standards are also taken into consideration during prototype development.

Chapter 2, *Electronic Document Management Systems (EDMS)*, focuses on how Spring can handle file upload and download in preparation for some custom document or record management portal development. Through the implementation of a prototype, this chapter discusses how to use Spring's `MultipartFile` interface together with `HttpServletRequest` and `MultipartHttpServletRequest` for processing documents of any rendition type, with or without encryption/decryption. Also, part of the chapter covers how clients can upload or download file to and from FTP server and how Spring container manage file repository transactions using client-side components such as AJAX.

Chapter 3, *Student Management Portal (SMP)*, showcases the data modeling part of Spring through the use of standard JDBC interfaces and popular object-relational mapping (ORM) frameworks such as Hibernate 4.x and MyBatis 3.x. Moreover, it also includes JPA configuration to add data persistency to the project. Although this chapter focuses heavily on container configuration, it manages to tackle how to generate data model entities through Spring annotations and map form models to views through Spring's standard tag libraries. On the side, it also demonstrates how to attach auditing functionality through the use of logging framework Log4J and/or Logback.

Chapter 4, *Human Resource Management System (HRMS)*, focuses on writing applications that deal with voluminous data presentation and automated reports with some business intelligence, like that of the HRMS. The prototype provides a mechanism to generate `.pdf`, `.doc`, and `.xls` reports through `ContentNegotiatingViewResolver` and other related view APIs. For common plugins, HRMS has a functionality that generates those documents through the use of POI and iText libraries. For colorful graphs and charts, this chapter includes GoogleChart and JFreeChart as the main libraries in HRMS for generating data visualizations from hardcoded or database records. Popular enterprise report generation tools such as JasperReports and DynamicReports are also part of the app. On the side, this chapter manages to include exception handling and unit testing in Spring.

Chapter 5, *Customer Feedback System (CFS)*, provides the mechanism to protect application such as CFS from spammers and bots. Applications such as forums or survey portals mainly implement CAPTCHA to prevent unwanted or automated spamming. In this chapter, Spring uses some of the popular CAPTCHA solutions, namely reCaptcha, JCaptcha, SimpleCaptcha, Kaptcha, and BotDetect, to enable protection for CFS. On the side, CFS has a Contact Us functionality that uses SendGrid to manage, secure, and monitor suspicious inbound and outbound e-mail traffic through its email server.

Chapter 6, *Hotel Management System (HMS)*, explains how to build adaptive and responsive web pages in applications that use the Spring framework. The chapter offers different solutions on how to make applications look friendly on mobile, tablets, and desktops. For intelligent themes, this chapter highlights ThemeResolver to play around with static resources (for example, CSS, JavaScript, and images) of the pages. On creating Single Page Applications (SPA), the chapter discusses using JavaScript objects in ExtJS and AngularJS to process data from the Spring MVC layers. On the other hand, the responsiveness of the HMS pages is discussed further using Twitter Bootstrap and Kickstrap, together with the adaptive tile templates created by Sitemesh and Tiles Framework. Spring integration, Thymeleaf and Spring Mobile is also included in this chapter.

Chapter 7, *Online Cart System (OCS)*, emphasizes workflows and security by creating a prototype of one of the market's popular solution, the e-commerce application. Aside from custom navigations shown in the previous chapters, this chapter illustrates other smart and advanced solutions to implement formalized business processes through Activiti BPMN 2.0, Spring Web Flow, and Portlet MVC Framework. This chapter also manages to get into the details of Spring Security to provide a comprehensive security solution for any Spring application.

Chapter 8, *Enterprise Resource Planning (ERP)*, helps create software that builds business processes through remote transactions web services just such as an ERP system. This chapter provides a skeleton for how to design interconnected Spring projects through RESTful and SOAP-based services. To start with, the projects have a simple @RestController implementation of the REST web service and we proceed to expand on some advanced integrations with JAX-WS, JAX-RS, Spring WS, CXF, Axis2, and XFire. On the other hand, the ERP successfully integrates Hessian, Burlap, and HttpInvoker to implement remote services between modules. AMQP and JMS have been integrated into this chapter to implement a thin layer of messaging protocol for event handling. This chapter also has side discussions on the 0Auth protocol for adding features on login authentication through Facebook and Twitter Spring Social modules.

Chapter 9, *Bus Ticketing Management System (BTS)*, implements browser-based applications using the Spring MVC specification. Not heavily loaded with Spring components, this chapter is streamlined to use JQuery, Prototype, DWR, and Dojo for data processing and presentation to some applications with a wide range of users, such as BTS. The conversion of data to JSON and XML is also highlighted through the use of the JAXB marshaller for the former and JSON mapping for the latter. Moreover, the chapter promotes JQGrid for intelligent tabular data presentation and GoogleChart JavaScript APIs for data visualization.

Chapter 10, *Social Task Management System (STMS)*, finalizes the extensibility of Spring through the use of Spring Data and Spring Integration modules. This chapter proves that the functional specification of an application can make use of the core and advanced Spring components with fewer libraries. Compacted into one module, this chapter has two applications that have the data repository and service layers with lesser code and fewer processes webbed together using Spring Integration's channels, service activators, bridges, splitters, and aggregators. Moreover, it illustrates the process to produce web services using inbound gateways and consume RESTful and SOAP-based services using the outbound gateways of Spring Integration.

# What you need for this book

Firstly, this book is intended for readers who have a background at least in Java SDK programming. This book does not cover anything about how to start dealing with Java as a language. Secondly, each chapter of this book enumerates the technical requirement to execute the respective Eclipse projects, but the following are the overall general requirements that the user must have:

- Any machine with at least 4 GB of RAM
- Java SDK 1.7.x
- Maven 3.2.x
- Eclipse STS 3.6 or higher
- Apache Tomcat 7.x
- Apache Solr 5.4
- Neo4J CE 2.2.10
- Apache ActiveMQ 5.2.x
- Apache Pluto 2.0.3
- RabbitMQ 3.5.6
- Erlang 7.1
- MongoDB 3.2
- MySQL 5.6
- VisualVM
- SoapUI 5.2.1
- iReport 5.6.x
- Google Chrome or Mozilla Firefox browser

Lastly, upgrading Java, Maven, and Tomcat versions will require users to recompile the existing Eclipse projects with some changes in Maven library versions to resolve compatibility issues.

# Who this book is for

This book has all the chapters for software developers who want to start exploring the Spring framework from its core, for experienced users who want to know more about fine-tuning and integrating the framework to other popular plugins, software frameworks, or tools to solve their work-related requirements, and for experts who want to experiment more with its extensibility in building feasible workarounds and custom-based architecture to solve their respective projects. Each chapter showcases an enterprise application prototype that serves as a guide to illustrate the technical details of how to go about each chapter. It is advisable to accompany each chapter with the Eclipse projects created, which are available for download. Each project may not pass for final production, but is assured to be a finished specimen for the study.

Since this book is a compendium of all the core and advanced concepts of the Spring Framework specification, it is advisable for Spring newbies to read, understand, and crunch Chapters 1 and 3. It is recommended to study the Eclipse projects for each chapter in order to grasp fully the content of the book.

# Conventions

In this book, you will find a number of text styles that distinguish between different kinds of information. Here are some examples of these styles and an explanation of their meaning.

All Java codes, and some XML configurations are written in this style:

```
package org.packt.edms.portal.model.form;
import java.util.List;
import org.springframework.web.multipart.MultipartFile;
public class MultipleFilesUploadForm {
    private List<MultipartFile> files;
    public List<MultipartFile> getFiles() {
        return files;
    }
    public void setFiles(List<MultipartFile> files) {
        this.files = files;
    }
}
```

The JavaScript codes of the book are written in this style:

```
<script type="text/javascript">
define(["dojo/request/xhr","dojo/dom","dojo/on","dojo/domReady!"],
       function(xhr,dom,on){
          var tripId = $('#tripid').val();
          var param = '{ id: tripId }';
          function listDestinations(){ // see the sources    }
            on(dom.byId("custSearchBtn"),
                   "click",callAjaxListing);    } );
</script>
```

Pure HTML codes use it's a style like this:

```
<body>
  <div id="sf-wrapper">
    <div class="container-fluid">
        <div class="row-fluid">
            <div class="span12"> <!--  see the sources -->
        </div></div></div></div>
  </body>
```

There will be a highlight on certain areas of the code whenever a point is being pointed out:

```
Login user = loginDao.getLogin(username.trim());
        try {
         boolean enabled = true;
           boolean accountNonExpired = true;
           boolean credentialsNonExpired = true;
           boolean accountNonLocked = true;
           return new CustomerUserDetails
               (user.getUsername(),user.getEncPassword(), enabled,
                accountNonExpired,credentialsNonExpired,
                accountNonLocked,getAuthorities(user.getId(),
                loginDao.getUserRoleIds(user.getId()))));
        } catch (Exception e) {
           throw new RuntimeException(e);
        }
```

The view names and other general links are written in this style: /ocs/login.html

Filesystem paths, and some API classes and interfaces are in strong style:

**/bpmn/cartevents.bpmn20.xml**

**Server issues**, **errors**, and **exceptions** are written in screen text style.

Warnings or important notes appear in a box like this.

 Tips and tricks appear like this.

# Reader feedback

Feedback from our readers is always welcome. Let us know what you think about this book—what you liked or disliked. Reader feedback is important for us as it helps us develop titles that you will really get the most out of.

To send us general feedback, simply e-mail feedback@packtpub.com, and mention the book's title in the subject of your message.

If there is a topic that you have expertise in and you are interested in either writing or contributing to a book, see our author guide at www.packtpub.com/authors.

# Customer support

Now that you are the proud owner of a Packt book, we have a number of things to help you to get the most from your purchase.

# Downloading the example code

You can download the example code files for this book from your account at http://www.packtpub.com. If you purchased this book elsewhere, you can visit http://www.packtpub.com/support and register to have the files e-mailed directly to you.

You can download the code files by following these steps:

1. Log in or register to our website using your e-mail address and password.
2. Hover the mouse pointer on the **SUPPORT** tab at the top.
3. Click on **Code Downloads & Errata**.
4. Enter the name of the book in the **Search** box.

5. Select the book for which you're looking to download the code files.
6. Choose from the drop-down menu where you purchased this book from.
7. Click on **Code Download**.

You can also download the code files by clicking on the **Code Files** button on the book's webpage at the Packt Publishing website. This page can be accessed by entering the book's name in the Search box. Please note that you need to be logged in to your Packt account.

Once the file is downloaded, please make sure that you unzip or extract the folder using the latest version of:

- WinRAR / 7-Zip for Windows
- Zipeg / iZip / UnRarX for Mac
- 7-Zip / PeaZip for Linux

The code bundle for the book is also hosted on GitHub at `https://github.com/PacktPu blishing/springmvcblueprints`. We also have other code bundles from our rich catalog of books and videos available at `https://github.com/PacktPublishing/`. Check them out!

# Errata

Although we have taken every care to ensure the accuracy of our content, mistakes do happen. If you find a mistake in one of our books—maybe a mistake in the text or the code—we would be grateful if you could report this to us. By doing so, you can save other readers from frustration and help us improve subsequent versions of this book. If you find any errata, please report them by visiting `http://www.packtpub.com/submit-errata`, selecting your book, clicking on the Errata Submission Form link, and entering the details of your errata. Once your errata are verified, your submission will be accepted and the errata will be uploaded to our website or added to any list of existing errata under the Errata section of that title.

To view the previously submitted errata, go to `https://www.packtpub.com/books/con tent/support` and enter the name of the book in the search field. The required information will appear under the Errata section.

# Piracy

Piracy of copyrighted material on the Internet is an ongoing problem across all media. At Packt, we take the protection of our copyright and licenses very seriously. If you come across any illegal copies of our works in any form on the Internet, please provide us with the location address or website name immediately so that we can pursue a remedy.

Please contact us at `copyright@packtpub.com` with a link to the suspected pirated material.

We appreciate your help in protecting our authors and our ability to bring you valuable content.

# Questions

If you have a problem with any aspect of this book, you can contact us at `questions@packtpub.com`, and we will do our best to address the problem.

# 1
# Creating a Personal Web Portal (PWP)

This chapter is all about creating a robust and simple personal web portal that can serve as a personal web page, or a professional reference site, for anyone. Usually, these kinds of websites are used as mashups, or dashboards, of centralized sources of information describing an individual or group.

Technically, a personal web portal is a composition of web components like CSS, HTML, and JavaScript, woven together to create a formal, simple or exquisite presentation of any content. It can be used, in its simplest form, as a personal portfolio or an enterprise form like an e-commerce content management system. Commercially, these portals are drafted and designed using the principles of the Rich-client platform or responsive web designs. In the industry, most companies suggest that clients try easy-to-use-tools like PHP frameworks (for example, **CodeIgniter**, **Laravel**, **Drupal**) and seldom advise using JEE-based portals.

Aside from the software processes and techniques that will be discussed in this chapter, the main goal is for the reader to have a quick but detailed review of the main recipe of Spring MVC 4.x implementation, and to know the importance of **Java Enterprise Edition** (**JEE**) concepts behind any Java Enterprise frameworks.

In this chapter, you will learn how to:

- Implement a complete Spring MVC framework
- Configure DispatcherServlet in a Spring MVC project
- Learn types of controllers and their current features
- Use controller annotations
- Map URLs to controllers

- Use different types of models in dispatching objects
- Validate form domain objects using Validator
- Convert and transform request parameter values into other object types
- Configure views
- Configure and implement e-mail transactions
- Deploy Spring MVC projects

# Overview of the project

The **personal web portal (PWP)** created publishes a simple biography, and professional information, one can at least share through the Web. The prototype is a session-driven one that can do dynamic transactions, like updating information on the web pages, and posting notes on the page without using any back-end database.

Through using wireframes, below are the initial drafts and design of the web portal:

- **The Home Page**: This is the first page of the site that shows updatable quotes, and inspiring messages coming from the owner of the portal. It contains a sticky-note feature at the side that allows visitors to post their short greetings to the owner in real-time.

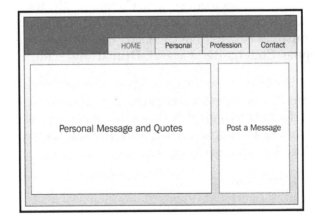

- **The Personal Information Page**: This page highlights personal information of the owner including the owner's name, age, hobbies, birth date, and age. This page contains part of the blogger's educational history. The content is dynamic and can be updated at any time by the owner.

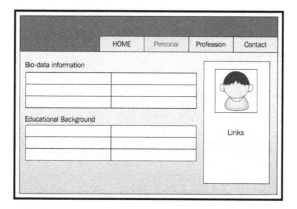

- **The Professional Information Page**: This page presents details about the owner's career background. It lists down all the previous jobs of the account owner, and enumerates all skills-related information. This content is also updatable.

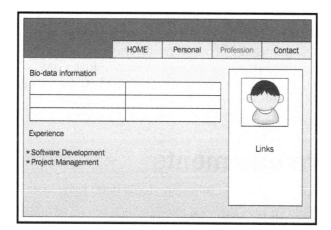

- **The Reach Out Page**: This serves as the contact information page of the owner. Moreover, it allows visitors to send their contact information, and specifically their electronic mail address, to the portal owner.

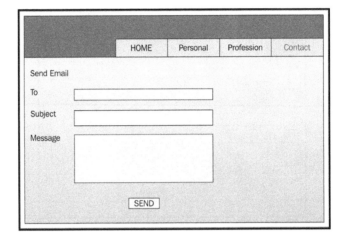

- **Update pages**: The **Home**, **Personal** and **Professional** pages have updateable pages for the owner to update the content of the portal. The prototype has the capability to update the information presented in the content at any time the user desires.

This simple prototype, called PWP, will give clear steps on how to build personal sites, from the ground up, using Spring MVC 4.x specifications. It will give enthusiasts the opportunity to start creating Spring-based web portals in just a day, without using any database backend. To those who are new to the Spring MVC 4.x concept, this chapter will be a good start in building full-blown portal sites.

# Technical requirements

In order to start the development, the following tools need to be installed onto the platform:

- Java Development Kit (JDK) 1.7.x
- Spring Tool Suite (Eclipse) 3.6
- Maven 3.x
- Spring Framework 4.1
- Apache Tomcat 7.x

- Any operating system

First, the JDK 1.7.x installer must be installed. Visit the site `http://www.oracle.com/tec` `hnetwork/java/javase/downloads/jdk7-downloads-1880260.html` to download the installer.

Next, set up the Spring Tool Suite 3.6 (Eclipse-based) which will be the official Integrated Development Environment (IDE) of this book. Download the Spring Tool Suite 3.6 at `https` `://spring.io/tools/sts`.

# Setting-up the development environment

This book recommends the **Spring Tool Suite** (**Eclipse**) 3.6 since it has all the Spring Framework 4.x plug-ins, and other dependencies needed by the projects. To start us off, the following image shows the dashboard of the STS IDE:

Conversely, Apache Maven 3.x will be used to build and deploy the project for this chapter. Apache Maven is a software project management and comprehension tool. Based on the concept of a **project object model** (**POM**), Maven can manage a project's build, reporting and documentation from a central piece of information (`https://maven.apache.org/`).

There is already a Maven plugin installed in the STS IDE that can be used to generate the needed development directory structure. Among the many ways to create Spring MVC projects, this chapter focuses on two styles, namely:

- Converting a dynamic web project to a Maven specimen
- Creating a Maven project from scratch

# Converting a dynamic web project to a Maven project

To start creating the project, press *CTRL + N* to browse the menu wizard of the IDE. This menu wizard contains all the types of project modules you'll need to start a project. The menu wizard should look similar to the following screenshot:

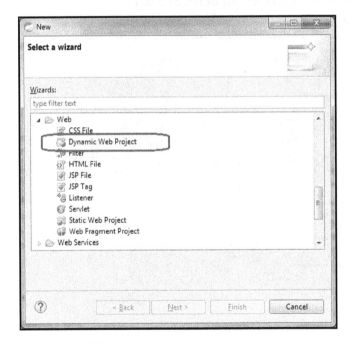

Once on the menu, browse the **Web** option and choose **Dynamic Web Project**. Afterwards, just follow the series of instructions to create the chosen project module until you reached the last menu wizard, which looks like the following figure:

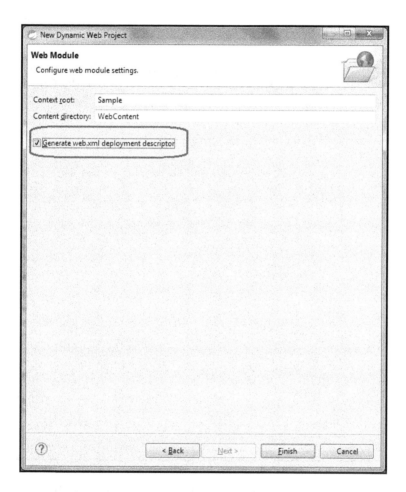

This last instruction (**Web Module** panel) will auto-generate the deployment descriptor (web.xml) of the project. Always click on the **Generate web-xml deployment descriptor** checkbox option. The deployment descriptor is an XML file that must reside inside the /WEB-INF/ folder of all JEE projects. This file describes how a component, module or application can be deployed. A JEE project must always be in the web.xml file otherwise the project will be defective.

Since the Spring 4.x container supports the Servlet Specification 3.0 in Tomcat 7 and above, `web.xml` is no longer mandatory and can be replaced by `org.springframework.web.servlet.support.AbstractAnnotat ionConfigDispatcherServletInitializer` or `org.springframework.web.servlet.support.AbstractDispatche rServletInitializer` class.

The next major step is to convert the newly created dynamic web project to a Maven one. To complete the conversion, right-click on the project and navigate to the **Configure | Convert Maven Project** command set, as shown in the following image:

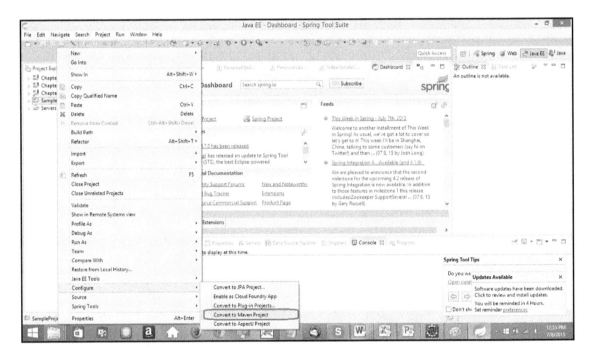

It is always best for the developer to study the directory structure of the project folder created before the actual implementation starts. The following is the directory structure of the Maven project after the conversion:

The project directories are just like the usual Eclipse dynamic web project without the
`pom.xml` file.

# Creating a Maven project from scratch

Another method of creating a Spring MVC web project is by creating a Maven project from
the start. Be sure to install the Maven 3.2 plugin in STS Eclipse. Browse the menu wizard
again, and locate the **Maven** option. Click on the **Maven Project** to generate a new Maven
project.

After clicking this option, a wizard will pop up, asking if an archetype is needed or not to create the Maven project. An archetype is a Maven plugin whose main objective is to create a project structure as per its template. To start quickly, choose an archetype plugin to create a simple Java application here. It is recommended to create the project using the archetype `maven-archetype-webapp`. However, skipping the archetype selection can still be a valid option.

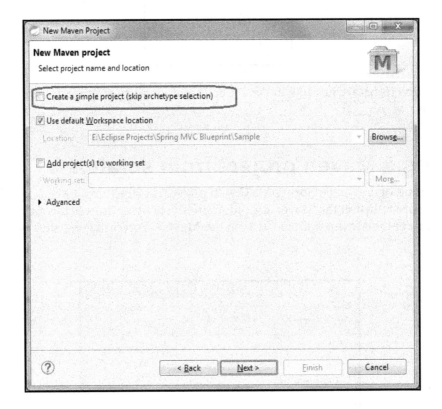

After you've done this, proceed with the **Select an Archetype** window shown in the following screenshot. Locate `maven-archetype-webapp` then proceed with the last process.

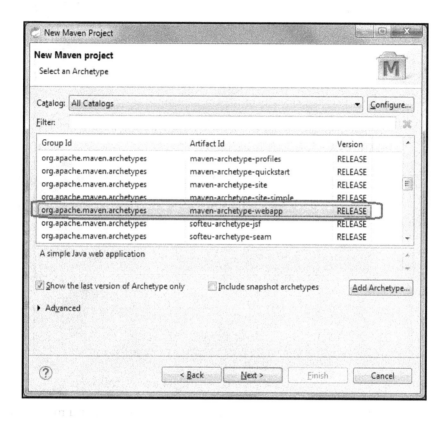

The selection of the Archetype `maven-archetype-webapp` will require the input of Maven parameters before ending the whole process with a new Maven project:

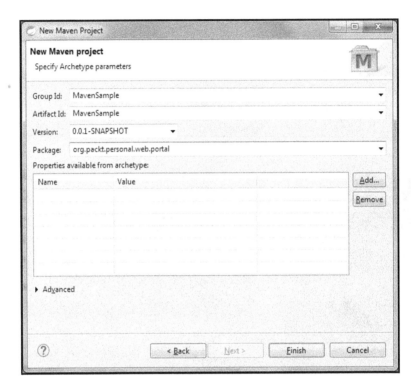

The required parameters for the Maven group or project are as follows:

- Group ID (`groupId`): This is the ID of the project's group and must be unique among all the project's groups.
- Artifact ID (`artifactId`): This is the ID of the project. This is generally the name of the project.
- Version (`version`): This is the version of the project.
- Package (`package`): The initial or core package of the sources.

For more information on Maven plugin and configuration details, visit the documentation and samples on the site `http://maven.apache.org/`.

After providing the Maven parameters, the project source folder structure will be similar to the following screenshot:

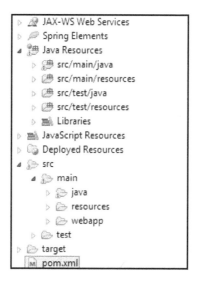

# The pom.xml file

The basic fundamental unit of work in Maven is the pom.xml file. This XML file is the main part of the Maven project folder structure, and is always located in the base directory of the project. The file contains all the necessary archetype plugins and dependencies for project building and deployment.

The PWP has this pom.xml file that builds sources, creates project WAR files, and deploys the projects with web.xml to the Tomcat server.

```xml
<project xmlns="http://maven.apache.org/POM/4.0.0"
xmlns:xsi="http://www.w3.org/2001/XMLSchema-instance"
xsi:schemaLocation="http://maven.apache.org/POM/4.0.0
http://maven.apache.org/xsd/maven-4.0.0.xsd">
   <modelVersion>4.0.0</modelVersion>
   <groupId>org.packt.spring.codes</groupId>
   <artifactId>ChapterOne</artifactId>
   <version>0.0.1-SNAPSHOT</version>
   <packaging>war</packaging>
   <name>ChapterOne</name>
   <description>Personal Web Portal</description>
```

```xml
<!-- properties -->
<properties>
  <spring.version>4.1.2.RELEASE</spring.version>
  <servlet.api.version>3.1.0</servlet.api.version>
</properties>
<!-- dependencies -->

<dependencies>
  <dependency>
  <groupId>javax.mail</groupId>
  <artifactId>mail</artifactId>
  <version>1.4.3</version>
</dependency>

<dependency>
  <groupId>org.springframework</groupId>
  <artifactId>spring-core</artifactId>
  <version>${spring.version}</version>
</dependency>

<dependency>
  <groupId>org.springframework</groupId>
  <artifactId>spring-beans</artifactId>
  <version>${spring.version}</version>
</dependency>

<!-- Rest of the dependencies in sources -->
</dependencies>

<build>
  <finalName>spring-mvc-maven-webapp-from-scratch</finalName>
    <plugins>
      <!-- Apache Tomcat 7 Maven Plugin -->
      <--
      <plugin>
        <groupId>org.apache.tomcat.maven</groupId>
        <artifactId>tomcat7-maven-plugin</artifactId>
        <version>2.2</version>
        <configuration>

          <url>http://localhost:8080/manager/text</url>
          <path>/ch01</path>
          <username>admin</username>
          <password>admin</password>
        </configuration>
      </plugin>
      -->
      <plugin>
```

```
      <groupId>org.apache.maven.plugins</groupId>
      <artifactId>maven-compiler-plugin</artifactId>
      <version>3.1</version>
      <configuration>
        <source>1.7</source>
        <target>1.7</target>
      </configuration>
    </plugin>
    <!-- Mojo Maven Plugin -->
      <plugin>
        <groupId>org.codehaus.mojo</groupId>
        <artifactId>tomcat-maven-plugin</artifactId>
        <version>1.1</version>
        <configuration>
          <url>http://localhost:8080/manager/text</url>
          <server>TomcatServer</server>
          <path>/ch01</path>
        </configuration>
      </plugin>
    </plugins>
  </build>
</project>
```

After setting the development and deployment environment, it is time to start configuring out the Spring MVC component of PWP.

# Project deployment

Apache Tomcat 7 will be used as the application server for this chapter. There are two popular Maven plugins that can be used to deploy applications to Tomcat: the Apache Maven plugin and the Mojo Maven plugin. By default, this book uses the Mojo Maven plugin.

To deploy a Maven project to Tomcat using the Mojo Maven plugin, the following configuration must be followed:

1. Locate the `user/conf/tomcat-users.xml` file on the Tomcat server and add the desired user with administrator rights. Information like role, username and password of the added user must be added inside the `<tomcat-user>` tag. A sample configuration is shown in the following code snippet:

```
<role rolename="manager"/>
<role rolename="admin"/>
<user username="admin" password="admin"
```

```
roles="admin,manager "/>
```

- Now save the file.

2. Locate the `file ~/.m2/settings.xml` in Maven. If the file is non-existent, download Maven from its site and copy the `settings.xml` to `~/.m2`. Open the file and locate the `<servers>` tag. Insert the following tag inside the `<servers>` tag.

```xml
<server>
  <id>TomcatServer</id>
  <username>admin</username>
  <password>admin</password>
</server>
```

- The `<id>` is any desired name for the Tomcat server that will be later called by the `pom.xml` plugin for Tomcat 7. The `<username>` and `<password>` are the server credentials manually added in `/conf/tomcat-users.xml` above. Save the file.

3. Open `pom.xml` and add the following Maven plugin for Tomcat 7 server.

```xml
<plugin>
  <groupId>org.codehaus.mojo</groupId>
  <artifactId>tomcat-maven-plugin</artifactId>
  <version>1.1</version>
  <configuration>
    <url>http://localhost:8080/manager/text</url>
    <server>TomcatServer</server>
    <path>/ch01</path>
  </configuration>
</plugin>
```

The `<configuration>` settings contain information of where to deploy the project (`<url>`), what context root to use (`<path>/`), and the server name (`<server>`) used in the `settings.xml` file.

To deploy using the Apache Tomcat7 Maven plugin, the `<configuration>` tag only needs the `<username>` and `<password>` tags of the administration console, including the `<url>` and the `<path>`.

# Maven deployment process

All projects are deployed in the Tomcat 7 server using the Maven plugin installed in STS. Follow the steps below to properly deploy the Spring MVC projects.

1. Be sure to have a correctly configured Maven project with the appropriate POM configuration shown in the preceding figure.
2. Right-click on the project and locate **Run As** in the menu options. Then, locate **Maven build...** in the sub-menu option, to configure the Maven goals for the first time. Maven goal is a task or command that is executed to build and manage Maven projects.

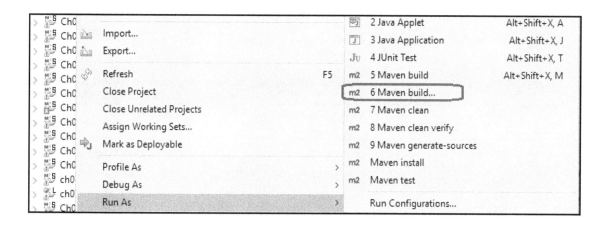

3. After this, a Maven configuration panel will pop up to write the needed goals for deployment, and to launch the deployment process. If the Mojo Maven plugin is used, write on the Goals textbox the following: clean install tomcat:deploy. If the Apache Tomcat7 Maven plugin is used, the goals must be: clean install tomcat7:deploy. Aside from these goals, there are some that can be essential for management like remove, update and re-deploy.

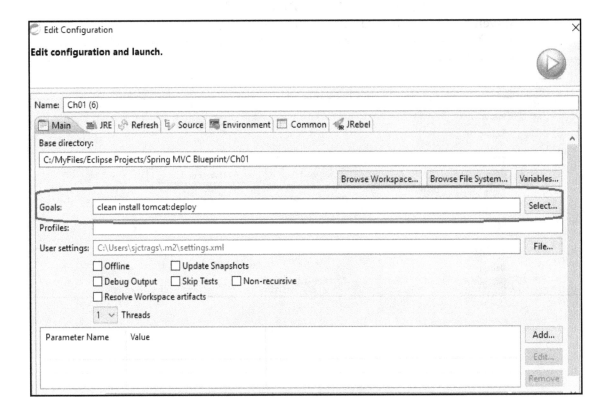

4. Click the **Run** button to launch the deployment. All the Maven execution logs will be shown on the console. The outcome of the deployment will be either a **BUILD SUCCESS** or a **BUILD FAILURE**.

# Project libraries and dependencies

Configure pom.xml to add the major Spring Framework 4.x libraries (JAR files) for the PWP project. These dependency modules are the following:

- **spring-core (Spring core module)**: This contains the core components of the framework which includes the Inverse of Control principle and Dependency Injection (DI).
- **spring-beans (Spring bean module)**: This contains the bean generation using BeanFactory and fetches injected beans using the method getBean().
- **spring-context (Spring context module)**: Built by the core and bean modules that provide the interfaces of ApplicationContext with some features like resource bundling, internationalization, and scheduling.
- **spring-context-support (Spring context support module)**: This module contains the classes needed for integrating third-party applications to a Spring Application Context.
- **spring-web**: This contains the web features of the Spring Framework which includes the initialization of the IoC container using servlet listeners and a web-oriented application context.
- **spring-webmvc (Spring MVC module)**: This is the module that has the MVC implementations and features.
- **spring-tx (Spring Transaction module)**: This contains transaction management on Bean object declarations with some special interfaces for all the POJO objects.

Aside from the other non-framework libraries, the following are auxiliary JAR files that support the Spring Framework 4.x core libraries:

- servlet-api: This contains all the classes and interfaces that describe the interaction between a servlet class and the runtime environment provided for the instance of a class within the bound of the servlet container.
- jsp-api: This contains all the classes that implement the JspPage interface.
- jstl: This contains all the classes and interfaces for Taglib support for all JSP pages.
- javax-mail: This provides a platform-independent and protocol-independent framework to build mail and messaging applications.
- javax.validation: This provides JSR-303 annotations for Java Bean validation.

All of these dependencies must be added to the pom.xml of the Maven project.

# Overview of the Spring MVC specification

The Spring MVC framework derives its specification from the **Model-View-Controller** (**MVC**) design pattern that separates the application into layers such as business, logic, navigation and presentation. The principle behind this design pattern is to create a de-coupled or loosely-coupled architecture, which is more flexible than the tightly-coupled frameworks.

Technically, Spring MVC works starts with a `DispatcherServlet` that dispatches requests to handlers, with configurable handler mappings, view resolution, locale, time zone and theme resolution, as well as support for uploading files. The default handler is based on the `@Controller` and `@RequestMapping` annotations, offering a wide range of flexible handling methods. With the introduction of Spring 3.0, the `@Controller` mechanism also allows you to create RESTful Web sites and applications, through the `@PathVariable` annotation and other features (`http://docs.spring.io/`).

The following diagram depicts how `DispatcherServlet` manages the whole MVC framework while, at the same time, avoiding the *Fat Controller syndrome*.

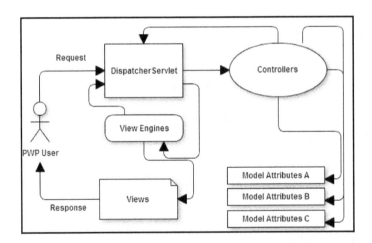

The `org.springframework.web.servlet.DispatcherServlet` is an actual servlet in the `web.xml` file of your web application, declared using the standard `servlet` tags. Just like any typical servlets, it recognizes request transactions through URL mappings. This servlet serves as the front controller of the whole MVC project.

Since this PWP project is written using the Spring Framework 4.x specification, the implementations always starts by declaring the `DispatcherServlet`.

# The project development

All the nuts and bolts involved in developing the PWP from scratch will be discussed in this topic. Each of the four web pages, including their internal processes, will be scrutinized using the codes of the project. The Spring MVC concepts will focus on the following areas:

- Configuration of `DispatcherServlet`
- Configuration of Spring container
- Creating controllers
- Types of attributes
- Validation
- Type conversion and transformation
- E-mail support configuration
- Views and `ViewResolvers`

# Configuring the DispatcherServlet

We start creating the Spring MVC project by configuring the DispatcherServlet API class. The Spring MVC framework has the `DispatcherServlet` at the center of all request and response transactions as illustrated in the preceding figure.

From the point of view of the PWP, the `DispatcherServlet` starts receiving requests when the user starts running pages on the web browser. The processes are enumerated as follows:

- When the container receives a request from a path, the `DispatcherServlet` checks whose controller is mapped to the path name.
- Then, the controller acknowledges the request with the appropriate service methods (for example, `GET`, `POST`, `PUT`, `HEAD`), executes the appropriate transaction method with the given model(s), and then returns the view name to the `DispatcherServlet`.
- Then, the `DispatcherServlet` checks which type of view resolver has been configured from its container. Through the view resolver, the `DispatcherServlet` will know the appropriate view that matches the given request.
- Finally, the `DispatcherServlet` will process the transport of model data to the view for presentation or rendition.

The PWP has the following configuration for the `DispatcherServlet`:

```xml
<?xml version="1.0" encoding="UTF-8"?>
<web-app xmlns:xsi="http://www.w3.org/2001/XMLSchema-instance"
  xmlns="http://java.sun.com/xml/ns/javaee"
  xmlns:web="http://java.sun.com/xml/ns/javaee/web-app_2_5.xsd"
  xsi:schemaLocation="http://java.sun.com/xml/ns/javaee
  http://java.sun.com/xml/ns/javaee/web-app_3_0.xsd"    id="WebApp_ID"
  version="3.0">
<display-name>ChapterOne</display-name>

<!-- Declare Spring DispatcherServlet -->
<servlet>
  <servlet-name>pwp</servlet-name>
  <servlet-class>
    org.springframework.web.servlet.DispatcherServlet
  </servlet-class>
</servlet>
<servlet-mapping>
  <servlet-name>pwp</servlet-name>
  <url-pattern>*.html</url-pattern>
</servlet-mapping>

<!-- Spring accepted extension declared here below -->
<mime-mapping>
  <extension>png</extension>
  <mime-type>image/png</mime-type>
</mime-mapping>

</web-app>
```

Just like any typical JEE servlet, the tags `<servlet>` and `<servlet-mapping>` are used to declare the dispatcher servlet `DispatcherServlet`:

```xml
<servlet>
  <servlet-name>pwp</servlet-name>
  <servlet-class>
    org.springframework.web.servlet.DispatcherServlet
  </servlet-class>
</servlet>
<servlet-mapping>
  <servlet-name>pwp</servlet-name>
  <url-pattern>*.html</url-pattern>
</servlet-mapping>
```

The `<servlet-name>` tag does not only stand for the name of the servlet, but is also related to the name of a Spring container which will be tackled later. The `<url-pattern>` indicates which type of valid URLs will be recognized by the `DispatcherServlet` during request-response transactions. In our preceding configuration, it shows that all URL must have an extension `.html` in order for the requests to be processed by the servlet.

When it comes to file types, the `DispatcherServlet` only considers content types declared with the `<mime-mapping>` tag. In this project, we only have PNG files needed by the portal.

```
<mime-mapping>
  <extension>png</extension>
  <mime-type>image/png</mime-type>
</mime-mapping>
```

# Creating the Spring container

After we've configured the `DispatcherServlet`, the Spring MVC container must be created. The interface `org.springframework.context.ApplicationContext` is Spring's more advanced container. The implementation of this object manages other objects of the portal application that will be known later as beans. All beans are injected into this container so that the portal will just "fetch" them once they are needed in several transactions.

There are two ways to create a Spring MVC container and these are:

- XML-based configuration
- JavaConfig-based configuration

# Spring container configuration using XML

Using our STS IDE, the ApplicationContext (`applicationContext.xml`) can be created using the Spring Eclipse plugin. Following is the menu wizard showing the plugin for the Spring Framework module:

On the wizard, click on the **Spring Bean Configuration File** option which will guide you to the next instruction panel. This is the selection of the XSD namespaces needed by the `applicationContext.xml` for the Spring components.

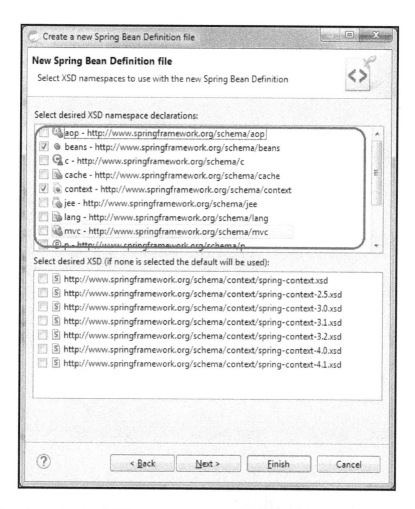

After choosing the necessary XSD namespaces needed for bean injections and configurations, the PWP's XML-based container will look like the following configuration:

```xml
<?xml version="1.0" encoding="UTF-8"?>
<beans xmlns="http://www.springframework.org/schema/beans"
   xmlns:xsi="http://www.w3.org/2001/XMLSchema-instance"
   xmlns:aop="http://www.springframework.org/schema/aop"
   xmlns:context="http://www.springframework.org/schema/context"
   xmlns:oxm="http://www.springframework.org/schema/oxm"
   xmlns:tx="http://www.springframework.org/schema/tx"
   xmlns:mvc="http://www.springframework.org/schema/mvc"
   xsi:schemaLocation="http://www.springframework.org/schema/aop
http://www.springframework.org/schema/aop/spring-aop-4.1.xsd
```

```
http://www.springframework.org/schema/oxm
http://www.springframework.org/schema/oxm/spring-oxm-4.1.xsd
http://www.springframework.org/schema/beans
http://www.springframework.org/schema/beans/spring-beans-4.1.xsd
http://www.springframework.org/schema/tx
http://www.springframework.org/schema/tx/spring-tx-4.1.xsd
http://www.springframework.org/schema/context
http://www.springframework.org/schema/context/spring-context-4.1.xsd
http://www.springframework.org/schema/mvc
http://www.springframework.org/schema/mvc/spring-mvc-4.1.xsd">

    // all beans injected here
</beans>
```

The `applicationContext.xml` is loaded, accessed, and read by the `DispatcherServlet`. The convention used so the `DispatcherServlet` recognizes the container is to name our `applicationContext.xml` file using the format `dispatcherServletName-servlet.xml`, wherein the `dispatcherServletName` is the name indicated by the `<servlet-name>` tag:

```
<servlet>
  <servlet-name>pwp</servlet-name>
  <servlet-class>
    org.springframework.web.servlet.DispatcherServlet
  </servlet-class>
</servlet>
```

Thus, the PWP's `applicationContext.xml` file is named `pwp-servlet.xml`. The default filename of an XML-based Spring container must always follow the convention `[dispatcher-servlet-name]-servlet.xml`.

# Spring container configuration using JavaConfig

The other type of implementation of the Spring MVC container is through the `JavaConfig` classes. In the `JavaConfig` method, every component tag has its respective annotation equivalent. Following is the equivalent configuration of the preceding XML-based setup.

```
package org.packt.personal.web.portal.config;
import org.springframework.context.annotation.Configuration;

@Configuration
public class PersonalWebPortalConfig {   }
```

The @Configuration annotation indicates that this class contains one or more bean methods (usually getters) annotated with @Bean that returns manageable beans of the container. Some references call this class a configurator class.

The two implementations are incomparable, but some projects mix them. XML-based Spring MVC containers become cumbersome when the files get larger, while annotation-based ones can be managed since they are just POJO-based. JavaConfig is a better approach when it comes to using a **rapid application development (RAD)** strategy. The reason for this is that when the number of components in the project increases, JavaConfig can only just manage the dependencies among beans through autowiring, which the XML cannot impose since the codes are decoupled from the dependency injection process. Debugging is also easy, since bug detection will be done during compilation, unlike in the XML-style where errors will be detected right after the deployment or execution of the application.

On the issue of mixing them, the project must choose which configuration is going to be bootstrapped by the container. If it is the JavaConfig, it must use the @ImportResource to load all the injected beans from the XML:

```
@Configuration
@ImportResource("classpath:pws-servlet.xml")
public class PersonalWebPortalConfig {    }
```

If the XML-based configuration is used instead, the XML must use <context:component-scan="org.packt.personal.web.portal"/> to locate the @Configuration class and load all @Bean autowired in it.

In general, the XML-based method is preferred, whenever an Enterprise application is being developed, because XML is still widely used in systems integration techniques. Some legacy systems also preferred the XML-based container.

The PWP project has an XML-based and JavaConfig-based container.

# Configuring the Spring container

Before we create controllers for our PWP project, the Spring container must be ready for bean injections and component declarations. First, our Spring MVC container must be annotation-driven so that we can utilize the annotation stereotypes used by the current Spring Framework specification in configuring containers.

To enable the use of annotations inside classes, the following tag must be appearing in the `pwp-servlet.xml`:

```
<mvc:annotation-driven />
```

Second, when the `<annotation-driven>` tag is enabled, the container must automatically scan all component classes that are part of the Spring MVC web project. This will be enabled through inserting the following tag into the `pwp-servlet.xml`.

```
<context:component-scan
    base-package="org.packt.personal.web.portal" />
```

The base-package attribute indicates the base folder of the development directory structure (`src`) where all components and beans are located. Declaring this tag enables auto-detection of the bean components in the project, which includes the controllers.

Drop all static resources like the CSS files into the `ch01/webapp` folder. Declare the default servlet handler in order to allow the access of those static resources from the root of the web application even though the `DispatcherServlet` is registered at the context root `ch01`.

```
<mvc:default-servlet-handler />
```

Then, use the `<mvc:resources>` element to point to the location of the static resources with a specific public URL pattern.

```
<mvc:resources mapping="/css/**" location="/css/" />
```

The complete XML-based Spring container of PWP is shown as follows:

```
<?xml version="1.0" encoding="UTF-8"?>
<beans xmlns="http://www.springframework.org/schema/beans"
   xmlns:xsi="http://www.w3.org/2001/XMLSchema-instance"
   xmlns:aop="http://www.springframework.org/schema/aop"
   xmlns:context="http://www.springframework.org/schema/context"
   xmlns:oxm="http://www.springframework.org/schema/oxm"
   xmlns:tx="http://www.springframework.org/schema/tx"
   xmlns:mvc="http://www.springframework.org/schema/mvc"
   xsi:schemaLocation="http://www.springframework.org/schema/aop
      http://www.springframework.org/schema/aop/spring-aop-4.1.xsd
      http://www.springframework.org/schema/oxm
      http://www.springframework.org/schema/oxm/spring-oxm-4.1.xsd
      http://www.springframework.org/schema/beans
      http://www.springframework.org/schema/beans/
         spring-beans-4.1.xsd
      http://www.springframework.org/schema/tx
      http://www.springframework.org/schema/tx/spring-tx-4.1.xsd
      http://www.springframework.org/schema/context
```

```
    http://www.springframework.org/schema/context/
        spring-context-4.1.xsd
    http://www.springframework.org/schema/mvc
    http://www.springframework.org/schema/mvc/spring-mvc-4.1.xsd">

  <mvc:annotation-driven />
  <mvc:default-servlet-handler />
  <mvc:resources mapping="/css/**" location="/css/" />
</beans>
```

The JavaConfig equivalent of our XML-based container will have this equivalent code:

```
import org.springframework.context.annotation.Bean;
import org.springframework.context.annotation.ComponentScan;
// Rest of the imports in sources

@Configuration
@ComponentScan(basePackages="org.packt.personal.web.portal")
@EnableWebMvc
public class PWPConfiguration extends WebMvcConfigurerAdapter {

  @Override
    public void addResourceHandlers(ResourceHandlerRegistry        registry)
{
       registry.addResourceHandler("/css/**").
addResourceLocations("/css/");
    }
}
```

The @EnableWebMvc annotation is equivalent to <mvc:annotation-driven /> in the
XML-based version . Lastly, the @ComponentScan annotation is equivalent to
the <context:component-scan base-package=" org.packt.personal.web.portal
"/> we have in our pwp-servlet.xml. To allow recognition to static resources, the
application must override the resource handler method.

# Creating the controllers

The PWP project will consist of four content pages each having its own use request
transaction. Users can update three of the four contents using session handling. In order to
implement services to each page, controller class must be created with the
stereotype @Controller instead of extending controller base classes or Spring-specific
APIs. The home page of PWP has the following controller declaration:

```
@Controller
public class IndexController {   }
```

Each `controller` class has more than service or handler methods. Each service method is being mapped to the user's request by the `DispatcherServlet`. A valid service or handler method must have a `@RequestMapping` stereotype written on top of the method or function signature. A sample controller with a service method is shown as follows:

```
@Controller
public class IndexController {

  @RequestMapping(value="/index", method=RequestMethod.GET)
  public String getIndex(Model model) {
    model.addAttribute("greetings",  "Welcome Page");
    return "index";
  }
}
```

A service method is mapped to at least one URL or path, and has an HTTP method declared. The preceding sample `getIndex()` is mapped to the `/index.html` and processes a `GET` request transaction.

There are actually four general classifications of a controller and these are the following:

- **A controller that calls a page only**: These controllers simply provide services that call view names like the following sample:

  ```
  @Controller
    public class IndexController {

      @RequestMapping(value="/index",
      method=RequestMethod.GET)
      public String getIndex() {
        return "index";
      }
    }
  ```

- **A controller that brings model(s) to views**: This group of controllers transport models to the view for presentation purposes. A controller can pass an `org.springframework.web.ModelAndView` to successful view pages with an object containing all the necessary objects, like in the following snippet:

  ```
  @Controller
    public class IndexController {

      @RequestMapping(value="/index",
      method=RequestMethod.GET)
      public ModelAndView getIndex() {
        Map<String, Object> model = new HashMap<>();
  ```

```
      model.put("greetings",  "Welcome Page");
      return new ModelAndView("index", "model", model);
   }

}
```

- On the other hand, the most modern and simple way of transporting model data is through the use of the `org.springframework.ui.Model` object, wherein all objects transported to the views are either `@ModelAttribute` or `@SessionAttribute`. A simple sample on this approach is given as follows:

```
@Controller
  public class IndexController {

    @RequestMapping(value="/index",
    method=RequestMethod.GET)
    public String getIndex(Model model) {
      model.addAttribute("greetings",  "Welcome Page");
      return "index";
    }
  }
```

- **A controller that has multi-services or multi-actions**: Controllers that have more than one service or action:

```
@Controller
public class IndexController {

  @RequestMapping(value="/index",
  method=RequestMethod.GET)
  public String getIndex(Model model){
    model.addAttribute("greetings",  "Welcome Page");
    return "index";
  }

  @RequestMapping(value="/index_post",
    method=RequestMethod.POST)
    public String postIndex(Model model) {
      model.addAttribute("greetings",  "Welcome Page");
      return "index";
    }
}
```

- **A controller that accepts request parameters (form controllers)**: These controllers have a form view and a success view. The form view accepts request parameters from the client. Then the request will be mapped to the service method, which will process all the request data. The result will be transported as a model, or as an attribute, to the corresponding view. Following is a sample snippet:

```
@Controller
@SessionAttributes(value={"statusSess", "homeSess"})
@RequestMapping("/pwp/index_update")
public class IndexUpdateController {

@Autowired
private Validator indexValidator;

@InitBinder("homeForm")
public void initBinder(WebDataBinder binder) {
binder.setValidator(indexValidator);
}

@RequestMapping(method=RequestMethod.GET)

public String initForm(Model model) {
Home homeForm = new Home();
model.addAttribute("homeForm", homeForm);
return "index_update";
}

@RequestMapping(method=RequestMethod.POST)
public String submitForm(Model model,
@ModelAttribute("homeForm")
@Validated Home homeForm, BindingResult binding) {
model.addAttribute("homeForm", homeForm);
String returnVal = "index";
if(binding.hasErrors()) {
returnVal = "index_update";
} else {
model.addAttribute("homeSess", homeForm);
model.addAttribute("statusSess", "undefault");
}
return returnVal;
}
}
```

# The PWP controllers

This project utilizes all the preceding controller classification except for multi-action controllers. Following is the finished product of the PWP that highlights the home page. All content pages have an equivalent update transaction for updating their content. The home page, in particular, is invoked through the URL
`http://localhost:8080/ch01/pwp/index.html` where `ch01` is the context root. With this URL, `DispatcherServlet` will look for the controller that has the service method bearing the path `/pwp/index`. Once the match is found, the service method calls the appropriate view with the data model, if there is one. The final step will be loading the content desired by the user.

A complete home page controller class with the default values of the cone is shown as follows:

```
package org.packt.personal.web.portal.controller;

import java.util.ArrayList;
import java.util.Date;
import java.util.HashMap;
import java.util.List;
import java.util.Map;
```

```java
import org.packt.personal.web.portal.model.form.Home;
import org.packt.personal.web.portal.model.form.PostMessage;
// Rest of the code in the sources

@Controller
@SessionAttributes("posts")
@RequestMapping("pwp")
public class IndexController {

  @ModelAttribute("posts")
  public List<PostMessage> newPosts() {
    return initPost();
  }

  @RequestMapping(value="/index", method=RequestMethod.GET)
  public String getIndex(Model model,  @ModelAttribute("posts")
    List<PostMessage> posts,
    @ModelAttribute("postForm") PostMessage postForm) {

      Home home = new Home();
      home.setMessage(initMessage());
      home.setQuote(initQuote());
      model.addAttribute("home",  home);
        if(posts == null) posts = newPosts();
        if(validatePost(postForm)) {
          postForm.setDatePosted(new Date());
          posts.add(postForm);
        }
        model.addAttribute("posts",  posts);
      return "index";
  }

  @RequestMapping(value="/index_redirect",
    method=RequestMethod.GET)
  public RedirectView updateIndex() {
    return new RedirectView("/ch01/pwp/index_update.html");
  }

  public String initQuote() {
    String message = "Twenty years from now you will be more
      disappointed by the things .......... -Mark Twain";
    return message;
  }

  public String initMessage() {
    String message = "Having a positive outlook on life is a      crucial
part of finding inspiration. In the paragraph above,       ......";
    return message;
```

```
  }

  public List<PostMessage> initPost() {
    List<PostMessage> posts = new ArrayList<>();
    PostMessage post = new PostMessage();
    post.setSubject("Welcome!");
    post.setDatePosted(new Date());
    post.setPostedMsg("Hello visitors!Feelfree to post on my
    portal!");

    posts.add(post);
    return posts;
  }

  public boolean validatePost(PostMessage post) {
    try {
      if(post.getSubject().trim().length() == 0 ||
      post.getPostedMsg().trim().length() == 0) {
        return false;
      }
    }
    catch(Exception e) {
      return false;
    }
    return true;
  }
}
```

The method `getIndex()` is responsible for loading the home page initially. The default content for message and content are given by two methods, namely `initMessage()` and `initPost()`. The `initPost()` method initially populates the right navigation panel of the home page where all the posts will be listed. This posting feature will be elaborated on further in the next topics.

Generally, all these default methods are essential to generate the home page when no session data are available to replace this default content.

The update page on the home page will be invoked by clicking the **Update** button. Each portal has an **Update** button except for the **Reach Out** page. After clicking the **Update** button on the home page, `DispatcherServlet` will look for the service that has the URL path `/pwp/index_redirect`. There are two general ways to implement redirection and these are the following:

- **Using the RedirectView API**: This process of redirection is done through implementation of the handler method that returns `org.springframework.web.servlet.view.RedirectView`.

Following are some snippets that show how to implement redirection.

```
@RequestMapping(value="/index_redirect",
                method=RequestMethod.GET)
  public RedirectView updateIndex() {
    return new RedirectView("/ch01/pwp/index_update.html");
  }

@RequestMapping(value="/index_redirect",
                method=RequestMethod.GET)
  public String updateIndex() {
    return (redirect:"/ch01/pwp/index_update.html");
  }
```

- **Using the <c:url> JSTL tag**: This process is a direct process of redirection and being configured on the view page.

```
<c:url var=indexUpdate" value="/pwp/index_update.html"/>
<a href="<c:out value="${indexUpdate }"/>">Update Home</a>
```

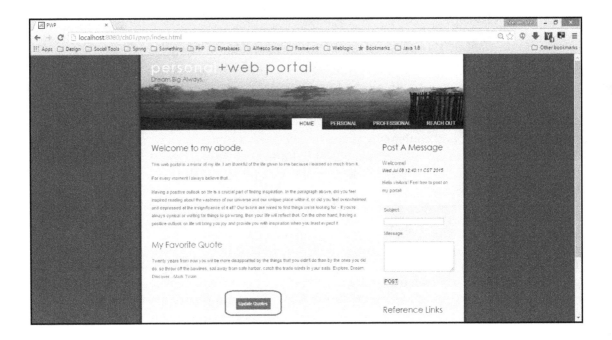

After redirection to the update page, the home page has two important pieces of content information that need to be updated, and these are the message and quote portions of the page:

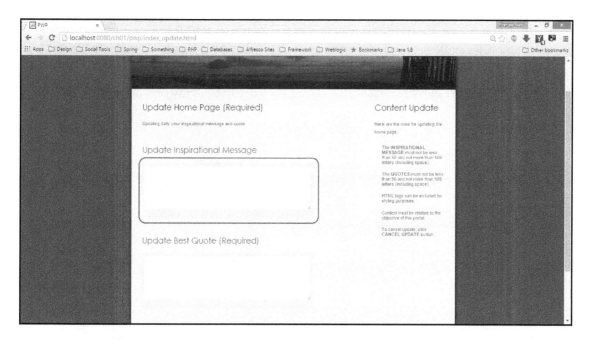

All update pages have validators to check the attributes of the form data. On the home page, users cannot input quotes or messages that are less than 50 and more than 500 alphanumeric characters. Validation and object type checking occurs only if our controllers have form views. A controller that has form and success views is implemented in a different way. Following is a template of a form controller that is used by the PWP project:

```
package org.packt.personal.web.portal.controller;

import java.util.ArrayList;
import java.util.Date;
import java.util.List;

import org.packt.personal.web.portal.converter.AgeConverter;
import org.packt.personal.web.portal.converter.BirthDateConverter;
// Rest of the codes in the sources
@Controller
@SessionAttributes(value = {"pStatusSess", "personSess"})
@RequestMapping("/pwp/personal_update")
public class PersonalUpdateController {
```

```
@Autowired
Validator personalValidator;

@InitBinder("personForm")
public void initBinder(WebDataBinder binder) {
  binder.setValidator(personalValidator);
  binder.registerCustomEditor(Integer.class, "biography.age",
  new AgeConverter());
  binder.registerCustomEditor(Integer.class, "education.year",
  new YearConverter());
  binder.registerCustomEditor(Date.class, "biography.birthDate",
  new BirthDateConverter());
}

@RequestMapping(method=RequestMethod.GET)
public String initForm(Model model) {
  Biography bio = new Biography();
  Education educ = new Education();
  Personal personForm = new Personal();
  personForm.setBiography(bio);
  personForm.setEducation(educ);
  references(model);
  model.addAttribute("personForm", personForm);
  return "personal_update";
}


@RequestMapping(method=RequestMethod.POST)
public String submitForm(Model model,
@ModelAttribute("personForm") @Validated Personal personForm,
BindingResult binding) {
  model.addAttribute("personForm", personForm);
  String returnVal = "personal";
  if(binding.hasErrors()) {
    references(model);
    returnVal = "personal_update";
  } else {
    model.addAttribute("personSess", personForm);
    model.addAttribute("pStatusSess", "undefault");
  }
  return returnVal;

}

public void references(Model model) {
  List<String> hobbiesList = new ArrayList<String>();
  hobbiesList.add("Not Applicable");
  hobbiesList.add("Singing");
  hobbiesList.add("Painting");
```

```
    hobbiesList.add("Traveling");
    hobbiesList.add("Writing");
    hobbiesList.add("Swimming");
    model.addAttribute("hobbiesList", hobbiesList);
    // Rest of the code in sources
  }
}
```

Although there is no restriction as to what, and how many, handler methods are needed in a typical controller class, a form controller has to maintain having only one `@RequestMapping` stereotype declared at the class level. The path indicated must be the controller's form view.

The preceding controller has two service operations namely the `initForm()` and `submitForm()` methods. The `initForm()` service is always a GET method, which always initializes the form view. It also binds the form domain object that contains the request data from the user. The `submitForm()` is a POST service that is executed after form submission. This automatically extracts the validated domain object from the form and transports any model to the result views.

The `references()` method is used to populate the form components found in the form view. **Java Collection Framework (JCF)** is used to contain all the data which can be hardcoded or which is from a data store.

The usual exception during form-handling happens when the form-backing object, or the model, is not set to bind with the form view. Whenever the browser calls the `initForm()`, the following exception will be encountered.

```
java.lang.IllegalStateException:
  Neither BindingResult nor plain target object
    for bean name 'home' available as request attribute
      at o.s.w.s.s.BindStatus.<init>(BindStatus.java:141)
```

In order for `submitForm()` to access the form-backing object, the `@ModelAttribute` annotation is needed to be declared in its parameters. An `@ModelAttribute` local parameter indicates that the argument will be retrieved from the form view. If not present in the form view, the argument must be instantiated first in the `initForm()`, and bound to the form view. Moreover, Spring MVC throws an exception when errors occur during request binding, by default. That is why in `submitForm()`, one of the arguments is for `BindIngResult` where we can extract all errors during the request transaction. The `BindingResult` argument needs to be positioned right after our form-backing object, which is a rare case when it comes to the `@RequestMapping` order of arguments.

If this rule is violated, the following exception will be thrown:

```
java.lang.IllegalStateException:
Errors/BindingResult argument declared without preceding model     attribute
```

# Using @ModelAttribute and @SessionAttributes

The **Personal Web Portal** (**PWP**) application does not have database connectivity since the main highlight in this chapter are the raw Spring MVC 4 components. Also, it has no Spring security attached to it from the core, so there are no login/logout transaction for the user. All controllers in the PWP use a lot of @ModelAttribute and @SessionAttributes data.

The @ModelAttribute data are actually the same with request attributes. These are objects created from one single request dispatching. Moreover, these data are also called **request-scoped data**, which means that these data values are only valid within one request-response transaction.

One use of @ModelAttribute is to bind the form domain object to the form view page. On an incoming request transaction, any models with @ModelAttributes are called before any controller handler method. The following initForm() method is one example of this scenario.

```
@RequestMapping(method=RequestMethod.GET)
  public String initForm(Model model,
  @ModelAttribute("profesionalForm")
  Professional professionalForm) {
    return "professional_update";
  }

@RequestMapping(method=RequestMethod.GET)
  public String initForm(Model model) {
    Professional professionalForm = new Professional();

    model.addAttribute("professionalForm", professionalForm);
    references(model);
    return "professional_update";
  }
  public void references(Model model) {
    List<String> hobbiesList = new ArrayList<String>();
    hobbiesList.add("Not Applicable");
    hobbiesList.add("Singing");
    hobbiesList.add("Painting");
    hobbiesList.add("Traveling");
    hobbiesList.add("Writing");
    hobbiesList.add("Swimming");
```

```
        model.addAttribute("hobbiesList", hobbiesList);

        List<String> readingsList = new ArrayList<String>();
        readingsList.add("Not Applicable");
        readingsList.add("Novel");
        readingsList.add("Magazine");
        readingsList.add("Newspaper");
        readingsList.add("Diaries");
        model.addAttribute("readingsList", readingsList);

        List<String> educLevelList = new ArrayList<String>();
        educLevelList.add("Not Applicable");
        educLevelList.add("Doctoral");
        educLevelList.add("Masters");
        educLevelList.add("College");
        educLevelList.add("Vocational");
        educLevelList.add("High School");
        model.addAttribute("educLevelList", educLevelList);
    }
```

To initialize the @ModelAttribute, it must be injected with an object value just like we have in the PWP project:

```
@ModelAttribute("greetings")
  public List<String> getGreetings() {
    return Greetings.allGreets();
  }
```

The @SessionAttributes, on the other hand, are used by the controller to declare session objects during session handling. Equally, these attributes are the session attributes in a typical JEE web component. As long as the session is not terminated, session data are always accessible for update and retrieval. Sessions were used in the PWP project to store values for all the dynamic content transactions. Here is a code snippet that shows how to declare, initialize and update values that are @SessionAttributes.

```
@Controller
@SessionAttributes("posts")
@RequestMapping("pwp")
public class IndexController {

  @ModelAttribute("posts")
  public List<PostMessage> newPosts() {
    return initPost();
  }

  @RequestMapping(value="/index", method=RequestMethod.GET)
  public String getIndex(Model model,  @ModelAttribute("posts")
```

```
        List<PostMessage> posts,
        @ModelAttribute("postForm") PostMessage postForm) {

          Home home = new Home();
          home.setMessage(initMessage());
          home.setQuote(initQuote());
          model.addAttribute("home", home);

          if(posts == null) posts = newPosts();
          if(validatePost(postForm)) {
            postForm.setDatePosted(new Date());
            posts.add(postForm);
          }

          model.addAttribute("posts", posts);
          return "index";
      }
      // Other codes refer to sources
  }
```

The @SessionAttributes are declared on the controller level and are initialized as with any @ModelAttribute. Always initialize the session data to avoid the following error:

```
Servlet.service() for servlet [pwp] in context with path [/ch01] threw
exception [Expected session attribute 'posts'] with root cause
    org.springframework.web.HttpSessionRequiredException: Expected session
attribute 'posts'
```

In order for the service operations to access the session attribute argument, be sure to have a @ModelAttribute parameter on the local parameter of the service depicting the attribute data:

```
public String getIndex(Model model, @ModelAttribute("posts")
  List<PostMessage> posts,
  @ModelAttribute("postForm") PostMessage postForm) {
  }
```

These two attributes trigger the information workflow of the PWP project, even without the help of any web services or data store.

# Form domain objects

Binding to the form view using @ModelAttribute, forms domain objects that are plain POJOs, and are used to save request parameter values from the user. Sometimes these objects are also called form data models. See the following domain:

```
package org.packt.personal.web.portal.model.form;

public class Home {

    private String message;
    private String quote;

    public String getMessage() {
        return message;
    }

    public void setMessage(String message) {
        this.message = message;
    }

    public String getQuote() {
        return quote;
    }

    public void setQuote(String quote) {
        this.quote = quote;
    }
}
```

Instantiation of this model will be found in the initForm() method and the binding to the form view page will be implemented using the **Spring Form Taglib** directive:

```
<%@ taglib prefix="form"  uri="http://www.springframework.org/tags/form"%>
```

The Spring MVC <form> tag has its own form components that can be readily mapped to the setters of the form domain objects. These topics will be highlighted in Chapter 3, *Student Management Portal (SMP)*, of this book. The following JSP code snippet shows how the binding is done through the <form> tag:

```
<form:form commandName="homeForm" method="post">
  <div class="form_settings">
    <!-- insert the page content here -->
    <h2>Update Inspirational Message</h2>
    <p><form:textarea path="message" rows="8" cols="50"/></p>
    <span><form:errors path="message" cssStyle="color:       #ff0000;
"/></span>
```

```
<br/> <br/> <br/>

<h2>Update Best Quote (Required)</h2>
<p><form:textarea path="quote" rows="8" cols="50"/></p>
<span><form:errors path="quote"  cssStyle="color:      #ff0000;
"/></span>
<br/> <br/> <br/>

<p style="padding-top: 15px; padding-left: 20px"><input
class="submit"
type="submit" value="Update Home Page"></p>
</div>
</form:form>
```

There are instances when a form view page contains several request parameters which need to be subdivided into groups.

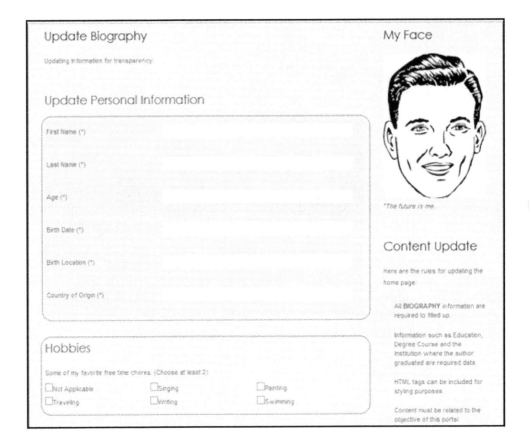

Given this situation, the best strategy is to decompose the huge flat domain POJO into several specific form domain models, each containing related data. Then, create a main POJO component class, which will hold all smaller domain models. This class will be represented as the form-backing object for the form view. A sample implementation of the preceding content page is shown as follows:

```
package org.packt.personal.web.portal.model.form;

public class Personal {

  private Biography biography;
  private Education education;

  public Biography getBiography() {
    return biography;
  }
  public void setBiography(Biography biography) {
    this.biography = biography;
  }
  public Education getEducation() {
    return education;
  }
  public void setEducation(Education education) {
    this.education = education;
  }
}

package org.packt.personal.web.portal.model.form;
import java.util.Date;
import java.util.List;

public class Biography {
  private String firstName;
  private String lastName;
  private Integer age;
  private Date birthDate;
  private String location;
  private String country;
  private List<String> hobbies;
  private List<String> readings;
  // The getters and the setters
}

package org.packt.personal.web.portal.model.form;
public class Education {

  private String educLevel;
```

```
    private String institution;
    private String degree;
    private String specialization;
    private Integer year;

    // The getters and the setters
}
```

The binding of the component will be quite different compared to the usual domain model. To bind all biography attributes to the form components, it is important to access first the `getter` method of the biography object, then through this we can now access all the setters of its attributes. The following example is a clear picture of the complicated binding:

```
<form:form commandName="personForm" method="post">
  <div class="form_settings">
  <!-- insert the page content here -->

    <h2>Update Personal Information</h2>
    <table style="width:100%; border-spacing:0;">
    <tr><td>First Name (*)</td>
      <td><form:input path="biography.firstName"/></td>
      <td><form:errors path="biography.firstName" cssStyle="color:
#ff0000"/></td>
    </tr>
    <tr><td>Last Name (*)</td>
      <td><form:input path="biography.lastName"/></td>
      <td><form:errors path="biography.lastName" cssStyle="color:
#ff0000"/>
    </tr>
    <!-- Rest of the script in the sources -->
  </table>

  <!-- Rest of the code in sources -->
</form:form>
```

# The ViewResolver and view configuration

The interface `ViewResolver` is responsible for the mapping of the view names to the actual view pages. It also provides the view interface, which addresses the request of a view to the view technology. In this PWP project, all of our pages are written in JSP-JSTL so the view interface used is `org.springframework.web.servlet.view.JstlView`. The project's view resolver is implemented inside the Spring container in this way:

```
<bean id="viewResolver"
  class="org.springframework.web.servlet.view.
ResourceBundleViewResolver">
  <property name="basename">
    <value>config.views</value>
  </property>
</bean>
```

The views are also declared in the custom property file
`./src/config/views.properties`:

```
hello.(class)=org.springframework.web.servlet.view.JstlView
hello.url=/jsp/hello_world.jsp

index.(class)=org.springframework.web.servlet.view.JstlView
index.url=/jsp/index.jsp

index_update.(class)=org.springframework.web.servlet.view.JstlView
index_update.url=/jsp/index_update.jsp

// See the sources
```

There are three popular generic `ViewResolver` implementations that developers always use and these are:

- `InternalResourceViewResolver`: This is implemented whenever all the actual view pages are stored inside `/WEB-INF/jsp`. It has two sets of properties, namely a prefix or suffix that needs to be configured to generate the final view page URL.

```
<bean
  class="org.springframework.web.servlet.view.
      InternalResourceViewResolver">
    <property name="viewClass"
    value="org.springframework.web.servlet.view.JstlView"/>
    <property name="prefix">
      <value>/WEB-INF/</value>
    </property>
    <property name="suffix">
      <value>.jsp</value>
    </property>
</bean>
```

- The prefix indicates the location of the actual views, while the suffix tells the controller the allowed extension of all the actual pages. By default, `InternalResourceViewResolver` resolves the view names into view objects of type `JstlView` if the JSTL library is present in the classpath. If the view template is not the default, the `viewClass` property must be explicitly declared and mapped to other view templates like `org.springframework.web.servlet.view.tiles2.TilesView` if tiles are to be used.

- `XmlViewResolver`: If you want to declare each individual view-mapping to the actual page in an XML format, then this implementation best fits the project. A sample implementation is shown as follows:

```
<bean id="helloWorld"
  class="org.springframework.web.servlet.view.JstlView">
  <property name="url"
    value="/WEB-INF/helloWorld.jsp" />
</bean>
```

- `ResourceBundleViewResolver`: This implementation is the most flexible among the three, because the only thing needed here is a property containing all the view mappings. Moreover, one has the capability to combine different view technology in just one project, for the purpose of mixing together presentation layers.

A Spring MVC project can have more than resolvers, given that the order property in all definitions is defined to set order levels of 0 having the highest priority. The following code shows the ordering technique:

```
<bean
  class="org.springframework.web.servlet.view.
InternalResourceViewResolver">
    <property name="prefix">
      <value>/WEB-INF/</value>
    </property>
    <property name="suffix">
      <value>.jsp</value>
    </property>
    <property name="order" value="2" />
</bean>

<bean class= "org.springframework.web.servlet.view.XmlViewResolver">
  <property name="location">
    <value>/WEB-INF/views.xml</value>
  </property>
```

```
    <property name="order" value="1" />
</bean>

<bean class=
"org.springframework.web.servlet.view.ResourceBundleViewResolver">
    <property name="basename" value="views" />
    <property name="order" value="0" />
</bean>
```

By convention, the `InternalResourceViewResolver` is always given the least priority because it takes a little time to map the view name directly to the actual pages before all the remaining resolvers. This might give conflict to other mappings if other resolvers are not fast enough in mapping views.

## Actual view pages

The view template used in this project is JSP-JSTL, since the view interface used to map to JSP pages is `org.springframework.web.servlet.view.JstlView`. It is no longer recommended to use scriptlets.

Obviously, the actual view pages use some EL language components like the implicit object `sessionScope`. EL language is part of the `jsp-api.jar` libraries, so it is still acceptable to use its components. Moreover, we also used some JSTL tags like `<c:out/>` and `<c:url/>`. The tag `<c:out/>` is always recommended to output values of EL expression `${}`, especially in generating reports wherein lots of the data are handled by EL expressions. The attribute `escapeXml` means that all words that are HTML tags will be captured, and thus they will be rendered on the page as HTML components. But most importantly, redirection implemented inside the view page must use URL rewriting so that when cookies are cut-off, the session data will still be shared by all controllers and views.

## Validating Form Data

All form domain objects must be validated using the `org.springframework.validation.Validator` interface and annotations supported by JSR 303. The validation interface is implemented to create a set of validation rules as per the form view. A sample implementation used in PWP's home content page is shown as follows:

```
package org.packt.personal.web.portal.validator;

import org.packt.personal.web.portal.model.form.Home;
import org.springframework.stereotype.Component;
```

```
import org.springframework.validation.Errors;
import org.springframework.validation.ValidationUtils;
import org.springframework.validation.Validator;

public class IndexValidator implements Validator {
  @Override
  public boolean supports(Class<?> clazz) {
    return Home.class.equals(clazz);
  }

  @Override
  public void validate(Object obj, Errors errors) {
    Home homeForm = (Home) obj;
    ValidationUtils.rejectIfEmptyOrWhitespace(errors,
      "message", "message.empty");
    ValidationUtils.rejectIfEmptyOrWhitespace(errors,
      "quote", "quote.empty");

    if(homeForm.getMessage().length() > 500) {
      errors.rejectValue("message",
        "message.maxlength");
    }
    if(homeForm.getMessage().length() < 50) {
      errors.rejectValue("message",
        "message.minlength");
    }

    if(homeForm.getQuote().length() > 500) {
      errors.rejectValue("quote", "quote.maxlength");
    }
    if(homeForm.getQuote().length() < 50) {
      errors.rejectValue("quote", "quote.minlength");
    }
  }

}
```

It validates checks if the user entered a content message and quotes greater than 50, but not greater than 500 alphanumeric. The validator interface has two abstract methods to implement, namely:

- `public boolean supports()`: This method checks what type of `@ModelAttribute` object is being validated. `@SessionAttributes` are also included in this Boolean method.

- `public void validate()`: If the preceding method confirms correctly the `@ModelAttribute` to be validated, this method will be executed next, dealing with all data values of the domain object.

Validators are components of the Spring MVC project. Spring MVC 4 uses the `@Autowired` stereotype to call the instance of the validator in the controller class. To enable the validator, the `setValidator()` method of `org.springframework.web.bind .WebDataBinder` has to be invoked inside the `initBinder()` method. To avoid complications, it is recommended to set one validator per `initBinder()` since we can create more than one `initBinder()` inside a form controller.

For situations like in PWP where both the `@SessionAttributes` and `@ModelAttribute` are utilized by the operations, `initBinder()` is recommended to be explicitly mapped to the specific attribute for the validator. Otherwise, the following exception shown will be encountered:

```
SEVERE: Servlet.service() for servlet [pwp] in context with path
[/ch01] threw exception [Request processing failed; nested exception is
java.lang.IllegalStateException: Invalid target for Validator
[org.packt.personal.web.portal.validator.IndexValidator@5b4ca52d]:
undefault] with root cause
    java.lang.IllegalStateException: Invalid target for Validator
[org.packt.personal.web.portal.validator.IndexValidator@5b4ca52d]:
undefault
```

To retrieve the result of the validation on a `@ModelAttribute` as per `initBinder()`, be sure to use the `@Validated` stereotype with the model argument declared in the `submitForm()` method. Following is a code that shows how to declare and enable validation in a form controller:

```
@Autowired
  private Validator indexValidator;

  @InitBinder("homeForm")
  public void initBinder(WebDataBinder binder) {
    binder.setValidator(indexValidator);
  }

  @RequestMapping(method=RequestMethod.POST)
  public String submitForm(Model model,    @ModelAttribute("homeForm")
@Validated Home homeForm,    BindingResult binding) {
    model.addAttribute("homeForm", homeForm);
    String returnVal = "index";
    if(binding.hasErrors()) {
      returnVal = "index_update";
```

```
    } else {
      model.addAttribute("homeSess", homeForm);
      model.addAttribute("statusSess", "undefault");
    }
    return returnVal;
  }
```

## Validation using JSR 303

Aside from custom validation using the validator interface, Spring 4.x container supports annotations under the JSR 303 specifications that are applied directly to Java beans, used by the classes to impose specific validation rules. The following EmailController uses @NotNull to check if the two objects are not null, otherwise an error will be detected by the BindingResult.

```
@Controller
@RequestMapping("/pwp/contact")
public class EmailController {

  @NotNull
  @Autowired
  private SimpleMailMessage emailTemplate;

  @NotNull
  @Autowired
  private JavaMailSender emailSender;
  // See the sources
}
```

Aside from @NotNull, annotations like @Pattern, and @Size are also widely used in string matching and collection size restrictions, respectively.

## Domain data type conversion and filtering

The main purpose of the initBinder() is not purely to validate, but to bind request parameter data to the form domain model. It checks if the request parameter data matches the type of variables in the form-backing object. It provides conversion processes to data in order to avoid type mismatch and other related exceptions. The method has built-in property editors that you can use to check types. Some are custom editors of the type java.beans.PropertyEditorSupport that check complicated matches with added custom transactions.

In the Personal portal page, there are data that needs to be converted into proper object types like age and birth date.

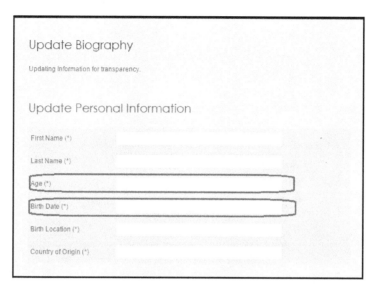

Remember that `request` parameter data are all, by default, `String` objects. The custom property editor can be helpful in converting `String` data to other types, just to fit in the form-backing object's `setter` methods. Following is a custom editor for this page:

```
package org.packt.personal.web.portal.converter;
import java.beans.PropertyEditorSupport;

public class AgeConverter extends PropertyEditorSupport {

  @Override
  public void setAsText(String text) throws
  IllegalArgumentException {
    Integer age = 0;
    try {
      age = Integer.parseInt(text.trim());
    } catch(Exception e) {
      age = 18;
    }
    setValue(age);
  }
}

package org.packt.personal.web.portal.converter;
```

```
import java.beans.PropertyEditorSupport;
import java.text.ParseException;
import java.text.SimpleDateFormat;
import java.util.Date;

public class BirthDateConverter extends PropertyEditorSupport {

  @Override
  public void setAsText(String text) throws
  IllegalArgumentException {
    SimpleDateFormat format = new
    SimpleDateFormat("mm/yy/dd");
    Date birthDate;
    try {
      birthDate = format.parse(text.trim());
    } catch (ParseException e) {
      // TODO Auto-generated catch block
      birthDate = new Date();
    }
    setValue(birthDate);
  }
}
```

# E-mail configuration

The Reach Out page opens an electronic communication between the portal owner and the portal reader or user. The Spring Framework supports e-mail operations with the `org.springframework.mail` package as the root level package with the following API classes:

- `MailSender`: The central interface for sending e-mails is the `MailSender` interface.
- `SimpleMailMessage`: The simple value object encapsulating the properties of a simple mail such as from and to (plus many others) is the class.
- `MailException`: The root exception of all e-mail checked exceptions which provide a higher level of abstraction over the lower level mail system exceptions.
- `JavaMailSender`: The interface that adds specialized `JavaMail` features such as MIME message support to its superclass `MailSender` interface.
- `MimeMessageHelper`: A class that comes in pretty handy when dealing with `JavaMail` messages without using verbose JavaMail APIs.
- `MimeMessagePreparator`: A callback interface for the preparation of `JavaMail` MIME messages.

This project sends three forms of e-mail template, namely the basic text-based e-mail, HTML-based e-mail and template-based e-mail. Following is PWP's way of sending an HTML-based e-mail.

```java
public void sendMailHTML(Email emailForm) {
   String  fromEmail = emailForm.getSendTo();
   String toEmail = emailForm.getSendTo();
   String emailSubject = emailForm.getSubject();
   String emailBody = emailForm.getMessage();

   MimeMessage mimeMessage =
   emailSender.createMimeMessage();
   try {
     MimeMessageHelper helper = new
     MimeMessageHelper(mimeMessage, true, "utf-8");
     mimeMessage.setContent("<i><b>"+emailBody
     +"</b></i>", "text/html");
     helper.setFrom(fromEmail);
     helper.setTo(toEmail);
     helper.setSubject(emailSubject);

   } catch (MessagingException e) {}
   /*
   uncomment the following lines for attachment
   FileSystemResource
   file = new FileSystemResource("sample.jpg");
   helper.addAttachment(file.getFilename(), file);
   */

   emailSender.send(mimeMessage);
   System.out.println("Mail sent successfully.");

}
```

# The Personal Web Portal (PWP) project

This chapter highlighted how to create a simple Spring MVC project using only its core components. Moreover, the chapter highlighted some of the components used by the PWP that can be used also by anybody to start learning Spring MVC from its core. Learning core components is essential to establish better understanding on how the base framework works, starting from configuring the controller, up to the implementation of `PropertyEditorSupport` for data binding enhancement and object type conversion. This chapter has given a picture of how to start a base Spring MVC project.

Following are full web pages of the PWP:

- Let us look at the home page:

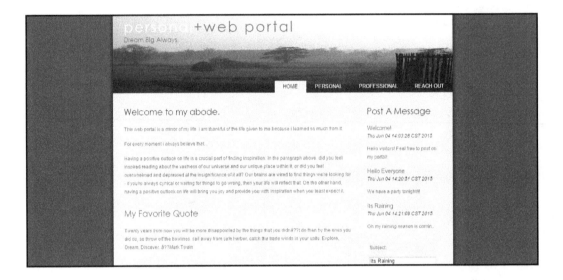

- Now let's look at the personal page:

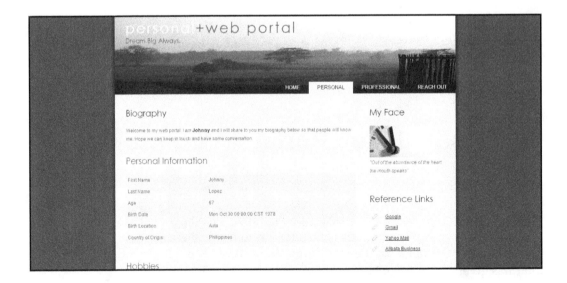

- Now, the professional page:

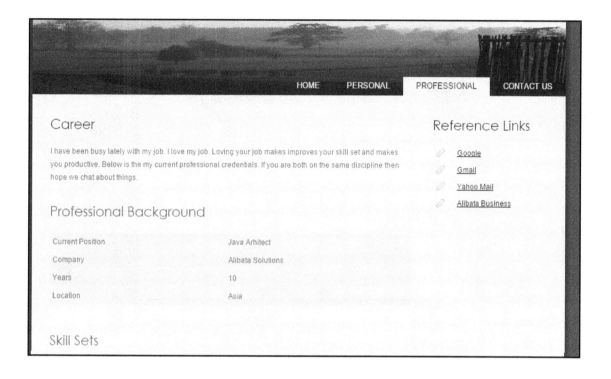

- And finally the reach out page:

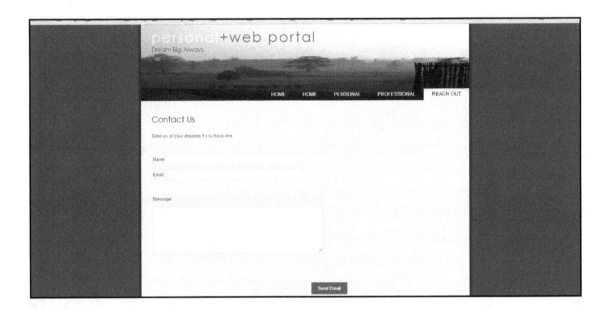

**Web design theme**

The theme used by this project is inspired by, and based on, templates from `http://creativecommons.org`.

# Challenge yourself

Create a personal portfolio website using Spring MVC. The site should consist of the following pages:

- **Home page**: Consists of your picture, biography, academic information and other personal-related information.
- **Update page**: Updates the information presented on the homepage. See to it that the home page is always updated once this is executed.
- **Contact Us**: Provides e-mail support for those who want to email the owner.

# Summary

Using the basic Spring Framework 4.x APIs, web portal creators can create their own platform to promote their personal philosophy, business, ideology, religion, and other concepts. Although it is an advantage to use existing portal platforms made in other language like PHP and Python, it is still fulfilling to design and develop our own portal based on an open-source framework. The PWP is just prototype software that needs to be upgraded to have a backend database, security, and other social media plugins, in order to make the software commercially competitive.

The next chapter will be about creating a simple document repository focusing on document management. If your personal web portal needs to have a Dropbox-like feature for any types of documents, then the next chapter will help you build that feature.

# 2
# Electronic Document Management Systems (EDMS)

One of the most essential enterprise content management systems nowadays is the electronic content management (ECM) system. Companies resort to this kind of web ecosystem to provide solutions for managing their legal documents, hospital records, e-mails, billing invoices and other collaboration-related files. These software solutions store all those unstructured data, to promote paperless transactions that help companies minimize their costs when managing huge cabinets of documents.

The ECM solution is the integration of different sub-components including record management, document management, workflow and process management, collaboration solution, and security modules. Some of the popularly known ECM platforms that are used by many companies worldwide are: EMC Documentum, Alfresco, Apache Lenya, Liferay and OpenCMS.

The chapter will particularly focus on the implementation of uploading and downloading files that is considered the main feature of a **DMS**. To discuss the process of creating this feature, a software specimen called **Electronic Document Management System** (EDMS) will be created, to guide the reader on how to start with DMS using the Spring MVC 4.x specification.

In this chapter, you will learn how to:

- Configure a Spring MVC container for file uploading
- Implement and design uploading of files
- Use a MultipartFile interface
- Create file validations
- Learn the different solutions for file uploading using Spring MVC 4.x

- Deploy Spring MVC projects
- Encrypt and decrypt stored files

# Overview of the project

The software specimen focuses only on the uploading and downloading solutions. It gives a simple conceptual framework on how to use the Spring MVC framework in creating a document library. No database management system will be used, except if the metadata are required to be backed up for future retrieval. All documents will be saved directly into the file system.

The simple prototype has the following pages:

- **The Home Page**: This is the faÃ§ade of the software, containing the logo, main content and ads of the site. All general links and functionalities are found on this page. This page also contains the login functionality of the application:

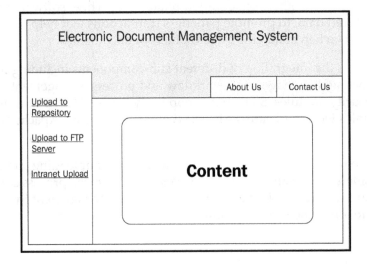

- **The Upload Page**: This is where the user will upload the document(s). The page asks for a file and needs to be redirected to the location of the file. It will also ask for some information related to the document, such as rendition types, the name of the uploader, and date of upload. Clicking the upload button will trigger the uploading transaction, given all requirements are met.

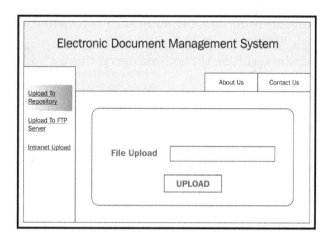

- **The Download Page**: This page is a prototype that renders a table of all the files uploaded, and creates download links per document.

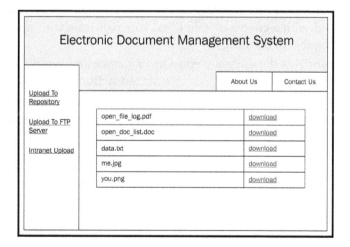

Given the preceding wireframes, the strength of the prototype will be in the uploading and downloading of any types of documents with validation constraints. The file uploading operations will cover implementation on how to:

- Upload single and multiple documents to the local repository or file system using the core IO streams
- Upload documents to FTP servers
- Upload documents using AJAX libraries such as JQuery data form plugins and JQuery generic library
- Upload documents with encryption and decryption for added security

On the other hand, the downloading solution will focus on typical file downloads and FTP file retrieval, which technically is a process of downloading files too.

# Technical requirement

This project will use the same installers and tools listed in Chapter 1, *Creating a Personal Web Portal (PWP)*, but there are some additional components and libraries that are required to be part of the STS project.

The Maven dependencies that need to be added are the following:

- **commons-fileupload**: This dependency consists of classes and interfaces needed to create an easy, robust, and high-performance, file upload capability in servlet-based web applications; this library parses HTTP submitted using the POST method, and with a content type of "multipart/form-data", and exposes the polished request to the caller.
- **commons-io**: This dependency consists of classes and interfaces that support file reading, writing and other management transactions.
- **commons-net**: This dependency consists of a set of classes and interfaces that provide a fundamental protocol access to establish handshake transactions like FTP/FTPS access.

The library's commons-fileupload and commons-io are needed for the file uploading and downloading, while the commons-net are needed for dropping and retrieving files into an FTP server.

Since AJAX transactions will be part of the prototype, the following JavaScript libraries need to be included in the project:

- `jquery-2.1.4.min.js`: The compressed version of the JQuery library; JQuery is a JavaScript library that can manipulate HTML, DOM, and CSS, handle HTML events, can implement AJAX transactions and provides other utilities like animations and effects.
- `jquery.form.min.js`: This is a JavaScript library that processes form elements in an HTML page.

The preceding JavaScript libraries are separately used to implement uploading of files using the AJAX mechanism.

# The pom.xml

The `pom.xml` file still consists of the core Spring MVC components of `Chapter 1`, *Creating a Personal Web Portal (PWP)*, with the addition of the following dependencies:

```
<dependency>
<groupId>commons-net</groupId>
<artifactId>commons-net</artifactId>
<version>3.3</version>
</dependency>
<dependency>
    <groupId>commons-fileupload</groupId>
    <artifactId>commons-fileupload</artifactId>
    <version>1.3.1</version>
</dependency>
<dependency>
  <groupId>commons-io</groupId>
  <artifactId>commons-io</artifactId>
  <version>2.2</version>
</dependency>
```

# The process flow

The following is an overview of the design:

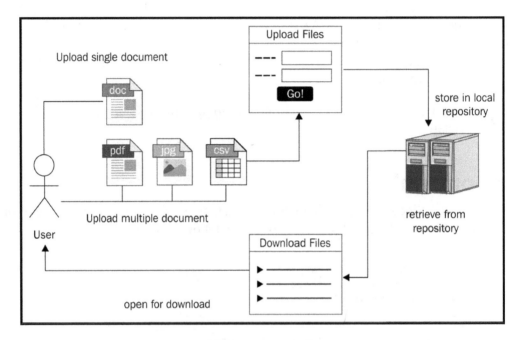

The EDMS starts when the user clicks any of the three following options for uploading:

- **Upload to Repository**: This creates a copy of the uploaded file and stores it in the hard disk with or without encryption.
- **Upload to FTP Server**: This retrieves the file from a fixed local storage, and then creates a copy of it in the FTP server location. In order to copy the file, the user needs to input a valid username and password into the FTP server machine.
- **Intranet Upload**: This allows the user to upload the file via a JavaScript client code, and then store the file locally, just like a typical upload to repository strategy.

These three transactions can upload single or multiple documents as desired by the user.

After the form submission, the request will be parsed by the commons-upload libraries, then map the multipart/form-data object to the MultipartFile implementation. The handler method assigned to the request can now extract the file uploaded through the MultipartFile, and eventually store the object into the file system, or to the FTP server, using commons-io and old IO API classes.

Once uploaded, EDMS has the capability to read all uploaded documents in order for the user to download them again. Either the documents are stored in the file system, or the FTP server, controllers can retrieve them and map them on a view that can provide the download links per file.

The discussion will revolve around the details of how to set up a document library module, like EDMS, using the Spring MVC 4.x specification.

# The project development

All the nuts and bolts involved in developing this portal will show how to implement basic Spring MVC software.

- Configuration of the `DispatcherServlet`
- Configuration of the Spring container
- Creating controllers
- Validation
- Views and ViewResolvers
- Encryption and decryption of files
- Creating error views for generic exceptions

# Configuring the DispatcherServlet

There are two ways to perform file-uploading transactions, and the easiest and most immediate way is to use the Servlet 3.1 multipart request process. In order to configure this option, we add the tag `<multipart-config>` inside the `<servlet>` tag declaration of `DispatcherServlet`. The next step, which involves configuring the Spring MVC container, will discuss multipart request processes.

Aside from the `<multipart-config>` tag, there are no additional settings that have been added to the `web.xml`. The deployment descriptor (`web.xml`) still contains the `<servlet>` tag for the front controller's declaration. Even though EDMS uploads files of all different content types, it is not a requirement to include all of those mime-types in the servlet's resources.

The following is the complete content of the `web.xml` file:

```xml
<?xml version="1.0" encoding="UTF-8"?>
<web-app xmlns:xsi="http://www.w3.org/2001/XMLSchema-instance"
xmlns="http://java.sun.com/xml/ns/javaee"
xmlns:web="http://java.sun.com/xml/ns/javaee/web-app_2_5.xsd"
xsi:schemaLocation="http://java.sun.com/xml/ns/javaee
http://java.sun.com/xml/ns/javaee/web-app_3_0.xsd" id="WebApp_ID"
version="3.0">
  <display-name>ChapterTwo</display-name>
  <!-- Declare Spring DispatcherServlet -->
  <servlet>
     <servlet-name>edms</servlet-name>
     <servlet-
class>org.springframework.web.servlet.DispatcherServlet</servlet-class>
     <multipart-config>
          <max-file-size>104857600</max-file-size>
          <max-request-size>104857600</max-request-size>
     </multipart-config>
  </servlet>
  <servlet-mapping>
     <servlet-name>edms</servlet-name>
     <url-pattern>*.html</url-pattern>
  </servlet-mapping>

</web-app>
```

# Creating the Spring container

In order for the Spring Framework to recognize requests from file-uploading transactions, it must have the following API components installed into the framework:

- **Servlet API Multipart Request**: This is the standard API for file uploading since Servlet 3.0
- **Apache Commons FileUpload APIs**: This is a non-standard and external library

The Servlet 3.1 API classes for a multipart request are already part of the Servlet container, but can be configured further to indicate where to store the uploaded file, and to set the maximum size (in bytes) of the file(s) to be uploaded. The setup of this is done within the definition of the `DispatcherServlet` with the use of the `<multipart-config>` tag. The configuration of the EDMS involves some of the following properties:

- `max-file-size`: This property sets the maximum size limit of the uploaded files in bytes. The default value is -1 which means no limit in size.
- `max-request-size`: This property sets the maximum size limit of all the multipart/form-data requests in bytes. The default value is -1 which means it is unlimited when it comes to the size.
- `location`: This property sets the default directory location of all the uploaded documents.
- `file-size-threshold`: This property sets the maximum allowable size (in bytes) of uploaded files that can be written to the disk. The default value, which is 0, states that the container should never write bytes to disk.

The EDMS configures only two properties, namely the `<max-file-size>` and the `<max-request-size>`. If the transaction exceeds the maximum limit set for each property above, an exception like we see in the following will be thrown:

```
org.springframework.web.multipart.MultipartException:
Could not parse multipart servlet request;
```

To enable multipart handling using Apache Commons FileUpload, the library must first be installed, and then a resolver must be injected into the container for the `DispatcherServlet` to access it. In the case of EDMS, the following is the resolver configured to handle file uploading using Commons FileUpload:

```
<bean id="multipartResolver"
        class="org.springframework.web.multipart.commons.
        CommonsMultipartResolver">
    <property name="maxUploadSize" value="104857600" />
        <!-- 100MB -->
        <!-- max size of file in memory (in bytes) -->
    <property name="maxInMemorySize" value="1048576" />
        <!-- 1MB -->
</bean>
```

Once the `DispatcherServlet` receives the request from the client, the task to process the transaction is delegated by the servlet to the resolver declared. When the resolver receives the request, it then maps and parses the request into multipartfiles and parameters to create an instance of the `MultipartHttpServletRequest`.

The `CommonsMultipartResolver` consists of optional properties that can be further configured to optimize the uploading process and these options are:

- `uploadTempDir`: This property sets the temporary directory where uploaded files are saved. The default value is the servlets container's default temporary folder for the web applications.
- `maxUploadSize`: This property sets the maximum allowable size of files to be uploaded in bytes. The default value is -1 which means unlimited size.
- `maxInMemorySize`: This property sets the maximum allowable size needed before the uploaded files can be saved in the temporary folder. The default value is 10240 bytes.

The EDMS has configured only two properties, namely the `maxUploadSize` and `maxInMemorySize`. If there is no resolver declared and file uploading proceeds, the following exception will be encountered by the EDMS:

```
java.lang.IllegalStateException, java.io.IOException]:
    java.lang.IllegalArgumentException: Expected
MultipartHttpServletRequest:
        is a MultipartResolver configured?
```

# Creating exception handling for multipart requests

In the case that EDMS encounters exceptions thrown by the file uploading, it has the capability to handle the exception through the `org.springframework.web.servlet.handler.SimpleMappingExceptionResolver`. This resolver registers one, or more, exception resolver beans that recognize exceptions encountered by any transaction, especially requests, and maps these beans to the error pages declared in its view mappings. Ways of handling exceptions in several Spring MVC applications will be discussed in the next chapters. In EDMS, all the `java.lang` exception classes are mapped to the error view `file_error`.

```
<bean class="org.springframework.web.servlet
  .handler.SimpleMappingExceptionResolver">
    <property name="exceptionMappings">
      <props>
        <prop key="java.lang.Exception">file_error</prop>
      </props>
    </property>
</bean>
```

# Creating the controllers

The EDMS has these main controllers implementing the options for file uploading and downloading transactions. The EDMS custom controllers are as follows:

- UploadSingleFileController: This form controller responds to the common FileUpload multipart request transaction, and processes the MultipartFile in order to save the single file into the file system store.
- UploadMultipleFileController: This is a form controller that has the same response as UploadSingleFileController; the only difference is that the request consists of more than one file to be dropped into the file system.
- UploadSingleFileFtpController: This is a special form controller that asks for a file to be uploaded into the FTP server, username and password of the server.
- UploadSingleFileAjax: This is a typical controller that has two services that handle uploading forms through JQuery plugins and another one that handles form transactions using JQuery form data plugin.
- UploadEncryptFileController: This is a form controller that asks for the file and encrypts it using the Bouncy Castle Crypto API, before saving it to the file system.
- DownloadFileController: This is a typical controller used to download a desired file on the list.
- DowloadFileFtpController: This is a typical controller used to retrieve a file from an FTP server.
- DownloadEncryptFileController: This is the controller that needs to be called to decrypt file that has been encrypted.

# Uploading a single document

The UploadSingleFileController responds to a request from a form that carries a document or file that needs to be uploaded to the server. The EDMS stores its uploaded documents or files within the web server home folder, owing to easy security configuration and management. The service, or handler, method mapped to the request, extracts the multipart object, and creates a copy of the file to the location using OutputStreams class.

The following snippet shows the service method with the process of uploading the file to the location:

```
@RequestMapping(method = RequestMethod.POST)
public String submitForm(
    Model model,
    @Validated @ModelAttribute("singleFileForm")
                SingeFileUploadForm singleFileForm,
        BindingResult bindingResult) {
  String returnVal = "view_file_form";

  if (bindingResult.hasErrors()) {
    model.addAttribute("singleFileForm",
                                singleFileForm);
    returnVal = "upload_single_form";
  } else {
    MultipartFile multipartFile =
                    singleFileForm.getFile();

    try {
// creates the file system folder or repository
        File dir =
                    createUploadDirectory("tmpFiles");
// copies the file on server
      returnVal = uploadSingleFile(dir, multipartFile,
                            model, singleFileForm);
    } catch (Exception e) {
      model.addAttribute("singleFileForm",
                            singleFileForm);
      returnVal = "upload_single_form";
    }
  }
  return returnVal;
}
```

The method known as `createUploadDirectory()` asks for the name of the upload directory, verifies it exists, and if not, creates it for the succeeding file uploading. The following is the code of the method:

```
private File createUploadDirectory(String dirName){
    String rootPath = System.getProperty("catalina.home");
    File dir = new File(rootPath + File.separator +
                                    dirName);
    if (!dir.exists())
      dir.mkdirs();
    return dir;
}
```

After directory verification and creation, the method known as `uploadSingleFile()` is now called to copy the original file to the upload directory using `BufferedOutputStream`. The `java.io.BufferedOutputStream` class manages the copying of the bytes content in a source file to a destination file through a single batch of byte transfer. This makes the process faster than any other per byte, or per character, writing method.

```java
private String uploadSingleFile(File dir,
    MultipartFile multipartFile, Model model,
    SingeFileUploadForm singleFileForm) throws IOException{
    File serverFile = new File(dir.getAbsolutePath()
      + File.separator
          + multipartFile.getOriginalFilename());
    BufferedOutputStream stream = new BufferedOutputStream(
        new FileOutputStream(serverFile));
    byte[] bytes = multipartFile.getBytes();
    stream.write(bytes);
    stream.close();
    model.addAttribute("singleFileForm", singleFileForm);
      return "view_file_form";
}
```

# Uploading multiple documents

Spring allows the uploading of more than one document, which is done by mapping the array of multipart objects to the request. The custom controller of the EDMS, namely `UploadMultipleFileController`, has a service that extracts the array of multipart objects, which consists of a list of uploaded files ready to be uploaded into the local repository. The implementation is just an extended version of how to upload the single document. The code for the service method, that processes the bulk of files for uploading, is as follows:

```java
@RequestMapping(method = RequestMethod.POST)
public String submitForm(
  Model model,
  @Validated @ModelAttribute("multipleFileUploadForm")
        MultipleFilesUploadForm multipleFileUploadForm,
    BindingResult bindingResult) {
  String returnVal = "view_files_form";
  if (bindingResult.hasErrors()) {
      model.addAttribute("multipleFileUploadForm",
                  multipleFileUploadForm);
      returnVal = "upload_multiple_form";
  } else {
      List<MultipartFile> docFiles =
              multipleFileUploadForm.getFiles();
```

```
            if (docFiles.size() > 0 || docFiles != null) {
            Iterator<MultipartFile> iterate =
                              docFiles.iterator();
    // accesses the repository otherwise creates it
            File dir = createUploadDirectory("tmpFiles");
            // retrieve all the files objects
            while (iterate.hasNext()) {
            MultipartFile multipartFile =
                              iterate.next();
            returnVal = uploadIndividualFile(dir,
                    multipartFile, model, multipleFileUploadForm);
            }
        model.addAttribute("multipleFileUploadForm",
                        multipleFileUploadForm);
            }  }
        return returnVal;
    }
```

First, the `@Controller` has the `createUploadDirectory()` that verifies and creates the directory if it does not exist, just like in the previous topic. Then it retrieves the full list of the MultipartFile from the request to be processed by `uploadIndividualFile()`, which will upload every file to the upload directory. The method uses `BufferedOutputStream` to manage fixed memory allocation for the bytes transfer, and also to make the performance fast.

```
    private String uploadIndividualFile(File dir,
        MultipartFile multipartFile, Model model,
        MultipleFilesUploadForm multipleFileUploadForm){
        try {
            byte[] bytes = multipartFile.getBytes();

    // accesses the file from the source folder and copies it
    // to the repository
            File serverFile = new File(dir.getAbsolutePath()
            + File.separator
            + multipartFile.getOriginalFilename());
            BufferedOutputStream stream = new
                        BufferedOutputStream(
            new FileOutputStream(serverFile));
            stream.write(bytes);
            stream.close();
                return "view_files_form";
        } catch (Exception e) {
        model.addAttribute("multipleFileUploadForm",
                        multipleFileUploadForm);
        return "upload_multiple_form";
    }  }
```

# Uploading single or multiple documents into the FTP server

The only EDMS controller that manages all multipart objects for FTP server uploading is the UploadSingleFileFtpController, which only implements single file FTP uploads. This process needs the Apache Commons Net API that has the necessary classes to help EDMS with FTP operations like creating connections, retrieving a list of all the files from the FTP, uploading files to the FTP, downloading files from the FTP, and other files and directory manipulations possible using the FTP protocol.

The uploading starts with instantiating the org.apache.commons.net.ftp.FTPClient class. We then use the connect() method of the FTPClient, access the FTP server, and evaluate the connection status. If it's successful, use the login() method of the same class, using the valid credentials of the FTP server ,otherwise the login operation will become invalid.

Once logged into the server, read and extract the stream object of the file that needs to be uploaded. Using the storeFile() method of the FTPClient class, pass the desired complete name of the file once uploaded, and the stream object of the original file as the second argument. Always call the logout() and disconnect(), respectively, after a successful or unsuccessful FTP file upload. A solution found in EDMS is shown as follows:

```
@RequestMapping(method=RequestMethod.POST)
public String submitForm(Model model,
    @Validated @ModelAttribute("singleFtpForm")
    SingleFileUploadFtpForm singleFtpForm,
    BindingResult bindingResult) throws ServletException,
                        IOException{
    String returnVal = "view_file_ftp";
    if (bindingResult.hasErrors()) {
        model.addAttribute("singleFtpForm", singleFtpForm);
        returnVal = "upload_single_ftp";
    } else {
        model.addAttribute("singleFtpForm",singleFtpForm);
        FTPClient ftpClient = new FTPClient();
        FileInputStream inputStream = null;
        try {
            if (isFtpAccessValid(ftpClient, "<FTP URL here>",
                    singleFtpForm)) {
            // entry point to the FTP server
            ftpClient.enterLocalPassiveMode();
            // file byte type
            ftpClient.setFileType(FTP.BINARY_FILE_TYPE);
            // creates the file system folder or repository
            File dir = createUploadDirectory("tmpFiles");
```

```
                    // creates the empty file on server
                    File serverFile = new
                        File(dir.getAbsolutePath() + File.separator
                          + singleFtpForm.getFile().getOriginalFilename());
                    inputStream = new FileInputStream(serverFile);

                    // uploads the file, returns false if errors found
                    boolean uploaded = ftpClient.storeFile(
                            singleFtpForm.getFile().getOriginalFilename(),
                            inputStream);

                    if(!uploaded) throw new ServletException();
                    // logout the user, returned true if logout success
                    boolean logout = ftpClient.logout();
                    if(!logout) throw new ServletException();

                    // See the sources
                    } else { // Error page }

                    } catch (SocketException e) {  // Error page  }
                    catch (IOException e) { // Error page  }
                    finally {
                      try {
                        ftpClient.disconnect();
                      } catch (IOException e) { // Error page }
                }
            }
        return returnVal;
    }
```

First, the @Controller annotation checks if the user has access to the FTP server, and if the URL is a valid FTP endpoint through the isFtpAccessValid() method.

```
    public boolean isFtpAccessValid(FTPClient ftpClient, String ftpUrl,
    SingleFileUploadFtpForm singleFtpForm) throws SocketException, IOException{
        // the server FTP address
        String ftpServer = "<FTP URL here>";
        ftpClient.connect(ftpServer);

        // access the file system folder or repository
        // otherwise it creates it
        boolean login = ftpClient.login(singleFtpForm.getUsername(),
                        singleFtpForm.getPassword());
        return login;
    }
```

Then, it configures the FTP access properties and verifies the upload directory for the backup directory. From the request, the @Controller first creates the copy of the original file at the server, and then forwards it through the ftpClient.storeFile() method. If the FTP transfer is successful, the client will be logged out through ftpClient.logout(). Exceptions will be thrown if there are problems encountered along the way.

# Uploading single or multiple files asynchronously

Many of the intranet applications are heavily loaded with portlets, and sometimes portlets are composed of AJAX that can access the server asynchronously together with other HTTP transactions. AJAX driven portlets, or applications, can communicate with Spring MVC in whatever container, once files are to be uploaded into the document repository. The existence of Webscript Framework in Alfresco ECM gives EDMS the idea that somehow there will be ways that document(s) can be uploaded and downloaded using JavaScript.

The controller of EDMS that processes the client-side implementation for file uploading with the server-side counterpart is the UploadSingleFileAjax. The service can only process one document for uploading.

The EDMS prototype implements two types of asynchronous client-side implementations of file uploading and these are:

- **AJAX-driven file uploading using a JQuery Plugin**: This solution utilizes the jQuery form plugin that allows AJAX implementation for form transaction. The API has two main methods, ajaxForm() and ajaxSubmit(), that gather information from the form element to determine and manage form submission. To further optimize the process of submission, these two methods contain more options that fine-tune the request transaction. EDMS has implemented a simple solution that uses this JavaScript library:

```
function uploadJqueryForm(){
        $('#result').html('');
            $("#form").ajaxForm({
            success:function(data) {
                $('#result').html(data);
        },
        dataType:"text"
        }).submit();
    }
```

- **AJAX-driven file uploading using JQuery Form Data Plugin**: This solution utilizes the `FormData` object of the JQuery plugin, that contains a set of key/value pairs that needs to be transported using `XMLHttpRequest`. Its main use is to send form data independent from form transaction. The transmitted data is in the same format that the form's `submit()` method would use to send the data, if the form's encoding type were set to multipart/form-data. Since EDMS is a prototype, users can examine and evaluate which of the two client-side solutions can best provide optimized file uploading transactions. The following is the EDMS simple solution using this option:

```
function uploadFormData(){
    $('#result').html('');
  var oMyForm = new FormData();
  oMyForm.append("file", file.files[0]);
  $.ajax({
    url: 'http://localhost:8080/ch02//edms/call_ajax.html',
    data: oMyForm,
    dataType: 'text',
    processData: false,
    contentType: false,
    type: 'POST',
    success: function(data){
      $('#result').html(data);
    }
  });
}
```

On the server side, the controller `UploadSingleFileAjax` has a service that uses the interface `MultipartHttpServletRequest` to get the multipart object from the request. This is the easiest way to extract the said object(s) in order to start the uploading. The rest of the implementation is just the same with the `UploadSingleFileController` controller. The following is the service for this request:

```
@RequestMapping(value="/edms/call_ajax",
                method=RequestMethod.POST)
  public String getFile(Model model, MultipartHttpServletRequest
          request, HttpServletResponse response){
    Iterator<String> itr =  request.getFileNames();
    MultipartFile multipart = request.getFile(itr.next());
    try {
        byte[] bytes = multipart.getBytes();
        // Creating the directory to store file
        String rootPath = System.getProperty("catalina.home");
        File dir = new File(rootPath + File.separator +
                                    "tmpFiles");
        if (!dir.exists())
```

```
            dir.mkdirs();

        // Create the file on server
        File serverFile = new File(dir.getAbsolutePath()
          + File.separator + multipart.getOriginalFilename());
        BufferedOutputStream stream = new BufferedOutputStream(
             new FileOutputStream(serverFile));
        stream.write(bytes);
        stream.close();
        model.addAttribute("multipart", multipart);
    } catch (IOException e) {    }
    return "view_ajax";
}
```

# Uploading documents with encryption/decryption

Some ECM has a document management system that encrypts the file before uploading, in order to secure the files from hacking, or infiltration, once they are uploaded to the repository. There are lots of cryptography API solutions used for securing files, but EDMS uses the Bouncy Castle Crypto API library.

The Bouncy Castle Crypto package is a Java implementation of cryptographic algorithms; it was developed by the Legion of the Bouncy Castle. The package is organized so that it contains a lightweight API suitable for use in any environment (including the newly released J2ME), with an additional infrastructure to conform the algorithms to the JCE framework. The API includes packages that encrypt credentials, or files, using populate cryptography algorithms like RSA, DES, AES and other variants. For simplicity, the EDMS uses the DES type of encryption-decryption, which needs a key to proceed with the transaction. The code of the service method is shown as follows:

```
@RequestMapping(method = RequestMethod.POST)
public String submitForm(  Model model,
    @Validated ModelAttribute("singleFileEncryptForm")
            SingleFileEncryptForm singleFileEncryptForm,
    BindingResult bindingResult) {
  String returnVal = "view_file_encrypt";

  if (bindingResult.hasErrors()) {
      model.addAttribute("singleFileEncryptForm",
                 singleFileEncryptForm);
      returnVal = "upload_single_encrypt";
  } else {
  MultipartFile multipartFile =
        singleFileEncryptForm.getFile();
      try {
```

```
    // encrypts the file using DES Algorithm
      byte[] encContent =
                    encryptedContent(multipartFile, "12345678");
    // accesses the repository otherwise creates it
      File dir = createUploadDirectory("tmpFiles");
      FileOutputStream imageOutFile =
                    new FileOutputStream(dir.getAbsolutePath()
        + File.separator
                    + multipartFile.getOriginalFilename() +".signed");
      BufferedOutputStream stream =
                    new BufferedOutputStream(imageOutFile);
      stream.write(encContent);
      stream.flush();
      stream.close();
      imageOutFile.close();
      model.addAttribute("signedFileName",
      multipartFile.getOriginalFilename() +".signed");
          } catch (Exception e) {
        model.addAttribute("singleFileEncryptForm",
                            singleFileEncryptForm);
        returnVal = "upload_single_encrypt";
      }
    }
    return returnVal;
  }
```

After calling `createUploadDirectory()`, the `@Controller` will
execute `encryptedContent()` to extract the bytes content of the uploaded file and encode
it using a **cipher text**, or key, through a DES algorithm of Bouncy Castle APIs. This process
is found in the method `encryptDESFile()`.

 This application exposes the cipher text or keys as a request parameter or
hardcoded data, but it is recommended to store this in a keystore or a file
cabinet.

```
private byte[] encryptedContent(MultipartFile multipartFile,
                                    String cipher)
          throws Exception, IOException{
    File convFile = new File(
              multipartFile.getOriginalFilename());
    multipartFile.transferTo(convFile);
    FileInputStream imageInFile =
                new FileInputStream(convFile);
    byte imageData[] = new byte[(int) convFile.length()];
    imageInFile.read(imageData);
    byte[] bytes = encryptDESFile(cipher,imageData);
```

```
    imageInFile.close();
    return bytes;
}
private byte[] encryptDESFile(String keys, byte[] plainText) {
    BlockCipher engine = new DESEngine();

    byte[] key = keys.getBytes();
    byte[] ptBytes = plainText;
    BufferedBlockCipher cipher = new
        PaddedBufferedBlockCipher(new CBCBlockCipher(engine));
    cipher.init(true, new KeyParameter(key));
    byte[] rv = new
            byte[cipher.getOutputSize(ptBytes.length)];
    int tam = cipher.processBytes(ptBytes, 0,
                                    ptBytes.length, rv, 0);
    try {
        cipher.doFinal(rv, tam);
    } catch (Exception ce) {      }
    return rv;
}
```

To decrypt the file for download, the decryptDESFile() method must be called:

```
public byte[] decryptDESFile(String key, byte[] cipherText) {
    BlockCipher engine = new DESEngine();
    byte[] bytes = key.getBytes();
    BufferedBlockCipher cipher = new
            PaddedBufferedBlockCipher(
                CBCBlockCipher(engine));
    cipher.init(false, new KeyParameter(bytes));
    byte[] rv =
        new byte[cipher.getOutputSize(cipherText.length)];
    int tam = cipher.processBytes(cipherText, 0,
                            cipherText.length, rv, 0);
    try {
        cipher.doFinal(rv, tam);
    } catch (Exception ce) {    }
    return rv;
}
```

# Downloading individual documents from the file system

The EDMS has a controller, called DownloadFileController, that accepts the filename of the original document as a request parameter; accesses and evaluates the content types; creates an InputStream object copy of the files in the repository; and updates the content-disposition header using the HttpServletResponse.

The service implementation is shown as follows:

```
@RequestMapping(value = "/edms/download_single_file",
                method = RequestMethod.GET)
public String downloadFile(@RequestParam("fileName")
                String fileName,
                HttpServletRequest request,
                HttpServletResponse response) {

    // Creating the directory to store file
    String filePath = System.getProperty("catalina.home")
                    + File.separator
        + "tmpFiles" + File.separator + fileName;
    File downloadFile = new File(filePath);

    // get MIME type of the file
    ServletContext context = request.getServletContext();
    String mimeType = context.getMimeType(filePath);
    if (mimeType == null) {
      // set to binary type if MIME mapping not found
      mimeType = "application/octet-stream";
    }
    System.out.println("MIME type: " + mimeType);

    // set content attributes for the response
    response.setContentType(mimeType);
    response.setContentLength((int) downloadFile.length());

    // set headers for the response
    String headerKey = "Content-Disposition";
    String headerValue = String.format("attachment;
                                filename=\"%s\"",
        downloadFile.getName());
    response.setHeader(headerKey, headerValue);
    FileInputStream fis;
    try {
      fis = new FileInputStream(downloadFile);
      FileCopyUtils.copy(fis, response.getOutputStream());
    } catch (FileNotFoundException e) {  }
          catch (IOException e) { }
    return "";
}
```

# Downloading individual documents from the FTP server

The controller `DownloadFileFtpController` has a service that retrieves an uploaded file from the FTP server, for the user to download it from the view pages. The first phase of the solution uses the Apache Commons Net API, which is similar to the FTP upload service mentioned above. The only difference is that this solution uses the `FileOutputStream` object to write the object stream of the uploaded file to a new file, specified with the file name given. The API class `FtpClient` has a `retrieveFile` (String remote, `OutputStream` local) method that needs the downloadable file name (as it appears on the server) as its first argument, and to pass the output stream object as the second argument. EDMS has a simple solution indicated in the following code:

```
@RequestMapping(value = "/edms/download_single_ftp",
                method = RequestMethod.GET)
public String downloadFile(@RequestParam("fileName") String fileName,
@RequestParam("username") String username,
    @RequestParam("password") String password,
    HttpServletRequest request,
        HttpServletResponse response) {

    FTPClient ftpClient = new FTPClient();
    FileOutputStream fos = null;
    String ftpServer = "ftp.alibatabusiness.com";
    try {
    // pass directory path on server to connect
      ftpClient.connect(ftpServer);

    // pass username and password, returned true if
        // authentication is successful
    boolean login = ftpClient.login(username, password);
        if (login) {
      fos = new FileOutputStream(fileName);
      boolean download = ftpClient.retrieveFile(
        "C:\\Users\\sjctrags\\Downloads"
                                + fileName, fos);
    // logout the user, returned true if logout successfully
      boolean logout = ftpClient.logout();
      if (logout) { }
      } else {   }

    } catch (SocketException e) {
    } catch (IOException e) {
    } finally {
      try {
        fos.close();
        ftpClient.disconnect();
```

```
        } catch (IOException e) {}
    }
    return "view_file_ftp";
}
```

The controllers mentioned in the preceding code are the present implementation in the EDMS project for this chapter. Some functionalities like multiple file uploads to FTP server, and multiple file uploads using AJAX, will be left as an exercise for the reader. Speaking of AJAX, we can create client-side solutions for file uploading using Jackrabbit API with the Spring MVC container.

# The form domains

The EDMS has two domain models that generally represent a form for a single file upload, and one for a multiple file upload. These data will be passed to and from a multipart request transaction, through a defined controller and the view. Common to all domains, an interface org.springframework.web.multipart.MultipartFile must be present, because it is the representation of an uploaded file received in a multipart request. After form submission, the file contents are either stored in memory or temporarily on the disk. Once the service method has received the Multipartfile object, it is copied to the session-level or persistent store. The temporary storage used by the Multipartfile will be cleared at the end of request processing.

The form domain model, that will contain the single multipart object after form submission, must be implemented this way:

```
package org.packt.edms.portal.model.form;

import org.springframework.web.multipart.MultipartFile;

public class SingeFileUploadForm {
    private MultipartFile file;

    public MultipartFile getFile() {
        return file;
    }

    public void setFile(MultipartFile file) {
        this.file = file;
    }
}
```

The other form domain that contains multiple files for upload must look like this:

```
package org.packt.edms.portal.model.form;

import java.util.List;
import org.springframework.web.multipart.MultipartFile;

public class MultipleFilesUploadForm {
  private List<MultipartFile> files;
    public List<MultipartFile> getFiles() {
        return files;
    }

    public void setFiles(List<MultipartFile> files) {
        this.files = files;
    }
}
```

These domain objects will still contain more information than EDMS, as the requirement covers more features and workflows.

# The views

The view and view resolvers are similar to that of our PWP prototype in Chapter 1, *Creating a Personal Web Portal (PWP)*. Nothing has changed except for the actual view pages. The pages are typical of an HTML view consisting of the head and body HTML tags. It contains the Spring Form Taglib and JSTL libraries to create a form <form:form> tag. It is recommended to set the request method to POST, although there are complicated implementations where PUT is the method setting. The commandName property of the <form:form> tag contains the name of the backing bean, bound to the appropriate domain model discussed above.

One very essential setting for all the actual pages used in EDMS is the use of the enctype="multipart/form-data" attribute in the <form:form> tag, through which the browser learns how to encode the form as a multipart request. The next important attribute is the input tag, with the type property set to file, through which the uploaded file is placed. Since validation needs to be part of the EDMS, the <form:errors> tag defines where the error message of the specified field will be displayed in the view. Finally, the input tag, with the type property set to upload, is used for the upload button.

The following code is the actual view page of uploading a single document:

```
<%@ page language="java" contentType="text/html; charset=ISO-8859-1"
    pageEncoding="ISO-8859-1"%>
<%@ taglib prefix="c"  uri="http://java.sun.com/jsp/jstl/core"%>
<%@ taglib prefix="form"  uri="http://www.springframework.org/tags/form"%>
<!DOCTYPE html PUBLIC "-//W3C//DTD HTML 4.01 Transitional//EN"
"http://www.w3.org/TR/html4/loose.dtd">
<html>
<head>
<meta http-equiv="Content-Type" content="text/html; charset=ISO-8859-1">
<title>Insert title here</title>
</head>
<body>
    <form:form commandName="singleFileForm" method="POST"
                enctype="multipart/form-data">
        File to upload: <input type="file" name="file" /><br />
        <form:errors path="file"/>
        <input type="submit" value="Upload">
         Press here to upload the file!
    </form:form>
</body>
</html>
```

Part of the view pages is the `file_error` view, which is called once `DispatcherServlet` encounters an error during the request dispatch process. The page shows the exception message that can be custom made or generic. The EDMS has only one generic actual view page, and it is shown as follows:

```
<%@ page language="java" contentType="text/html; charset=ISO-8859-1"
    pageEncoding="ISO-8859-1"%>
<!DOCTYPE html PUBLIC "-//W3C//DTD HTML 4.01 Transitional//EN"
"http://www.w3.org/TR/html4/loose.dtd">
<html>
<head>
<meta http-equiv="Content-Type" content="text/html; charset=ISO-8859-1">
<title>Insert title here</title>
</head>
<body>
    <h2>File Uploading Eror</h2>
    <p> ${ exception }
</body>
</html>
```

# The validators

The EDMS will not be complete without an engine that checks whether the file(s) is (are) valid for uploading. The criteria that document storage must consider during the validation process can be any of the following:

- The maximum and/or minimum file size the user must upload
- The total size of the files uploaded or the quota of the whole multipart request
- The maximum number of files the system can upload per request
- The content types of the files to be uploaded into the repository
- The filename convention that the system follows (not mandatory)
- Any attributes from the document that the process wants to filter

The setup and configuration of the `@InitBinder` and `@Autowired` components in the controllers are just the same as with the PWP in `Chapter 1`, *Creating a Personal Web Portal (PWP)*. Just to give you an idea how validation is being implemented in the EDMS, an actual code with regard to validating multiple file uploads, is shown as follows:

```
package org.packt.edms.portal.validator;

import java.util.List;

import org.packt.edms.portal.model.form.MultipleFilesUploadForm;
import org.springframework.validation.Errors;
import org.springframework.validation.Validator;
import org.springframework.web.multipart.MultipartFile;

public class MultipleFileValidator implements Validator{

  @Override
  public boolean supports(Class<?> clazz) {
    // TODO Auto-generated method stub
    return MultipleFilesUploadForm.class.equals(clazz);
  }

  @Override
  public void validate(Object obj, Errors error) {
    MultipleFilesUploadForm form = (MultipleFilesUploadForm) obj;
    List<MultipartFile> files = form.getFiles();
    boolean isValid = true;
    StringBuilder sb = new StringBuilder("");
    for(MultipartFile file:files)
    {
      if(file.getSize() == 0)
      {
```

```
        isValid = false;
        sb.append(file.getOriginalFilename()+" ");
      }
    }
    if(!isValid)
      error.rejectValue("files","error.file.size",new
String[]{sb.toString()},"File size limit exceeded");
  }
}
```

# The EDMS project

This chapter provides different solutions to how to start with a document uploader and downloader module. Although a full ECM application involves integration of different features like collaboration modules, records management plugins, watermarking, annotation plugins, and workflow management, it is still the document repository that is being most utilized by the client, including the flexibility of the software to upload and download any content types. Since Spring Framework 4.x supports file uploading, it will be just as easy for the developers to innovate techniques on file management as to spend time on basic uploading measures.

The following is the EDMS home page, which has all the types of uploading documents:

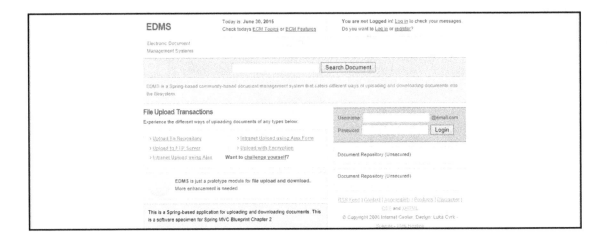

**Web design theme**
The theme is based on the pool of open source templates from `http://ww`
`w.solucija.com/`.

# Challenge yourself

Create an E-book web store that has the following features:

- **Library page**: This shows all the list of e-books in PDF format ready to be downloaded by any readers online.
- **Admin page**: A secured page that is used by any custodian or manager in uploading e-books for the viewers to download. This page uploads PDF files only.

# Summary

Spring MVC Framework 4.x still supports single and multiple file uploading using the `MultipartFile` class. Anyone can start creating a file manager, or a personalized document repository, in their own portals, using the steps provided by this chapter. Since the EDMS is a prototype, this still has to be upgraded by adding some ECM features with security.

The next chapter will introduce how the Spring Framework can store data into a relational database management system. The PWP and EDMS can use database management systems to store their data and metadata. We will have an in-depth understanding of how to go about data connectivity in Spring Framework 4.x in the next chapters

# 3
# Student Management Portal (SMP)

University and college web portals have always been the façade of an organization to promote their mission and vision, and endorse their academic standards and expertise. Aside from good marketing and external promotion, an academic institution can be labeled "high-end" if all internal transactions, from academic affairs to administration, are automated, which spares faculty and staff from doing redundant tasks.

Management information systems for academic institutions always cover major transactions like online student applications, student management for scores and performance, scheduling, attendance monitoring, and course list development. All these automated transactions are done manually by officers and administrators, which may cause overheads on resources, time and cost.

Many of the school management systems are written in PHP or Ruby Rails, possibly because of the easy syntax these languages exhibit, or the availability of pre-packaged snippets online available for instant use.

This chapter will discuss how to start a student management portal that caters for the same administration, academic and student modules, but uses the systematic organized techniques of the Spring 4 specification. This chapter needs a grounding in the topics in Chapter 1, *Creating a Personal Web Portal (PWP)* and some of the components in Chapter 2, *Electronic Document Management Systems (EDMS)*, but new concepts will be introduced which are appropriate for developing SMPs from the ground up. As seen from the previous chapters, the price of building Spring MVC applications is not only for the sake of the the new knowledge you acquire, but also for the maintainability and the manageability of codes after project delivery.

In this chapter, you will learn how to:

- Use relational database management system for Spring applications
- Implement DAO and services layers
- Use Spring Framework JDBC abstraction
- Use Hibernate 4.x Framework
- Use MyBatis 3.x Framework
- Implement audit trails and logging using AOP

# An overview of the project

This software is a typical management information system for academic institutions that has administrative functions are always automated. This type of information relies heavily on the data store from which they can create archived reports, profiles, master tables and current snapshots of data. Through integrating the concept of relational database management systems, the accuracy, and integrity, of simultaneous and redundant access to these data, are monitored and audited periodically.

The software contains the following major pages, which provide some basic functionality needed by core academic software systems:

- **The main page**: This wireframe shows the façade of the institution. To attract aspirants and transferees, we plan for this page to contain some marketing concepts, like the presence of some audio-visual images, news scoops, and other campus-related images.

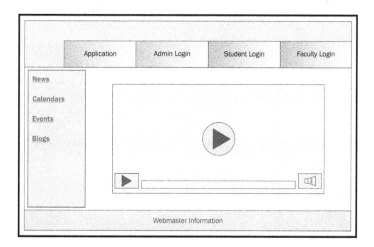

- **The admin page**: This page adds, removes, updates and retrieves all master lists of courses, departments, students, faculty members and applicants. Only administrators can access this page.

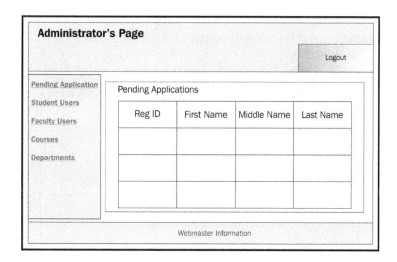

- **The faculty page**: This page is to be accessed by any valid faculty member of the institution wherein they can input grades, manage students' performance, and manages their course loads and schedules.

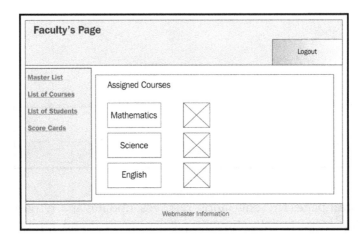

- **The student page**: This wireframe is dedicated to the page that manages student profiles and scholastic information. The student's individual grades, courses they are enrolled in, and the overall courses they took with the GPA, are all the concerns of this area.

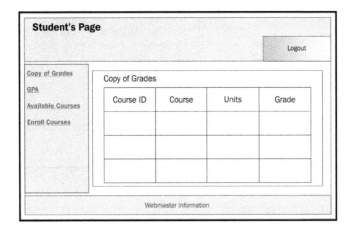

All the sub-links of the above major wireframes are also planned to be web pages showing tables, and form components, for input-output transactions.

The project highlighted in this chapter is just a typical university, or college, management system, except that this will be implemented in Spring MVC 4.

# Technical requirements

This chapter has provided four types of implementation, wherein each has its own set of POM libraries. Their purpose is just to give enthusiasts the options of where to start implementating the business requirements given above.

The following are the implementation types of this **Student Management Portal** (**SMP**):

- **Implementation A**: Using Spring JDBC plugin
- **Implementation B**: Using Spring and MyBatis framework
- **Implementation C**: Using Spring and Hibernate framework
- **Implementation D**: Using Spring, JPA, and Hibernate framework

# Implementation A – using the Spring JDBC plugin

This type of implementation needs the following libraries to be added into the previous libraries you had on PWP (Chapter 1, *Creating a Personal Web Portal (PWP)*) and EDMS (Chapter 2, *Electronic Document Management Systems (EDMS)*):

- `spring-jdbc`: This is a Spring abstraction that opens the database connection for the software; executes all the queries and transactions created at the data layer part; returns a list of all records; handles all exceptions; handles commit and rollback transactions; and closes the connection, statement and result set.
- `mysql-connector-java`: This is an abstraction that provides standard-based drivers and implementations of all SQL libraries.
- `commons-dbcp` and `commons-dbcp2`: This provides API classes for connection pooling which enhances performance of the application.
- `com.mchange`: This is a set of simple libraries used as driver managers which provides standard DataSource objects.

# Implementation C – using Spring and MyBatis frameworks

This implementation type needs the following libraries to start the development:

- `spring-jdbc`
- `spring-orm`: This contains Spring support classes used by the application to integrate with Hibernate, **Java Persistence API (JPA)** and **Java Data Objects (JDO)** for resource management, **data access object (DAO)** implementations, and transaction strategies.
- `cglib`: The **Byte Code Generation Library** is a high-level API, used to generate and transform Java byte codes. It is used by AOP testing data access frameworks to generate dynamic proxy objects, and intercept field access.
- `mybatis`: This contains all the main API classes and interfaces of the MyBatis framework, which automates the mapping between SQL databases and objects in Java.
- `mybatis-spring`: This is a set of API classes and interfaces which integrates MyBatis seamlessly with Spring through creating and building MyBatis mappers and SqlSessions that can be understood by Spring specification; it translates MyBatis exceptions into Spring `DataAccessExceptions`, and finally, it lets you build your application code free of dependencies on MyBatis, Spring or MyBatis-Spring.
- `commons-dbcp` and `commons-dbcp2`
- `mysql-connector-java`
- `com.mchange`

# Implementation B – using Spring and Hibernate frameworks

- `spring-jdbc`
- `spring-orm`
- `aopalliance`: This is a set of classes and interfaces that support AOP, and interoperability, among different AOP implementations in Spring and other frameworks or platforms.
- `hibernate-core`: This is a set of classes and interfaces that provide data persistence to relational databases.

- `hibernate-c3p0`: Hibernate's classes for connection pooling.
- `mysql-connector-java`
- `com.mchange`

# Implementation D – using Spring, JPA and Hibernate Frameworks

- `hibernate-entitymanager`: `EntityManager` is part of the persistence API that contains the methods such as persist, merge, remove, find, and many others needed for SQL transactions.
- `hibernate-jpa-2.0-api`: This is the persistence framework for object relational mapping, which is based on **POJO** (**Plain Old Java Object**) and was conceived from EJB2. It can be used in both EJB and non-EJB context.
- `aopalliance`
- `hibernate-core`
- `hibernate-c3p0`
- `mysql-connector-java`
- `com.mchange`
- `spring-jdbc`
- `spring-orm`

Other libraries needed by the SMP project are the following:

- `spring-aop`: Spring's support for AOP
- `log4j`: The framework for logging
- `spring-tx`: Spring's libraries for transaction management

# Software design overview

This project implementation follows the Spring MVC configuration and setup presented in our section on the PWP (`Chapter 1`, *Creating a Personal Web Portal (PWP)*). The only formal addition in here, is the data layer part, since there will be a database management server involved in the operation of the whole SMP transactions, from login authentication, to archiving of records.

Two layers will be added into the implementation and these are the data access object layer and the service layer. We first set up the DAO layer, which is needed for data persistency. This is the only layer that directly accesses the database server, given the appropriate driver manager and credentials. All data objects contain SQL transactions that will directly access the database concerned. Generally, the DAO must be as light as possible to simply provide a connection to the database, but sometimes it is abstracted so there is a different database backend.

The other is the service layer. This layer provides algorithms to the data retrieved from the DAO layer, in order to be sent back to the client. Sometimes a service caters for more than one DAO, just to fulfil the requirement of a certain module.

Both DAO and service layers are important to the final structure of the implementation. The following is the diagram that shows the flow of data from the DAO layer up to the controller:

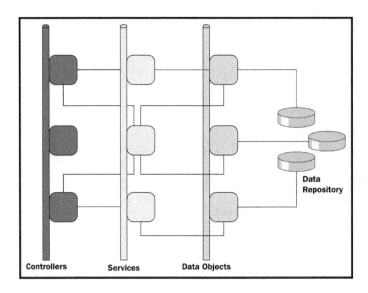

# Configuring the DispatcherServlet

Just like in Chapters 1 and 2, we still follow the convention in declaring the
DispatcherServlet. Using JavaConfig, a class known
as AbstractAnnotationConfigDispatcherServletInitializer is created, to avoid
declaring the servlet in a deployment descriptor.

The only difference now is that there will be separate containers catering for the JDBC
configuration, DAO bean and service beans. If an XML-based ApplicationContext is
used, the deployment descriptor must implement a listener called
a ContextLoaderListener, in order to import all those ApplicationContexts files
needed by the DispatcherServlet.

```
<context-param>
    <param-name>contextConfigLocation</param-name>
    <param-value>
            /WEB-INF/jdbc.xml
            /WEB-INF/dao_services.xml
    </param-value>
</context-param>
<listener>
<listener-class>
    org.springframework.web.context.ContextLoaderListener
 </listener-class>
</listener>
```

The filenames are written as context param values of the contextConfigLocation.

On the other hand, the following code is the JavaConfig counterpart of the
implementation above:

```
@Configuration
@ImportResource({"/WEB-INF/jdbc.xml",
                 "/WEB-INF/dao_services.xml"})
public class SMPConfig {
    // @Bean definitions here...
}
```

# The SMP database

SMP uses the following ERD design, done using MySQL WorkBench. The database server is MySQL Server 6.x.

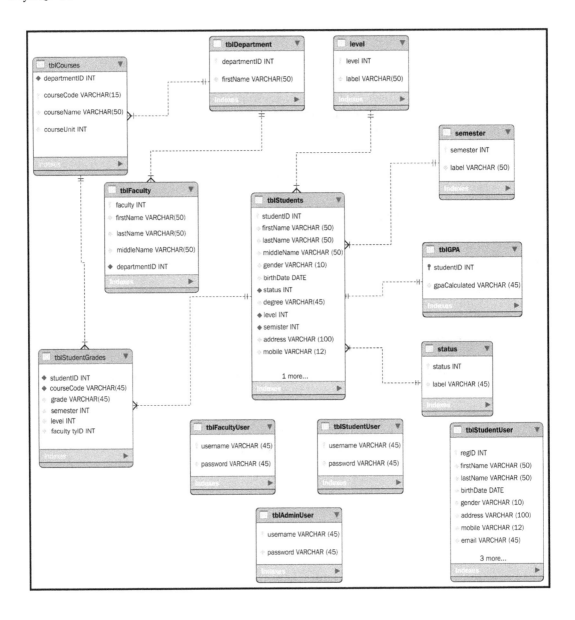

# Creating the Spring containers

The creation of Spring containers varies among the four types of implementation of SMP presented in the technical requirements, since each type has its own different set of libraries to be injected into the container. Here are the different SMP implementations.

# Implementation A – using a Spring JDBC plugin

The first container to be created is the JDBC container, which highlights the driver manager and the JDBC support classes. Since the book will use the XML type of `ApplicationContext` configuration, the following is a bean, which contains the usual database properties, namely the database URI, username, password and the driver class.

## jdbc.xml

The main and first content of this `ApplicationContext` container must be the following:

```
<bean id="dataSource"
class="org.springframework.jdbc.datasource.DriverManagerDataSource">
    <property name="driverClassName"
            value="com.mysql.jdbc.Driver"/>
    <property name="url" value="jdbc:mysql://localhost:3306/smp"/>
    <property name="username" value="root"/>
    <property name="password" value="username"/>
</bean>
<bean id="jdbcTemplate"
        class="org.springframework.jdbc.core.JdbcTemplate">
            <property name="dataSource">
                <ref bean="dataSource"/>
            </property>
</bean>
```

Since the `DriverManagerDataSource` does not support a connection-pooling capability, it is expensive for the application when a new user connects to the database, since it will open a new physical connection to cater for the new user. Thus another configuration has been made which highlights data-pooling from the `com.mchange` library:

```
<bean id="dataSource"
        class="com.mchange.v2.c3p0.ComboPooledDataSource">
            <property name="driverClass">
                <value>com.mysql.jdbc.Driver</value>
            </property>
            <property name="jdbcUrl">
```

```
                    <value>jdbc:mysql://localhost:3306/smp</value>
            </property>
            <property name="user">
                    <value>root</value>
            </property>
            <property name="password">
                    <value>admin</value>
            </property>
            <property name="minPoolSize">
                    <value>5</value>
            </property>
            <property name="acquireIncrement">
                    <value>5</value>
            </property>
            <property name="maxPoolSize">
                    <value>100</value>
            </property>
            <property name="maxStatementsPerConnection">
                    <value>180</value>
            </property>
    </bean>
    <!-- JDBC Template -->
    <bean id="jdbcTemplate"
        class="org.springframework.jdbc.core.JdbcTemplate">
            <property name="dataSource">
                <ref bean="dataSource"/>
            </property>
    </bean>
```

The Spring JDBC has two popular popular classes and these are the `JdbcTemplate` and the `NamedParameterJdbcTemplate`. The API used for any general SQL transactions is the `JdbcTemplate`, which has its own implementation of JDBC interfaces. The only advantage that developers can benefit from, in using `JdbcTemplate`, is its easy-to-use methods that can directly access the database. But, there are problems encountered in using a `JdbcTemplate` which:

- Sometimes requires lots of codes to be written just to extract the data from the repository, such as implementing the `RowMapper`, instantiating the `ResultSet`, and creating some logic just to extract the list of records.
- Recommends risky methods, or a series of try-catch statements, in order to handle exception handling.
- Sometimes requires manual calls to transaction management.
- Reuses lengthy SQL codes just to implement SQL transactions.

Conversely, the `NamedParameterJdbcTemplate` is used if there are lots of constrained SQL statements in the data access layer. Instead of the placeholder question mark (?), we use names to indicate parameters, for instance:

```
public  void setCourses (Course e){
String query="insert into courses values(:id,:course_name,:units)";
Map<String,Object> map=new HashMap<String,Object>();
map.put("id",e.getId());
map.put("courseName",e.getCourseName());
map.put("units",e.getUnits());
template.execute(query,map,new PreparedStatementCallback() {
    @Override
    public Object doInPreparedStatement(PreparedStatement ps)
            throws SQLException, DataAccessException {
        return ps.executeUpdate();
    }
});
}
}
```

But before this query is used, the `NamedParameterJdbcTemplate` must also be injected into the JDBC container:

```
<!-- JDBC Template -->
<bean id="namedJdbcTemplate"
class="org.springframework.jdbc.core.namedparam.NamedParameterJdbcTemplate"
>
        <property name="dataSource">
                <ref bean="dataSource"/>
        </property>
  </bean>
```

The second container that needs to be configured is the `dao_services.xml`. The beans injected inside these containers needs the JDBC support beans to be configured in the `jdbc.xml` file. In order to avoid a `NullPointerException`, the following is the correct way of connecting two containers. The following configuration file shows the collections of beans from the `@Repository` and `@Service` classes to be injected into the Spring container.

# dao_services.xml

This configuration contains mainly of the DAO configuration:

```
<import resource="jdbc.xml"/>

    <bean id="applicationDao"
class="org.packt.academic.student.portal.dao.impl.ApplicationDaoImpl">
```

```
        <property name="jdbcTemplate" ref="jdbcTemplate"></property>
    </bean>
    <bean id="applicationService"
class="org.packt.academic.student.portal.service.impl.ApplicationServiceImp
l">
        <property name="applicationDao" ref="applicationDao"></property>
    </bean>
    <bean id="loginDao"
class="org.packt.academic.student.portal.dao.impl.LoginDaoImpl">
        <property name="jdbcTemplate" ref="jdbcTemplate"></property>
    </bean>
    <bean id="loginService"
class="org.packt.academic.student.portal.service.impl.LoginServiceImpl">
        <property name="loginDao" ref="loginDao"></property>
    </bean>
```

 Instead of bean dependency injection (DI), @Autowired annotation is preferred by many for decoupling and code clarity purposes. Some areas of the application mix both DI and @Autowired.

We use the `<import resource=""/>` tag to combine two XML-based containers which maintain the continuity of bean injection.

The last container that SMP requires is the main container, which is the `smp-servlet.xml`. Just like PWP (Chapter 1, *Creating a Personal Web Portal (PWP)*) and EDMS (Chapter 2, *Electronic Document Management Systems (EDMS)*), the bean injections are almost the same, except for some data-related injections. The following file carries all the essential and main Spring MVC bean classes needed to set up the whole application.

## smp_servlet.xml

The main Spring configuration file contains the major MVC configuration for SMP.

```
<context:component-scan base-package="org.packt.academic.student.portal"/>
    <aop:aspectj-autoproxy proxy-target-class="true">
      <aop:include name="auditLogger"/>
    </aop:aspectj-autoproxy>

  <mvc:annotation-driven />
  <mvc:default-servlet-handler />
  <mvc:resources mapping="/layout/scripts/**"
                 location="/layout/layout/" />
  <mvc:resources mapping="/layout/styles/**"
                 location="/layout/scripts/" />
```

```
    <!-- View Resolver -->
  <bean id="viewResolver"
class="org.springframework.web.servlet.view.ResourceBundleViewResolver">
    <property name="basename">
      <value>config.views</value>
    </property>
  </bean>
  <!-- Resource Bundle -->
    <bean id="messageSource"
class="org.springframework.context.support.ResourceBundleMessageSource">
        <property name="basename"><value>config.errors</value></property>
    </bean>
    // Codes here just see source
  <mvc:interceptors>
      <mvc:interceptor>
          <mvc:mapping path="/smp/admin_login.html" />
          <bean
class="org.packt.academic.student.portal.interceptor.LoginInterceptor"/>
      </mvc:interceptor>
      <mvc:interceptor>
          <mvc:mapping path="/smp/admin_logout.html" />
          <bean
class="org.packt.academic.student.portal.interceptor.LogoutInterceptor"/>
      </mvc:interceptor>
  </mvc:interceptors>
<bean id="auditLogger"
class="org.packt.academic.student.portal.audit.AuditLogServices"/>
```

Since we have new static resources, all <mvc:resources> will be mapped to different CSS, images and JS files. There are also new features that will be found inside the projects, and these are in the AOP, which is needed for audit-trailing and logging. Also, the interceptors will be discussed as an important session, request and security-handling mechanism for view pages.

# Implementation B – using Spring and MyBatis frameworks

This implementation uses a framework that is very simple and easy to use, whose main objective is to provide low-level JDBC codes that automate executing the SQL commands, store results into Java objects, and persist data into tables by passing data objects into the framework.

If you need an Object Relational Mapping (ORM) framework that is easy to manage and use, then MyBatis is the best choice for your SMP implementation. The following are some advantages of using MyBatis:

- It spares developers from a series of boilerplated codes
- It is easy to learn from scratch
- It works with small, medium or large-scale databases, either with modern or legacy databases
- It is purely SQL-based
- It can be integrated with third-party caching libraries for better performance
- It induces better performance

The Spring container must initialize all new drivers and properties for MyBatis configuration in this application. The following is the resulting XML configuration if the Mybatis Framework is used as an ORM.

# jdbc.xml

The primary configuration of the JDBC and MyBATIS must be found here:

```xml
<bean id="dataSource"
    class="org.apache.commons.dbcp2.BasicDataSource"
    destroy-method="close">
    <property name="driverClassName"
                value="com.mysql.jdbc.Driver"/>
    <property name="url"
                value="jdbc:mysql://localhost:3306/smp"/>
    <property name="username" value="root"/>
    <property name="password" value="admin"/>
</bean>
<bean id="sqlSessionFactory"
        class="org.mybatis.spring.SqlSessionFactoryBean">
    <property name="dataSource" ref="dataSource" />
    <property name="configLocation"
                value="classpath:config/mybatis-config.xml" />
</bean>
    <bean class="org.mybatis.spring.mapper
                        .MapperScannerConfigurer">
        <property name="basePackage"
                value="org.packt.academic.student.portal.mapper" />
</bean>
<bean id="transactionManager"
        class="org.springframework.jdbc
                .datasource.DataSourceTransactionManager">
```

```
        <property name="dataSource" ref="dataSource" />
    </bean>
```

The driver manager used here is `org.apache.commons.dbcp2.BasicDataSource` which is the Apache Commons DBCP connection-pooling library, but the `ComboPooledDataSource` in Type A can still be used instead. After the database credentials are configured, include the `org.springframework.jdbc.datasource.DataSourceTransactionManager` for scoping/controlling the SQL transactions. Then, configure the MyBatis and Spring connectivity through configuring the `org.mybatis.spring.SqlSessionFactoryBean`. This MyBatis central configuration has three properties that need to be filled by information, and these are:

- `DataSource`: The database configuration
- `ConfigLocation`: The location where the mapper configuration file resides

The `SqlSessionFactoryBean` also provides the `SqlSession` object.

Next, and finally, configure the `org.mybatis.spring.mapper.MapperScannerConfigurer` that scans all the mapper classes.

The `JavaConfig` equivalent of this container will look like this:

```
@Configuration
@MapperScan("org.packt.academic.student.portal.mapper ")
public class SMPMybatisConfig {
    @Bean
    public DataSource getDataSource() {
        BasicDataSource dataSource = new BasicDataSource();
        dataSource.setDriverClassName("com.mysql.jdbc.Driver");
        dataSource.setUrl("jdbc:mysql://localhost:3306/smp");
        dataSource.setUsername("root");
        dataSource.setPassword("admin");
        return dataSource;
    }
    @Bean
    public DataSourceTransactionManager transactionManager() {
        return new DataSourceTransactionManager(getDataSource());
    }
    @Bean
    public SqlSessionFactory sqlSessionFactory() throws Exception {
        SqlSessionFactoryBean sessionFactory = new SqlSessionFactoryBean();
        sessionFactory.setDataSource(getDataSource());
        return sessionFactory.getObject();
```

```
        }
    }
```

The `dao_services.xml` will not contain injected DAO and service beans anymore. All the classes need to be declared to `@Transactional`, given that their methods are public. MyBatis does not work well with `@Transactional` private methods.

MyBatis has internal annotation support to transactional database operations. To enable this annotation, the configuration file must declare an annotation-driven manager:

## dao_services.xml

Using the `spring-tx` libraries, transaction manager is simply created through a simple line:

```
<import resource="jdbc.xml"/>
<tx:annotation-driven transaction-manager="transactionManager"/>
```

On the main container `smp-servlet.xml`, everything is same as in Type A.

# Implementation C – using Spring and Hibernate frameworks

The Hibernate framework is an ORM tool that simplifies data creation, data manipulation and data access to the SMP database. In addition to MyBatis, this is another strategy to implement SQL transactions. Here are the advantages of using Hibernate over other ORM frameworks:

- Hibernate has built-in caches so it is fast. There are two types of cache in the Hibernate framework: the first level cache and the second level cache. The first level cache is enabled by default.
- It has its own **HQL** (**Hibernate Query Language**), which is an object-oriented version of SQL. It generates database independent queries, so you don't need to write database specific queries. Using HQL spares you from creating length SQL statements.
- The Hibernate framework provides the facility to create database tables automatically. Therefore, there is no need to create tables in the database manually, and also we can update the tables automatically.
- The Hibernate framework has built-in query statistics and database status because it supports a query cache.

First, we configure the JDBC container using the Hibernate configuration details. The XML configuration file must consist of all the beans needed to integrate Spring to the Hibernate framework, and all the database properties for the application is shown as follows:

# jdbc.xml

The primary configuration of the JDBC and Hibernate must be found here:

```
<bean id="dataSource" class="org.apache.commons.dbcp2.BasicDataSource"
destroy-method="close">
    <property name="driverClassName"
              value="com.mysql.jdbc.Driver"/>
    <property name="url"
              value="jdbc:mysql://localhost:3306/usmp"/>
    <property name="username" value="root"/>
    <property name="password" value="admin"/>
</bean>
<bean id="sessionFactory"
    class="org.springframework.orm
            .hibernate4.LocalSessionFactoryBean">
    <property name="dataSource" ref="dataSource" />
    <property name="configLocation"
              value="classpath:config/hibernate.cfg.xml" />
</bean>
<tx:annotation-driven />
    <bean id="transactionManager"
          class="org.springframework.orm
                .hibernate4.HibernateTransactionManager">
    <property name="sessionFactory" ref="sessionFactory" />
</bean>
```

The `hibernate.cfg.xml` file is the Hibernate configuration file containing all the Hibernate properties, and all model classes used by the application. This file is located in our `config` folder.

# hibernate.cfg.xml

All the core Hibernate configuration details are found in this file:

```
<?xml version='1.0' encoding='utf-8'?>
<!DOCTYPE hibernate-configuration PUBLIC
        "-//Hibernate/Hibernate Configuration DTD 3.0//EN"
        "http://www.hibernate.org/dtd/hibernate-configuration-3.0.dtd">
<hibernate-configuration>
  <session-factory>
```

```xml
        <property name="dialect">
                org.hibernate.dialect.MySQLDialect
        </property>
        <property name="show_sql">true</property>
        <mapping resource="config/model/Tblapplication.hbm.xml"/>
        <mapping resource="config/model/Tblstudents.hbm.xml"/>
         // more codes in the source
    </session-factory>
</hibernate-configuration>
```

Using XML configuration, all data models are mapped to the framework using `*.hbm.xml` files. If annotation is used for model-mapping, the appropriate XML configuration for the JDBC container is this:

```xml
<bean id="dataSource" class="org.apache.commons.dbcp2.BasicDataSource"
destroy-method="close">
        <property name="driverClassName"
                    value="com.mysql.jdbc.Driver"/>
        <property name="url"
                    value="jdbc:mysql://localhost:3306/smp"/>
        <property name="username" value="root"/>
        <property name="password" value="admin"/>
</bean>
        <bean id="sessionFactory"
          class="org.springframework.orm
                .hibernate4.LocalSessionFactoryBean">
          <property name="dataSource" ref="dataSource" />
          <property name="annotatedClasses">
          <list>
            <value>
            org.packt.academic.student.portal.model.data.Tbladminuser
            </value>
            <value>
            org.packt.academic.student.portal.model.data.Tblcourses
            </value>
            <value>
        org.packt.academic.student.portal.model.data.Tblregistration
            </value>
          <value>
            org.packt.academic.student.portal.model.data.Tblstudents
          </value>
            </list>
          </property>
         <property name="annotatedPackages">
          <list>
           <value>org.packt.academic.student.portal.model.data</value>
            </list>
         </property>
```

```
<property name="configLocation"
        value="classpath:config/hibernate.cfg.xml" />
</bean>
<tx:annotation-driven />
    <bean id="transactionManager"
      class="org.springframework.orm
        .hibernate4.HibernateTransactionManager">
    <property name="sessionFactory" ref="sessionFactory" />
```

Part of the `org.springframework.orm.hibernate4.LocalSessionFactoryBean` includes two properties that are needed to declare all annotated model classes and these are:

- `annotatedClasses`: This property accepts a list of annotated classes used in this SMP application
- `annotatedPackages`: This property accepts a list of packages where all annotated model classes reside.

The project prefers to set the `annotatedPackages` because it will not make the container bloated.

Whether the Hibernate model-mapping is XML-based, or annotation-based, the configuration always starts with the datasource. Just like in Type A and B implementations, we can use the `BasicDataSource` of Apache or the `ComboPooledDataSource` of `com.mchange` for this bean.

Next, is the configuration of our `SessionFactory` object. It is a thread-safe, immutable cache of compiled mappings for a single database. Sometimes literature calls it a factory for `org.hibernate.Session` instances and a client of `org.hibernate.connection.ConnectionProvider`. Optionally, this class maintains a second-level cache of data that is reusable between transactions at a process or cluster level. To instantiate the `SessionFactory` object, we will be using `org.springframework.orm.hibernate4.LocalSessionFactoryBean`, which is similar in role to the same-named class in the `orm.hibernate3` package. However, in practice, it is closer to the `AnnotationSessionFactoryBean`, since its core purpose is to bootstrap a `SessionFactory` from package scanning.

Since Spring 4, the use `HibernateTemplate` is no longer recommended, so we need to create our `TransactionManager`. Use the class `org.springframework.orm.hibernate4.HibernateTransactionManager` for this time.

# Implementation D – using Spring, JPA and Hibernate frameworks

Another implementation of this SMP project is through the use of the JPA framework. JPA is a persistence framework and is used whenever an enterprise application uses vast amounts of data to store, retrieve, read, and update. Generally, as data gets huge, lots of code and configuration details are needed to maintain efficient access to the database.

JPA is just a specification or set of guidelines and it has no implementation classes in it. When used on top of Hibernate 4, it uses the Hibernate JPA implementations. JPA unifies the ORM standard for persistence because if the Hibernate JPA is directly used, it will depend solely on Hibernate JPA, and switching to another JPA specification would be difficult. Thus, it is conventional to instantiate, and use, specific JPA specification on top of any ORM.

For the JPA framework, the JDBC configuration file might look the same as the Hibernate configuration file, but it includes JPA properties like the one shown as follows.

# jdbc.xml

The primary configuration of the JDBC and JPA is done here:

```xml
<bean id="dataSource" class="org.apache.commons.dbcp2.BasicDataSource"
destroy-method="close">
    <property name="driverClassName"
                  value="com.mysql.jdbc.Driver"/>
    <property name="url"
                  value="jdbc:mysql://localhost:3306/smp"/>
    <property name="username" value="root"/>
    <property name="password" value="admin"/>
</bean>
<tx:annotation-driven transaction-manager="transactionManager" />
    <bean id="transactionManager"
        class="org.springframework.orm.jpa.JpaTransactionManager">
        <property name="entityManagerFactory"
                  ref="entityManagerFactory" />
    </bean>
    <bean id="entityManagerFactory"
class="org.springframework.orm.jpa.LocalContainerEntityManagerFactoryBean">
        <property name="persistenceXmlLocation"
                  value="classpath:config/persistence.xml" />
        <property name="dataSource" ref="dataSource" />
        <property name="packagesToScan"
          value=" org.packt.academic.student.portal.model.data " />
```

```
<property name="jpaVendorAdapter">
    <bean
class="org.springframework.orm.jpa.vendor.HibernateJpaVendorAdapter">
        <property name="showSql" value="true" />
        <property name="databasePlatform"
        value="org.hibernate.dialect.MySQLDialect" />
    </bean>
</property>
</bean>
```

Just like in any implementations presented in this chapter, we always start with datasource configuration. Then, the injection of the EntityManager is next in line, since it is associated with a persistence context. The EntityManager is the JPA connection to the database, which has methods such as persist, merge, remove, which we will find are very important in SQL transactions. Many applications require multiple database connections during their lifetime. For instance, in a web application, it is common to establish a separate database connection, using a separate EntityManager instance, for every HTTP request.

The EntityManager is produced by an implementation of EntityManagerFactory. This project uses org.springframework.orm.jpa.LocalContainerEntityManagerFactoryBean, which has properties needed to fully process the connection. Part of the property is the persistenceXmlLocation, which needs the location of the persistence.xml. Since Spring 3, persistence.xml is no longer recommended, because all the JPA Entity models are scanned using the property packagesToScan. Lastly, the jpaVendorAdapter, which interfaces any ORM framework, must be injected with the org.springframework.orm.jpa.vendor.HibernateJpaVendorAdapter, since we will be using Hibernate Framework 4. The following figure summarizes the whole API connectivity of the JPA specification:

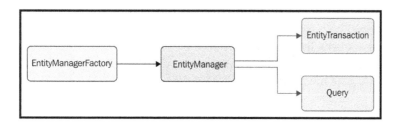

## The persistence.xml

A JPA persistence unit is a logical grouping of user-defined persistable classes (entity classes, embeddable classes and mapped superclasses) with related settings. Defining a persistence unit is required by JPA. Persistence units are defined in a `persistence.xml` file, which has to be located in the classpath. One `persistence.xml` file can include definitions for one or more persistence units. The use of this file is already an option from Spring 3.1 onwards.

```xml
<?xml version="1.0" encoding="UTF-8"?>
<persistence version="2.1" xmlns="http://xmlns.jcp.org/xml/ns/persistence"
xmlns:xsi="http://www.w3.org/2001/XMLSchema-instance"
xsi:schemaLocation="http://xmlns.jcp.org/xml/ns/persistence
http://xmlns.jcp.org/xml/ns/persistence/persistence_2_1.xsd">

<persistence-unit name="profilePersistency">
      <provider>org.hibernate.ejb.HibernatePersistence</provider>
<class>org.packt.academic.student.portal.model.data.Tblregistration.java</c
lass>
</persistence-unit>

</persistence>
```

The containers of the `dao_services.xml` contain all the injected beans from DAO objects and the service layer. The `smp-servlet.xml` remains the same.

# The Data Access Object (DAO) layer

The Student Management Portal (SMP) has packages under the DAO layer, namely the `org.packt.academic.student.portal.dao` and `org.packt.academic.student.portal.dao.impl`. To maintain loosely-coupled architecture, it would be best to first write the interface for all the DAO classes before their implementation. All of the four implementations follow the same interface blueprint. For instance, the `ApplicationDao`, which contains all database operations for the student application module, has the following DAO interface:

```java
public interface ApplicationDao {
  public void setPendingApp(Application application);
  public List<Application> getPendingApp();
  public Application getPending(Integer regId);
  public void setRegister(Application application);
  public void deletePending(Application application);
  public void setStudentAccount(Application application);
  }
```

When it comes to the implementation, the four implementations differ from each other.

# Implementation A – using the Spring JDBC plugin

The implementation class for the `ApplicationDao`, with this implementation strategy, uses the injected `JdbcTemplate`, or the `NamedParameterJdbcTemplate` support classes for the SQL transactions. The following is the code for all of the methods given in the preceding interface.

```
@Repository
public class ApplicationDaoImpl implements ApplicationDao {
    private JdbcTemplate jdbcTemplate;
    public JdbcTemplate getJdbcTemplate() {
        return jdbcTemplate;
    }

    public void setJdbcTemplate(JdbcTemplate jdbcTemplate) {
        this.jdbcTemplate = jdbcTemplate;
    }

    @Override
    public void setPendingApp(Application application) {
        String sql = "INSERT INTO tblRegistration (firstName, middleName,
lastName, birthDate, gender, address, mobile, email, username, password)"
                + " VALUES (?, ?, ?, ?, ?, ?, ?, ?, ?, ?)";
        jdbcTemplate.update(sql, application.getFirstName(),
application.getMidName(), application.getLastName(),
            application.getBirthDate(), application.getGender(),
application.getAddress(), application.getMobile(), application.getEmail(),
application.getUsername(), application.getPassword());
    }

    @Override
    public List<Application> getPendingApp() {
        String sql = "SELECT * FROM tblRegistration";
        List<Application> listPending = jdbcTemplate.query(sql,
                new RowMapper<Application>() {

            @Override
            public Application mapRow(ResultSet rs, int rowNum)
                    throws SQLException {
                Application application = new Application();
                application.setRegId(rs.getInt("regId"));
                application.setFirstName(rs.getString("firstName"));
                application.setMidName(rs.getString("middleName"));
                application.setLastName(rs.getString("lastName"));
```

```java
            application.setBirthDate(rs.getDate("birthDate"));
            application.setGender(rs.getString("gender"));
            application.setAddress(rs.getString("address"));
            application.setMobile(rs.getString("mobile"));
            application.setEmail(rs.getString("email"));
            return application;
            }
      });
      return listPending;
   }

   @Override
   public Application getPending(Integer regId) {
      String sql = "SELECT * FROM tblRegistration WHERE regId
            return jdbcTemplate.queryForObject(sql, new
                     RowMapper<Application>() {
            @Override
            public Application mapRow(ResultSet rs, int rowNum)
                     throws SQLException{
         Application application = new Application();
         application.setRegId(rs.getInt("regId"));
application.setFirstName(rs.getString("firstName"));
         application.setMidName(rs.getString("middleName"));
         application.setLastName(rs.getString("lastName"));
      application.setBirthDate(rs.getDate("birthDate"));
      application.setGender(rs.getString("gender"));
         application.setAddress(rs.getString("address"));
      application.setMobile(rs.getString("mobile"));
      application.setEmail(rs.getString("email"));
            application.setUsername(rs.getString("username"));
      application.setPassword(rs.getString("password"));
         return application;
         }
      }, regId);
   }

   @Override
   public void setRegister(Application application) {
      String sql = "INSERT INTO tblStudents (firstName, middleName, lastName,
birthDate, gender, address, mobile, email, status, degree, level,
semester)"
                  + " VALUES (?, ?, ?, ?, ?, ?, ?, ?, ?, ?, ?, ?)";
      jdbcTemplate.update(sql, application.getFirstName(),
      application.getMidName(), application.getLastName(),
application.getBirthDate(), application.getGender(),
application.getAddress(), application.getMobile(),
application.getEmail(),0, "",0,0);
   }
```

```
@Override
public void deletePending(Application application) {
  String sql = "DELETE FROM tblRegistration WHERE
                  regId=?";
    jdbcTemplate.update(sql, application.getRegId());
  }
  // More codes in the source
}
```

The JdbcTemplate has the following methods, which are used by the SMP Dao Layer:

| JdbcTemplate Methods | Functionality |
|---|---|
| public int update(String query) | insertion, update and deletion of records |
| public int update(String query,Object... args) | insertion, update and deletion of records using PreparedStatement with given arguments |
| public void execute(String query) | execution of DDL query |
| public T execute(String sql, PreparedStatementCallback action) | execution of the queries that uses PreparedStatement callback |
| public T query(String sql, ResultSetExtractor rse) | fetching records using ResultSetExtractor |
| public List query(String sql, RowMapper rse) | fetching records using RowMapper |

The NamedParameterJdbcTemplate has only one method to override:

```
pubic T execute(String sql,Map map,PreparedStatementCallback psc)
```

All DAO classes have the annotation @Repository, which is a Domain-Driven Design strategy for encapsulating storage, retrieval, and search behavior, which emulates a collection of objects. The advantages of having these annotations are the following:

- All DAO classes will be eligible for persistence exception translation
- All DAO classes can undergo AOP mechanism

# Implementation B – using Spring and MyBatis Frameworks

In MyBatis, the DAO interfaces are technically called the mapper interface. Using the XML-based mapper configuration, all the implementations of the mapper interfaces are written in the `dao_mapper.xml`. In the case of `ApplicationMapper`, the implementation of all its methods is found in `/mybatis/mapper/application_mapper.xml` of the SMP classpath. Here is a snapshot of the content of `application_mapper.xml`:

```xml
<?xml version="1.0" encoding="UTF-8" ?>
<!DOCTYPE mapper PUBLIC "-//mybatis.org//DTD Mapper 3.0//EN"
  "http://mybatis.org/dtd/mybatis-3-mapper.dtd">

<mapper
namespace="org.packt.academic.student.portal.mapper.ApplicationMapper" >
 <insert id="setPendingApp"
parameterType="org.packt.academic.student.portal.model.data.Tblregistration
" >
   insert into tblRegistration (firstName, middleName, lastName, birthDate,
gender, address, mobile, email, username, password)
    values ( #{firstName,jdbcType=VARCHAR}, #{middleName,jdbcType=VARCHAR},
#{lastName,jdbcType=VARCHAR}, #{birthDate,jdbcType=DATE},
#{gender,jdbcType=VARCHAR},
#{address,jdbcType=VARCHAR}, #{mobile,jdbcType=VARCHAR},
#{email,jdbcType=VARCHAR}, #{username,jdbcType=VARCHAR},
#{password,jdbcType=VARCHAR})
 </insert>
  <select id="getPendingApp" resultMap="applicationResult">
    SELECT * FROM tblRegistration
  </select>
  <resultMap
type="org.packt.academic.student.portal.model.data.Tblregistration"
id="applicationResult">
    <id property="regId" column="regId" />
    <result property="firstName" column="firstName" />
    <result property="middleName" column="middleName" />
    <result property="lastName" column="lastName" />
    <result property="birthDate" column="birthDate" />
    <result property="gender" column="gender" />
    <result property="address" column="address" />
    <result property="mobile" column="mobile" />
    <result property="email" column="email" />
  </resultMap>
  <select id="getPending" resultMap="applicationResult2"
          parameterType="int">
    SELECT * FROM tblRegistration WHERE regId = #{regId}
```

```
    </select>
    <resultMap
type="org.packt.academic.student.portal.model.data.Tblregistration"
id="applicationResult2">
    <id property="regId" column="regId" />
    <result property="firstName" column="firstName" />
    <result property="middleName" column="middleName" />
    <result property="lastName" column="lastName" />
    <result property="birthDate" column="birthDate" />
    <result property="gender" column="gender" />
    <result property="address" column="address" />
    <result property="mobile" column="mobile" />
    <result property="email" column="email" />
    </resultMap>
    <insert id="setRegister"
parameterType="org.packt.academic.student.portal.model.data.Tblstudents" >
        insert into tblStudents (firstName, middleName, lastName, birthDate,
gender, address, mobile, email, status, degree, level, semester)
        values ( #{firstName,jdbcType=VARCHAR},
#{middleName,jdbcType=VARCHAR}, #{lastName,jdbcType=VARCHAR},
#{birthDate,jdbcType=DATE}, #{gender,jdbcType=VARCHAR},
#{address,jdbcType=VARCHAR}, #{mobile,jdbcType=VARCHAR},
#{email,jdbcType=VARCHAR}, #{status,jdbcType=INTEGER},
#{degree,jdbcType=VARCHAR}, #{level,jdbcType=INTEGER},
#{semester,jdbcType=INTEGER})
    </insert>
    <delete id="deletePending"
parameterType="org.packt.academic.student.portal.model.data.Tblregistration
" >
        DELETE FROM tblRegistration WHERE regId = #{regId}
    </delete>
// more codes in the source
</mapper>
```

This SMP will have at least 10 mapper configuration files. All the XML mappers will be registered inside the `mybatis-config.xml` file. A sneak peek of the MyBatis configuration file (`/config/mybatis-config.xml`) for the SMP application is shown as follows:

```
<?xml version="1.0" encoding="UTF-8" ?>
<!DOCTYPE configuration
  PUBLIC "-//mybatis.org//DTD Config 3.0//EN"
  "http://mybatis.org/dtd/mybatis-3-config.dtd">
<configuration>
 <mappers>
  <mapper resource="/mybatis/mapping/application_mapper.xml" />
  <mapper resource="/mybatis/mapping/login_mapper.xml" />
   // more mappers below
 </mappers>
```

```
</configuration>
```

Using the annotation-based MyBatis, XML mappers are no longer used, but annotations are applied on the mapper interfaces. In our `ApplicationMapper`, this is a sample snippet:

```
public interface ApplicationMapper {
@Insert(insert into tblRegistration (firstName, middleName,
    lastName, birthDate, gender, address, mobile, email,
    username, password)
  values ( #{firstName,jdbcType=VARCHAR}, #{middleName,jdbcType=VARCHAR},
#{lastName,jdbcType=VARCHAR}, #{birthDate,jdbcType=DATE},
#{gender,jdbcType=VARCHAR},
#{address,jdbcType=VARCHAR}, #{mobile,jdbcType=VARCHAR},
#{email,jdbcType=VARCHAR}, #{username,jdbcType=VARCHAR},
#{password,jdbcType=VARCHAR})
)
  public void setPendingApp(Tblregistration registration);
  // more codes in the source
}
```

# Implementation C – using Spring and Hibernate frameworks

The model classes of this implementation have a `SessionFactory` injected into them to provide sessions. The session objects should not be kept open for a long time because they are not usually thread safe, and they should be created and destroyed as needed. The main function of the session is to offer create, read and delete operations for instances of the mapped entity classes in Hibernate transactions. On the `ApplicationDao`, data object implementation must look like this:

```
@Repository
public class ApplicationDaoImpl implements ApplicationDao {
  @Autowired
  private SessionFactory sessionFactory;
  public void setPendingApp(Tblregistration registration) {
    Session session =
              this.sessionFactory.getCurrentSession();
        session.persist(registration);
  }

  @SuppressWarnings("unchecked")
  public List<Tblregistration> getPendingApp() {
    Session session =
              this.sessionFactory.getCurrentSession();
```

```
    List<Tblregistration> pendingList =
            session.createQuery("from Tblregistration").list();
    return pendingList;
  }
  // More codes in source
}
```

The popular methods used by the session in executing SQL transactions, here in the SMP project, are:

| Hibernate Session Methods | Functionality |
| --- | --- |
| `void persist(Object object)` | Makes a transient instance persistent |
| `void persist(String entityName, Object object)` | Makes a transient instance persistent |
| `Object merge(String entityName, Object object)` | Copies the state of the given object onto the persistent object with the same identifier |
| `Object merge(Object object)` | Copies the state of the given object into the persistent object with the same identifier. |
| `Object get(Class clazz, Serializable id)` | Returns the persistent instance of the given entity class with the given identifier, or null if there is no such persistent instance |
| `Query createQuery(String queryString)` | Creates a new instance of query for the given HQL query string |
| `void delete(Object object)` | Removes a persistent instance from the datastore |
| `void delete(String entityName, Object object)` | Removes a persistent instance from the datastore |

All these methods automatically call the transaction method `commit()`, so calling the said method will lead to an exception. If the requirement asks for a new session, where the methods `commit()` and `rollback()` are needed to be invoked programmatically, then the `Transaction` object must be instantiated. An example of this scenario is shown as follows:

```
public void setRegister(Tblstudents applicant) {
  Session session = this.sessionFactory.openSession();
  Transaction transaction = session.beginTransaction();
  session.persist(applicant);
  transaction.commit();
  session.close();
}
```

# Implementation D – using Spring, JPA and Hibernate frameworks

Using the JPA framework, the DAO implementation class looks like this:

```
@Repository
public class ApplicationDaoImpl implements ApplicationDao {
  @PersistenceContext
  private EntityManager entityManager;
  public void setPendingApp(Tblregistration registration) {
    entityManager.persist(registration);
        entityManager.flush(); ();
  }

  @SuppressWarnings("unchecked")
  public List<Tblregistration> getPendingApp() {
      String qlString = "SELECT * FROM Tblregistration t";
      TypedQuery< Tblregistration > query =
        entityManager.createQuery(qlString, Tblregistration.class);
    return query.getResultList();
  // More codes in source
  }
```

The `EntityManager` is used to access a database in a particular unit of work. This is declared already in the JDBC container. This object is declared the `@PersistentContext`, which means it is a unique entity instance, with a lifecycle and is managed by a particular entity manager. The scope of this context can either be the transaction, or an extended unit of work.

To insert an entity into the database, the following methods are used:

- `Merge`: Deals with new entities to be inserted into the tables
- `Persist`: Deals with both new and detached entities; detached entities are previous entities inserted into the table

To force the insertion of the entity, and to synchronize the persistence context, the `flush()` is invoked after calling the merge or persist methods.

To read data, use the `java.persistence.Query` or the
`java.persistence.TypedQuery`.

To update records, the merge method is used.

The deletion of an entity is executed with the remove method of the `EntityManager`, after
the entity has been loaded into the `PersistenceContext`, with the help of the find
method.

# The service layer

Just like with the DAO layer, each implementation type has its own implementation of
service classes. But all of the implementations have both
`org.packt.academic.student.portal.service` and
`org.packt.academic.student.portal.service.impl` packages. The purpose of the
business layer is to implement business logic with the use of the DAO objects.

# Implementation A – using the Spring JDBC plugin

Given the `LoginService` interface of the SMP as follows:

```
public interface LoginService {
  public boolean isAdminUser(Login login);
  public boolean isStudentUser(Login login);
  public boolean isFacultyUser(Login login);
}
```

The implementation of this interface is just a typical `Transactional` class.
A `@Transactional` class starts with a transaction on each method start, and commits it on
each method exit (or rollback, if the method was failed due to an error). Note that since the
transactions are in the method's scope, and inside method we are using DAO, the DAO
method will be executed within same transaction.

By using the annotation `@Service`, the class will recognized as having the role to
implement the business logic of the application. All its methods will be monitored using
Aspect and PointCuts in AOP. The following is SMP's implementation of
the `LoginService`.

```
@Service
public class LoginServiceImpl implements LoginService {
  private LoginDao loginDao;
```

```
public LoginDao getLoginDao() {
  return loginDao;
}

public void setLoginDao(LoginDao loginDao) {
  this.loginDao = loginDao;
}
@Override
public isAdminUser(Login login) {
  Login dbData = loginDao.getAdmin(login);
  if(dbData == null){
    return false;
  }
  return true;
}
// More codes in source
}
```

 Avoid using @Transactional to read operations because it becomes useless and ignored by the framework.

# Implementation B – using Spring and MyBatis frameworks

This implementation is slightly difference in its process of implementing the service classes. The following is the LoginServiceImpl counterpart of the Spring-MyBatis implementation:

```
@Service
@Transactional(propagation = Propagation.REQUIRED, rollbackFor =
Exception.class)
public class LoginServiceImpl implements LoginService {
  @Autowired
  private LoginMapper loginMapper;

  public boolean isAdminUser(String username, String password) {
    Map<String, String> map = new HashMap<String, String>();
    map.put("username", username);
    map.put("password", password);
    Tbladminuser user = loginMapper.getAdmin(map);
    if(user == null){
      return false;
    }
```

```
    return true;
  }
      // More codes in source
}
```

The service class must always be `@Transactional` and must define the
`Propagation.REQUIRED`, which means the transaction can be newly created or reused if
necessary.

# Implementation C – using Spring and Hibernate frameworks

This implementation uses the same concept as Implementation A.

# Implementation D – using Spring, JPA and Hibernate frameworks

Just like Implementation C, this strategy also uses the same concept as Implementation A.

# The data domain layer

If views are mapped to form domain objects, table schema are mapped to data domain
objects. It is the depiction of a table schema definition that can be used for inserting,
updating, removing and reading records. In JPA implementation, these data domain classes
are called entity classes. In Hibernate these are called persistent classes. In MyBatis and
Spring JDBC, these are just POJOs.

# Implementation A – using a Spring JDBC plugin

Given the `Tblregistration` table, SMP's domain class for this table is shown as follows:

```
public class Tblregistration {
  private String firstName;
  private String midName;
  private String lastName;
  private Date birthDate;
  private String gender;
  // More on the source
```

```
public String getUsername() {
  return username;
}
public void setUsername(String username) {
  this.username = username;
}
 // More on the source
}
```

# Implementation B – using Spring and MyBatis frameworks

Spring JDBC and MyBatis uses typical POJO as their data domain classes.

# Implementation C – using Spring and Hibernate frameworks

Persistent classes in the Hibernate ORM framework use annotations to depict constraint keys, column names and types, and other schema attributes. The following is the persistent class for the `tblRegistration` schema:

```
@Entity
@Table(name = "tblregistration", catalog = "smp")
public class Tblregistration implements java.io.Serializable {

  private Integer regId;
  private String firstName;
  private String lastName;
  // More on the source

  @Id
  @GeneratedValue(strategy = IDENTITY)

  @Column(name = "regId", unique = true, nullable = false)
  public Integer getRegId() {
    return this.regId;
  }

  public void setRegId(Integer regId) {
    this.regId = regId;
  }
```

```
@Column(name = "firstName", nullable = false, length = 50)
public String getFirstName() {
  return this.firstName;
}

public void setFirstName(String firstName) {
  this.firstName = firstName;
}
// More on the source
}
```

The following annotations are used in the preceding class:

- `@Entity`: The annotation that marks the class as an entity.
- `@Table`: The annotation that specifies the table name where data of this entity is to be persisted. If you don't use the `@Table` annotation, Hibernate will use the class name as the table name by default.
- `@Id`: The annotation that marks the identifier for this entity.
- `@Column`: The annotation that specifies the details of the column for this property or field. If the `@Column` annotation is not specified, the property name will be used as the column name by default.

The `@GeneratedValue` annotation is used to generate a unique identifier for the objects of persistent class. This can be customized, or auto-generated, depending on the requirement. The strategies that can be used for this ID generation are assigned increment, sequence, hilo, native, identity, seqhilo, uuid, guid, select, foreign, and sequence-identity.

# Implementation D – using Spring, JPA and Hibernate frameworks

JPA implementation of its entity class is quite similar to that of Hibernate but without the `catalog` attribute of the `@Table` annotation.

```
import javax.persistence.GeneratedValue;
import static javax.persistence.GenerationType.IDENTITY;

@Entity
@Table(name = "tblregistration)
public class Tblregistration implements java.io.Serializable {

  private Integer regId;
  private String firstName;
```

```
private String lastName;
// More on the source

@Id
@GeneratedValue(strategy = IDENTITY)

@Column(name = "regId", unique = true, nullable = false)
public Integer getRegId() {
  return this.regId;
}

public void setRegId(Integer regId) {
  this.regId = regId;
}
// More on the source
}
```

# The controllers

All the service classes are called by the controllers in order to perform request-response transactions. Only the service layer is exposed to the controllers. Chapter 1, *Creating a Personal Web Portal (PWP)* has guided this implementation in creating different @Controller classes.

# The validators and type conversion

Since there is a lot of form information needed by SMP, it has several validator classes to check, if the user has the correct inputs. PropertyEditors are also needed to convert input parameter data to date, time, and other objects, before inserting them into the tables. The rules in Chapter 1, *Creating a Personal Web Portal (PWP)* have guided SMP in creating these classes.

# The interceptors

Interceptors are popular in the Struts 2 framework, but Spring MVC can implement interceptors to manage sessions, logging, and auditing a user authentication process. The concept of an interceptor is similar to the filters in a typical Java Enterprise model but not exactly the same.

In order to create a handler interceptor, we must make use of `org.springframework.web.servlet.HandlerInterceptor`. The `HandlerInterceptor` defines three methods that can be used for pre-processing and post-processing requests:

- `PreHandle`: This is called before a URL is executed, and returns a Boolean value. When it returns true, the handler execution chain continues, whereas when it returns false, the `DispatcherServlet` stops the execution of the entire request-response transaction.
- `PostHandle`: This is called after a URL is executed.
- `AfterCompletion`: This is called after the result view page has been executed.

The SMP project uses interceptors to check the number of visitors to the portal, the duration a user has used the portal, and to authenticate the user. The following is a sample interceptor used in the administrator's login.

```
public class LoginInterceptor extends HandlerInterceptorAdapter{
  @Override
  public void afterCompletion(HttpServletRequest request,
      HttpServletResponse response, Object handler,
              Exception ex) throws Exception {
    // More on the source
  }
  @Override
  public boolean preHandle(HttpServletRequest request,
      HttpServletResponse response, Object handler)
              throws Exception {
    long timeStarted = System.currentTimeMillis();
    HttpSession session = request.getSession();
    session.setAttribute("timeStarted", timeStarted);

    return true;
  }
  @Override
  public void postHandle(HttpServletRequest request,
      HttpServletResponse response, Object handler,
      ModelAndView modelAndView) throws Exception {
    HttpSession session = request.getSession();
      long timeStarted =
            (long) session.getAttribute("timeStarted");
      long timeUsed = System.currentTimeMillis() - timeStarted;
      session.setAttribute("timeUsed", timeUsed);
  }
}
```

# The Aspect, Advice and PointCut

One of the major features of any system is audit trailing or user logging. The system must handle the logging of all transactions that a user has executed in a portal. Not only that, it must also complete information on the logging of transactions from the moment the user has opened the application.

Interceptors can be used here, but the most appropriate solution is the Aspect Oriented Programming (AOP) support of Spring MVC 4.x, since the nature of execution of auditing and logging can be configured to cut across different classes. We simply used some of Aspects for logging service methods and formulate some of PointCut to be executed mostly by `@After` advice. An example of SMP logger is shown as follows:

```
@Aspect
public class AuditLogServices {
    private static Logger mainLogger = Logger.getLogger("generic");
    @Before("execution(*
        org.packt.academic.student.portal.service.impl.*.*(..))
        && target(service)")
    public void log(Object service) {
      mainLogger.info("Accessing {}" +
                service.getClass().getSimpleName());


    }
@AfterThrowing(pointcut = "loggingPoincut()", throwing = "e")
public void logAfterThrowing(JoinPoint joinPoint, Throwable e) {
    mainLogger.error("Exception in {}.{}() with cause = {}",
joinPoint.getSignature().getDeclaringTypeName(),
            joinPoint.getSignature().getName(), e.getCause(), e);
    }


}
```

The logger framework used by the portal is Log4J framework, which has the following configuration:

```
<?xml version="1.0" encoding="UTF-8"?>
<!DOCTYPE log4j:configuration PUBLIC "-//log4j/log4j Configuration//EN"
"log4j.dtd">
<log4j:configuration xmlns:log4j="http://jakarta.apache.org/log4j/">
    <appender name="Appender1"
            class="org.apache.log4j.ConsoleAppender">
        <layout class="org.apache.log4j.PatternLayout">
            <param name="ConversionPattern" value="%-7p %d [%t] %c
                                                %x - %m%n"/>
        </layout>
```

```
    </appender>
    // More on sources
</log4j:configuration>
```

# The views

SMP just used typical JSP-JSTL views using the ResouceBundleViewResolver. All the implementations and concepts are just adapted from Chapter 1, *Creating a Personal Web Portal (PWP)*.

**The Theme**
The theme of this portal was derived from the templates authored by http ://www.os-templates.com/.

# The Student Management Portal (SMP)

Building an information system using any programming language and frameworks is very tough, since all the details of the requirement must be considered starting with login transactions, content of the pages, functionalities highlighted by the system, security and integrity of the data saved, and retrieved from its data store. The following is the finished product of the SMP. This is the only project in this book that is written in many versions starting from **Spring JDBC support**, **Spring-MyBatis integration**, **Spring-Hibernate integration** and **Spring-Hibernate-JPA implementation**.

The following screenshot shows the main page of SMP:

The administration login panel:

The pending student account transaction:

# Challenge yourself

Using the above solution, create an online bookstore that has an administrator, and manager and customer profiles. The following are the functionalities in every profile:

- **Administration profile**: This page must add new manager and costumer accounts or disable accounts.
- **Manager profile**: This page can access the book inventory, which means a manager can add, remove or archive books; manage the stock; and manage prices of books.
- **Customer profile**: On this page you can order by adding things into its personalized cart.

The online bookstore has login and logout transactions. It has a built-in audit trail for security purposed. Use MySQL server as the database server.

# Summary

The EDMS application is a prototype that exhibits how to integrate a relational database management system to a Spring MVC application. This chapter showcases a few of the popular Object Relational Mapping (ORM) frameworks such as Hibernate 4.x, MyBatis 3.x and JPA 2.x, that provide different database abstraction layers for Spring's database transactions. Although the database technology used is MySQL, the process of configuration applies is the same as other relational database management systems (RDBMS) like in Microsoft SQL Server and Oracle 11g/12C, except with some extra properties to their additional drivers.

NoSQL databases like MongoDB, and its integration to Spring MVC, will be discussed in `Chapter 10`, *Social Task Management System (STMS)*.

# 4
# Human Resource Management System (HRMS)

The Human Resources Management System is a module of **Enterprise Resource Planning (ERP)** that involves processes and activities related to payroll systems, sales and marketing, and manpower allocation. This kind of information system involves routines and packages present in the data processing departments of most companies.

Some basic functional specifications of an HRMS include payroll transactions, time and attendance evaluation, performance monitoring, benefits administration, training and learning management, employee profiling, scheduling, leave management, and other analytics. All these processes need a database management system for CRUD transactions, archiving, and generations of voluminous reports. Chapter 3, *Student Management Portal (SMP)*, has guides in implementing different strategies, or options, on data modeling and datysical views all have an .ftl extension. It is advisable to design a layout first before coding the FTL files. From the layout, we build a template (adabase configuration for Spring MVC 4 web projects. Data sources are always at the center of any data processing activities, thus, the concepts in Chapter 3, *Student Management Portal (SMP)*, will be needed here.

This chapter will introduce developers to how to integrate reports and basic analytics for data presentation and printing.

The techniques and tools to be highlighted here are flexible, and can be integrated into any information systems written in the Spring 4.x MVC specification, that have a lot of report and data analytics.

In this chapter, you will learn how to:

- Use the different types of Views and ViewResolvers
- Integrate Freemarker and the Velocity plugin for view handling
- Generate graphs and charts using a JFreeChart plugin
- Generate graphs and charts using a Google Chart plugin
- Generate documents for presentation and download using POI and IText plugins
- Generate reports using JasperReports and DynamicReports
- Generate XML, JSON, Excel, Word and RTF documents
- Generate RSS and ATOM feeds
- Apply types of exception handling in Spring 4 MVC
- Use a Spring test framework for test-driven development and testing

# Overview of the project

The **Human Resource Management System** (**HRMS**) project simulates how a human resources department works. The basic activities featured in the system include employee profile management, leave management, attendance monitoring, project performance evaluation, training and career enrichment assessment, and company information dissemination. Just like any typical information system, HRMS has its own administrator module for user and role management. In the meantime, all security is database-driven.

The software design started with the following wireframes suited to start a HRMS prototype with valid functional specifications:

- **The main page**: Since the proposed system is an intranet type to be accessed only by employees of a company, the final design for the home page is simply the login page with a signup page at the side.

- **The admin page**: The only role of the admin page is to activate, de-activate, penalize, and monitor HRMS access and traffic. The administrator's page has some graphs, charts, and reports related to the users of the system.

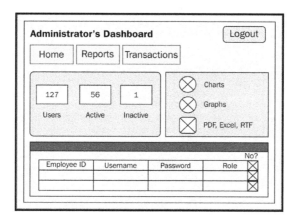

- **The HR manager page**: All the HR transactions are found on this page. It is loaded with analytics and reports regarding employees' profiles, performance, leave, and career information.

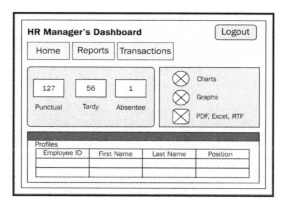

- **The employee page**: Basically this page contains the profile information of the employee's account. This is always updated by the user. Other than the personal data sheet, this page contains reports on, an employee's attendance, reports and company news updates disseminated by the HR manager.

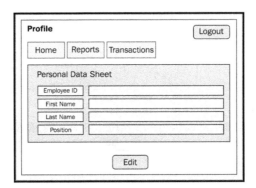

- **The reports page**: This page presents buttons and links that lead to viewing and downloading certain data from the database, using different types of rendition like HTML, WORD, RTF, EXCEL, PDF, XML, JSON, or TXT. The administrator, HR manager, and employee pages contains their own reports page.

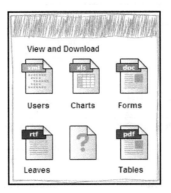

- **The charts page**: The data analysis part is found on this page. This shows charts and graphs on the frequency and distribution of the different variables under study, for example the classification of employees according to age range, sex, performance, department, roles, and position. This page allows these charts and graphs to be viewed or downloaded.

# Technical requirements

All the core configuration setup has already been discussed in the previous chapters. The focus of this chapter is to integrate Spring MVC applications with plugins and libraries that can be used to render data in many forms.

Rendition is the process of creating a copy of the original document in a different format such as PDF, HTML, TEXT, or any valid formats. In web applications, we consider HTML as our default format for data presentation.

Aside from rendition types, we need to highlight some libraries that can help the application process all ordinal and nominal data into a visual representation.

# iText 5.x

iText is an open source API that can be downloaded from `http://itextpdf.com`. It is a powerful and efficient tool for PDF, HTML, RTF, and XML documents generation. iText has a huge support on a variety of fonts to be used in the document. The code structure of iText allows you to generate any of the supported types of documents with a common code.

The iText library contains classes to generate PDF text in various fonts, generate tables in a PDF document, add watermarks to pages, and so on. There are many more features available with iText; just visit the site for more technical documentation.

There are two kinds of libraries HRMS uses for document transformation and these are:

- `com.lowagie`: The original iText PDF Library by Bruno Lowagie
- `com.itextpdf`: The current library created by iText Software Corp.

# Apache POI

Apache POI is a powerful Java library used to work with different Microsoft Office file formats such as Excel, PowerPoint, Visio, MS Word, and other Microsoft-based rendition types. This can be used both in web applications and in standalone applications using the Java Swing API. The name POI is an acronym for Poor Obfuscation Implementation, which means that the libraries are created in a complicated way, which might be impossible to be disassembled. Visit `http://poi.apache.org/` for more technical documentation.

The HRMS needs the two libraries from POI, namely:

- `org.apache.poi`: The core POI packages
- `org.apache.poi` (`poi-ooxml`): The POI API for XWPF for the WordprocessingML class (Windows 2007 and above)

# JExcelAPI

This is an open source Java API that is integrated into any web and standalone applications to read Excel spreadsheets, and to generate Excel spreadsheets dynamically. In addition, it contains a mechanism that allows Java applications to be read in a spreadsheet, modify cells, and write out a new spreadsheet.

The JExcelAPI allows non-Windows platforms to execute pure Excel document generation. To find out more about the library, visit `http://jexcelapi.sourceforge.net/`.

To utilize the API classes, HRMS included the following Maven artifact:

- `net.sourceforge.jexcelapi` (jxl): The core library for JExcelAPI

# JasperReports

When it comes to small or huge data, JasperReports can generate many rendition types given a set of data input. Moreover, it provides the necessary features to generate dynamic reports that include data retrieval, using JDBC (Java Database Connectivity), with its own parameters, expressions, variables, and groups. JasperReports also includes advanced features, such as custom data sources, scriptlets, and sub-reports. The overall features and maturity of JasperReports makes it the open-source version of Crystal Reports. More about the features of JasperReports is written at `http://jasperreports.sourceforge.net`.

The HRMS uses JasperReports for generating PDF, Excel, Word, RTF, JSON, and XML documents from human resources data.

The main Maven artifact for JasperReports is:

- `net.sf.jasperreports`

This needs the other Maven dependencies to work and these are:

- `log4j`: Library for logging
- `commons-digester`: Library for reading XML configuration for internal Java object initialization and configuration
- `com.itextpdf`: Library for Jasper PDF generation
- `commons-digester`: Library for Jasper Excel generation
- `org.apache.poi (poi-ooxml)`
- `xerces (xercesImpl)`: Library for DOM parsing
- `org.codehaus.castor (castor)`: XML data-binding framework
- `com.fasterxml.jackson.core (jackson-databind)`, `com.fasterxml.jackson.core (jackson-annotations)`: Library for Jasper JSON generation

And since there are transactions involving XML parsing, we need to import the Spring API for JAXB parsing:

```
<dependency>
        <groupId>org.springframework</groupId>
        <artifactId>spring-oxm</artifactId>
        <version>${spring.version}</version>
</dependency>
```

# iReport 5.6.0 Visual Designer

iReport is a free, open source report designer for JasperReports, which is used to create sophisticated and voluminous layouts containing charts, images, sub-reports, crosstabs, and other report-related features. The tool can access database tables and fields data through JDBC, TableModels, JavaBeans, XML, Hibernate, CSV, and custom sources. The ultimate goal of the iReport tool is to generate and publish reports as PDF, RTF, XML, XLS, CSV, HTML, XHTML, text, DOCX, or OpenOffice files. This tool is used throughout HRMS development in generating Jasper documents. This tool can be downloaded from `http://c ommunity.jaspersoft.com/project/ireport-designer`.

# DynamicReports

DynamicReports is based on JasperReports, which is evidently why the majority of its API classes are so dependent on the JasperReports library. The only advantage of this tool is its straightforward, short, and handy codes, which are used to create reports and to produce documents for display, print, and export. It allows the creation of dynamic report designs without the use of iReport or any visual report designer. This plugin supports popular formats such as PDF, Excel, and Word. Read about DynamicReports at `http://dynamicre ports.org/`.

The Maven artifact for this is:

- `net.sourceforge.dynamicreports` (`dynamicreports-core`): The main library for DynamicReports plugin

# Freemarker Template Language (FTL)

Freemarker Template Language or FTL is a Java-based, open source, template engine that can be used in a standalone or servlet-based application as a rendition tool. In web applications, this is used to create dynamic layouts of menu pages. An FTL page can contain simple HTML tags with some programming constructs like conditions, loops, switch statements, and template mappings. Some template mappings have placeholders or EL variables that can be dynamically supplied by any controllers or services. All codes of FTL are written in a text file with the extension `.ftl`. More information and documentation about FTL is found in its site `http://freemarker.org/`.

HRMS used this plugin to generate dynamic HTML-based reports with templates. To recognize FTL, the POM must include the following Maven artifact:

- `org.freemarker`: FreeMarker core APIs

# Velocity

Apache Velocity is a Java-based template engine that provides a template language to reference objects defined in Java code. It aims to ensure clean separation between the presentation tier and business tiers in a web application (the Model-View-Controller design pattern). Read about Velocity at `http://velocity.apache.org/`.

HRMS uses this tool in some parts of the pages, while some use FTL. The following are the libraries needed to implement Velocity templates:

- `commons-collections`: Helps accelerate performance by providing powerful data structures and data handling
- `org.apache.velocity`: The Velocity core APIs
- `org.apache.velocity` (`velocity-tools`): The Velocity supporting APIs

# JFreeChart

JFreeChart is an API used for creating and displaying charts such as bar, pie, graphs, plots, and other analytics for an application. It supports several output types like Swing components, image files (including PNG and JPEG), and vector graphics file formats (including PDF, EPS, and SVG). JFreeChart is open source and distributed under the terms of LGPL. More descriptions on its API classes and methods are found at `http://www.jfre e.org/jfreechart/`.

HRMS has included this library as an option for the generation of graphs through its Maven artifact:

- `jfree` (`jfreechart`): The core library of JFreeChart

And before we start using the API classes, JFreeChart has a servlet that needs to be declared in the `web.xml`:

```
<servlet>
    <servlet-name>chart</servlet-name>
    <servlet-class>
        org.jfree.chart.servlet.DisplayChart
    </servlet-class>
</servlet>
    <servlet-mapping>
        <servlet-name>chart</servlet-name>
        <url-pattern>/hrms/chart</url-pattern>
    </servlet-mapping>
```

# Google Chart

The Google Chart API is a free and lightweight tool for static and dynamic charts generation integrated into any web application. HRMS uses charts4j, a lightweight wrapper to the Google Chart API, which makes incorporating charts into your Spring web application much easier compared to using its core APIs. Visit the site `https://develope rs.google.com/chart/` which contains all libraries for client-side data visualization and `https://code.google.com/p/charts4j/` for the server-side counterpart. The artifact needed to import the char4j library for server-side transactions is:

- `com.googlecode.charts4j` (`charts4j`): The core library of Google Charts

# ROME

ROME is a popular plugin for the generation of RSS and ATOM feeds in an application. Among its features are parsing feeds, generating feeds, converting feeds from a concrete feed to a SyndFeed and vice versa, parsing modules, and generating modules. HRMS uses this project for the generation of news information delivered by company heads daily. More about its API classes is found at `http://rometools.github.io/rome/`.

The following are the required Maven plugins for RSS generation:

- `Rome`: The core API for RSS and ATOM feeds generation
- `Rometools` (rome): The implementation classes of the core APIs

# Software testing libraries

Spring MVC 4.x comes with a very powerful test framework that supports both unit and integration testing. To utilize the API classes, CFS included the following Maven artefact for MVC component testing:

```
<dependency>
    <groupId>org.springframework</groupId>
    <artifactId>spring-test</artifactId>
    <version>${spring.version}</version>
    <scope>test</scope>
</dependency>
```

# The HRMS database

In the same way as in Chapter 3, *Student Management Portal (SMP)*, the project will be using MySQL 6.x DBMS as its data storage and manager. The schema is named **hrms,** which has the following ERD:

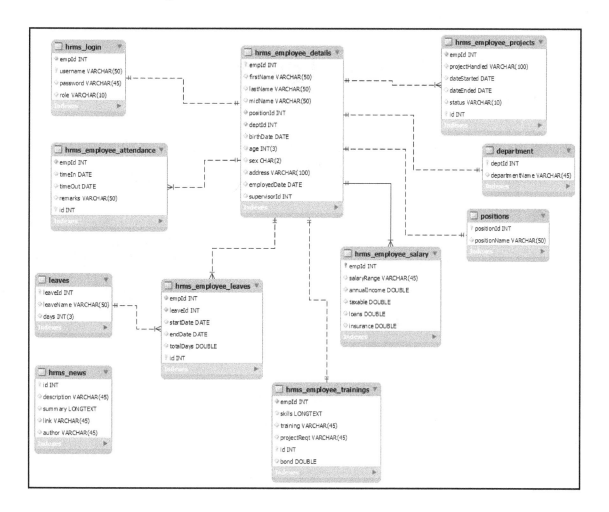

# Data modeling framework

Chapter 3, *Student Management Portal (SMP)*, presented the use of the different types of implementing database transactions in Spring MVC 4.x applications. HRMS will be using the **Hibernate 4.x Framework** to implement its CRUD transactions and for caching and performance monitoring.

# Integrating charts and graphs

The HRMS project uses two plugins for data analysis and presentation, and these are JFreeChart and Google Charts libraries. All data is stored in its MySQL database.

The **Administrator's dashboard** has a page /hrms/admin_charts.html which highlights the frequency and the distribution of users based on user roles, status, activities, and length of employment. The software decided to use the JFreeChart plugin for further analysis.

The **HR Manager's dashboard** has a view /html/hr_charts.html which presents all charts and graphs for the company's employee distribution based on sex, length of employment, performance, attendance, turnover rate, skills and human resources, and number of resources per positions. The plugin for the data visualization is Google Chart.

The **Employee's page** is simply a profile-type account module that has a frequency chart comtaining employees' number of absences, and tardiness which has been incurred daily, monthly, and yearly. All the data will be coming from their attendance logs. JFreeCharts and Google Charts are both used in /html/employee_attendance.html.

# Configuring the ViewResolver

For typical JSP view pages, the HRMS project will still use the previous chapters' viewResolver configuration:

```
<bean id="viewResolver"
    class="org.springframework.web.servlet.view
                      .ResourceBundleViewResolver">
        <property name="basename">
            <value>config.views</value>
        </property>
        <property name="order" value="0"/>
</bean>
```

Since HRMS will be using more than one viewResolvers, we will be ranking all of them from highest to lowest priority, as discussed in Chapter 1, *Creating a Personal Web Portal (PWP)*. The viewResolver, which is ranked the highest, will be the first to map the views, and the lowest will always be the last. The `org.springframework.web.servlet.view.ResourceBundleViewResolver` will do the mapping first in the chain, since it has the order value of 0. Removing the order property in any of the viewResolvers will lead to HTTP status 404. Please refer to Chapter 1, *Creating a Personal Web Portal (PWP)*, with regard to viewResolver configuration.

# The administrator's analytics

The following are the components needed to successfully integrate charts and graphs to the administrator's page in a Spring MVC way.

# The DAO and service layers

A sample of the DAO implementation of HRMS, which retrieves the data for analysis, is the `LoginDaoImpl.java`. This class gives the current number of users who are administrators, HR managers, and typical employees.

```
@Repository
public class LoginDaoImpl implements LoginDao {

    // See code from sources
    @Transactional
    @SuppressWarnings("unchecked")
    @Override
    public List<HrmsLogin> getAdminUsers() {
        Session session = this.sessionFactory.getCurrentSession();
        Criteria crit = session.createCriteria(HrmsLogin.class);
        crit.add(Restrictions.like("role","admin"));
        List<HrmsLogin> users = crit.list();
        return users;
    }

    @Transactional
    @SuppressWarnings("unchecked")
    @Override
    public List<HrmsLogin> getHrUsers() {
        Session session = this.sessionFactory.getCurrentSession();
        Criteria crit = session.createCriteria(HrmsLogin.class);
        crit.add(Restrictions.like("role","hr"));
```

```
        List<HrmsLogin> users = crit.list();
        return users;
    }
    @Transactional
    @SuppressWarnings("unchecked")
    @Override
    public List<HrmsLogin> getEmployeeUsers() {
        Session session = this.sessionFactory.getCurrentSession();
        Criteria crit = session.createCriteria(HrmsLogin.class);
        crit.add(Restrictions.like("role","employee"));
        List<HrmsLogin> users = crit.list();
        return users;
    }
}
```

To organize all the data from the DAO layer, the class `LoginServiceImpl` will apply the necessary algorithm to consolidate all the data needed for plotting. The method `mapUsers()` below retrieves all the frequency of users by roles. This will be collected and stored in a `HashMap`. The method `getUserList()` returns a list collection that contains all users of the HRMS.

```
@Service
public class LoginServiceImpl implements LoginService {
    @Autowired
    private LoginDao loginDao;
    // See the sources
    @Override
    public Map<String, Integer> mapUsers() {
            Map<String, Integer> tblUsers = new HashMap<>();
            tblUsers.put("admin", loginDao.getAdminUsers().size());
            tblUsers.put("employee", loginDao.getHrUsers().size());
            tblUsers.put("hr", loginDao.getHrUsers().size());
            return tblUsers;
    }
    @Override
    public List<HrmsLogin> getUserList() {
            return loginDao.getLoginUsers();
    }
// See the sources
}
```

All data must be stored in a collection object, to be visualized by the APIs of JFreeChart. The following diagram shows the flow of data from before it reached the view pages. This is how data is transferred to controllers using the Java Collections Framework:

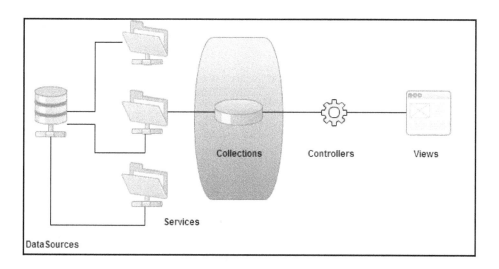

# The controllers

The plotting of data is done by the controllers. It is through this layer that the application interacts with the JFreeChart libraries. The service layer must provide the controller with the final data to be processed by JFreeChart. The following is the controller that plots all the data provided by LoginServiceImpl.

```java
@Controller
public class AdminJFreeChartController {
  @Autowired
  private LoginService loginService;

  @RequestMapping(value = "/hrms/admin_charts",
                  method = RequestMethod.GET)
  public String getCharts(Model model, HttpServletRequest request,
            HttpServletResponse response) throws
                            ServletException, IOException {
    String adminBarChart = createBarCharts(request, response);
    String adminLineChart = createLineGraph(request, response);
    // See the sources

    model.addAttribute("adminBarChart", adminBarChart);
    model.addAttribute("adminLineChart", adminLineChart);
```

```
    // See the sources
    return "admin_charts";
}

private String createBarCharts(HttpServletRequest request,
            HttpServletResponse response) throws
                ServletException, IOException {
        Map<String, Integer> tblUsers = loginService.mapUsers();
        DefaultCategoryDataset dataset =
                    new DefaultCategoryDataset();
        dataset.addValue(tblUsers.get("admin"),
                "Admin", "Admin");
        dataset.addValue(tblUsers.get("hr"),
                "HR Mgr", "HR Mgr");
        dataset.addValue(tblUsers.get("employee"),
                "Employees", "Employees");
        final JFreeChart chart =
                ChartFactory.createBarChart(
    "Frequency Bar Chart", "User Type", "No. of Users", dataset,
    PlotOrientation.VERTICAL, true, true, false);
        chart.setBackgroundPaint(Color.white);
        final TextTitle subtitle = new TextTitle(
        "The frequency Bar Chart of Alibata Business Inc.
                employees from 1990 - 2016.");
        subtitle.setFont(new Font("Calibri", Font.PLAIN, 12));
        chart.addSubtitle(subtitle);
    // See the sources
    }
}
```

## Line chart

A line chart, or line graph, displays information as a series of data points (markers) connected by straight line segments. In JFreeChart, all data structures from the service layer will be used as an input to the JFreeChart class, which is a chart class implemented using the Java 2D APIs. Afterwards, datasets will be produced by the plotter classes of JFreeChart. The current version supports bar charts, line charts, pie charts, and XY plots (including time series data).

JFreeChart coordinates several objects to achieve its aim of being able to draw a chart on a Java 2D graphics device: a list of title objects (which often includes the chart's legend), a plot, and a dataset (the plot in turn manages a domain axis and a range axis). The dataset to be plotted is created through the DefaultCategoryDataset that has a method addValue() which accepts three parameters namely the data value, the X-column, and the Y-column of the graph.

The following code shows one way of populating the `DefaultCategoryDataset`:

```
private DefaultCategoryDataset createDataset(HashMap turnOverRates) {
   DefaultCategoryDataset dataset = new DefaultCategoryDataset( );
   dataset.addValue( 5 , "resignation" , "2010" );
   dataset.addValue( 10 , "resignation" , "2011" );
   dataset.addValue( 8 , "resignation" ,  "2012" );
   dataset.addValue( 10 , "resignation" , "2013" );
   dataset.addValue( 7 , "resignation" , "2014" );
   dataset.addValue( 8 , "resignation" , "2015" );
   return dataset;
}
```

The JFreeChart is instantiated through the `ChartFactory` class, which contains a collection of static utility methods for creating some standard ready-made charts in JFreeChart. This method, known as `ChartFactory.createLineChart()`, has the direct process of creating the object. Classes like `java.awt.Color`, `java.awt.Font` and `org.jfree.chart.title.TextTitle` can help build the details and look and feel of the final drawing.

To draw the chart, the `ChartRenderingInfo` class must be instantiated. This contains a structure for storing rendering information that needs to be built every time the `JFreeChart.draw()` method is executed. The types of rendering information will be defined by `StandardEntityCollection` which is an implementation of `org.jfree.chart.entity.EntityCollection` that contain `org.jfree.chart.entity.ChartEntity` objects such as coordinates, area, URL, tooltip information, and other chart features. And finally, there is the method `ChartUtilities.writeImageMap()`, which is needed to write the final drawing into a Writer object either for saving or for web presentation. The final code for implementing a line chart using the JFreeChart library is as follows:

```
private String createLineChart(HttpServletRequest request,
   HttpServletResponse response) throws
                  ServletException, IOException {
String file = "";
JFreeChart chart = ChartFactory.createLineChart(
"Turnover Rates", "Years", "No. of Resignation",
            createDataset(),PlotOrientation.VERTICAL,
            true,true,false);
chart.setBackgroundPaint(Color.white);
final TextTitle subtitle = new TextTitle(
   "The chart shows the distribution of turnover rates.");
subtitle.setFont(new Font("Calibri", Font.PLAIN, 12));
chart.addSubtitle(subtitle);
ChartRenderingInfo info = new ChartRenderingInfo
```

```
                              (new StandardEntityCollection());
  HttpSession session = request.getSession();
  PrintWriter out = response.getWriter();
  try {
      file = ServletUtilities.saveChartAsPNG(chart, 700,
                          300, info, session);
      ChartUtilities.writeImageMap(out, "imgMap", info, false);
      out.flush();
  } catch (IOException e) { e.printStackTrace(); }

  String filename = request.getContextPath +"/hrms/chart?filename="
                                        + file;

  return filename;
  }
```

The line chart will look something like this:

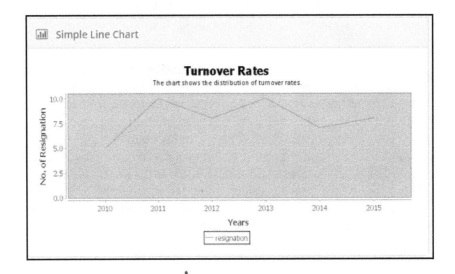

## XY line chart

The *XY* chart (scatter) is based on one data series consisting of a list of *x* and *y* values. Each value pair $(x,y)$ is a point in a coordinate system. Here, one value determines the horizontal (*X*) position, and the other determines the vertical (*Y*) position. The graph compares the rate of increase and decrease in the hiring of supervisors, managers, and clerks in a company.

Using the `ChartFactory.createXYLineChart()`, an *XY* chart object with default settings will be created. Using the collection of data sources injected by the service layer, a dataset called the `XYDataset` object will be created, which contains a series *(x,y)* wherein *X* are the independent variables and *Y* are the dependent ones. All these datasets are plotted using the `XYPlot` class which is a general class for plotting data in the form of *(x, y)* pairs. It needs an `XYItemRenderer` to draw the final data plotting. An example of an `XYItemRenderer` is `XYLineAndShapeRenderer` which plots a *(x,y)* pair with shapes along with the connecting lines.

The implementation of the above *XY* chart is shown as follows:

```
private String createXYLineChart(HttpSession session,
   String title, String xtitle, String ytitle, int width,
   int height, String useMap, PrintWriter pw, HashMap data) {
XYDataset xydataset = getXYDataset(data);
String filename = "";

JFreeChart chart =
     ChartFactory.createXYLineChart(title, xtitle,
              ytitle, xydataset, PlotOrientation.VERTICAL,
              true, true, true);
chart.setTitle(new TextTitle(title, new Font("Calibri",
              Font.ITALIC, 12)));
chart.getTitle().setFont(new Font("Calibri", Font.PLAIN, 12));
chart.setBackgroundPaint(Color.white);
   final XYPlot plot = chart.getXYPlot( );
XYLineAndShapeRenderer renderer =  new XYLineAndShapeRenderer( );
renderer.setSeriesPaint( 0 , Color.RED );
renderer.setSeriesPaint( 1 , Color.GREEN );
renderer.setSeriesPaint( 2 , Color.YELLOW );
renderer.setSeriesStroke( 0 , new BasicStroke( 4.0f ) );
renderer.setSeriesStroke( 1 , new BasicStroke( 3.0f ) );
renderer.setSeriesStroke( 2 , new BasicStroke( 2.0f ) );
plot.setRenderer( renderer );
ChartRenderingInfo info =
         new ChartRenderingInfo(new StandardEntityCollection());
try {
   filename = ServletUtilities.saveChartAsPNG(chart,
                     width, height, info, session);
   ChartUtilities.writeImageMap(pw, useMap, info, false);
   pw.flush();
} catch (IOException e) { e.printStackTrace(); }

return filename;
}
private XYDataset getXYDataset(Map data) {
List<Integer> supervisorHirees = data.get("supervisor")
```

```
XYSeries xyseries1 = new XYSeries("Supervisor");
Xyseries1.add((Integer) 1, (Integer) supervisorHirees.get(0));
Xyseries1.add((Integer) 5, (Integer) supervisorHirees.get(1));
xyseries1.add((Integer) 10, (Integer) supervisorHirees.get(2));
// see the sources
XYSeriesCollection xyseriescollection =
                          new XYSeriesCollection();
xyseriescollection.addSeries(xyseries1);
return xyseriescollection;
}
```

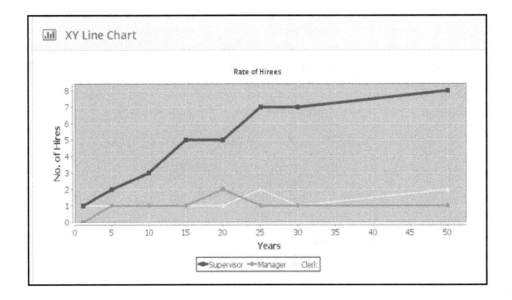

## 2D bar chart

A bar chart uses different orientation (horizontal or vertical) bars to show comparisons in various categories. One axis (the domain axis) of the chart shows the specific domain being compared, and the other axis (the range axis) represents discrete values. The bar chart under the admin dashboard was used to study the distribution of users who always frequently access the application.

The `ChartFactory.createBarChart()` method is used by the controller to create the bar chart object with default settings like title, data sets, and dimensions. The service layer, again, will provide data sources that are used to generate the datasets used in the bar graphs called `CategoryDataset`. These types of data sets need to be plotted using the class `CategoryPlot`, a type of a plotter. The details and descriptions of the X-axis and the Y-axis can be configured through the class `CategoryAxis` and `NumberAxis`, respectively. The following is the implementation of the bar chart.

```
private String createBarCharts(HttpServletRequest request,
    HttpServletResponse response) throws
    ServletException, IOException {
Map<String, Integer> tblUsers = loginService.mapUsers();

DefaultCategoryDataset dataset = new DefaultCategoryDataset();
dataset.addValue(tblUsers.get("admin"), "Admin", "Admin");
dataset.addValue(tblUsers.get("hr"), "HR Mgr","HR Mgr");
dataset.addValue(tblUsers.get("employee"),  "Emp", "Emp");
final JFreeChart chart = ChartFactory.createBarChart(
        "Frequency Bar Chart", "User Type", "No. of Users",
         dataset, PlotOrientation.VERTICAL,
         true, true, false);
chart.setBackgroundPaint(Color.white);
final TextTitle subtitle = new TextTitle(
   "The frequency Bar Chart of Alibata from 1990 - 2016.");
subtitle.setFont(new Font("Calibri", Font.PLAIN, 12));
chart.addSubtitle(subtitle);
final CategoryPlot plot = chart.getCategoryPlot();
plot.setForegroundAlpha(0.5f);

plot.setBackgroundPaint(Color.lightGray);
plot.setDomainGridlinesVisible(true);
plot.setDomainGridlinePaint(Color.white);
plot.setRangeGridlinesVisible(true);
plot.setRangeGridlinePaint(Color.white);

final CategoryAxis domainAxis = plot.getDomainAxis();
domainAxis.setCategoryLabelPositions(
                            CategoryLabelPositions.UP_45);
domainAxis.setLowerMargin(0.0);
domainAxis.setUpperMargin(0.0);
final NumberAxis rangeAxis = (NumberAxis) plot.getRangeAxis();
rangeAxis.setLabelAngle(0.5 * Math.PI / 2.0);
ChartRenderingInfo info =
        new ChartRenderingInfo(new StandardEntityCollection());
HttpSession session = request.getSession();
PrintWriter out = response.getWriter();
String filename = ServletUtilities.saveChartAsPNG(chart, 700, 300,
                                        info, session);
ChartUtilities.writeImageMap(out, "imgMap", info, false);
String file = request.getContextPath() + "/hrms/chart?filename="
                                        + filename;
return file; }
```

This is what the output of the code will look like:

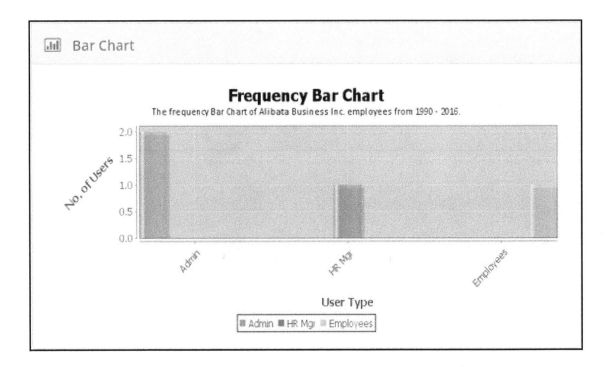

## 2D pie chart

A pie chart is a chart, which is divided into sectors, wherein each arc length of the sector is proportional to the quantity it represents. The type of data sets that works with pie charts belong to the `PieDataset` class, which is a general purpose dataset where values are associated with keys. And the pie chart object with a default setting is created through the `ChartFactory.createPieChart()` method. The following is the implementation of the pie chart depicted in the diagram given below it:

```
private String createPieChart(HttpServletRequest request,
    HttpServletResponse response) throws
    ServletException, IOException {
Map<String, Integer> tblUsers = loginService.mapUsers();

final DefaultPieDataset dataset = new DefaultPieDataset();
dataset.setValue("Administrator",tblUsers.get("admin"));
dataset.setValue("HR Manager", tblUsers.get("hr"));
dataset.setValue("Employee", tblUsers.get("employee"));
```

```
final JFreeChart chart = ChartFactory.createPieChart("User Types ",
                    dataset, true, true, false);
chart.setBackgroundPaint(Color.white);
final TextTitle subtitle = new TextTitle(
            " The chart shows the classification of users.");
subtitle.setFont(new Font("Calibri", Font.PLAIN, 12));
chart.addSubtitle(subtitle);

ChartRenderingInfo info =
        new ChartRenderingInfo(new StandardEntityCollection());
HttpSession session = request.getSession();
PrintWriter out = response.getWriter();
String filename = ServletUtilities.saveChartAsPNG(
            chart, 700, 300, info, session);
ChartUtilities.writeImageMap(out, "imgMap",
            info, false);
String file = request.getContextPath() +  "/hrms/chart?filename="
                                    + filename;
return file;
}
```

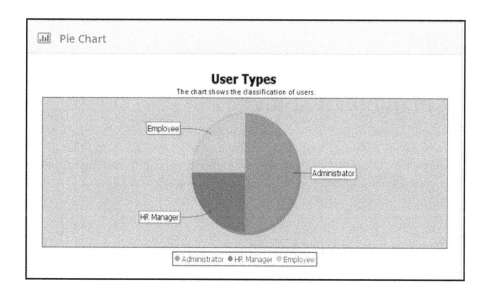

## Other JFreeChart graphs

Other than line charts, 2D bar charts, XY plots, and 2D pie charts, JFreeChart can generate complicated graphical presentations of data-like time series charts, bubble charts, 3D pie charts, scatter plots, 3D bar graphs, and stacked bar graphs. The HRMS prototype offers all of these data visualizations that assist administrators in managing their users.

# The view pages

JFreeChart's `ServletUtilities` class saves images with expiration inside a temporary folder indicated by `System.getProperty("java.io.tmpdir")` which is known as the `<Tomcat>/temp` folder. All the paths pointing to all the images in `<Tomcat>/temp` are passed by the `@Controller`, to the view pages, to be rendered on screen as stream objects. A sample JSP view snippet is shown as follows:

```
<!-- /widget-header -->
  <div class="widget-content">
    <img src="${ adminBarChart }" class="chart-holder"
            border=0 usemap="#imgMap">
    <!-- /bar-chart -->
  </div>
```

where `adminBarChart` is the file path returned by the `@Controller` shown previously.

# The HR manager's analytics

All the data visualization found in this module uses Google Chart. The purpose is to have a comparison between JFreeChart and Google Chart when it comes to code length, the difficulty in using the APIs, and the quality of the plotting. The following are the components needed to successfully integrate charts and graphs into the HR manager's dashboard.

## The DAO and service layers

The way that we write our service classes here is just the same as that of the administrator. All services must provide the Google Chart APIs with the data sources stored in collection objects to avoid complications in generating data sets on the controller layer.

# The controllers

Just like the administrator's dashboard, the HR manager has a page that plots everything on one page; all the needed analytics are included in one view for all charts and graphs. The following controller calls for all chart generation under the Google Chart plugin:

```
@Controller
public class HRGoogleChartController {

private final XYSeries series = new XYSeries("Data");
@RequestMapping(value = "/hrms/hr_charts",
                method = RequestMethod.GET)
public String getCharts(Model model)
                     throws ServletException, IOException {
    String pieChart = drawPieChart();
    String pieChart2D = drawPieChart2d();
    String lineGraph = drawLineGraph();
    String drawLineDetailed = drawLineDetailed();
    String barGraph =    drawBarGraph();
    String scatterPlot = drawScatterHandler();

    model.addAttribute("pieChart3DD", pieChart3D);
    model.addAttribute("pieChart2D", pieChart2D);
    model.addAttribute("lineGraph", lineGraph);
    model.addAttribute("drawLineDetailed", drawLineDetailed);
    model.addAttribute("barGraph", barGraph);
    model.addAttribute("scatterPlot", scatterPlot);
    return "hr_charts";
}
```

# Line chart

Constructing an object of the LineChart type starts with the GCharts API class. There are several factory methods of GCharts, and it is through newPieChart() method that we can instantiate a line chart object. Plotting data is also centralized by the class Plot. It has a set of factory methods and we used the newPlot() method to create a data set. A line chart is rendered within the browser using SVG or VML. The following is a straightforward implementation of the line graph.

```
public String drawLineGraph() {
    final Plot plot = Plots.newPlot(Data.newData(
                    hrManagerService.getUserPerYear()));
    final LineChart chart = GCharts.newLineChart(plot);
    chart.setTitle("Growth of Alibata System Inc. (Estimated Plot)");
    chart.setSize(720, 360);
```

```
    return chart.toURLString();
}
```

Here is Google Chart's simple line chart:

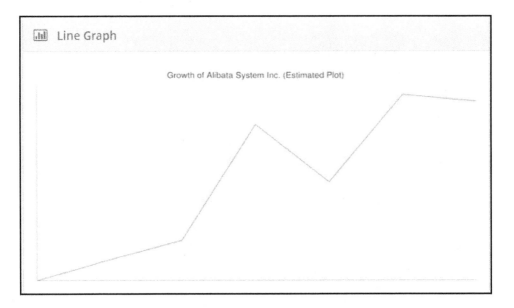

Google Chart can provide some improvement to the original implementation without many additional lines of codes. A detailed line graph of the original version above just took a few mutator methods to overlay some labels and entities. The newly enhanced line chart has the following code implementation, which is almost the same as the original one:

```
public String drawLineDetailed() {
    final Plot plot = Plots.newPlot(Data.newData(
                    hrManagerService.getUserPerYear())));
    LineChart chart = GCharts.newLineChart(plot);
    chart.setTitle("Growth of Alibata System Inc.
                (Estimated Plot)");
    chart.addHorizontalRangeMarker(0, 95.5, Color.GRAY);
    chart.setGrid(80.2, 80.2, 7, 7);

    chart.addXAxisLabels(AxisLabelsFactory.newAxisLabels(
    Arrays.asList("2010-2011", "2011-2013", "2013-present"),
    Arrays.asList(10.6, 50.00, 80.00)));
    chart.addYAxisLabels(AxisLabelsFactory
        .newNumericAxisLabels(0, 20.00, 40.00, 60.00,
                        80.00, 90.00, 100.00));
    chart.setSize(720, 360);
```

```
    return chart.toURLString();
}
```

Here is Google Chart's detailed line chart:

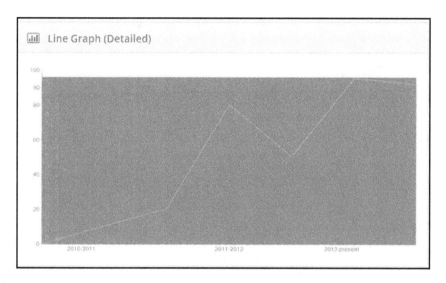

# Bar chart

A bar chart is constructed with the `GCharts.newBarChart()` static factory method. The Google Chart library supports vertical and horizontal bar charts. Bars also might come from a vector (simple bar graph) or series (stacked or grouped bar graphs). HRMS implemented a stacked bar chart as shown above. The graph shows the rate of a head count increase, in three departments of the company, namely sales, marketing, and implementation. Datasets of bar charts are generated using the `Plots.newBarChartPlot()` method. Having more than one data series means that stacked bar charts need to be drawn and a sample implementation is shown as follows:

```
public String drawBarGraph() {
    BarChartPlot sales = Plots.newBarChartPlot(
            Data.newData(hrManagerService.getSalesPerYear()),
            Color.BLUEVIOLET, "Sales Department");
    BarChartPlot marketing = Plots.newBarChartPlot(
            Data.newData(hrManagerService.getMarketingPerYear()),
            Color.ORANGERED, "Marketing Department");
    BarChartPlot implementation = Plots.newBarChartPlot(
            Data.newData(hrManagerService.getImplemPerYear()),
            Color.LIMEGREEN, "Implementation Department");
    BarChart chart = GCharts.newBarChart(sales, marketing,
```

```
                                    implementation);

        AxisStyle axisStyle = AxisStyle.newAxisStyle(Color.BLACK, 13,
                            AxisTextAlignment.CENTER);
        AxisLabels score = AxisLabelsFactory.newAxisLabels
                        ("Score", 50.0);
        score.setAxisStyle(axisStyle);
        AxisLabels year= AxisLabelsFactory.newAxisLabels("Year", 50.0);
        year.setAxisStyle(axisStyle);

        return chart.toURLString();
    }
```

This is what Google Chart's stacked bar chart looks like:

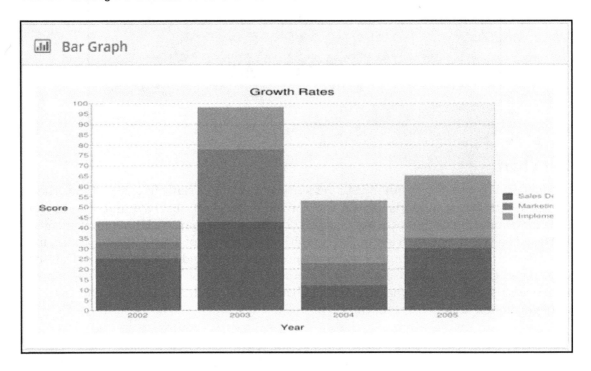

## Other Google Chart graphs

Other charts that the APIs can generate are Venn diagrams, 3D bars and pie charts, scatter plots, maps, and QR codes.

The HRMS also provides features like an automated master list generation of users, attendance sheets, employee leave, and other HR forms available for record-keeping.

# The view pages

Unlike JFreeChart, Google Chart classes have a `toURLString()` method that auto-generates a URL where the images will be displayed. It does not save images at the filesystem, but anyone can save the images manually. The following view page shows how an image is rendered based on the URL `pieChart` passed by the `@Controller`:

```
<div class="widget-content">
    <img alt="Google Pie Chart" src="${ pieChart }"
        class="chart-holder" width="538" height="250"/>
    <!-- /bar-chart -->
</div>
```

And the captured value of the URL `pieChart` is:

```
http://chart.apis.google.com/chart?cht=p3&chs=720x360&chd=e:JmgAQAGa&chts=0
00000,15&chl=18-20|21-30|31-40|%3E%3D+40&chco=CACACA,DF7417,951800,01A1DB&c
hdl=18-20|21-30|31-40|%3E%3D+40&chtt=Alibata+System+Inc.+Employees+%28by+Ag
e%29
```

# Integrating reports

The application HRMS has integrated lots of plugins that can be integrated to the Spring MVC 4.x framework. Different tools can offer different types of rendition transformation but HRMS always defaults the rendition type to an HTML format.

# PDF document generation using iText 5.x

Among the libraries for PDF generation, iText 5.x is the current and most widely used tool for generating PDF files, for sending attachments, receipt generation, and for other HR form automation, like HRMS, that we can see in this project.

To set up the elements of the PDF document like the layout, paper size, and its metadata, we need to create a helper class, which will become our view class for rendering PDF documents. In creating the PWP application in `Chapter 1`, *Creating a Personal Web Portal (PWP)*, it was mentioned there that a view class is responsible for rendering content, and exposing the model. A single view exposes multiple model attributes, and may vary depending on the technology used for rendering. The default view is the `org.springframework.web.servlet.view.JstlView`, which renders JSP-based reports.

Now, iText provides a class called `AbstractView`, which needs to be subclassed to create an iText 5.x-compliant view transformation. The following is HRMS's iText implementation of `AbstractView` that generates a master list of users:

```
public abstract class HRPDFBuilder extends AbstractView {
    public HRPDFBuilder() {
        setContentType("application/pdf");    }
    @Override
    protected boolean generatesDownloadContent() {
        return true;    }
    @Override
    protected void renderMergedOutputModel(
        Map<String, Object> model,
        HttpServletRequest request, HttpServletResponse response)
          throws Exception { .. }
// See the sources
}
public class HrPDFBuilderImpl extends HrPDFView {
    @SuppressWarnings("unchecked")
    @Override
    protected void buildPdfDocument(Map<String, Object> model,
        Document doc, PdfWriter writer, HttpServletRequest request,
        HttpServletResponse response)    throws Exception {
    List<HrmsLogin> users = (List<HrmsLogin>)
                        model.get("allUsers");
    doc.add(new Paragraph("Master List of Users"));
    PdfPTable table = new PdfPTable(4);
    table.setWidthPercentage(100.0f);
    table.setWidths(new float[] {3.0f, 2.0f, 2.0f, 2.0f});
    table.setSpacingBefore(10);
    // See the sources
    for (HrmsLogin user : users) {
        table.addCell(user.getHrmsEmployeeDetails().getEmpId()+"");
        table.addCell(user.getUsername());
        table.addCell(user.getPassword());
        table.addCell(user.getRole());
    }
  doc.add(table);
  }
}
```

The `HrPDFBuilderImpl` is a custom view that will be used to map PDF rendition pages inside the views.properties. Then, the `ResourceBundleViewResolver` must recognize this new `customView` class that contains all the utilities for rendering an iText 5.x-compliant PDF document. In the HRMS project, we have a view name of `pdfView` inside `views.properties` that has mapped it to the `HrPDFBuilderImpl`:

```
pdfView.(class)=
        org.packt.human.resource.portal.views.HrPDFBuilderImpl
```

This view name will be called by the controller designed for generating the user master list in PDF format, together with the model containing all the records from the data source.

```
@Controller
public class AdminDownloadController {
@Autowired
private LoginService loginService;

// See the sources
@RequestMapping(value = "/hrms/downloadPDF",
                method = RequestMethod.GET)
public ModelAndView downloadPDF() {
    List<HrmsLogin> allUsers = loginService.getUserList();
    return new ModelAndView("pdfView", "allUsers", allUsers);
}
}
```

The following is the PDF document generated by `HrPDFBuilderImpl`, which can be viewed and downloaded from the page.

| Master List of Users | | | |
|---|---|---|---|
| Employee ID | Username | Password | Role |
| 1234567 | admin | admin | admin |
| 2312235 | allan | allan | admin |
| 7678834 | jesette | jesette | employee |
| 1233455 | jesse | jesee | employee |
| 5567321 | mabel | mabel | hr |

# Excel sheet generation using POI

On the other hand, to generate an Excel document using Apache POI within Spring MVC 4.x, another custom view is needed that will extend the AbstractView API of POI, for the purpose of overriding the method known as `buildExcelDocument()`.

```
public abstract class AbstractExcelView extends AbstractView {
    private static final String CONTENT_TYPE =
        "application/vnd.openxmlformats-
            officedocument.spreadsheetml.sheet";
    private static final String EXTENSION = ".xlsx";
```

```java
        private String url;
        public AbstractExcelView() {
            setContentType(CONTENT_TYPE);  }
        public void setUrl(String url) {
            this.url = url;    }
        // See the sources
    }
    public class HrExcelBuilder extends AbstractExcelView{
        @SuppressWarnings("unchecked")
        @Override
        protected void buildExcelDocument(Map<String, Object> model,
                HSSFWorkbook workbook, HttpServletRequest request,
                HttpServletResponse response)    throws Exception {
        List<HrmsLogin> users = (List<HrmsLogin>)
                            model.get("allUsers");
        HSSFSheet sheet = workbook.createSheet("User List");
                        sheet.setDefaultColumnWidth(30);
        CellStyle style = workbook.createCellStyle();
        Font font = workbook.createFont();
        font.setFontName("Arial");
        HSSFRow header = sheet.createRow(0);
        header.createCell(0).setCellValue("Employee ID");
        header.getCell(0).setCellStyle(style);
        header.createCell(1).setCellValue("Username");
        header.getCell(1).setCellStyle(style);
        // See the sources
        int rowCount = 1;
        for (HrmsLogin account : users) {
          HSSFRow aRow = sheet.createRow(rowCount++);
          aRow.createCell(0).setCellValue(
                  account.getHrmsEmployeeDetails().getEmpId());
          aRow.createCell(1).setCellValue(account.getUsername());
          aRow.createCell(2).setCellValue(account.getPassword());
          aRow.createCell(3).setCellValue(account.getRole());
        }
      }
    }
```

Just like in iText 5.x, the `ResourceBundleViewResolver` must recognize this new custom view class by declaring a view name to it in the `views.properties`:

```
excelView.(class)=
            org.packt.human.resource.portal.views.HRExcelBuilder
```

Lastly, any controller can just call `excelView` with the list of records called `allUsers`, which is needed by `HrExcelBuilder` for Excel sheet generation.

# Excel sheet generation using JExcelAPI

Just like POI, this plugin follows the same process from building a custom view up to the `ResourceBundleViewResolver` recognition. The only difference is that our custom view subclasses the `AbstractJExcelView` class of `JExcelAPI`.

Both POI and `JExcelAPI` output the same type of worksheet.

The Excel sheet of the master list of users is something like this:

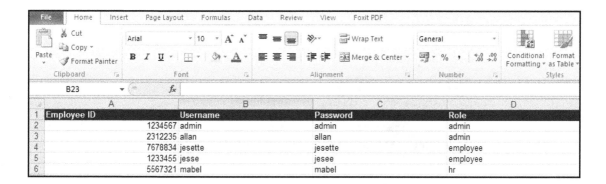

# Report generation using JasperReports

Before the Jasper-Spring MVC integration happens, the first thing to do is to open an **iReport Visual Designer**, and create JRXML, which is a reusable template that can be used by the Jasper report engine to populate data from any data sources. This XML template includes various sections like title, query string, fields, page header and footer, column header and footer, and other needed entities for the report layout.

Report fields represent the mapping of data between data source and report template. Fields can be combined in the report expressions to obtain the desired output. When declaring report fields, the data source should supply data corresponding to all the fields defined in the report template. On the template report, fields are indicated by `$F{ }` like `$F{empId}`, `$F{username}`, `$F{password}` and `$F{role}`.

The template looks like this when open in an XML editor:

```
<?xml version="1.0" encoding="UTF-8"?>
<jasperReport xmlns="http://jasperreports.sourceforge.net/jasperreports"
xmlns:xsi="http://www.w3.org/2001/XMLSchema-instance"
xsi:schemaLocation="http://jasperreports.sourceforge.net/jasperreports
```

```
http://jasperreports.sourceforge.net/xsd/jasperreport.xsd" name="JRStudent"
pageWidth="595" pageHeight="842" columnWidth="555" leftMargin="20"
rightMargin="20" topMargin="20" bottomMargin="20" uuid="574a8abb-
c648-42c3-9dd1-b9cc61394ed4">
    <property name="ireport.zoom" value="1.0"/>
    <property name="ireport.x" value="0"/>
    // See the sources
    <field name="role" class="java.lang.String"/>
    <background>
        <band splitType="Stretch"/>
    </background>
    <columnHeader>
        // See the sources
    </columnHeader>
    <detail>
        // See the sources
    </detail>
    <columnFooter>
        <band height="45" splitType="Stretch"/>
    </columnFooter>
    <pageFooter>
        <band height="54" splitType="Stretch"/>
    </pageFooter>
    <summary>
        <band height="42" splitType="Stretch"/>
    </summary>
</jasperReport>
```

The following screenshot shows an iReport editor with a new template at the design stage:

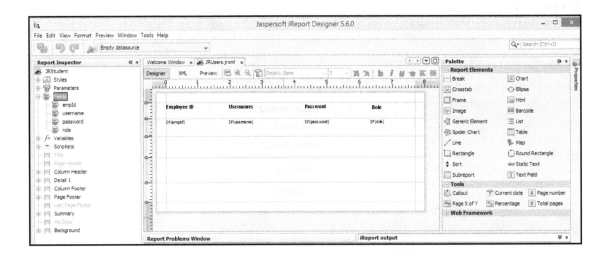

Once the JRXML (template) has been signed-off, it needs to be compiled by iReport to generate its `.jasper` equivalent. The JASPER file is the one executed by Spring MVC. Thus, two files are needed by Spring MVC: the JRXML and its JASPER file. All of the files are found in our `classpath:/config` folder.

There are four ways that HRMS is used to integrate `JasperReports` plugins into Spring MVC 4.x:

- **Direct execution of the JASPER file and a direct call to all the APIs inside the controller**: One of the controllers of an HRMS creates a master list of users in three different formats, namely PDF, RTF, and DOCX format. The implementations do not rely on any views and a `viewResolver` configuration in the `ApplicationContext`. The code is shown as follows:

```
@RequestMapping(value = "/hrms/pdfreport",
                method = RequestMethod.GET)
public String generatePDF(ModelMap model,
    HttpServletRequest request, HttpServletResponse response)
    throws ServletException, IOException,
    JRException, NamingException {
      usersList = loginService.getUserList();
      AdminJasperBase dsUsers=new AdminJasperBase(usersList);
      Map<String,Object> params = new HashMap<>();
      params.put("users", usersList);
      JasperReport jasperReport = getCompiledFile
                                 ("JRUsers", request);
      JasperPrint jasperPrint = JasperFillManager.
                                 fillReport(jasperReport,
                                 params, dsUsers);
      response.setContentType("application/x-pdf");
      response.setHeader("Content-disposition", "inline;
      filename=Master List of Users.pdf");
      final OutputStream outStream = response.
                                      getOutputStream();
      JasperExportManager.exportReportToPdfStream
                                 (jasperPrint,outStream);
      return null;
  }
  private JasperReport getCompiledFile(String fileName,
      HttpServletRequest request) throws JRException {
      File reportFile = new File("./config/JRUsers.jasper");
      JasperReport jasperReport = (JasperReport)
      JRLoader.loadObject(this.getClass().getClassLoader()
          .getResourceAsStream("config/JRUsers.jasper"));
      return jasperReport;
  }
```

```
@RequestMapping(value = "/hrms/rtfreport", method =
                RequestMethod.GET)
public String generateRTF(ModelMap model,
  HttpServletRequest request,HttpServletResponse response
  ) throws ServletException, IOException, JRException,
  NamingException {
// See the sources
JasperReport jasperReport = getCompiledFile
                            ("JRUsers", request);
JasperPrint jasperPrint =JasperFillManager
  .fillReport(jasperReport, params, dsUsers);
ByteArrayOutputStream rtfStream = null;
try {
final JRRtfExporter rtfExporter = new JRRtfExporter();
rtfStream = new ByteArrayOutputStream();
rtfExporter.setParameter(JRExporterParameter.JASPER_PRINT,
                        jasperPrint);
rtfExporter.setParameter(JRExporterParameter.OUTPUT_STREAM,
                        rtfStream);
rtfExporter.exportReport();
rtfResume = rtfStream.toByteArray();
}
catch (final JRException e) { }
catch (final RuntimeException e) { }
response.setContentType("application/rtf");
response.setHeader("Content-disposition", "inline;
filename= Master List of Users.rtf");
final OutputStream outStream = response.getOutputStream();
outStream.write(rtfResume);
outStream.flush();
outStream.close();
return null;
}
@RequestMapping(value = "/hrms/docxreport",
                method = RequestMethod.GET)
public String generateDOCX(ModelMap model,
  HttpServletRequest request,HttpServletResponse response)
  throws ServletException, IOException,JRException,
  NamingException {
  byte[] docResume = null;
  try {
  final JRDocxExporter docExporter = new JRDocxExporter();
  docStream = new ByteArrayOutputStream();
  docExporter.setParameter(JRDocxExporterParameter
                            .JASPER_PRINT,jasperPrint);
  docExporter.setParameter(JRDocxExporterParameter
                            .OUTPUT_STREAM,docStream);
  docExporter.setParameter(JRDocxExporterParameter
```

```
                            .FLEXIBLE_ROW_HEIGHT, Boolean.TRUE);
        docExporter.exportReport();
        docResume = docStream.toByteArray();
        }
        catch (final JRException e) { }
        catch (final RuntimeException e) { }
        response.setContentType("application/vnd
            .openxmlformats-officedocument.wordprocessingml
            .document");
        response.setHeader("Content-disposition", "inline;
        filename=helloWorldReport.docx");
        final OutputStream outStream=response.getOutputStream();
        outStream.write(docResume);
        outStream.flush();
        outStream.close();
        return null;
    }
```

- **Using built-in views of Spring MVC 4.x**: HRMS uses these APIs in generating some data rendered in CSV, PDF, and HTML. These view classes are:

    - `org.springframework.web.servlet.view.jasperreports.JasperReportsMultiFormatView`: This is a `JasperReports` view class that allows actual rendering of a format to be specified at runtime using a parameter contained in the model:

    ```
    modelMap.put("datasource", dsUsers);
    modelMap.put("format", "pdf");
    ```

    - `org.springframework.web.servlet.view.jasperreports.JasperReportsCsvView`: This is a specific view for CSV report rendition

    - `org.springframework.web.servlet.view.jasperreports.JasperReportsPdfView`: This is a specific view for PDF report rendition

    - `org.springframework.web.servlet.view.jasperreports.JasperReportsHtmlView`: This is a specific view for HTML report rendition

    - `org.springframework.web.servlet.view.jasperreports.JasperReportsXlsView`: This is a specific view for XLS report rendition

    - `org.springframework.web.servlet.view.jasperreports.JasperReportsXlsxView`: This is a specific view for XLSX report rendition

Before we utilize the above views, these must be injected into the
`ApplicationContext` with the data source and the JRXML path.

```
<bean id="multiViewReport"
    class="org.springframework.web.servlet.view
            .jasperreports.JasperReportsMultiFormatView">
    <property name="url"
                    value="classpath:config/JRUsers.jrxml"/>
    <property name="reportDataKey" value="jrDatasource"/>
</bean>
<bean id="adminJasperPDFView"
    class="org.springframework.web.servlet.view
            .jasperreports.JasperReportsPdfView">
    <property name="url">
        <value>classpath:config/JRUsers.jrxml</value>
    </property>
    <property name="subReportDataKeys">
        <value>jrDatasource</value>
    </property>
</bean>
<bean id="adminJasperCSVView"
    class="org.springframework.web.servlet.view
            .jasperreports.JasperReportsCsvView">
    <property name="url">
        <value>classpath:config/JRUsers.jrxml</value>
    </property>
    <property name="subReportDataKeys">
        <value>jrDatasource</value>
    </property>
</bean>
<bean id="adminJasperHtmlView"
    class="org.springframework.web.servlet.view
            .jasperreports.JasperReportsHtmlView">
    <property name="url">
        <value>classpath:config/JRUsers.jrxml</value>
    </property>
    <property name="subReportDataKeys">
        <value>jrDatasource</value>
    </property>
</bean>
```

For the `JasperReportsMultiFormatView`, the controller must be the same with
the master list generation shown as follows:

```
@RequestMapping(value = "/hrms/pdfMultiView",
                method = RequestMethod.GET)
public String generatePDFMultiView(ModelMap model) {
    usersList = loginService.getUserList();
```

```
AdminJasperBase dsUsers=new AdminJasperBase(usersList);
model.addAttribute("jrDatasource", dsUsers);
model.addAttribute("format", "pdf");

return "multiViewReport";
}
```

A different controller is written for specific views and must be similar to what HRMS has for CSV rendition for leaves as follows:

```
@RequestMapping(method = RequestMethod.GET ,
                value = "/hrms/csvLeaves")
public ModelAndView generateCsvReport(ModelAndView
                                      modelAndView){
usersList = loginService.getUserLeaves();
AdminJasperBase dsUsers = new AdminJasperBase(usersList);
Map<String, Object> parameterMap = new HashMap<>();
    parameterMap.put("datasource", dsUsers);
modelAndView = new ModelAndView("adminJasperCSVView",
                                parameterMap);
return modelAndView;
}
```

- Using the typical way of mapping views through ResourceBundleViewResolver or XmlViewResolver: By default, HRMS uses ResourceBundleViewResolver for mapping views. Using this integration type, the controller must be written like this:

```
@RequestMapping(method = RequestMethod.GET ,
                value = "/hrms/pdfAbsences")
public ModelAndView generatePdfAbsences(ModelAndView
                                        modelAndView){
    usersList = loginService.getUserAbsences();
    AdminJasperBase dsUsers=new AdminJasperBase(usersList);
    Map<String, Object> parameterMap = new HashMap<>();
    parameterMap.put("datasource", dsUsers);
    modelAndView = new ModelAndView("absentView,
                                    parameterMap);
    return modelAndView;
}
```

The view name `absentView` will be mapped to the JASPER file in the `views.properties`:

```
absentView.(class)=org.springframework.web.servlet.view
                   .jasperreports.JasperReportsPdfView
absentView.url=classpath:/config/JRAbsences.jasper
```

```
absentView.reportDataKey= datasource
```

- Using the
  `org.springframework.web.servlet.view.jasperreports.JasperReport
  sViewResolver`: This viewResolver translates all the JASPER files automatically using a specific view class or multiple views. The only precaution here is to be sure the paths of the JASPER files are correct and the resolver is a high priority (the order must be near 0). HRMS has the following configuration:

```
<bean id="jasperResolver"
    class="org.springframework.web.servlet.view
            .jasperreports.JasperReportsViewResolver">
  <property name="prefix" value="classpath:/config/"/>
  <property name="suffix" value=".jasper"/>
  <property name="subReportDataKeys">
      <value>jrDatasource</value>
  </property>
  <property name="viewNames">
      <value>JR*</value>
  </property>
  <property name="viewClass">
      <value>org.springframework.web.servlet.view
          .jasperreports.JasperReportsMultiFormatView</value>
  </property>
  <property name="order" value="2"/>
</bean>
```

And the controller for this configuration must be implemented in this manner:

```
@RequestMapping(value = "/hrms/pdfReportResolver",
                method = RequestMethod.GET)
public ModelAndView generatePDFResolver(ModelMap modelMap,
                              ModelAndView modelAndView) {
    usersList = loginService.getUserList();
    AdminJasperBase dsUsers =  new AdminJasperBase(usersList);
    modelMap.put("datasource", dsUsers);
    modelMap.put("format", "pdf");
    modelAndView = new ModelAndView("JRUsers", modelMap);
    return modelAndView;
}
```

 ModelMap contains only the data without the view name. ModelAndView has both.

JasperReports is one of the widely-used rendition tools found in most of the Spring MVC applications because of its flexibility when it comes to implementation and support of rendition formats that it can offer to many reporting requirements. Moreover, it can collaborate with Google Charts and JFreeChart APIs to render the images in PDF or DOCX formats.

# Report generation using DynamicReports

If the requirement asks for a more dynamic way of designing reports, the dynamic reports tool is more appropriate to use. HRMS has a module where controllers no longer depend on JRXML and JASPER files in rendering data into PDF formats. In DynamicReports, a design is created by a pure simple Java code. Since it is generated at runtime, any controller can implement any logic-injecting different scenario-based layout. This logic decides how the report will look like, unlike the static reports JasperReports templates where the defined design cannot be changed at runtime. The following controller shows an implementation snippet of a PDF rendition using DynamicReports APIs, as follows:

```
private LoginService loginService;
private List<HrmsLogin> usersList;

@RequestMapping(value = "/hrms/dyna_report", method = RequestMethod.GET)
public String printWelcome7(ModelMap model,
   HttpServletRequest request, HttpServletResponse response)
     throws ServletException, IOException, JRException,
        NamingException, Exception {
 JasperReportBuilder report = DynamicReports.report();
 usersList = loginService.getUserList();
 if(usersList != null){ throw new ReportNotFoundException(); }
 AdminJasperBase dsUsers =  new AdminJasperBase(usersList);
 report.columns(Columns.column("Employee Id", "empId",
                 DataTypes.stringType()),
             Columns.column("Username", "username",
                 DataTypes.stringType()),
             Columns.column("Password", "password",
                 DataTypes.stringType()),
             Columns.column("Role", "role",
                 DataTypes.stringType()))
         .title(Components.text("Master List of Users")
         .setHorizontalAlignment(HorizontalAlignment.CENTER))
         .pageFooter(Components.pageXofY.setDataSource(dsUsers);
 report.build();
 response.setContentType("application/pdf");
 response.setHeader("Content-disposition", "inline;
                              filename=dnynamicReport.pdf");
```

```
try {
    final OutputStream outStream = response.getOutputStream();
report.toPdf(outStream);
    outStream.flush();
    outStream.close();
} catch (DRException e) { throw new ReportNotFoundException(); } catch
(Exception e){  throw new ReportNotFoundException(); }
    return null;
}
```

From the implementation, no viewResolver call or JASPER execution is found anywhere in the code. For ad hoc reporting, this is the best choice to use; besides, this can be used side-by-side with the static design of iReport through sub-reports purposes.

# Report generation using ContentNegotiatingViewResolver

The `org.springframework.web.servlet.view.ContentNegotiatingViewResolver` is an implementation of ViewResolver, which renders a particular model data with a view name into different media types like XML, JSON, PDF, XLS, and HTML. `ContentNegotiatingViewResolver` does not resolve a view by itself, but delegates to other ViewResolvers that can also be configured inside its bean. The order property needs to be set to a higher precedence than the others.

HRMS has this bean configuration for the `ContentNegotiatingViewResolver`:

```xml
<bean id="viewResolver4" class="org.springframework.web.servlet.view
                .ContentNegotiatingViewResolver">
<property name="order" value="3" />
<property name="mediaTypes">
    <map>
      <entry key="json" value="application/json" />
      <entry key="xml" value="application/xml" />
      <entry key="pdf" value="application/pdf" />
      <entry key="html" value="text/html" />
      <entry key="xlsx"
            value="application/vnd.openxmlformats-
                        officedocument.spreadsheetml.sheet" />
    </map>
</property>
<property name="defaultViews">
    <list>
        <!-- JSON View -->
        <bean class="org.springframework.web.servlet.view
```

```
                                    .json.MappingJackson2JsonView">
            <property name="objectMapper" ref="adminLoginMapper"/>
        </bean>

        <!--   XML view -->
        <bean class="org.springframework.web.servlet.view
                                    .xml.MarshallingView">
            <constructor-arg>
                <bean class="org.springframework.oxm
                            .castor.CastorMarshaller">
                <property name="targetClass"
                  value="org.packt.human.resource.portal
                            .model.data.HrmsLogin"/>
                <property name="mappingLocation"
                  value="classpath:/config/login-mapping.xml" />
            </bean>
          </constructor-arg>
        </bean>

        <!--   PDF view -->
        <bean class="org.packt.human.resource.portal
                                        .views.PDFView">
        </bean>
        <!--   XLSX "Excel" view -->
        <bean class="org.packt.human.resource.portal
                                        .views.ExcelView">
        </bean>
      </list>
    </property>
    <property name="ignoreAcceptHeader" value="true" />
</bean>
```

In configuring this kind of resolver, be sure to have the appropriate and complete set of libraries for all the media types indicated. Also include all the dependencies involved as per the core library. Since there is an XML rendition, the Spring Core OXM library is included to support XML output generation, using JAXB2 with its dependencies Xerxes and Castor APIs. The libraries Jackson-databind and Jackson-annotations provide JSON output support. The iText 5.x library is also needed to provide the PDF generation library to support PDF output. Lastly, HRMS chose Apache POI library for this resolver to help produce XLS formatted reports.

By default, there is a class called PathExtensionContentNegotiationStrategy, which is used by the resolver to detect the URL extension of the view name, since the rendition process will be dependent on the content types. Then, a class called ParameterContentNegotiationStrategy will accept the request parameter of the former to be mapped with the media types indicated in the viewResolver, in order to proceed with the transformation. If the media type is not there, the default parameter name is format. It is mandatory to always use `ignoreAcceptHeader`, in order to disregard HTTP headers during the transformation process, since HRMS is only after the model.

When it comes to controller implementation, we only need to create one and all the indicated media types will be generated.

```
@RequestMapping(value = "/hrms/userList_nego",
                method = RequestMethod.GET)
 public  List<HrmsLogin>  get(Model model) {
     usersList = loginService.getUserList();
     model.addAttribute("allUsers", usersList);
     return usersList;
   }
```

Accessing `http://localhost:8080/ch04/hrms/userList_nego.xml` will show the following output:

```
This XML file does not appear to have any style information associated with it. The document tree is shown below.

▼<array-list>
  ▼<HrmsLogin xmlns:xsi="http://www.w3.org/2001/XMLSchema-instance" empId="1234567" xsi:type="HrmsLogin">
     <username>admin</username>
     <password>admin</password>
     <role>admin</role>
  </HrmsLogin>
  ▼<HrmsLogin xmlns:xsi="http://www.w3.org/2001/XMLSchema-instance" empId="2312235" xsi:type="HrmsLogin">
     <username>allan</username>
     <password>allan</password>
     <role>admin</role>
  </HrmsLogin>
  ▼<HrmsLogin xmlns:xsi="http://www.w3.org/2001/XMLSchema-instance" empId="7678834" xsi:type="HrmsLogin">
     <username>jesette</username>
     <password>jesette</password>
     <role>employee</role>
  </HrmsLogin>
  ▼<HrmsLogin xmlns:xsi="http://www.w3.org/2001/XMLSchema-instance" empId="1233455" xsi:type="HrmsLogin">
     <username>jesse</username>
     <password>jesee</password>
     <role>employee</role>
  </HrmsLogin>
  ▼<HrmsLogin xmlns:xsi="http://www.w3.org/2001/XMLSchema-instance" empId="5567321" xsi:type="HrmsLogin">
     <username>mabel</username>
     <password>mabel</password>
     <role>hr</role>
  </HrmsLogin>
</array-list>
```

While `http://localhost:8080/ch04/hrms/userList_nego.json` will show this JSON data on the screen:

```
"hrmsLoginList":[{"username":"admin","hrmsEmployeeDetails":
"empId":0,"department":null,"positions":null,"firstName":null,"lastName":null,"midName":null,"birthDate":null,"age":0,"sex":null,"address":null,"employedDate":null,"supervisorId":0,"hrm
gins":[],"hrmsEmployeeProjectses":[],"hrmsEmployeeTrainingses":[],"hrmsEmployeeLeaveses":[],"hrmsEmployeeSalaries":[],"hrmsEmployeeAttendances":[],"handler":
}},"password":"admin","role":"admin"},{"username":"allan","hrmsEmployeeDetails":
"empId":0,"department":null,"positions":null,"firstName":null,"lastName":null,"midName":null,"birthDate":null,"age":0,"sex":null,"address":null,"employedDate":null,"supervisorId":0,"hrm
gins":[],"hrmsEmployeeProjectses":[],"hrmsEmployeeTrainingses":[],"hrmsEmployeeLeaveses":[],"hrmsEmployeeSalaries":[],"hrmsEmployeeAttendances":[],"handler":
}},"password":"allan","role":"admin"},{"username":"jesette","hrmsEmployeeDetails":
"empId":0,"department":null,"positions":null,"firstName":null,"lastName":null,"midName":null,"birthDate":null,"age":0,"sex":null,"address":null,"employedDate":null,"supervisorId":0,"hrm
gins":[],"hrmsEmployeeProjectses":[],"hrmsEmployeeTrainingses":[],"hrmsEmployeeLeaveses":[],"hrmsEmployeeSalaries":[],"hrmsEmployeeAttendances":[],"handler":
}},"password":"jesette","role":"employee"},{"username":"jesse","hrmsEmployeeDetails":
"empId":0,"department":null,"positions":null,"firstName":null,"lastName":null,"midName":null,"birthDate":null,"age":0,"sex":null,"address":null,"employedDate":null,"supervisorId":0,"hrm
gins":[],"hrmsEmployeeProjectses":[],"hrmsEmployeeTrainingses":[],"hrmsEmployeeLeaveses":[],"hrmsEmployeeSalaries":[],"hrmsEmployeeAttendances":[],"handler":
}},"password":"jesse","role":"employee"},{"username":"mabel","hrmsEmployeeDetails":
"empId":0,"department":null,"positions":null,"firstName":null,"lastName":null,"midName":null,"birthDate":null,"age":0,"sex":null,"address":null,"employedDate":null,"supervisorId":0,"hrm
gins":[],"hrmsEmployeeProjectses":[],"hrmsEmployeeTrainingses":[],"hrmsEmployeeLeaveses":[],"hrmsEmployeeSalaries":[],"hrmsEmployeeAttendances":[],"handler":
}},"password":"mabel","role":"hr"},"allUsers":[{"username":"admin","hrmsEmployeeDetails":
"empId":0,"department":null,"positions":null,"firstName":null,"lastName":null,"midName":null,"birthDate":null,"age":0,"sex":null,"address":null,"employedDate":null,"supervisorId":0,"hrm
gins":[],"hrmsEmployeeProjectses":[],"hrmsEmployeeTrainingses":[],"hrmsEmployeeLeaveses":[],"hrmsEmployeeSalaries":[],"hrmsEmployeeAttendances":[],"handler":
}},"password":"admin","role":"admin"},{"username":"allan","hrmsEmployeeDetails":
"empId":0,"department":null,"positions":null,"firstName":null,"lastName":null,"midName":null,"birthDate":null,"age":0,"sex":null,"address":null,"employedDate":null,"supervisorId":0,"hrm
gins":[],"hrmsEmployeeProjectses":[],"hrmsEmployeeTrainingses":[],"hrmsEmployeeLeaveses":[],"hrmsEmployeeSalaries":[],"hrmsEmployeeAttendances":[],"handler":
}},"password":"allan","role":"admin"},{"username":"jesette","hrmsEmployeeDetails":
"empId":0,"department":null,"positions":null,"firstName":null,"lastName":null,"midName":null,"birthDate":null,"age":0,"sex":null,"address":null,"employedDate":null,"supervisorId":0,"hrm
gins":[],"hrmsEmployeeProjectses":[],"hrmsEmployeeTrainingses":[],"hrmsEmployeeLeaveses":[],"hrmsEmployeeSalaries":[],"hrmsEmployeeAttendances":[],"handler":
}},"password":"jesette","role":"employee"},{"username":"jesse","hrmsEmployeeDetails":
"empId":0,"department":null,"positions":null,"firstName":null,"lastName":null,"midName":null,"birthDate":null,"age":0,"sex":null,"address":null,"employedDate":null,"supervisorId":0,"hrm
gins":[],"hrmsEmployeeProjectses":[],"hrmsEmployeeTrainingses":[],"hrmsEmployeeLeaveses":[],"hrmsEmployeeSalaries":[],"hrmsEmployeeAttendances":[],"handler":
}},"password":"jesse","role":"employee"},{"username":"mabel","hrmsEmployeeDetails":
"empId":0,"department":null,"positions":null,"firstName":null,"lastName":null,"midName":null,"birthDate":null,"age":0,"sex":null,"address":null,"employedDate":null,"supervisorId":0,"hrm
gins":[],"hrmsEmployeeProjectses":[],"hrmsEmployeeTrainingses":[],"hrmsEmployeeLeaveses":[],"hrmsEmployeeSalaries":[],"hrmsEmployeeAttendances":[],"handler":
}},"password":"mabel","role":"hr"}]}
```

# Generating reports using HTML

Spring uses `org.springframework.web.servlet.view.JstlView` class to render JSP pages that use the Java Standard Tag Library (JSTL). This view class is the default view mapping of the `InternalResourceViewResolver` but it is manually mapped to physical views in views.properties when the `ResourceBundleViewResolver` is used.

Aside from JSP-JSTL, Velocity and FreeMarker are two languages that can be used as view technologies within Spring MVC applications. The languages are template engines and are used more when dissecting HTML pages into layouts.

The template engine is a component that processes fixed text and data as input, integrates certain processing rules to this input, and generates a text document containing the data. These engines are a very useful requirement when it comes to dynamic web page creation, rendition transformation, and e-mail formatting.

## FreeMarker Template Language (FTL)

Unlike JSP, FreeMaker (FTL) is not dependent on the servlet architecture or on HTTP. This is best when used in the generation of HTML web pages, particularly in applications following the MVC (Model-View-Controller) pattern.

HRMS provides a way to separate the logic from the web design concerns in all its pages. This separation is useful for clear and easy maintenance of code, since changes in the headers, footers, and content look and feel won't bother the logic side that builds the rendition.

The use of FTL starts with the configuration of `org.springframework.web.servlet.view.freemarker.FreeMarkerViewResolver` as the viewResolver. The bean `freemarkerConfig`, which defines the Freemarker configuration, is injected into the `ApplicationContext`. It has properties like:

- `templateLoaderPath`: The path where we will store all our .ftl templates
- `freemarkerVariables`: FTL expression variables used globally in views
- `defaultEncoding`: The encoding setting of all the views in the project
- `freemarkerSettings`: Configuration settings related to FTL

Other than the viewResolver, it is recommended to set some FTL configuration details in a property file (`hrms_freemarker.properties`) that registers the following details:

```
datetime_format=yyyy-MM-dd HH:mm:ss
date_format=yyyy-MM-dd
time_format=HH:mm:ss
number_format=0.######;
boolean_format=true,false
whitespace_stripping=true
tag_syntax=square_bracket
url_escaping_charset=UTF-8
classic_compatible=true
```

Lastly, the physical views all have an `.ftl` extension. It is advisable to design a layout first before coding the FTL files. From the layout, we build a template (`admin_template.ftl`) that may include all the generic and detailed web design components of HRMS pages. The following is a skeleton of an FTL template used in the project:

```
<#macro adminLayout>
  <html>
    <!-ALL CSS and JS scripts -->
    <body>
      <table border="1" cellspacing="0" cellpadding="0">
        <#include "tbl_header.ftl"/>
        <#include "tbl_body.ftl"/>
      </table>
      <#include "tbl_footer.ftl"/>
    </body>
  </html>
</#macro>
```

After the template, we implement the other FTL files to be included into the template, namely `tbl_header.ftl`, `tbl_body.ftl`, and `tbl_footer.ftl`, which are all for data presentation.

## tbl_header.ftl

The following code is a sample Freemarker header template for the web page:

```
<tr>
    <th>Employee ID</th>
    <th>Username</th>
    <th>Password</th>
    <th>Role</th>
</tr>
```

## tbl_body.ftl

The following code is a sample Freemarker body template for the web page:

```
<#list model["allUsers"] as user>
  <tr>
    <td>${user.hrmsEmployeeDetails.empId}</td>
    <td>${user.username}</td>
    <td>${user.password}</td>
    <td>${user.role}</td>
  </tr>
</#list>
```

## tbl_footer.ftl

The following code is a sample Freemarker footer template for the web page:

```
<h6>Data Courtesy of Alibata Systems Inc.</h6>
```

After coding all the required FTL template files, we use `admin_template.ftl` to generate our view, which will be called by the assigned controllers. One of the final view implementations is our page `/hrms/admin_users_page_ftl`, which is presented here:

```
<#import "admin_template.ftl" as layout>
<@layout.adminLayout>
  <div><h1>Transaction Data - Valid Users</h1></div>
</@layout.adminLayout>
```

To study further about expressions and template programming in FTL, visit the site `http://freemarker.org/index.html`.

# Velocity

Another option for JSP-based view implementation is through the use of Velocity. Both are incomparable since Velocity's syntax is simpler and more distinct, while FreeMarker's heavier syntax allows the support of JSP tags. Velocity has its own pool of plugins in VelocityTools, which can be used instead of some JSTL tags for processing. Velocity gives a better performance generally than FreeMarker.

First, the viewResolver `org.springframework.web.servlet.view.velocity.VelocityLayoutViewResolver` must be configured with the following settings:

- `cache` enables the setting of the "cacheLimit" property to the default limit (1024) or to 0, respectively; by default this is true
- `prefix` is used to locate the .vm files
- `layoutUrl` initializes the layout template to use
- `suffix` determines the extension of the files which is `.vm`

Then, we need to set the `VelocityConfigurer` bean to configure Velocity for web usage. HRMS uses the simplest way to use this class through specifying the `resourceLoaderPath` property.

After the entire configuration, Velocity's view pages can now be implemented, starting from the template. The `admin_layout.vm` has the same objective as the former FTL template, which lists all the users of HRMS.

```
<html>
  <head>
    <title>Spring & Velocity</title>
    <!-CSS and JS scripts -->
  </head>
    <body>
      <div>
        #parse("/WEB-INF/admin_vm/hrms/header.vm")
      </div>
      <div>
        $screen_content
      </div>
      <div>
        #parse("/WEB-INF/admin_vm/hrms/footer.vm")
      </div>
    </body>
</html>
```

This is the only part where Velocity will have some overhead, and it's on the parsing of each of its template components. Here, then are the implementations of each component, namely `header.vm` and `footer.vm`:

## header.vm

The following code is a sample Velocity header template for the web page:

```
<div style="background: #E0E0E0; height: 80px; padding: 5px;">
  <div style="float: left">
      <h1>Admin - The User List</h1>
  </div>
</div>
```

## footer.vm

The following code is a sample Velocity footer template for the web page:

```
<div
    style="background: #E0E0E0; text-align: center; padding: 5px;
          margin-top: 10px;">
    Aibata Systems Inc.
</div>
```

Comparing the two template engines, VM files contains mostly HTML mark-up tags which makes it easier and simpler to use than FreeMarker.

After coding all templates, we now code the final view `/hrms/admin_users_page_vm` which is shown as follows:

```
<h2>User list</h2>
<table border="1">
<tr>
  <th>Employee ID</th>
  <th>Username</th>
  <th>Password</th>
  <th>Role</th>
</tr>
#foreach($user in $allUsers)
    <tr>
      <td>$user.hrmsEmployeeDetails.empId</td>
      <td>$user.username</td>
  <td>$user.password</td>
  <td>$user.role</td>
    </tr>
#end
```

```
</table>
```

The final view does not import the entire `admin_layout.vm` but contains only the body of the page. Velocity does the reverse of FreeMarker, wherein the view page content is imported by the layout and becomes the value of its expression `$screen_content`. For more details on how to understand advanced Velocity syntax, visit `http://wiki.apache.org/velocity/CodeStandards`.

HRMS provides both of the template engines for rendering proper JSP pages. Sometimes, developers need more than just the use of JSTL tags like page layout and component creation, which can be handled properly by the template engine.
`Chapter 5`, *Customer Feedback System (CFS)*, will discuss more about template engines and how they affect responsive web design in several Spring MVC 4.x applications.

# Generating news feeds

HRMS contains a newsletter page, which generates RSS and Atom feeds. Web feeds are used to publish (in an XML format) information from blogs, breaking news, and multimedia that are frequently updated. Web feeds are very important to publishers because they can automate the syndication process. These feeds are also important for readers because they are kept updated on the news and other information.

Web feeds can also aggregate many feeds to a single place. Feed readers are used to read web feeds. There are currently two types of web feeds and these are RSS (Really Simple Syndication) and Atom.

## RSS feeds

RSS 2.0 is the latest RSS version. An RSS document is made up of the full content, or the summary, along with the metadata (date, author, and so on), and is published as an XML document. RSS only supports text and escaped HTML and is used for smaller content types only.

HRMS uses the ROME (Rss and atOM utilitiEs) plugin to generate web feeds for the newsletter page. This library is used to override the Spring MVC 4.x abstract class for RSS feed generation of the `org.springframework.web.servlet.view.feed.AbstractRssFeedView`. There are two methods that are required to be implemented:

- `buildFeedMetadata`: This method is needed to establish the feed's core metadata using the channel class

- buildFeedItems: This method generates the feed information and returns a collection of item objects to the channel

The channel object holds all the metadata and feed information. The custom implementation of the AbstractRssFeedView will look like the following snippet:

```
public class HrmsRssViewBuilder extends AbstractRssFeedView{
@Override
protected void buildFeedMetadata(Map<String, Object> model,
            Channel feed, HttpServletRequest request) {
    feed.setTitle("HRMS News Feeds");
    feed.setDescription("HRMS News Feeds");
    feed.setLink("https://www.packtpub.com/");
    super.buildFeedMetadata(model, feed, request);
}

@SuppressWarnings("unchecked")
@Override
protected List<Item> buildFeedItems(Map<String, Object> model,
                HttpServletRequest req, HttpServletResponse resp)
                            throws Exception {
    List<HrmsNews> news = (List<HrmsNews>) model.get("allNews");
    List<Item> items = new ArrayList<Item>(news.size());
for(HrmsNews topic : news ){
        Item item = new Item();
        Content content = new Content();
        content.setValue(topic.getSummary());
        item.setContent(content);
        item.setTitle(topic.getDescription());
        item.setLink(topic.getLink());
        item.setPubDate(new Date());
        items.add(item);
    }
    return items;
}
}
```

Then we create a view name and map it with the custom RSS view class above, in order to be recognized by the ResourceBundleViewResolver:

```
rss_hrms_feeds.(class)=org.packt.human.resource.portal.views
                                            .HrmsRssViewBuilder
```

The controller that provides the data and calls the view name is simply implemented this way:

```
@Controller
public class AdminFeedsController {
@Autowired
private NewsService newsService;
private List<HrmsNews> newsList;

@RequestMapping(value="/hrms/rss_feeds", method=RequestMethod.GET)
public String createRSSFeeds(Model model){
    newsList = newsService.readAllNews();
    model.addAttribute("allNews", newsList);
    return "rss_hrms_feeds";
}
// See the sources
}
```

# Atom Feeds

Atom is a new format and is purpose-developed to overcome some of the limitations that are present in RSS 2.0. Atom1.0 has two separate tags, namely `<summary>` and `<content>` tags, which accommodate a range of content types, including text, escaped HTML, well-formed XHTML, and XML. It allows entries to link to the feed or standalone entries. Atom can use XML Encryption and XML Digital Signature to encrypt.

Just like with RSS feed generation, Spring MVC 4.x has an abstract view class `org.springframework.web.servlet.view.feed.AbstractAtomFeedView` that supports Atom feed generation. It uses the same library, ROME, to implement the custom view class.

As with RSS, there are also two methods that need to be implemented:

- `buildFeedMetadata`: This method establishes the feed's core metadata using the Feed model class
- `buildFeedItems`: This method generates the feed information and returns a collection of entry objects

Atom uses the feed object to carry the metadata and feed information. The following is the newsletter implementation for the ATOM generation:

```
public class HrmsAtomViewBuilder extends AbstractAtomFeedView {
@Override
protected void buildFeedMetadata(Map<String, Object> model,
```

```
                    Feed feed,
       HttpServletRequest request) {
  feed.setTitle("User Feeds News");
     feed.setId("tag:hrmsUserTypes");
     feed.setUpdated(new Date());
  }


  @Override
  protected List<Entry> buildFeedEntries(Map<String, Object> model,
          HttpServletRequest req, HttpServletResponse response)
                        throws Exception {
     List<HrmsNews> news = (List<HrmsNews>) model.get("allNews");
     List<Entry> entries = new ArrayList<Entry>(news.size());
     for(HrmsNews topic : news ){
          Entry entry = new Entry();
          entry.setId(topic.getId()+"");
          entry.setTitle(topic.getDescription());
  Content summary = new Content();
          summary.setValue(topic.getSummary());
          entry.setSummary(summary);
          Link link = new Link();
          link.setType("text/html");
          link.setHref(topic.getLink());

          List arrLinks = new ArrayList();
          arrLinks.add(link);
          entry.setAlternateLinks(arrLinks);
          entry.setUpdated(new Date());
          entries.add(entry);
     }
  return entries;
  }
  }
```

We create a view name to be mapped to the preceding custom view class:

```
atom_hrms_feeds.(class)=org.packt.human.resource.portal.views
                                        .HrmsAtomViewBuilder
```

The controller is implemented in a similar way to the RSS feed generation.

# Handling exceptions

Most of the applications related to analytics and report generation are prone to HTTP Status 404, which means that the pages were pulled out for some confidential reasons or that the page has technical glitches. Sometimes erroneous data sources give the pages HTTP Status 500 or 503. To avoid such intentional or unintentional problems, we need to create an exception-handling mechanism for our applications.

HRMS implemented three ways to shield its pages from unwanted HTTP Status Error messages and these are:

- **Implementing a custom exception class**: Normally this solution is best for an application which has a list of custom classes that needed to be implemented per controller:

```
@ResponseStatus(value=HttpStatus.NOT_FOUND,
            reason="Employee Not Found")
public class ReportNotFoundException extends Exception {
    public ReportNotFoundException(){
        super("ReportNotFoundException");    }
}
@ExceptionHandler(ReportNotFoundException.class)
public ModelAndView handleEmployeeNotFoundException(
            HttpServletRequest request, Exception ex) {
    ModelAndView modelAndView = new ModelAndView();
    modelAndView.addObject("exception", ex);
    modelAndView.addObject("url",
            request.getRequestURL());
            modelAndView.setViewName("error");
        return modelAndView; }
```

- **Using** `@AdviceController`: Implementing `@AdviceController` is just implementing a full blown Spring component, which can contain the global exception handler, model attributes and initbinder, which can be automatically triggered when an uncaught exception happens in any of the `@Controllers`:

```
@ControllerAdvice
public class HRMSExceptionHandler {
    @ExceptionHandler(SQLException.class)
    public String handleSQLException(HttpServletRequest
            request, Exception ex){
        return "database_error";    }
    @ResponseStatus(value=HttpStatus.NOT_FOUND,
            reason="IOException occured")
    @ExceptionHandler(IOException.class)
```

```
public void handleIOException(){
    //returning 404 error code page
    }    }
```

- **Using** `HandlerExceptionResolver`: This implements the global exception handler through `HandlerExceptionResolver` and maps exceptions to resources like HTML or JSP error pages:

```
public class AdminHrmsExceptionResolver extends
        SimpleMappingExceptionResolver {

@Override
public String buildLogMessage(Exception ex,
        HttpServletRequest request) {
    return "Admin Module exception: " +
        ex.getLocalizedMessage();
    }
}
<!-- declare in hrms-servlet.xml -->
<bean id="adminHrmsExceptionResolver"
        class="org.packt.human.resource.portal
            .views.AdminHrmsExceptionResolver">
        <property name="exceptionMappings">
            <map>
                <entry key="Exception"
                        value="hrms_error"></entry>
            </map>
        </property>
        <property name="defaultErrorView"
                    value="hrms_error" />
</bean>
<!-- hrms_error is a view page -->
```

# Software testing

This chapter will introduce the Spring test framework, which is an integral part of the framework essential for testing all components of the MVC application. There are levels of where to start testing our HRMS application:

- **Unit testing**: This test focuses on the logic and data models of the controller wherein all dependencies are mocked or stubbed; there is no involvement of the Spring container

- **Integration testing**: This test focuses on controller logic, validation, and data binding or serialization enforced by the framework; there is some involvement with the Spring container but only in parts
- **MVC testing**: This test focuses on the whole stack of the application, from the controller to the database, through the service and data access layers

# Building the test class for unit testing

To start any test, we need to create a test class with
`@RunWith(SpringJUnit4ClassRunner.class)` and
`@ContextConfiguration(locations = {...})` annotations. The former indicates that the test class must be executed under Spring's JUnit facilities, while the latter indicates which XML files contains the `ApplicationContext`. Test methods are preceded by an annotation `@Test` and all models are `@Autowired` for testing.

```
@RunWith(SpringJUnit4ClassRunner.class)
@ContextConfiguration("file:src/main/webapp/WEB-INF/hrms-servlet.xml")
public class LoginServiceTest {

@Autowired
private LoginService loginService;

@Test
public void testRole(){
    String testUser = "admin";
    String testpass = "admin";

    String testRole = loginService.checkRole(testUser, testpass);
    Assert.assertEquals("admin", testRole);

}
```

# Building the test class for integration testing

The test classes for integration testing is the same as with unit testing but with the annotation `@WebAppConfiguration`, which means that the Spring container can be involved in the testing process. It has a `MockMvc` class that mocks the Spring MVC infrastructure. The following is an initial setup for a Spring integration testing:

```
@RunWith(SpringJUnit4ClassRunner.class)
@WebAppConfiguration
@ContextConfiguration("file:src/main/webapp/WEB-INF/hrms-servlet.xml")
public class LoginValidationTest {
```

```
private MockMvc mockMvc;

@Before
public void setup() {
    MockitoAnnotations.initMocks(this);
    ResourceBundleViewResolver viewResolver =
            new ResourceBundleViewResolver();
    viewResolver.setBasename("config.views");
    mockMvc =
        MockMvcBuilders.standaloneSetup(loginController).
    setViewResolvers(viewResolver).build();
    when(loginValidator.supports(any(Class.class)))
            .thenReturn(true);
}
// see the sources
}
```

All the concerned components involved in testing are preceded by the @Mock annotation. Integration testing involves controller-view, control-model, and controller-rendition testing. HRMS has a sample test class that depicts integration testing, which is shown as follows:

```
@Test
public void loginWithOutModel() throws Exception {
    this.mockMvc.perform(get("/hrms/login.html"))
            .andExpect(status().isOk())
            .andExpect(forwardedUrl("/jsp/login.jsp"));
}

@Test
public void loginWithModel() throws Exception {
    this.mockMvc.perform(get("/hrms/login.html"))
            .andExpect(status().isOk())
            .andExpect(forwardedUrl("/jsp/login.jsp"))
            .andExpect(model().attribute("loginForm",
                    any(LoginForm.class)));
}
@Test
public void loginWithModelAndErrors() throws Exception {
    when(loginService.validUser("admin",
                            "admin")).thenReturn(true);
    when(loginService.checkRole("admin",
                            "admin")).thenReturn("admin");
    this.mockMvc.perform(post("/hrms/login.html")
            .param("username", "admin")
            .param("password", "admin"))
            .andExpect(status().isOk())
            .andExpect(forwardedUrl("/jsp/admin_index.jsp"))
            .andExpect(model()
```

```
                       .attributeHasFieldErrors("loginForm", "username"));
    }
```

## Building the test class for MVC testing

Testing the whole application involves testing the controller with its views, models, and validator framework. A sample test class that shows the whole application testing is as follows:

```
@SuppressWarnings("rawtypes")
    @Test
    public void loginError() throws Exception {
        when(loginService.validUser("admin", "admin"))
                    .thenReturn(true);
        doAnswer(new Answer() {
                @Override
                public Object answer(InvocationOnMock
                    invocationOnMock) throws Throwable {
                    Errors errors =
                      (Errors) invocationOnMock.getArguments()[1];
                    errors.rejectValue("username",
                       "error.login.username");
                    return null;
                }
        }).when(loginValidator).validate(any(LoginForm.class),
                    any(Errors.class));
        mockMvc.perform(post("/hrms/login").param("username",
                    "admin").param("password","admin"))
                .andExpect(status().isOk())
                .andExpect(view().name("login"));
    }
```

# JVM memory management

Graphs and report generation always cause an OutOfMemoryError in any JEE-based applications. This chapter recommends adding the following VM options to the application server to avoid an application crash:

```
-Xmx1000M
-Xms500M
-XX:PermSize=256M
```

The following screenshot shows a snapshot of memory usage in HRMS during user testing. Using VisualVM, the heap snapshots were captured before and after the memory management has been applied to the JVM. The following screenshot shows that, before memory management, the HRMS consumes more heap space as the plugins generate all the graphs and charts. Adjusting the minimum and maximum heap spaces stabilizes the amount of heap space used.

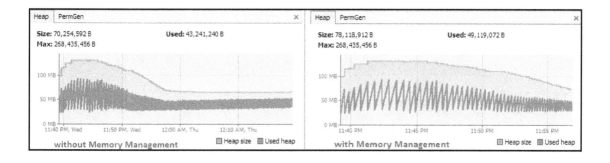

# Client-side visualization

Some applications allow features that will generate data analysis through JavaScript, which is supported mainly by Spring. GoogleChart, for instance, has a visualization API that consists of JavaScript classes that can generate charts and graphs. This topic will be discussed in `Chapter 8`, *Enterprise Resource Planning (ERP)*.

**The theme**
The theme of this portal was derived from the templates authored at `http://www.egrappler.com`.

# The Human Resource Management System (HRMS)

This HRMS is just only one of the real-world applications that need a lot of reports and charts for data visualization purposes. Many business owners and SEO consultants demand features that plot down data movement, create forecasts, and project coordinate points. The only limitation of this chapter is that it cannot give us an efficient solution in dealing with a huge amount of data. The book will deal with big and unstructured data analysis using Spring MVC 4.x in the next chapters.

## Challenge yourself

Create a simple online stock trading application that monitors the present and past stock of some random companies. It will generate line, and bar graphs, which can be downloaded as PDF files.

## Summary

This chapter has presented valid and popular solutions for how to integrate Spring 4.x MVC applications, with different rendition features aside from JSP views. Although there are many possible study areas, this chapter chose to study the feasibility of human resource management systems written in Spring, with all their involved reports and data analysis. With the proper memory management, the prototype has proven the ability of the framework to render data into charts or graphs, which can be downloaded in PDF or in an image format. The project also studied the feasibility of integrating the software to RSS feeds and Atom publishing protocol, which are a modern-day trick for checking updates on published sites. But the most interesting is highlighted in the different rendition generation we see in JasperReports and DynamicReports which many companies are doing nowadays.

# 5
# Customer Feedback System (CFS)

Lots of e-Commerce systems allow users to post their feedback on certain products, businesses or services for marketing and production purposes. Nowadays, many blogs and sites offer a feedback system in order to give insights to the business owners and their marketing teams on how to improve their business, products and/or overall customer experience.

Some feedback management services like `www.surveymonkey.com` offer survey forms to clients, not only to get feedback but also suggestions and recommendations. Some are in forums formats such as TripAdvisor, Reddit, and Travelocity, which provide an excellent user experience just gathering feedback on delicacies, hotels, restaurants, places and parks. Other systems are in the forms of blogs containing social plugins like Twitter, Facebook and Gmail, which gives people the ability to complain or commend items posted onto their blogs.

This chapter will highlight how to create a simple enterprise feedback system that will make use of the Spring MVC architecture. The software template will be a Post-It kind of a feedback system, with the capability to send user feedback using electronic mail. For audit purposes, all feedback will be archived in a database, and all e-mails will be monitored using SendGrid. In order to avoid e-mail spamming, **Denial of Service (DoS)** attacks and other exploitations, **Captcha** will be used in all input forms on the system.

In this chapter, you will learn how to:

- Use the different available Captcha plugins for Spring MVC 4.x
- Use SendGrid to monitor and manage e-mail transactions

# Overview of the project

The project featured in this chapter is a **Customer Feedback System** (**CFS**), which is a simple module that acts like a forum where customers can just post any topics regarding a product or an issue, through which other users can give feedback. This platform can also be considered as a simple collaboration tool where customers can exchange ideas, give suggestions, and promote their own concepts.

The feedback system has been planned to look like a generic prototype, classified between a survey and a forum type application. The following wireframe will give the overall picture of the system.

- **The topic page**: The system will have this façade open to guests, users or administrators who wants to drop in an issue for feedback. This can be customized further, for example, adding security or a login page. After posting a topic, anyone can edit, delete or respond to the issue through the buttons at the right side of the table list.

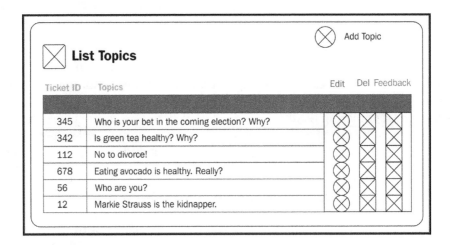

- **The add/edit topic page**: This is a form page for adding or editing a topic. It just contains basic information like the topic and its description.

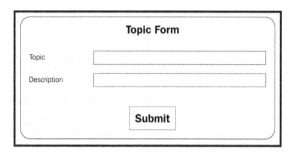

- **The feedback page**: If anyone would like to view the list of feedback on a certain topic or issue, there is a button at the far right of this page which will enumerate all user feedback.

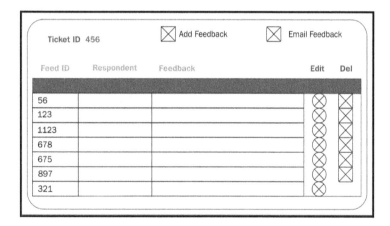

- **The add/edit feedback page**: This is the form page for posting feedback regarding a certain topic or ticket ID.

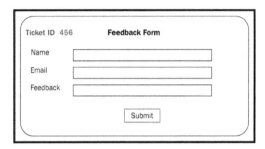

- **The e-mail form page**: If a user or customer wants their feedback delivered directly to the owner, then the <indexentry state="del" content="" dbid="0" tempid="4654">module is capable of sending their feedback via e-mail. The e-mail transaction is</indexentry> monitored and managed to avoid unwanted effects to the system.

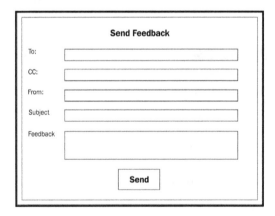

# Technical requirements

The project will start with the configuration and setup of the base Spring MVC 4.x platform. Refer to `Chapter 1`, *Creating a Personal Web Portal (PWP)* for all the processes. Then, the following libraries are required in the project for the implementation of a forum-based or survey-based feedback system.

# Captcha libraries

The following are the popular Captcha libraries used by the CFS to provide security to all forms for posting and dropping topics and feedback. The system does not have tight security because it is available to any respondents concerned with the topics.

## reCaptcha

The reCaptcha is the easiest plugin to be integrated into a Spring MVC application. It is an open-source plugin that provides ready-made Captcha images to be used in any sites. It does not require any coding either from the back-end or client-side side. This plugin is owned by Google and can be visited at `http://www.google.com/recaptcha`. The following Maven library is needed to successfully integrate reCaptcha to our CFS site:

- `net.tanesha.recaptcha4j` (recaptcha4j): The core API that provides a captcha on any JEE-based applications

## BotDetect

BotDetect is a Captcha generator used to secure any form validations to prevent automated and successive page posting. The OCR algorithms used to generate Captcha images here are complicated enough to be predicted by human eyes. It also offers Captcha audio alternatives to secure websites for people with impaired vision. More information about the plugin is found at `https://captcha.com/`. The current Maven BotDetect library for our CFS-BotDetect Captcha integration is:

- `com.captcha` (botdetect 3.0.alpha2): This is a new and and an in-progress BotDetect library used in integrating BotDetect Captch to JEE-based applications

The Maven library above will not work without this updated repository:

```
<repository>
  <id>captcha</id>
  <name>BotDetect Captcha Repository</name>
  <url>https://git.captcha.com/maven.git/blob_plain/HEAD:/</url>
</repository>
```

# JCaptcha

This stands for **Java Completely Automated Public Test to tell Computers and Humans Apart**, and is a 100% Java-based library. It is a highly programmable plugin that provides a robust and reliable Captcha implementation framework for any Java applications that need text, image or sound Captcha validation. This plugin has been used and tested in many GWT, Struts and Grails applications. Further documentation on JCaptcha can be found at h ttp://jcaptcha.sourceforge.net/. CFS needs the following Maven JCaptcha libraries and dependencies for a successful integration:

- com.octo.captcha (jcaptcha): This library provides a set of interfaces and implementations of generic and typed captcha and captcha factories.
- com.octo.captcha (jcaptcha-integration-simple-servlet): The main JCaptcha servlet that generates the Captcha images, sound and text.
- javax.media.jai (com.springsource.javax.media.jai.core): This library implements a set of core image-processing capabilities, including image tiling, regions of interest, deferred execution and a set of core image-processing operators, including many common points, areas, and frequency domain operators that are far more extensive than the existing imaging libraries of the Java platform.
- commons-collections: An Apache library that provides more optimized and powerful data structures for high-end processing.
- org.slf4j: This library provides a simple facade or abstraction for various logging frameworks (for example java.util.logging, logback, log4j), allowing the end user to plug in the desired logging framework at deployment time.

The default Maven repository for JCaptcha may not work currently, but the following repositories can be a good replacement:

```
<repository>
    <id>sourceforge-releases</id>
    <name>Sourceforge Releases</name>
    <url>https://oss.sonatype.org/content/
                repositories/sourceforge-releases</url>
</repository>
<repository>
    <id>com.springsource.repository.bundles.external</id>
    <name>SpringSource Enterprise Bundle Repository
        - External Bundle Releases</name>
    <url>http://repository.springsource.com/
                maven/bundles/external
    </url>
```

```
</repository>
```

# SimpleCaptcha

Another solution for form validation is SimpleCaptcha, which is a Java library for generating Captcha images. This solution has a straightforward and easy way of customizing the Captcha generation. The Maven library for this is:

- `com.liferay` (`nl.captcha.simplecaptcha`): The main APIs for `SimpleCaptcha` generation and customization

# Kaptcha

Kaptcha is a modern implementation of SimpleCaptcha. It is very easy to setup and use compared to SimpleCaptcha. The Captcha images are hard enough for only human eyes to read. The look and feel of the images are adjustable in Kaptcha since it has some configuration options that are needed to manage the code generation. Like SimpleCaptcha, this library is also easy to customize.

The Maven library for Kaptcha used by CFS is:

- `com.google.code` (kaptcha): This consists of the main APIs for Kaptcha

The preceding Maven library needs the following new repository in order to work:

```
<repository>
    <id>google-maven-snapshot-repository</id>
    <name>Google Maven Snapshot Repository</name>
    <url>https://m2repos.googlecode.com/svn/nexus</url>
        <snapshots>
            <enabled>true</enabled>
        </snapshots>
</repository>
```

# SendGrid library

SendGrid is an easily integrated, reliable, cloud-based e-mail infrastructure for maintaining and monitoring e-mail transactions. Its infrastructure is cost-effective and resource-efficient in providing e-mail delivery, scalability and real-time analytics along with flexible API's that make custom integration with different applications. CFS uses SendGrid to manage feedback sent through e-mail by customers or users.

The Maven library for SendGrid and its dependencies is shown as follows:

- `com.sendgrid` (`sendgrid-java`): These are Java helper classes for the SendGrid platform
- `org.json`: These are classes used for JSON decoding and encoding

# The CFS database

CFS uses a database to store all feedback and replies from customers on issues posted on the site. This is for traceability and audit trail purposes. The database is named **cfs** and has the ERD illustrated in the following figure.

# Data modeling framework

Just like in Chapter 4, *Human Resource Management System (HRMS)* this prototype will be promoting the Hibernate 4.x Framework. The following ERD design shows a simple schema definition for the applications, since the main objective is to store issues and feedback of site visitors on each issue.

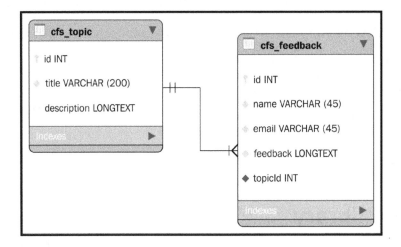

# The Captcha

CAPTCHA or Captcha stands for **Completely Automated Public Turing test to tell Computers and Humans Apart**, and is a type of challenge-response test implemented on many sites to ensure that no responses to the site are automated.

There are people who want to exploit the vulnerabilities and weaknesses of a system through running robots, spiders, and crawlers that produce automated responses to any form transactions to the system. Some users just want to create spam that will cause an overhead to system performance. Some just unintentionally log in to the system many times, because they forgot their credentials, but can in turn be considered as a threat to the portal if done with patterns. Given these many situations, the CAPTCHA test helps to identify which users are real human beings and which ones are bogus or auto-generated.

Generally, CAPTCHA is a verification test that is by many sign-up forms to avoid exploitation to the system. The following is an example of a Captcha attached to an e-mail verification form.

This is how an e-mail verification Captcha looks:

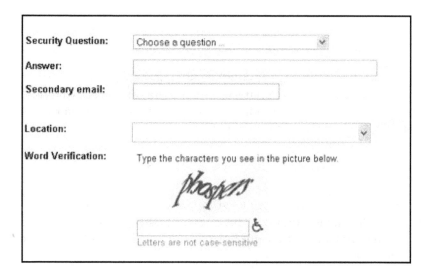

Captcha can use unpredictable and woven images, text or audio objects.

# Posting topics and issues

The CFS is a general application that tends to accept issues and topics from guests, customers and system users. User credentials are not needed because this portal can be open to the public, since part of the application's objective is to study marketing strategy and business roadmaps. Based on the wireframe, the main page will just list all the posted topics and will also provide an entry-point for topic posting.

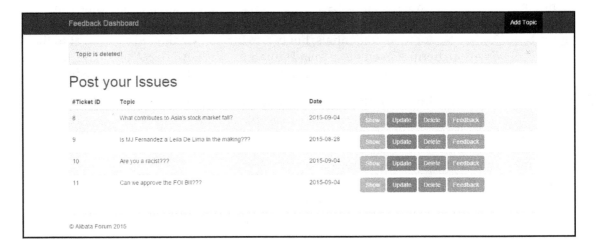

The preceding figure shows the implemented version of the wireframe for the topic listing. Anyone can post a topic, then edit, update, and delete it afterwards. Anyone can also give feedback on it. Since this is a public module, we need to attach Captcha to all form transactions, starting from posting a new topic.

# Adding topics

There are lots of Captcha implementations written in different languages, but only a few are feasible for Spring MVC 4.x integration. This chapter highlights five of the popular and well-known Captcha implementations for Spring MVC, and one of them is used by CFS for this feature of adding a new topic.

A topic metadata can include the issue itself, a description of the issue, the person who posted, an e-mail address, and the date posted. Some of this information is found on our form transaction for the new topic.

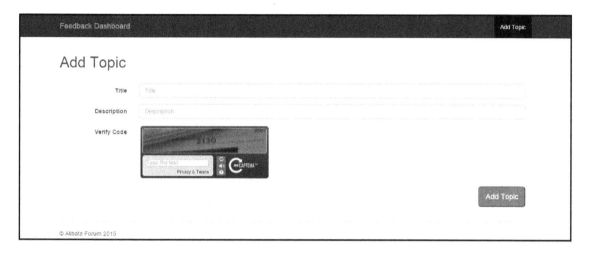

Obviously, as we can see from the preceding screenshot, **reCaptcha** is used as the official Captcha implementation for the said form. Before we start the implementation, we need to have a Gmail account to sign-up and generate both the private and public reCaptcha API keys.

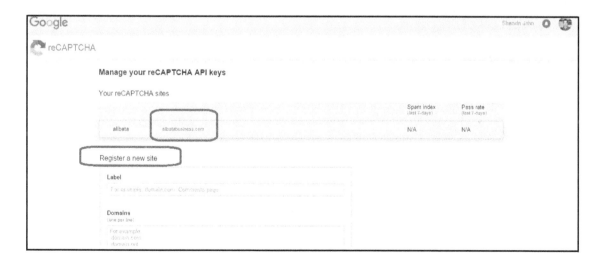

All Captcha validation will be done by assigned Google servers so as not to burden CFS with lots of coding tasks. Also, it entails tough security on the image generation of the Captcha, giving us the confidence that all Captcha transactions are reliable.

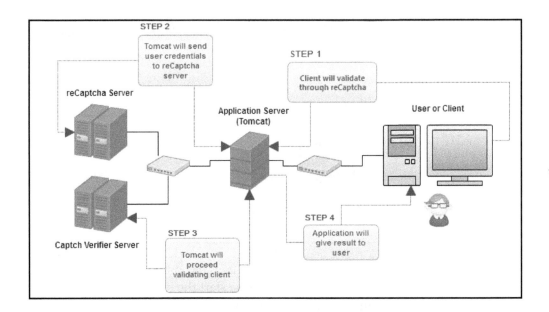

 The system must be connected to the Internet in order to connect to the reCaptcha server shown in the preceding diagram.

After getting the private and public keys from the server, the net.tanesha.recaptcha.ReCaptchaImpl object is injected as a bean with the private key as a property. This bean will be @Autowired into the controller, to process all Captcha input coming from the user.

## The reCaptcha controller

The controller contains all the needed DAOs and the reCaptcha object. It also receives two @RequestParams from the Captcha view. These two form element fields are the recaptcha_challenge_field, that contains information about the test presented to user, and the recaptcha_response_field that contains the user answer to the test. Aside from these inputs, reCaptcha APIs require a CFS remote address through the getRemoteAddr() method of the HttpServketRequest. In order to avoid conflicts with the operating system, it is advisable to set the system property, called `java.net.useSystemProxies`, to true, in order to allow JVM to use proxy automatically.

```
static {
        System.setProperty("java.net.useSystemProxies", "true");
    }
```

The overall controller for the reCaptcha integration must look like this:

```
@Controller
public class TopicFormController {

    static {
        System.setProperty("java.net.useSystemProxies", "true");
    }

    @Autowired
    private ReCaptcha reCaptcha;

    // see the sources
    @RequestMapping(value = "/cfs/topic_process_add",
                method = RequestMethod.POST)
    public RedirectView submitForAdd(
     @ModelAttribute("topicForm") @Validated TopicForm topicForm,
        HttpServletRequest request, BindingResult result,
         Model model, final RedirectAttributes redirectAttributes,
            @RequestParam("recaptcha_challenge_field")
                         String challangeField,
            @RequestParam("recaptcha_response_field")
                         String responseField) {
        RedirectView redirectView = new RedirectView();
        redirectView.setContextRelative(true);
        redirectView.setUrl("/cfs/topics.html");
        if (result.hasErrors()) {
            redirectView.setUrl("/cfs/topics.html");
        } else {
            redirectAttributes.addFlashAttribute("css", "success");
        String remoteAddress = request.getRemoteAddr();
        ReCaptchaResponse reCaptchaResponse =
         this.reCaptcha.checkAnswer(remoteAddress,
                challangeField, responseField);
        if(reCaptchaResponse.isValid()) {// see the sources}
            else { // see the sources    }
        return redirectView;
        }
    }
}
```

To validate the answer, `ReCaptchaImpl` has a method known as `checkAnswer()` which needs the address of the user and the two fields, response and challenge field, to verify if the user has got the correct captcha text.

## The reCaptcha View

To separate the logic from the view, CFS creates a tag file under the `WEB-INF/tags` folder, which contains the logic on how to import the reCaptcha API at the view level. The tag file contains the following code:

```
<%@ tag import="net.tanesha.recaptcha.ReCaptcha" %>
<%@ tag import="net.tanesha.recaptcha.ReCaptchaFactory" %>
<%@ attribute name="privateKey" required="true" rtexprvalue="false" %>
<%@ attribute name="publicKey" required="true" rtexprvalue="false" %>
<%
    ReCaptcha c = ReCaptchaFactory.newReCaptcha(publicKey, privateKey,
false);
    out.print(c.createRecaptchaHtml(null, null));
%>
```

The preceding `reCaptcha` class requires the private and the public key provided by the JSP view. The method `createRecaptchaHtml()` creates an HTML snippet that will render the testwhich usually looks like this:

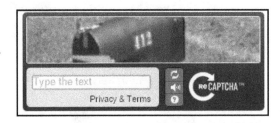

After creating the tag file it will be imported into the JSP view for the rendition of the challenge or test.

```
<%@ taglib prefix="tags" tagdir="/WEB-INF/tags" %>
<!-See the sources -->
<div class="col-sm-10">
   <tags:captcha
     privateKey="6Lf2rwsTAAAAACsFdaTempAjILAuK3GhMuZe3ZDK"
     publicKey="6Lf2rwsTAAAAIvxqJn7ZiIjCmE-
                          Jbb6Gw6Fcozo">
   </tags:captcha>
      </div>
```

# Editing topics

The CFS allows anyone to freely edit any topic posted, but they will also undergo a Captcha test. The Captcha library used in this feature is the BotDetect Captcha. After configuring the Maven requirement given above, the integration process starts with the declaration of its servlet `botdetect.web.http.CaptchaServlet` in the `web.xml`.

```
<servlet><servlet-name>BotDetect Captcha</servlet-name>
    <servlet-class>botdetect.web.http.CaptchaServlet
    </servlet-class>
</servlet>
<servlet-mapping>
    <servlet-name>BotDetect Captcha</servlet-name>
    <url-pattern>/botdetectcaptcha</url-pattern>
</servlet-mapping>
```

## The BotDetect controller

Then, on the controller side, validation of the Captcha test will be done simply by extracting the generated Captcha test `updateTopicCaptcha`, and the result of the test `getCaptchaCodeTextBox()`, which are both request parameters. The validation is simply written in a very simple code like this:

```
public boolean createBotCaptcha(BotModel
            botModel,HttpServletRequest request){
    Captcha captcha = Captcha.load(request, "updateTopicCaptcha");
    boolean isHuman = captcha.validate(request,
            botModel.getCaptchaCodeTextBox());
    if (isHuman)        return true;
    else return false
}
```

Another option is to implement this BotDetect validation under the validator of the edit form.

## The BotDetect view

The view page of the BotDetect must contain the taglib at the top of the view, and the HTML component that will show the BotDetect image, plus the text field that will contain the result of the test after submission.

```
<%@ taglib prefix="botDetect" uri="botDetect"%>
    // see the sources
<fieldset>
        <label for="captchaCodeTextBox" class="prompt">
```

```
      Retype the code:</label>
      <botDetect:captcha id="updateTopicCaptcha"
      codeLength="7" imageWidth="300"
        imageStyles="graffiti, graffiti2, halo, lego,  mass,
                     vertigo, strippy"/>
      <div class="validationDiv">
          <form:input path="botModel.captchaCodeTextBox" />
      </div>
  </fieldset>
    // see the sources
```

BotDetect allows the use of more than one of their own Captcha image styles such as graffiti, halo, mass, vertigo and strippy.

# Giving feedback

Any users can respond to any of the topics presented by CFS, including giving feedback on each. Each topic has its own list of feedback and the form for it is shown as follows:

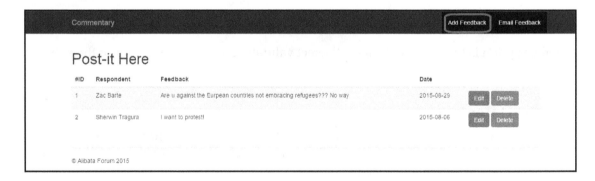

At the top of the form, a user will just click on the **Add Feedback** button to give their feelings on an issue. But, before they submit their entry, they will take a quick test from **Kaptcha**. After integrating the needed Maven requirement above, there are two ways to use Google Kaptcha:

- Creating a global
  servlet `com.google.code.kaptcha.servlet.KaptchaServlet` which must
  be declared in `web.xml` with its own defined mapping like `*.do`, in the case of
  CFS.
- Creating a `@Controller` that will use the settings of the image injected into the
  producer class, such as height, width, and font names.

```xml
<bean id="captchaProducer"
  class="com.google.code.kaptcha.impl.DefaultKaptcha">
  <property name="config">
    <bean class="com.google.code.kaptcha.util.Config">
      <constructor-arg>
        <props>
          <prop key="kaptcha.border">no</prop>
          <prop key="kaptcha.border.color">
            105,179,90 </prop>
          <prop key="kaptcha.textproducer.font.color">
            red </prop>
          <prop key="kaptcha.image.width">250 </prop>
          <prop key="kaptcha.textproducer.font.size">
            90 </prop>
          <prop key="kaptcha.image.height">90</prop>
          <prop key="kaptcha.session.key">code </prop>
          <prop key="kaptcha.textproducer.char.length">
            4 </prop>
          <prop key="kaptcha.textproducer.font.names">
            Arial, Arial, Microsoft Accor </prop>
        </props>
      </constructor-arg>
    </bean>
  </property>
</bean>
```

The current CFS uses the custom `@Controller` for the Kaptcha validation.

# The Kaptcha controller

Kaptcha uses an `HttpSession` to generate and verify Captcha codes. It starts by extracting
the codes in the controller and storing them in the session
variable `Constants.KAPTCHA_SESSION_KEY`. After submission, this key will again be
retrieved as a session variable for validation against the user's results in the test.

```java
@Controller
public class CaptchImageController {
    @Autowired
```

```java
        private Producer captchaProducer;

        @RequestMapping("/captcha/kaptcha-image.do")
        public ModelAndView handleRequest(
           HttpServletRequest request,
                HttpServletResponse response) throws Exception {
                response.setDateHeader("Expires", 0);
                response.setHeader("Cache-Control", "no-store,
                     no-cache, must-revalidate");
                response.addHeader("Cache-Control",
                    "post-check=0, pre-check=0");
                response.setHeader("Pragma", "no-cache");
                response.setContentType("image/jpeg");
                String capText = captchaProducer.createText();
                              request.getSession()
   .setAttribute(Constants.KAPTCHA_SESSION_KEY,
                capText);
                BufferedImage bi =
                        captchaProducer.createImage(capText);
                ServletOutputStream out =
                        response.getOutputStream();
                ImageIO.write(bi, "jpg", out);
                try {       out.flush();   }
                finally {  out.close(); }

                return null;
        }
```

To check if the user got the answer right to the validation test, the controller FeedbackFormController, which is responsible for feedback transactions, has a service method that calls validateKaptcha():

```java
@RequestMapping(value = "/cfs/feedback_process_add",
              method = RequestMethod.POST)
   public RedirectView submitForAdd(
      @ModelAttribute("feedbackForm") @Validated FeedbackForm
            feedbackForm,
         HttpServletRequest request, BindingResult result,
            Model model,
         final RedirectAttributes redirectAttributes) {
      // See the sources
     if (result.hasErrors()) {
      redirectView.setUrl("/cfs/feedbacks/" +
              feedbackForm.getTopicId());
     } else {
      redirectAttributes.addFlashAttribute("css", "success");
       String answer = request.getParameter("kaptchaAnswer");
        HttpSession session = request.getSession();
```

```
if (validateKaptcha(session, answer)) {
    redirectAttributes.addFlashAttribute("msg",
       "New feedback added successfully!");
     feedbackService.addFeedback(
            feedbackForm.getTopicId(), feedbackForm);
        redirectView.setUrl("/cfs/feedbacks/"
                + feedbackForm.getTopicId());
    } else {
        redirectView.setUrl("/cfs/feedbacks_add/"
                + feedbackForm.getTopicId());
    } }
return redirectView;        }

public boolean validateKaptcha(HttpSession session,
        String kaptchaResult){
    String code = (String)session.getAttribute(
    com.google.code.kaptcha.Constants.KAPTCHA_SESSION_KEY);
    if(code.equals(kaptchaResult)){ return true;      }
    return false;
} }
```

## The Kaptcha view

The Kaptcha view just needs the HTML snippet calling the controller that generates the image, plus some JQuery codes for image refresh purposes.

```
<div class="col-sm-10">
    <img src="/ch05/captcha/captcha-image.do" style="width: 250px"
        id="kaptchaImage"   style="margin-bottom: -3px"/>
    <input name="kaptcha" type="text" id="kaptcha" maxlength="10"
        class="chknumber_input" />
    <button type="submit" id="reloadKaptcha">Reload
      Kaptcha</button>
</div>
```

# Editing feedback

Aside from adding feedback, a user can edit any feedback posted. But it's not as easy as one would imagine; the edit feedback feature implements a SimpleCaptcha to avoid exploitation. Since SimpleCaptcha is a highly customizable solution, CFS allows a controller to generate the Captcha images.

## The SimpleCaptcha controller

There are two ways to implement SimpleCaptcha and they are: to globally use
`StickyCaptchaServlet` by default or to custom create a `SimpleCaptchaServlet`. If the
system is restricted to creating just one Captcha image or video per session, then the former
is used. If reloading is allowed then the latter is recommended. `StickyCaptchaServlet`
stores Captcha information at the session level. CFS uses its
custom `SimpleCaptchaServlet`, but has an available implementation for the "sticky" one.

The image is always generated using `Captcha.Builder()` API classes. The width and
length of the image is configured through the `Builder()` constructor. The Captcha API
class has a method `setText()` that needs some producers to help create the image,
like `DefaultTextProducer`, `ArabicTextProducer`, and `ChineseTextProducer`. Aside
from `setText()`, the main `Captcha` class has `addBackground()`, `addNoise()`
and `gimp()` to add art, blur, and tricks to the image, in order to make the text not-so-
readable. To end the generation, the `build()` method is called last, because it will flush-out
all the properties set for the image. Without the `build()`, an HTTP 500 status code will be
expected from the server.

If the `StickyCaptchaServlet` is used, the `Captcha` class must be injected as a bean,
together with all the properties mentioned above, and later, `@Autowired` in the controller
for image processing and validation.

```
<bean id="captchaBean" class="nl.captcha.CaptchaBean"
        scope="session">
    <constructor-arg index="0"><value>200</value></constructor-arg>
    <constructor-arg index="1"><value>50</value></constructor-arg>
    <property name="addBorder"><value>true</value></property>
        <property name="txtProd">
                <ref bean="textProducer"></ref></property>
        <property name="noiseProd">
                <ref bean="noiseProducer"></ref></property>
        <property name="gimpy">
            <ref bean="gimpyProducer"></ref></property>
        <aop:scoped-proxy/>
    </bean>

    <bean id="textProducer"
        class="nl.captcha.text.producer.DefaultTextProducer"/>
    <bean id="noiseProducer"
        class="nl.captcha.noise.CurvedLineNoiseProducer"/>
    <bean id="gimpyProducer"
        class="nl.captcha.gimpy.FishEyeGimpyRenderer"/>
```

Since the current CFS implementation allows reloading of an image, the following is the custom `SimpleCaptchaServlet` implementation:

```java
import nl.captcha.servlet.SimpleCaptchaServlet;
// See the sources

public class SimpleCaptchaCustomServlet extends
                    SimpleCaptchaServlet {

@Override
public void doGet(HttpServletRequest req,
  HttpServletResponse resp) throws ServletException, IOException {
    List<java.awt.Font> textFonts = Arrays.asList(
        new Font("Arial", Font.BOLD, 40),
        new Font("Courier", Font.BOLD, 40));
    Captcha captcha = new Captcha.Builder(250, 90).addText()
        .addBackground(
            new FlatColorBackgroundProducer(Color.YELLOW))
        .gimp(new FishEyeGimpyRenderer())
        .addNoise(new CurvedLineNoiseProducer())
        .addText(new DefaultTextProducer(5),
          new DefaultWordRenderer(Color.RED, textFonts))
        .build();

    CaptchaServletUtil.writeImage(resp, captcha.getImage());
    req.getSession().setAttribute(NAME, captcha);
  } }
```

To check whether the user has correctly answered the test before a successful feedback edit, the following method is called inside the request method:

```java
public static boolean validateSimpleCaptcha(HttpSession session, String
answer ) {
Captcha captcha = (Captcha) session.getAttribute(
                        Captcha.NAME );
String code = captcha.getAnswer();
if( code.equals( answer ) ) { return true;  }
return false;
  }
```

# The SimpleCaptcha view

Like Kaptcha, the view page of SimpleCaptcha simply contains the HTML snippets that contain the image rendition and the text box that will contain the result of the test.

```html
<div class="col-sm-10">
      <img id="simpleCaptcha"
```

```
                    src="/ch05/captcha/simple.png"/>
        <input type="text" maxlength="12" name="txtCaptchaAnswer"
           id="txtCaptchaAnswer" value="" style="width: 250"
           class="validate[required,minSize[8]]"/>
              <button type="submit" id="reloadSimpleCaptcha">Reload
              Kaptcha</button>
   </div>
```

# E-mail Feedback

Posting feedback is just one of the options the user has to let their side be heard by the management. One thing that users can do is to click on the **E-mail Feedback** button in the CFS, and just send their ideas to the concerned person who has issued the topic. The e-mail form is protected by JCaptcha to avoid e-mail spamming. Among all the Captcha implementation presented in this chapter, JCaptcha is the most flexible and highly-customizable type of Captcha. It has three types of services used for customizing the Captcha generation namely:

- Com.octo.captcha.service.image.DefaultManageableImageCaptchaSer
  vice: The class used for Captcha image generation
- Com.octo.captcha.service.sound.AbstractManageableSoundCaptchaSe
  rvice: The abstract class to be extended for Captcha sound implementation
- Com.octo.captcha.service.multitype.GenericManageableCaptchaServ
  ice: The class used for text, image, and sound implementation

CFS uses the com.octo.captcha.service.multitype.GenericManageableCaptchaService to guide the reader in how to create customization for any type of Captcha generation. The service constructor needs four parameters.

First, it needs to instantiate the com.octo.captcha.service.captchastore.CaptchaStore. This interface provides a way of temporarily storing Captcha with a unique key and the best implementation is com.octo.captcha.service.captchastore.FastHashMapCaptchaStore. Secondly, the service needs the Captcha settings or Captcha engine, which can be implemented in two ways: XML injection, using its predefined bean tags and properties, or code-based, using the API classes and methods. CFS chooses the latter way of implementing the engine. To implement the engine, you have to determine which type of Captcha is being created. Since CFS has focused on Captcha Image, we extend the more specific class com.octo.captcha.engine.image.ListImageCaptchaEngine, which uses the ImageCaptchaFactory.

Factories are the real creator of Captchas and need to be configured using the following API classes:

- Com.octo.captcha.component.word.wordgenerator.WordGenerator: This class is responsible for the generation of the text found on the image
- Com.octo.captcha.component.image.wordtoimage.WordToImage: A specific class used to generate image from text

The WordToImage API class needs some support classes that will help it build the image and these are:

- Com.octo.captcha.component.image.fontgenerator.FontGenerator: The class that enumerates the list of java.awt.Font objects with its properties
- Com.octo.captcha.component.image.backgroundgenerator.Background Generator: The class that generates the texture and color of the image background
- Com.octo.captcha.component.image.textpaster.TextPaster: The class that pastes the text on the background
- Com.octo.captcha.component.image.deformation.ImageDeformation: The class that generates the distortion of the image

After the engine, GenericManageableCaptchaService needs a third parameter, as the expiration time of the Captcha in seconds, a fourth parameter as the maximum size of the Captcha store in bytes, and the fourth parameter is the maximum usable Captcha store limit in bytes before garbage collection.

## The JCaptcha controller

The controller for this Captcha just calls the JCaptcha service for the generation of the image on the e-mail form. It also provides the validation method, which is also session-based. Some implementation places the validation process on the validation layer of the application.

The following is the CFS implementation for the controller:

```
@Resource(name = "imageCaptchaService")
private ImageCaptchaService imageCaptchaService;
@RequestMapping(value = "/cfs/captcha/e-mailCaptcha")
public String ImageCaptcha(HttpServletRequest request,
    HttpServletResponse response)
        throws ServletException, IOException {
    byte[] captchaChallengeAsJpeg = null;
```

```
        ByteArrayOutputStream jpegOutputStream = new
                    ByteArrayOutputStream();
    try {
      String sessionid = request.getSession().getId();
      BufferedImage challenge =
      imageCaptchaService.getImageChallengeForID(sessionid,
              request.getLocale());
      ImageIO.write(challenge, "jpeg", jpegOutputStream);
    } catch (Exception e) {      }
    captchaChallengeAsJpeg = jpegOutputStream.toByteArray();
    response.setHeader("Cache-Control", "no-store");
    response.setHeader("Pragma", "no-cache");
    response.setDateHeader("Expires", 0);
    response.setContentType("image/jpeg");
    ServletOutputStream responseOutputStream =
                        response.getOutputStream();
    responseOutputStream.write(captchaChallengeAsJpeg);
    responseOutputStream.flush();
    responseOutputStream.close();
    return null;
  }
```

On the other hand, the `E-mailFormController`, that processes the
`e-mailService`, calls the following method to validate the user's answer to the validation
test:

```
    public boolean validateJCaptcha(HttpSession session,
            String captchaResult){
    boolean validCaptcha = false;
    try {
        validCaptcha =
        imageCaptchaService.validateResponseForID(session.getId(),
                captchaResult);
        if(validCaptcha){   return true;     }
    }
    catch (CaptchaServiceException e) { return false; }
    return false;
  }
```

## The JCaptcha view

Just as with Kaptcha and SimpleCaptcha, we have no taglib or APIs to be imported in the
view side of the e-mail form. What we need here is the HTML code for the rendition of the
required JCaptcha generated image, and the text field for the result.

```
    <div class="col-sm-10">
        <img id="jcaptcha" src="/ch05/cfs/captcha/e-mailCaptcha" />
```

```
    <input type="button" value="refresh" onclick="refresh()" />
    <br/>
    <input type="text" name="captchTextResult" />
</div>
```

## The SendGrid service

Sending e-mail is always an entry point to site exploitation. It is always acceptable to use the JavaMail API in creating e-mail transaction processes, as presented in `Chapter 1`, *Creating a Personal Web Portal (PWP)*. But an application that uses JavaMail classes must implement Spring Security and other system security and firewalls, in order to ensure safe and reliable e-mail transactions. For public, or almost public, sites like CFS, an immediate solution is to use a cloud-based monitoring application like SendGrid for incoming and upcoming e-mails.

SendGrid has Web APIs that can be used by any platform including Spring MVC 4.x. But, to ensure security, SendGrid requires CFS to sign up for an account for the company's assessment. Afterwards, the account will show as pending at first, owing to the surveying the company will be conducting for the newly opened account.

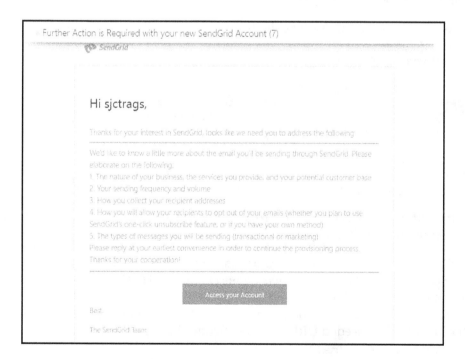

Once the account is approved, you can check through a SendGrid web service to see if the account created can access the Web APIs.

```
https://api.sendgrid.com/api/blocks.get.json?api_user=<username>&api_key=<p
assword>&to=sjctrags@yahoo.com&toname=Destination&subject=Example%20Subject
&text=testingtextbody&from=sjctrags@yahoo.com
```

Run the preceding web service and check the browser, which must have a JSON result:

```
[{"status": "5.7.9", "reason": "554 5.7.9 Message not accepted for policy
reasons. See http://postmaster.yahoo.com/errors/postmaster-28.html ",
"email": "sjctrags@yahoo.com"}]
```

As long as the status is not invalid, the application can now use the SendGrid Web API.

The process of SendGrid-Spring MVC 4.x integration starts with saving the username and password of the SendGrid account used in the above web service verification. These credentials must be stored in the property file, `sendgrid.properties`. It is not advisable to hardcode all essential SendGrid information inside the script.

```
sendgrid.api.user=<username>
sendgrid.api.key=<password>
```

In order to retrieve all the key-value pairs from a property file, CFS has injected `org.springframework.beans.factory.config.PropertyPlaceholderConfigurer` into the `ApplicationContext`:

```
<bean id="deployProperties"
class="org.springframework.beans.factory.config.
                                    PropertiesFactoryBean">
    <property name="location">
        <value>classpath:config/sendgrid.properties</value>
    </property>
</bean>
<context:property-placeholder properties-ref="deployProperties" />
```

After all the settings have been placed properly, the service layer of CFS pertaining to the e-mail transaction must be implemented.

The highlight API class is the `org.springframework.web.client.RestTemplate` API class. It is Spring's central class for synchronous client-side HTTP access. It simplifies communication with HTTP servers, and enforces RESTful principles. It handles HTTP connections, leaving application code to provide URLs (with possible template variables) and extract results. The needed URL, that asks SendGrid to perform a mail transaction, is ht tp://sendgrid.com/api/mail.send.json.

The response of the request can be any of the following return codes:

- 2XX: The API call was successful
- 4XX: The API call had an error in the parameters. The error will be encoded in the body of the response
- 5XX: The API call was unsuccessful; retry later

Together with this URL, SendGrid needs parameters to proceed with the mail transaction request and these are:

| to | Must be a valid e-mail address |
|---|---|
| toname | Must be a string. If the toparameter is an array, toname must be an array with the exact number of array elements as the to field |
| subject | Must be a valid string |
| text | The API call must include at least one of the text or html parameters |
| html | The API call must include at least one of the text or html parameters |
| from | Must be a valid e-mail address from your domain |
| cc | Must be a valid e-mail address |
| ccname | Must be a valid e-mail address |
| bcc | Must be a valid e-mail address |
| bccname | Must be a valid e-mail address |
| fromname | Must a valid string |
| replyto | Must be a valid e-mail address |

Some of these variables must be assigned to values before passing them to the RestTemplate class. The following is the SendGrid service implementation for the CFS application:

```
public class E-mailServiceImpl implements E-mailService {
    private RestTemplate restTemplate = new RestTemplate();
    @Value("${sendgrid.api.user}")
    private String sendgridApiUser;
    @Value("${sendgrid.api.key}")
    private String sendgridApiKey;

    @Override
```

```
public boolean send(E-mailFeedback message) {
    try {
        MultiValueMap<String, Object> vars = new
                LinkedMultiValueMap<String, Object>();
        vars.add("api_user", sendgridApiUser);
        vars.add("api_key", sendgridApiKey);
        vars.add("fromname", message.getSenderName());
        vars.add("from", message.getSenderE-mail());
        vars.add("bcc", message.getCcE-mail());
        vars.add("subject", message.getSubject());
        vars.add("text", "");
        vars.add("html", message.getBody());
        vars.add("to", message.getReceiverE-mail());
        vars.add("toname", message.getReceiverName());
        restTemplate.postForLocation(
                "http://sendgrid.com/api/mail.send.json", vars);
    } catch (Exception ex) { return false; }
    return true;
} }
```

**The Theme**

The theme of this portal was derived from the templates authored by http
://www.os-templates.com/.

# The Customer Feedback System (CSF)

Just like any other frameworks or platforms, Spring MVC 4.x can also implement or
customize some popular Captcha libraries to protect any lightweight, generic, and/or public
sites used to gather feedback, comments, or information, which do not really need tight
login protection or Spring Security. This chapter also gives you recommendations on how to
protect those sites with e-mail forms used to send information to different electronic mail
services worldwide. The following are some screenshots of CSF not mentioned in the above
discussion.

The **Update Topic** page (BotDetect Captcha):

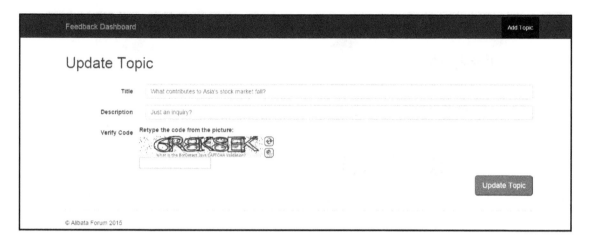

The **Update Feedback** page (SimpleCaptcha):

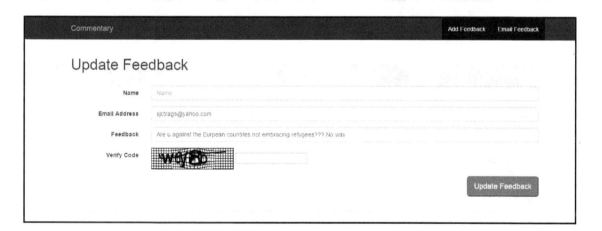

The **Add Feedback** page (Kaptcha):

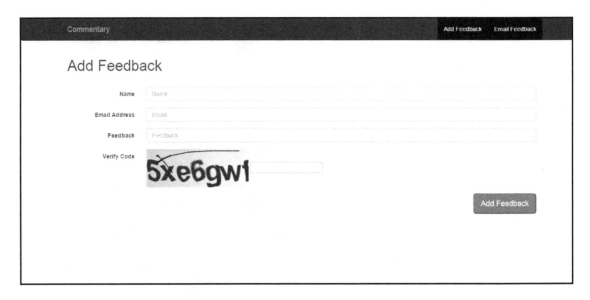

The **Email Feedback** form page (JCaptcha):

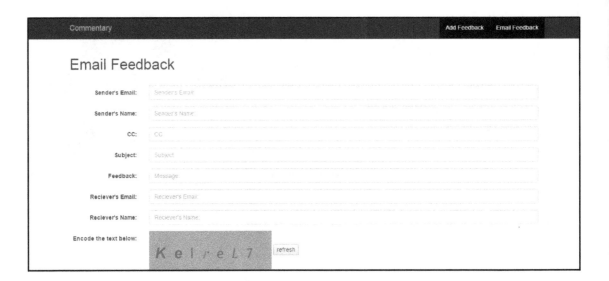

# Challenge yourself

Create an online Bulletin Board application for a college or university. Anyone from the institution must post their campus issues on this application, and anyone can provide feedback on each issue. Apply any of the Captcha implementations above. You can use any database or just `@ModelAttribute` and `@SessionAttributes` to store data. Hint: Study h ttps://www.reddit.com/.

# Summary

There are lots of ways to secure Spring MVC applications from unexpected attacks. The common way is to use third-party authentication modules, database authentication or any server-side security installations. This chapter talks about challenging the users to validate their intentions when accessing the software. Although not the ultimate solution, it provides delays which can help the administrator observe the nature of access of many visitors.

# 6
# Hotel Management System (HMS)

There are so many phases of web development that experts must take into consideration like the conceptual framework, technical foundation, data modeling, integration plan, hardware and network feasibility study, and web design. When it comes to sincerity, credibility, and impact to the user, stakeholders always prioritize the look and feel of the project. User experience is crucial to the final success of the project because our information-hungry society needs a dynamic, organized, adaptable, and responsive content.

This chapter will use the **Hotel Management System** (**HMS**) as the software prototype to study. The application will be used to emphasize how the application is done using Spring 4.x MVC and how it can comply with two interesting user experience recipes, namely adaptive and responsive web design. These two major design strategies for web designing will be discussed with the use of some tools and other third-party APIs applicable for Spring Framework implementation.

In this installment of the book, you will learn how to:

- Apply different themes using `ThemeResolver`
- Create and design enhanced layout for views using `Velocity`, `FreeMarker`, `Tiles`, and `SiteMesh`
- Create enhanced UI behavior using **AngularJS** and **ExtJS**
- Create responsive view pages using **Thymeleaf**, AngularJS, Twitter Bootstrap, and **Kickstrap**
- Create rich-client views using ExtJS
- Develop UI-enriched Spring MVC projects using Spring Roo's rapid development strategy
- Implement internationalization (i18n) to cater for different languages

# Overview of the project

This chapter is all about designing the appropriate, smart, and appealing user interface for a project. The challenge here is to create a HMS that will increase the volume of reservations through online bookings. The HMS to be developed must be on a par with other hotel booking pages and must attract more booking deals.

This HMS prototype is a feasibility study on how Spring MVC integrates with the different technology used for software that demands better user-experience for commercial purposes. The software is a combination of all the feasible solutions to let the readers choose which is the most desirable for their needs.

Since the focus of the chapter is more on the look and feel and behavior of the software's facade, some of the design dashboards that need to be implemented to achieve the desired user experience are:

- **Theme designs**: Web designers always think and plan the themes of any user interfaces they design. Mostly, they conduct study first on who will be the audience of the site. Then, they create a series of design templates and let customers choose which they prefer. They use tools like Adobe and CSS scripts to apply visuals, colors, texts, and layouts. HMS will show how theme creation is being integrated into Spring 4.x MVC.

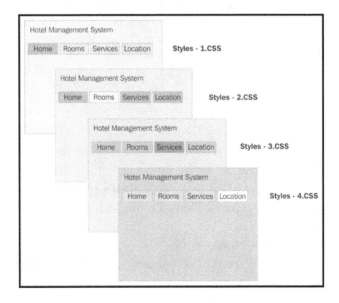

- **Templates**: Views are always treated as a magazine or newspaper where there are slices of templates depicting a layout. In this chapter, developers and designers must work on creating page fragments assembled together to form a complete page at runtime (dynamic pages). This is to avoid duplication of page parts, to optimize web content, and maintain consistency on the design trademark. The following image shows how a page is created by templates.

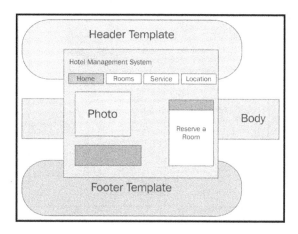

- **Rich client components**: Part of the user experience needed in the HMS is to have HTML components that directly interact with the server-side transactions. For instance, typical form handling in Spring needs form controllers in order to access databases while rich-client forms use JSON or XML in order to transact with the internal Spring services. Sometimes these form components are bundled with some CSS styles.

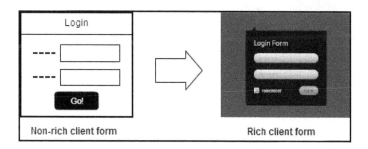

- **Responsive design**: HMS pages must be implemented in such a way that they can be opened in desktop computers, laptops, tablets, or mobiles without altering the UI layout.

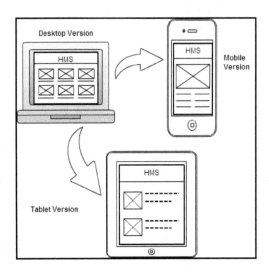

# Technical Requirements

Building HMS will not be too difficult as all the core components have already been implemented in Chapters 1, *Creating a Personal Web Portal (PWP)*, and Chapter 3, *Student Management Portal (SMP)*, ready for reuse. The requirement will be on the third-party tools which are mainly CSS and JavaScript frameworks. Some are Java-based libraries like Velocity and FreeMarker which have already been used in Chapter 4, *Human Resource Management System (HRMS)*.

We start the development by configuring our POM file and uploading our required CSS and JavaScript plug-ins to our /src/main/webapp folder.

# Angular JS

AngularJS is a JavaScript framework that can be added to an HTML page with the <script> tag. It extends HTML attributes with directives, and binds data to HTML with expressions. The framework extends the HTML DOM with additional attributes and makes it more responsive to user actions. Many of the applications which dynamically update the

HTML pages as the user interacts with the app use Angular JS because of its responsive client-side features. AngularJS is open source, completely free, and licensed under the Apache license version 2.0.

The two latest versions available from the website `https://angularjs.org/` are versions 1.4.x and 1.2.x. Version 1.4.x has faster compilation, enhanced bug-free syntax, improved scope-watching, inclusion of i18N features, and added support for animation. JS files can be downloaded from the site or we can import all the needed APIs using the following URL `http://ajax.googleapis.com/ajax/libs/angularjs/1.4.7/angular.min.js`.

# JQuery

JQuery is a cross-platform JavaScript extension for websites that provides certain CSS features and support for AJAX. It simplifies client-side scripting to make page navigation, parsing, animations, and even handling easier and more compact.

In this chapter, JQuery is just a support library which will help Angular JS, Bootstrap, and Kickstrap provide user responses in our HMS services.

JQuery is an open-source plugin and can be downloaded at `http://jquery.com/`. It has a URL `http://ajax.googleapis.com/ajax/libs/jquery/1.11.1/jquery.min.js` which can be used by the `<script>` tag to load all the libraries into the HTML page.

# Twitter Bootstrap

Twitter Bootstrap, or more commonly known as Bootstrap, is a frontend framework to develop web apps and sites fast. Bootstrap provides look-and-feel optimization of web components from grids, typographies, tables, forms, and buttons and provides process responsiveness for dropdowns, navigation, pop-up modals, pagination, breadcrumbs, tab, thumbnails and many other HTML components.

Versions 2.3.x and 3.x are two stable versions available online for manual download for URL import. The library consists of CSS for themes and JS for the client-side transactions. The CSS file can be imported through the `<link>` tag:

```
<link rel="stylesheet"
href="//netdna.bootstrapcdn.com/bootstrap/3.1.1/
    css/bootstrap.min.css">
```

The JS counterpart will be imported using the `<script>` tag:

```
<script src="//netdna.bootstrapcdn.com/bootstrap/3.1.1/
            js/bootstrap.min.js">
</script>
```

# Kickstrap

Kickstrap is a Twitter Bootstrap on steroids. It is heavily loaded with dynamic style sheets called `Less`. Less is a CSS pre-processor consisting of variables, mixins, functions, and many other techniques needed to generate CSS that can run client-side and server-side. The internal processing of Less uses `Rhino` but it rides on top of Nodes at the client-side.

Kickstrap is more maintainable, theme-friendly, and extendable than any other Bootstrap frameworks. This framework can be downloaded from `https://s3.amazonaws.com/kickstrap/Kickstrap+Downloads/kickstrap1.3.1.zip`.

# ExtJS

ExtJS is a pure JavaScript application framework for building interactive cross-platform web applications using techniques such as AJAX, DHTML, and DOM scripting. It has features like cross-browser compatibility, advanced MVC architecture, plugin-free charting, and modern UI widgets which makes it one of the most powerful client-side tools.

ExtJS 4.2.x has the stable core components and is used by HMS. The latest stable version ExtJS 5.1.x includes many new features along with support for **MVVM** (**Model-View-ViewModel**) architecture. This version is also a multi-device that supports tablets and touch screen desktops.

Both versions are commercially available at `http://www.sencha.com/products/download`. The open-source classic libraries (GPL) for version 4.2.x can be found at `http://cdn.sencha.com/ext/gpl/4.2.0/resources/css/ext-all.css` and `http://cdn.sencha.com/ext/gpl/4.2.0/ext-all.js`. Whereas the version 5.1.x classic libraries can be found at `http://cdn.sencha.com/ext/gpl/5.1.0/build/packages/ext-theme-classic/build/resources/ext-theme-classic-all.css` and `http://cdn.sencha.com/ext/gpl/5.1.0/build/ext-all.js`.

# Thymeleaf

Thymeleaf is a flexible Java templating engine library with the main objective of writing and processing HTML templates. Because it is lightweight, Thymeleaf known as being the best alternative to JSP view pages.

Even though it is simple and natural, Thymeleaf templates support **Spring EL** expressions implementation, internationalization, Spring MVC and Spring web flow integration, template caching, data table layout, and other template integration such as Tiles and Sitemesh.

To use Thymeleaf, add the following library in `POM.xml`:

- `org.thymeleaf` (`thymeleaf-spring4`): A set of classes and interfaces used to integrated Thymeleaf with Spring Framework 4.x.

# Apache Tiles Framework

Tiles is a free open-sourced template composition framework for modern Java applications designed to simplify complex user interfaces. It is based on a composite design pattern which states that a group of fragments can be treated as a single object. It has been successfully helpful in many MVC framework integrations.

Tiles defines page fragments which can be assembled to form a whole and complete page at runtime. The main goal is to avoid the duplication of common page elements by creating reusable templates which can be embedded within other tiles. These templates provide a consistent look and feel across an entire application.

To use Tiles in the HMS, the following Maven plugin must be included in our POM:

- `org.apache.tiles` (`tiles-core`): Consists of the basic core implementations of the APIs.
- `org.apache.tiles` (`tiles-jsp`): JSP support classes and tag libraries used in a JSP environment.
- `org.apache.tiles` (`tiles-extras`): Non-standard, non-generic, non-identifiable components that may be useful for Tiles fragments.
- `org.apache.tiles` (`tiles-template`): Common APIs used by Tiles to integrate with other templating technologies.
- `org.apache.tiles` (`tiles-el`): Support classes and tag libraries for EL.

# SiteMesh

Sitemesh is a page decorating framework that allows a clean separation of content from a presentation. Decorator Pattern allows behavior to be added to an individual object, either statically or dynamically, without affecting the behavior of other objects.

To integrate with the HMS, the following Maven plugin must be included in our POM.

- `org.sitemesh (sitemesh)`: A set of implementation classes and interfaces to implement SiteMesh.

# Spring mobile

**Spring Mobile** is an extension of the Spring MVC framework used for the development of mobile web applications. The Spring Mobile device contains API classes such as `LiteDeviceResolver`, which can detect devices like mobiles and tablets at the server side. The detection starts from evaluating browser requests which contain the site preference and other header information regarding the device. Given this header information, Spring Mobile will automatically adjust to provide users with the desired user experience.

In order for the HMS to use the Spring Mobile plug-in, we need to include the following Maven artefact in our POM file:

- `org.springframework.mobile` (SpringMobiledevice)

# Spring Roo

**Spring Roo** is a rapid development tool, not a framework, which helps create MVC applications. It helps developers focus on the domain model and business requirements while all the features will be generated by the tool itself.

To enable Spring Roo in our STS IDE, we need to follow the installation procedure below:

1. Open your STS IDE. Open the STS Dashboard through the toolbar indicated in the following figure:

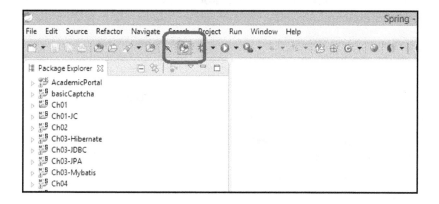

2. At the bottom of the Dashboard, locate and click the **Extensions** link.

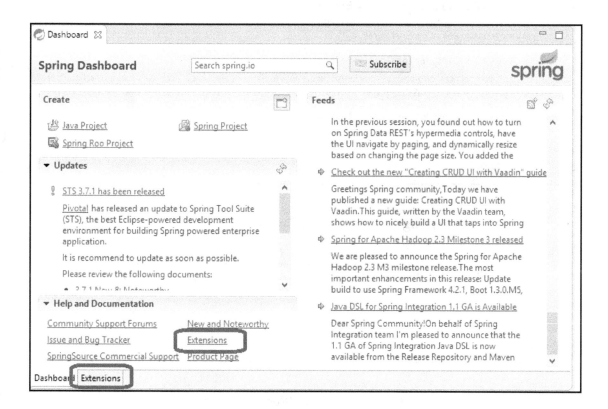

3. Afterwards, search for the `Spring Roo` and install Spring Roo (the current production release).

4. Click on the **Spring Roo** module and install.

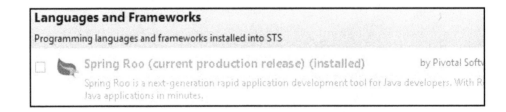

5. Then, search and install `Spring IDE` (Roo Extension).

6.  Lastly, restart your STS IDE.

# The HMS Database

The HMS schema design, shown in the following figure, will be implemented in MySQL Server 5.6.

This time the HMS will be using the **MyBatis 3.x Framework** to implement its SQL services.

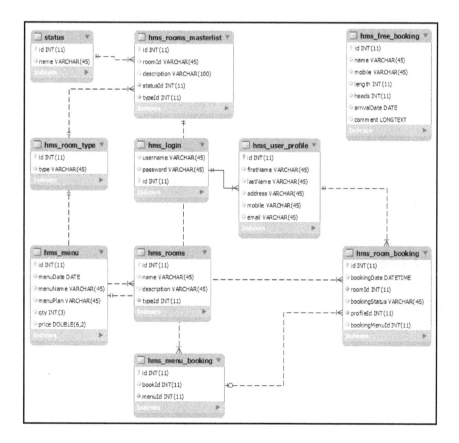

# User Experience (UX) design issues

Just like any typical marketing strategy, this chapter wants a HMS that will help market the amenities and services of a hotel establishment. We want the software to connect to people of any age level so that the management can persuade them to book one or more rooms any time of the year. This chapter wants to have software that is theme-ready so that developers will only worry about the content rather than the aesthetics.

To create usable, reliable, robust, credible, and persuasive web designs for the Spring MVC application, the following main design principles must be applied: **Adaptive Web Design (AWD)** and **Responsive Web Design (RWD)**.

Unfortunately, the Spring MVC Framework does not have an internal API to implement responsive and adaptive web designs but it can integrate some popular and stable external plugins and frameworks which can help it provide worldwide-accepted aesthetics for user interfaces.

## Adaptive web design

Adaptive Web Design is a strategy whereby designers create in advance several distinct layouts for different screen sizes of different devices. There are specific sets of web design layouts for mobile phones, tablets, and desktop computers and there are services at the backend that check what devices are publishing the content. These platform-specific designs detects the user's device through the @Controllers; then all instructions in the @Controller will be executed to deliver the pre-set layout and result for that particular device. So instead of a single huge layout going through several different-sized screens, we have one specific design loaded depending on the device detected.

## Responsive web design

Responsive Web Design is another web design strategy whereby designers only create a single template with a fluid layout that adjusts to the screen width of any devices. This single set of templates is needed to be created and maintained per theme. This strategy is an optimal way of providing a viewing experience to an MVC application because there is no need to create logic at the server-side to detect what devices view the content. So no matter how much you resize the screen, that same layout will automatically be loaded into the container and will respond to that device's resolution.

# Designing themes

To build a theme, the Spring application context must recognize different static resources like CSS, images, JavaScripts, and other layout templates in order to provide a better user experience. Spring has a built-in theme support which can be used to manage the look and feel and navigations of its applications. Also, it can use some popular client-side platforms to create the appropriate HTML backgrounds, foregrounds, and components to provide comfort and ease to users.

# Spring MVC theme support

Spring's theme support aims to utilize all the static resources to come up with a controller-managed resolution to enhance the overall look and feel of the application. The HMS without any third-party framework can manage its own user experience by creating combinations of static resources such as images, styles, scripts, and other art files to form themes. To avoid a *Status 404 error*, be sure to configure properly the static resource mapping of all resources exactly as per thr following:

```
<mvc:default-servlet-handler />
<mvc:resources mapping="/css/**" location="/css/" />
<mvc:resources mapping="/images/**" location="/images/" />
<mvc:resources mapping="/js/**" location="/js/" />
<mvc:resources mapping="/extjs/**" location="/extjs/" />
```

To use Spring MVC theme support, the project must inject the following main theme components, namely theme-aware resource bundles, theme resolvers, and theme change interceptors.

# The Spring Theme configuration

The theme configuration starts with creating various theme-aware source bundles which are all managed by the Spring interface org.springframework.ui.context.ThemeSource interface. Its implementation class known as org.springframework.ui.context.support.ResourceBundleThemeSource executes the chosen source bundle and enables the context loading of all source bundles which are all properties files. The keys value of the source bundles are the names of the resource and the values are the URIs or paths to resources which can be images, CSS, or JavaScript.

The bean configuration of the `ResourceBundleThemeSource` object is as follows:

```
<bean id="hmsThemeSource"
  class="org.springframework.ui.context.support
  .ResourceBundleThemeSource">
  <property name="basenamePrefix" value="config.hms_theme-" />
</bean>
```

This shows that a property named `basenamePrefix` is required to indicate the group and the location of the resources needed to be loaded into the container indicated in the `bean` declaration. A sample HMS property file found in the `config` folder that can be loaded by the preceding configuration is `hms_theme-booking.properties` which obviously has a prefix `hms_theme-`. The CSS resource found in this bundle is:

```
styleSheet=css/style-2.css
```

Afterwards, the HMS needs to create a bean that successfully implements `org.springframework.web.servlet.ThemeResolver`, an interface that is used to map all resources inside a source bundle to the physical views. There are three types of `ThemeResolver` implementations and it depends on how the application will manage the theme progression. The following implementations are:

- **FixedThemeResolver**: The default implementation of `ThemeResolver` which relies on the use fixed theme configuration. This style requires the property `defaultThemeName` to bet set otherwise it will provide the application a default theme name which is `theme`.
- **CookieThemeResolver**: The resolver that relies on a cookie handling mechanism and will require the properties `cookie name`, `cookie max age`, `defaultThemeName` and other cookie-related properties. This resolver is appropriate to stateless applications that depend on cookies with some expiration rules.
- **SessionThemeResolver**: The resolver that runs on user sessions where all the theme information is stored. In this type, the theme name must be set using the property `themeName`.

If no theme resolver is declared, `DispatcherServlet` will just consider `FixedThemeResolver` as the default resolver type.

The HMS uses `CookieThemeResolver` which is injected into the container as:

```
<bean id="hmsThemeResolver"
  class="org.springframework.web.servlet.theme.CookieThemeResolver">
  <property name="cookieMaxAge" value="1200" />
```

```
<property name="cookieName" value="hmscookie" />
<property name="defaultThemeName" value="main" />
</bean>
```

To complete the whole setup, the HMS needs to inject
`org.springframework.web.servlet.theme.ThemeChangeInterceptor` which allows
the changing of the theme resources on the view page per request transaction through a
certain configurable `request` parameter name. It is given a bean declaration of
`ThemeChangeInterceptor` as follows:

```
<bean id="themeChangeInterceptor"
  class="org.springframework.web.servlet.theme
  .ThemeChangeInterceptor">
  <property name="paramName" value="theme" /> </bean>
    <mvc:interceptors>
  <ref bean="themeChangeInterceptor"></ref></mvc:interceptors>
```

This provides the `/css/styles-2.css` resource to be used by a view page with the URI
`http://localhost:8080/ch06/hms/index?theme=booking` where `booking` is the
theme resource name pertaining to `hms_theme-booking.properties`, and `theme` is the
parameter name used by the interceptor. Changing the parameter value from
`theme=booking` to `theme=services` also changes the current theme to
`/css/styles-4.css`.

The following figure depicts the theme transition implemented in the HMS which can be
seen by clicking on **About Us** in the **Booking link** tab.

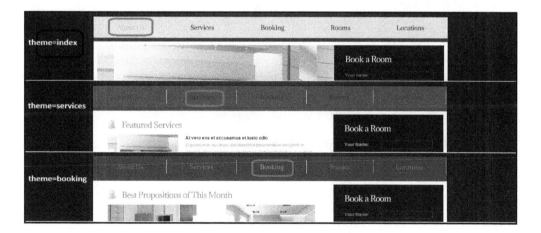

# Kickstrap Theme Designs

Spring's `ThemeResolver` has so many pitfalls and one is its inefficiency to build a full-blown user-interface stack. Some views of the projects are so heavily implemented with lots of necessary images and graphics leaving other views left undone. To cope with the timeline, the best solution is to use the Kickstrap toolkit for web designing. The Spring Framework can be integrated with Kickstrap with certain requirements.

Kickstrap is popularly known for its *ready-to-wear* theme strategy wherein it takes only a change in configuration to convert and replace the existing look and feel of the views. It offers several built-in themes like cerulean, spruce, cyborg, journal, and many others which are found in its `Kickstrap/theme` folder. Another advantage is its feature to add custom adaptive or responsive web themes.

# Kickstrap configuration

In order to utilize Kickstrap APIs, all view pages need to be a valid and complete HTML 5 document. Kickstrap looks for the `<!DOCTYPE html>` declaration found at the first part of the document just like the `/hms/kick/addbook.html` of the HMS which has the following code:

```
<%@ page language="java" contentType="text/html;
  charset=ISO-8859-1" pageEncoding="ISO-8859-1"%>
  <%@ taglib prefix="spring"
    uri="http://www.springframework.org/tags"%>
  <%@ taglib prefix="c"
    uri="http://java.sun.com/jsp/jstl/core"%>
  <%@ taglib prefix="fmt"
    uri="http://java.sun.com/jsp/jstl/fmt"%><!DOCTYPE html>
<html>
<head>
  <title>Add Room Booking</title>
  <spring:url value="/css/kickstrap.less" var="cssLess" />
  <spring:url value="/css/Kickstrap/js/less-1.3.3.min.js"
  var="jsLess" />
  <link rel="stylesheet/less" type="text/css" href="${ cssLess }">
  <script src="${ jsLess }"></script> </head>
  <body> <!-- refer to sources --> </body></html>
```

To start Kickstrap, HMS pages need to import the Kickstrap `Less` files, namely the `/css/kickstrap.less` and the `/css/Kickstrap/js/less-1.3.3.min.js`. Then, the following extra changes must be applied to the body of the views as indicated by the coding standard of the Kickstrap documentation:

- To avoid CSS conflicts, remove the margin on the body
- To avoid messing up the theme color, it is advisable to set the body's background color to white
- It is mandatory to use the `@baseFontFamily`, `@baseFontSize`, and `@baseLineHeight` attributes for setting the base fonts, colors, and sizes
- The general link color must be set using `@linkColor` and the link underlines must be configured using the property `:hover`

# Layout design types

Fixed and fluid layout designs are possible in Kickstrap. Both designs use only one specific grid layout; it's just that the fixed layout does not change even when the size of the browser or screen changes. In the fluid layout design, all components change proportionally in terms of the width and length of the screen dimension.

A layout is fixed whenever the dimension of the page uses the CSS selector `.container`. The views of this fixed grid container is defined by predefined CSS selectors `.row` which specifies the rows and `.spanN` which adds `N` appropriate number of columns to the container. The layout of `/hms/kick/addbook.html` is a 12-column grid and is written as:

```
<body>
  <div id="sf-wrapper">
  <div class="container">
  <div class="row">
  <div class="span12"> <!--  see the sources -->
  </div></div></div></div>
</body>
```

On the other hand, Kickstrap can create a fluid grid system by using the .container-fluid container with `.row-fluid` instead of `.row` for creating rows. Instead of exact pixel units, the fluid grid uses a percentage for column widths to ensure proper proportions for key screen resolutions and devices.

```
<body>
  <div id="sf-wrapper">
    <div class="container-fluid">
    <div class="row-fluid">
```

```
    <div class="span12"> <!--  see the sources -->
  </div></div></div></div>
</body>
```

Both fixed and fluid grid have a maximum of 12 columns to use on their containers.

# Responsive design in Kickstrap

Kickstrap also supports device type detection for proportional view changes through media queries. To enable responsive CSS in the HMS or any project, a customized CSS file must be created inside the `Kickstrap/css` folder. A folder `responsive` was created with the CSS file `hms-responsive.css` that contains the following media query implementation containing a new set of properties of the view once a new device screen resolution is detected:

```
/* Large desktop */
@media ( min-width : 1200px) {
  body {
    background-color: blue;
  }
}

/* Portrait tablet to landscape and desktop */
@media ( min-width : 768px) and (max-width: 979px) {
  body {
    background-color: green;
  }
}

// see the sources
}
```

After the customization, attach the `viewport` meta tag and import the newly created CSS file in all Kickstrap views.

```
<head>
  <meta name="viewport" content="width=device-width,
    initial-scale=1.0"><spring:url
    value="/css/Kickstrap/css/responsive/responsive.css"
  var="cssresp" />
  <link rel="stylesheet/less" type="text/css"
  href="${ cssresp }">
</head>
```

The preceding meta-tag is needed to allow and trigger the use of media queries within the view. The media query that maps the given layout is the one executed during screen detection. Kickstrap uses the following screen layout classification used for media queries: the implementation depends on the screen resolution of different devices as per the following classifications:

| Label | Layout width | Column width | Gutter width |
|---|---|---|---|
| **Large display** | 1200px and up | 70px | 30px |
| **Default** | 980px and up | 60px | 20px |
| **Portrait tablets** | 768px and above | 42px | 20px |
| **Phones to tablets** | 767px and below | Fluid columns, no fixed widths | |
| **Phones** | 480px and below | Fluid columns, no fixed widths | |

Furthermore, there are responsive utility classes offered by Kickstrap for showing and hiding content per device type. They can be found at `Kickstrap/bootstrap/less/responsive.less` the following table shows the available classes and their effect on a given media query layout.

| Class | Phones 767px and below | Tablets 979px to 768px | Desktops (Default) |
|---|---|---|---|
| .visible-phone | Visible | Hidden | Hidden |
| .visible-tablet | Hidden | Visible | Hidden |
| .visible-desktop | Hidden | Hidden | Visible |
| .hidden-phone | Hidden | Visible | Visible |
| .hidden-tablet | Visible | Hidden | Visible |
| .hidden-desktop | Visible | Hidden | Hidden |

## UI components styles

Kickstrap offers a toolkit for navigation, alert, modal, breadcrumb, or any web components that are ready for use by any view pages. For the HMS to make available these components, there are a list of class selectors needed to be used and some of the base styles are enumerated as follows:

- For basic table styling (for example, light padding and only horizontal dividers, add the base class `.table` to any `<table>`. To add more styles just append `.table-bordered`, `.table-hover`, or `.table-condensed` to the `.table` selector.

- For individual form controls, Kickstrap provides styling without requiring any CSS base class on the `<form>` or any large changes in mark-up. Form controls are stacked, with left-aligned labels on top. Styles for forms can be `.form-search` with `.search-query <input>`, `.form-inline`, and `.form-horizontal`.
- Button styles can be in any types like WARNING (`.btn btn-warning`), INFO (`.btn btn-info`), SUCCESS (`.btn btn-success`), DANGER (`.btn btn-danger`), and many others. When it comes to sizes, just add `.btn-large`, `.btn-small`, or `.btn-mini` selectors to the existing `.btn` styles.

To find out about the other components, visit the Kickstrap documentation at `http://getk ickstrap.com.s3-website-us-east-1.amazonaws.com/1.x/docs/`.

## Theme support

To configure the theme for the first time, open the file `Kickstrap/theme.less` and uncomment the two statements:

```
@import "Kickstrap/themes/cosmo/variables.less";
@import "Kickstrap/themes/cosmo/bootswatch.less";
```

The view `/hms/kick/addbook.html` now has a theme **Cosmo** eventually making a site looks like this:

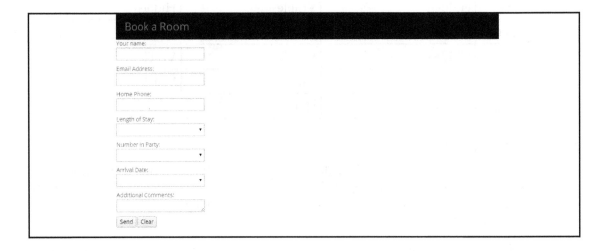

Afterwards, locate the `Kickstrap/theme` folder to choose what built-in theme is appropriate for the page. Edit the two lines above in the `theme.less` file and change the theme to `Cyborg`, for instance, the new page will be like this:

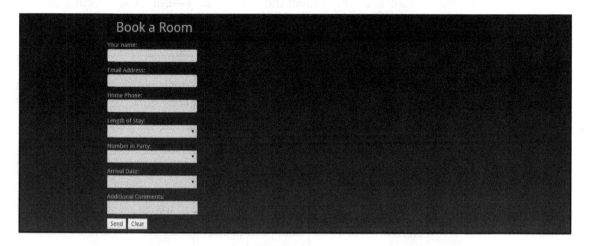

Aside from the built-in themes, future HMS Kickstrap themes can be customized since the plugin supports theme customization.

# Twitter Bootstrap theme design

Kickstrap is used whenever we have an immediate requirement to build a theme layout. Customizing some components will take us some time since we need to create some Less codes and compile some of them for our desired resolution to be implemented. For ground-up theming support, Twitter Bootstrap is the most widely used frontend framework in creating full-blown MVC applications. Some of the pages of the HMS are created through Bootstrap utilities. Also, the views of the CFS application in `Chapter 5`, *Customer Feedback System (CFS)*, are made up of Bootstrap components.

Just like its boilerplated version, Kickstrap, the maximum number of columns per screen container is also 12.

# Fixed grid layout design

The `Pending Guest Reservation` module of the HMS uses the Bootstrap 3+ framework for its user experience. Just like Kickstrap, it has some predefined CSS selectors that are associated to device screen sizes. To implement the fixed grid system, these selectors are needed in order to determine the view requirement and final look and feel of the module. The following table summarizes some of the key features of a grid system in Bootstrap 3+:

| Properties | Extra small devices Phones (<768px) | Small devices Tablets (≥768px) | Medium devices Desktops (≥992px) | Large devices Desktops (≥1200px) |
|---|---|---|---|---|
| CSS selectors | .col-xs-N | .col-sm-N | .col-md-N | .col-lg-N |
| Container width (MAX) | None (auto) | 750px | 970px | 1170px |
| Column width (MAX) | Auto | ~62px | ~81px | ~97px |
| Grid behavior | Horizontal at all times | Collapsed to start, horizontal above breakpoints | | |
| Gutter width | 15px on each side of a column (that is, 30px) | | | |
| .hidden-desktop | Visible | Hidden | Hidden | |

The N in each selector is equivalent to the number of columns a view page needs to utilize for the container of the layout. The class selector `col-md-5` means that there are five columns to be plotted in a row for a medium viewport screen layout.

The `Pending Guest Reservation` module has three view implementations and these are for tablet, mobile, and desktop screens. The tablet view `/hms/tabletpending.html` has a fixed grid layout of three rows and three columns which when opened in a tablet device will be:

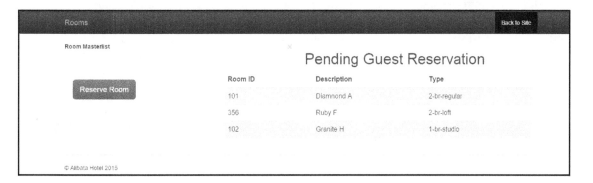

But when the browser is minimized, the page becomes a one-row and one-column container which is the default screen size like:

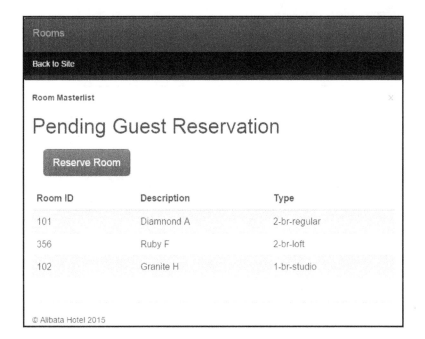

The default viewport size can be overridden through applying more flexible layouts that changes the column orientation. For instance, the view page `/hms/largepending.html` with a one-row-three column layout template does not look good on default devices because the `List of Rooms Reserved` column goes to the new line unexpectedly as shown in the following screenshot:

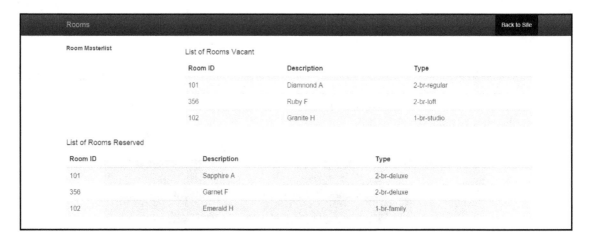

Once the site is opened in a mobile device the layout looks better because of the default one-column policy for smaller devices.

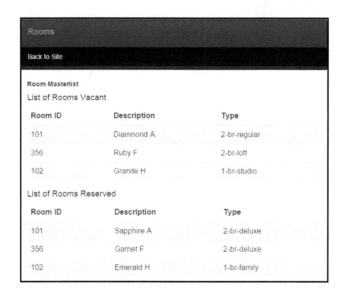

To preserve the one-row-three-column layout of the site on default screens, we need to apply a wrapping feature to impose the right layout. The new code will be similar to the following script:

```
<div class="container">
  <div class="row">
    <div class="col-sm-3 col-md-2">
    <div><!-refer to sources--></div>
  </div>
  <div class="col-sm-9 col-md-8">
    <div><!-refer to sources--></div>
  </div>
  <div class="col-sm-12 col-md-2">
    <div><!-refer to sources--></div>
  </div>
  </div>
</div>
```

With a small device like an android, the layout will looks fine since each column counts less than or equal to 12. But when opened in a medium device, the second column size will be followed wrapping the third column to lower pixels.

To enhance the layout, pages of our HMS or any applications must use media queries to maintain the default appropriate width and length of the viewport size.

# Fluid grid layout design

Fluid Grid is available only in Bootstrap 3.2 and above. To make the layout fluid, the container must have the selector class `.container-fluid` to allow the whole 100% resolution of the viewport. By default, this `.container-fluid` sets the horizontal margin to `auto` while the left and right padding is set to `15px` to offset the left and right margin of `-15px` per row.

# Responsive layout design in Bootstrap

Bootstrap 3+ is responsive and mobile friendly by default. Even though we created a fixed grid it will be eventually responsive. Just like Kickstrap, it has also responsive CSS classes used to manage and adjust the visibility of the view elements depending on the device type.

The following table shows the `.visible-` selector classes used in responsive layout design.

| Class Selectors | Description |
|---|---|
| **.visible-xs** | Elements visible only on extra small devices having screen width less than 768px; hidden on others. |
| **.visible-sm** | Elements visible only on small devices having screen width greater than or equal to 768px (that is, ≥768px) but less than 992px; hidden on others. |
| **.visible-md** | Elements visible only on medium devices having screen width greater than or equal to 992px (that is, ≥992px) but less than 1200px; hidden on others. |
| **.visible-lg** | Elements visible only on large devices having screen width greater than or equal to 1200px (that is, ≥1200px); hidden on others. |

The Pending Guest Reservation view pages have the following headers with visibility selectors where one of which will be displayed depending on the device detected:

```
<h1 class="visible-xs">For Mobile Users Only</h1>
<h1 class="visible-md">For  Tablet Users Only</h1>
<h1 class="visible-lg">For Desktop Users only</h1>
```

## UI components styles

Twitter Bootstrap 3.x has its own set of reusable HTML components and looks better than Kickstrap. It has lots of selectors and details and some of them are:

- You can create tables with basic styling that have horizontal dividers and small cell padding (8px by default), by just adding `.table` to the `<table>` element. To enable styles of tables just append to the existing selector the following: `.table-striped`, `.table-bordered`, `.table-hover`, `.table-condensed`.
- Bootstrap applies default styling to the `<form>` layout without any selector. The default style is the vertical form but there are three more horizontal (`.form-horizontal`) and inline (`.form-inline`) forms.
- Buttons in Bootstrap are colorful and can be of any of these types: WARNING (`.btn btn-warning`), INFO (`.btn btn-info`), SUCCESS (`.btn btn-success`), DANGER (`.btn btn-danger`), and many others. The sizes can be default (`.btn-default`), large (`.btn-lg`), small (`.btn-sm`), and very small .(`.btn-xs`). Other added properties are the blocked button (`.btn-blocked`) and the disabled button (`.disabled`).
- Bootstrap has an easy way of creating models or pop-up pages. The HMS has a button-triggered modal and a JavaScript-driven modal. The following screenshot is a sample modal of our HMS:

For further reference on the other components, visit the site `http://getbootstrap.com/components/` which has a series of samples and discussions on the fonts, images, and lots of components offered by Bootstrap for our Spring 4.x MVC applications.

# The Thymeleaf design

If `ThemeResolver` and the JavaScript-based Kickstrap and Bootstrap are not enough, a popular third party Java-based platform can be recommended to fulfill some UI requirements especially with form pages.

The HMS prototype used Thymeleaf to create its **Add Profile** page template which adds user information to the schema. Unlike JSP, implementing Thymeleaf as a view solution is just the same as creating web design templates rather than hardcore model mapping. Web resources are easier to delegate all over the page container because Thymeleaf does not require more tag libraries to be loaded into the container. Thymeleaf is a full HTML engine, meaning that the template file itself is an HTML file that can be rendered by any web browser. It is also an attribute-based template engine that is composed of HTML tag attributes.

When it comes to form handling, Thymeleaf is capable also of binding form-backing objects, generating result bindings, integrating property editors, conversion services, and validation error handling. Also, it has an internationalization support similar to what has been discussed in the previous chapters.

# Configuration

To start Thymeleaf with our HMS, we need to declare the `org.thymeleaf.spring4.view.ThymeleafViewResolver` bean, which acts as a bridge between Thymeleaf's template engine and Spring MVC's view rendering mechanism. It resolves template names and delegates them to a servlet context resource resolver.

```
<bean id="thymeleafViewResolver" class=
"org.thymeleaf.spring4.view.ThymeleafViewResolver">
  <property name="templateEngine" ref="templateEngine" />
  <property name="order" value="2" />
</bean>
```

Then, the `ThymeleafViewResolver` needs the `SpringTemplateEngine` instance for the Spring 4.x specification which establishes the Spring specific dialect as the default dialect.

```
<bean id="templateEngine"
  class="org.thymeleaf.spring4.SpringTemplateEngine">
  <property name="templateResolver" ref="templateResolver" />
</bean>
<bean id="templateResolver"
class="org.thymeleaf.templateresolver
.ServletContextTemplateResolver">
  <property name="prefix" value="/WEB-INF/templates/" />
  <property name="suffix" value=".html" />
  <property name="templateMode" value="HTML5" />
  <property name="cacheable" value="false"/>
  <property name="order" value="1" />
</bean>
```

 Enable the cacheable property before the project is deployed into the production server.

# Thymeleaf expressions

Thymeleaf contains a set of rules which implements the needed transactions for the views in Spring 4.x. This specific rule is based on the **Thymeleaf Standard Dialect** technically represented by the class called `org.thymeleaf.spring4.dialect.SpringStandardDialect`.

The following are the popular Thymeleaf rules on expressions which are slightly related to Spring EL syntax:

- The use of `${...}` and `*{...}` on most of its attributes
- The use of `${@myBean.doSomething()}` to access any beans in the application
- The use of `th:field`, `th:errors`, and `th:errorclass`, for form processing
- The attribute `#themes.code(...)` which can be synonymous to the `spring:theme` JSP custom tag
- The component builder expression `#mvc.uri(...)`, which can be used instead of the `spring:mvcUrl(...)` JSP custom function for Spring 4.1 and above

## Layout and theme

Thymeleaf supports Spring's `ThemeResolver`, Kickstrap, Twitter Bootstrap or any custom themes to be used in the application. The add profile view is a template so any UI framework or tool can be used.

To import external files, it uses the `th:href` modifier attribute to locate the URL of CSS files and the `th:src` modifier attribute to locate the URL of the JavaScript files needed for client-side processing. Each attribute uses link expression `@{...}` to declare the URL or paths.

```
<link rel="stylesheet" th:href="@{/css/styles.css}"
    type="text/css" media="screen"/>
  <script th:src="@{/js/functions.js}"
    type="text/javascript"></script>
  <script th:src="@{/js/jquery-min-1.9.1.js}"
    type="text/javascript"></script>
```

## Form handling using Thymeleaf

Thymeleaf preserves the HTML structure and just adds its own language-specific attributes on the document. the following is a Thymeleaf form snippet that adds a guest reservation:

```
<form id="guestForm" th:action="@{/guests/insert.html}"
  th:object="${user}" method="post">
    <div class="insertBlock">
    <span class="formSpan">
      <label for="usernameId"
      th:text="#{label.id}"></label>

      <input id="usernameId" type="text"
        th:field="*{id}" required="required"/>
```

```
        <br/>
    </span>
    <span class="formSpan">
      <label for="usernameId"
        th:text="#{label.username}"></label>
        <input id="usernameId" type="text"
        th:field="*{username}" required="required"/>
        <br />
    </span>
    <span class="formSpan">
      <label for="passwordId"
        th:text="#{label.password}"></label>
        <input id="passwordId" type="text"
          th:field="*{password}" required="required"/>
          <br />
    </span> </div>
    // see the sources
  </form>
```

The preceding form has an attribute `th:object` which is basically similar to the `commandName` attribute of Spring's form. To retrieve the object it must be inside the `${...}` block. The `th:action` attribute specifies what view page to call once the submit button is clicked.

## Rendering results

To iterate values on an HTML table, it uses the `th:each` attribute to retrieve all the data inside any arrays, List, Iterable, Maps, and any generic object that contains another object.

The following is one of the snippets in many of the Thymeleaf-made result view pages where the data is represented in a table:

```
<tbody>n<tr th:each="u : ${users}">
  <td th:text="${u.id}">id</td>
  <td th:text="${u.firstName}">firstName</td>
  <td th:text="${u.lastName}">lastName</td>
  <td th:text="${u.address}">address</td>
  // see the sources
  </tr>
</tbody>
```

# Internationalization support

To retrieve text messages from different `messages_{locale}`.properties, Thymeleaf needs the following components:

- `th:text` attribute, which evaluates its value expression and sets the result of this evaluation as the body of the tag it is in
- `#{msg.label}` expression specifying the key of the corresponding locale resource containing the text to be used by the `th:text`

The following is an example of a view page that retrieves resource bundle text messages:

```
<thead><tr>
  <th th:text="#{en.guest.id}">Id</th>
  <th th:text="#{en.guest.firstName}">Surname</th>
  <th th:text="#{en.guest.lastName}">Name</th>
  <th th:text="#{en.guest.address}">Country</th>
    // see the sources
</tr></thead>
```

# Thymeleaf layout design with fragments

To implement adaptive web design, layouts can be created but this time fragments are used. Thymeleaf needs us to define the fragments inside a template available for inclusion using the `th:fragment` attribute.

Give the following `/WEB-INF/thyme/templates/roomType.html` template:

```
<!DOCTYPE html>
<html xmlns="http://www.w3.org/1999/xhtml"
  xmlns:th="http://www.thymeleaf.org" lang="en">
<head>
<meta charset="UTF-8"/>
<title>Thymeleaf example</title>
<link rel="stylesheet" th:href="@{/css/styles.css}"
  type="text/css" media="screen"/>
<script th:src="@{/ch06/js/functions.js}"
  type="text/javascript"></script>
<script th:src="@{/ch06/js/jquery-min-1.9.1.js}"
  type="text/javascript"></script>
</head>
<body>
  <div th:fragment="body">
    <!- See the sources -->
  </div>
```

```
  </body>
  </html>
```

Any page can use `th:include` or `th:replace` to apply the templates depending on the layout design. The easiest syntax to include the template fragments inside a page is `templatename::domselector` or the equivalent `templatename::[domselector]`. Since the name of the template above is `roomType` and the fragment name is body, the page `roomTypesList.html` can have the following snippet:

```
<body>
   <div th:include=" roomType:: body"></div>
</body>
```

# Creating intelligent web components

Aside from web theme designs, an application such as the HMS will also gain more user attention if its specification includes creating web components that can easily interact with user needs and efficiently responds faster to numerous requests. The implementation of these intelligent HTML components must easily blend with the theme support discussed.

## AngularJS

One of the widely used frameworks in implementing web components that interacts with server containers is Angular JS. This solution is well-known in designing single page applications (SPAs) which are web applications that contain pages with multiple transactions happening at the back of the browser aside from the typical request-response transaction.

The strength of Angular JS is its efficient bi-directional binding of form models to the client that leads to the creation of form-intensive application stacks. This binding creates an MVC-enabled client-side infrastructure which includes all the theme components and presentation logic of the application. AngularJS can integrate with Kickstrap and Bootstrap for theme creation.

# Configuration

Implementing AngularJS scripts starts with telling the platform what part of the HTML document embodies the script with the use of the `ng-app` attribute. This attribute declares the module name of the script. Angular treats HTML as a DOM document so executing its scripts is like tagging the HTML tags for parsing in a way. The HMS has the admin page for adding room types which has the following document:

```
<html ng-app="hms">
  <head> </head>
  <body></body>
</html>
```

Then, the document must create a controller or controllers using the directive `ng-controller` to start implementing the Angular script. The declaration of `ng-controller` is done in`<body>` or any `<div>` tags.

On the other hand, the `ng-model` directive is applied to form components to data-bind the form field component to some named AngularJS model. Templates or data are written with double curly braces and the model name within it.

The view of the preceding directive is as follows:

```
<html ng-app="hms">
<!-See the sources -->
  <body ng-controller="roomTypeController">
<table class="table">
  <!-See the sources -->
  <tr ng-repeat="rtype in roomTypes">
    <td>{{rtype.id}}
    </td>
    <td>{{rtype.type}}
    </td>
  </tr>
</table>
<form class="form-horizontal" role="form" ng-submit="addRow()">
  <div class="form-group">
    <label class="col-md-2 control-label">ID</label>
    <div class="col-md-4">
      <input type="text" class="form-control" name="id"
        ng-model="id" />
    </div>
  </div>
  <div class="form-group">
    <label class="col-md-2 control-label">Type</label>
    <div class="col-md-4">
      <input type="text" class="form-control"
```

```
        name="type" ng-model="type" />
    </div>
  </div>
  <div class="form-group">
    <div style="padding-left:110px">
      <input type="submit" value="Submit"
        class="btn btn-primary"/>
    </div>
  </div>
</form>
</body>
</html>
```

# The Angular module

First, we need to create an `Angular` module which contains the vaue of `ng-app` and some list of dependencies which can be empty.

```
<script>
var hms = angular.module("hms", []);
hms.config(['$httpProvider', function ($httpProvider) {
  $httpProvider.defaults.headers.post['Content-Type'] =
  'application/x-www-form-urlencoded; charset=UTF-8';
}]);
```

Afterwards, the `ng-controller` will not be implemented just like a typical AJAX script which contains functions that will process request response transactions. All models coming from the server are represented as the set of properties assigned to the `$scope` object passed to the controller.

The `roomTypeController` retrieves all records from the server through the `GET` service `/ch06/hms/getRoomTypes` in JSON format. If no error is encountered during the response then `$scope.roomTypes = data`. Otherwise, a pop-up will be shown on screen with the error message.

Adding a new room type record needs a `POST` method transaction. After form submission, the document will execute the `addRow()` function to pass a new record in JSON format. The `$http` is a method that interfaces communication between the remote servers and the browser through JSON objects. The controller defines a dependency to the `$scope` and the `$http` module.

```
hms.controller('roomTypeController',
function($scope, $http) {
  $scope.roomTypes = [];
  $http({
```

```
    method : 'GET',
    url : '/ch06/hms/getRoomTypes'
}).success(function(data, status, headers, config) {
    $scope.roomTypes = data;
}).error(function(data, status, headers, config) {
    alert( "failure");
});

$scope.addRow = function() {
    var data = 'id=' + $scope.id + '&type=' +
    $scope.type;
    $http.post('/ch06/hms/addRoomType', data )
    .success(function(data, status, headers, config) {
        $scope.message = data;
        window.location = '#/ch06/hms/getRoomTypes';
        window.location.reload();
    })
    .error(function(data, status, headers, config) {
        alert( "failure message: " +
        JSON.stringify({data: data}));
    });
    $scope.id='';
    $scope.type='';
    }
}
);
</script>
```

# ExtJS

Just like AngularJS, ExtJS is also a JavaScript framework but known with its rich-client libraries for to its modeling UI widgets. ExtJS can send and receive JSON data to and from the server, respectively. In HMS, we use ExtJS 4.2.x to pass JSON data to create, read, delete, and update records.

## The application container

The HMS has a variation of the admin room type module using Ext JS 4.x.x. All Ext JS 4.2.x applications begin with a call to `Ext.application()` method. Ext is a singleton class and `application()` is a method of it that loads the `Ext.app.Application` class and starts it up with the supplied configuration after the page is ready for the request-response process.

```
Ext.application({
    name : 'hms',
```

```
      controllers: ['HmsRoomTypes'],
      launch : function () {
        Ext.widget('roomTypeList', {
          width : 500,
          height : 300,
          renderTo : 'output'
        });
      }
    }
  );
});
```

After creating the `Ext.app.Application` class for our HMS viewport, the following need to be implemented:

- The global settings for the application which includes the width and height of the main widget
- The controllers where all models and services are executed
- The models which include all data objects needed to be extracted from the server in the form JSON and records needed to be mapped and rendered to the views
- The store that caches all the models that we defined for our data
- The views that implements the data presentation of the application

# The data model

Most of the ExtJS applications have the `Ext.onready()` method which is a low-level technique of adding a listener that notifies the application when the document is ready (for example, it is usually used for initial loading and configuration). The HMS used `onReady()` to create the ExtJS model for our room type records from our database:

```
Ext.onReady(function () {
  Ext.define('hms.model.HmsRoomType', {
    extend: 'Ext.data.Model',
    fields: [
      {name: 'id', type: 'int'},
      {name: 'room_type', type: 'string'}
    ]
  });
});
```

All the data model definition extends the `Ext.data.Model` class which is part of the core libraries of Ext JS 4.2.x.

# The data store

Ext JS has a store that serves as a cache of all data objects used by the request-response transaction. Also, the store is needed to persist data retrieved from the server using a proxy.

```
Ext.define('hms.store.HmsRoomTypes', {
  extend : 'Ext.data.Store',
  storeId : 'roomTypes',
  model : 'hms.model.HmsRoomType',
  fields : ['id', 'room_type'],
  proxy: {
    type : 'ajax',
    url : '/ch06/api/getRoomTypes',
    reader: {
      type : 'json',
      root : 'roomTypes'
    }
  },
  autoLoad: true
});
```

The store has the following properties that need to be configured:

- `idProperty`: Pertains to the primary key or ID fields in the `model` class.
- `fields`: Defines all the properties (fields) and their data type of the model.
- `validations`: Used to apply validation types on the field.
- `proxy`: Used by the model or store to handle the loading and saving of the model data; the HMS used the AJAX proxy method which reads JSON data from a an endpoint service.

# The ExtJS view

After establishing the models and stores, the next implementation creates an ExtJS view which is usually an `Ext.grid.Panel` or is tabular in form but there are other grid components that can be used to be able to render properly our data. The following is the grid panel implementation for our admin room type module:

```
Ext.define('hms.view.RoomTypeList', {
  extend : 'Ext.grid.Panel',
  alias : 'widget.roomTypeList',
  title : 'HMS Room Type List',
  store : 'HmsRoomTypes',
  initComponent: function () {
    this.tbar = [{
```

```
            text : 'Add Room Type',
            action : 'add_room_type',
            iconCls : 'room-add'
        }];
        this.columns = [
            { header: 'ID', dataIndex: 'id', width: 50 },
            { header: 'Room Type', dataIndex: 'type', width: 100  },
            { header: 'Delete', width: 60,
              renderer: function (v, m, r) {
              // See the sources
            }, 100);
            return Ext.String.format('<div id="{0}"></div>', id);
        }
    }
    ];
    this.callParent(arguments);
    }
});
```

It is customary to create a layout on top of the panels and implement other sub-components on top of it like forms:

```
Ext.define('hms.view.RoomTypeForm', {
    extend : 'Ext.window.Window',
    alias : 'widget.roomTypeForm',
    title : 'Add Booking',
    width : 800,
    layout : 'fit',
    resizable: false,
    closeAction: 'hide',
    modal : true,
    config : {
      recordIndex : 0,
      action : ''
    },
    items : [{
      xtype : 'form',
      layout: 'anchor',
      bodyStyle: {
        background: 'none',
        padding: '5px',
        border: '0'
      },
      defaults: {
        xtype : 'textfield',
        anchor: '100%'
      },
      items : [{
```

```
      name : 'id',
      fieldLabel : 'ID'
    },{
      name: 'room_type',
      fieldLabel: 'Room Type'
    }]
  }],
  buttons: [{
    text: 'OK',
    action: 'add'
  },{
    text : 'Reset',
    handler : function () {
      this.up('window').down('form').getForm().reset();
    }
  },{
    text    : 'Cancel',
    handler: function () {
      this.up('window').close();
    }
  }]
});
```

# Controller

Lastly, create a controller that will consolidate all the components created from the start such as the models, stores, and view components.

```
Ext.define('hms.controller.HmsRoomTypes', {
  extend : 'Ext.app.Controller',
  stores : ['HmsRoomTypes'],
  views : ['RoomTypeList', 'RoomTypeForm'],
  refs : [{
    ref : 'formWindow',
    xtype : 'roomTypeForm',
    selector: 'roomTypeForm',
    autoCreate: true
  }],
  // See the sources
});
```

# The admin room type view

To call the application on our view pages, the JS file must be imported through the `<script>` tag:

```
<script type="text/javascript" src="../js/roomtypes.js"></script>
```

Then anywhere within the body, create a `<div>` tag with and ID indicated by the `renderTo` property of the `Ext.application()` method:

```
<body>
  <div id="output"> </div>
</body>
```

The following figure shows the final components found in our `/hms/ext/extroomtypesgrid.html` page:

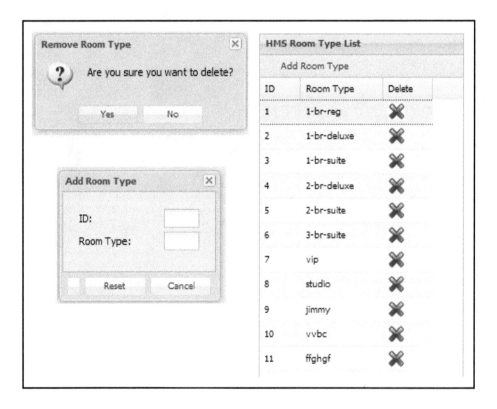

# Creating web layouts

A layout is a composition of fonts, colors, backgrounds, pages, and other sub-layouts which interact with one another to promote a brand. Technically, a layout is also called a **tile** which consists of different views that emerges as one bigger face for a profile, organization, or business used to promote an advocacy or goals. Together with web themes and components, Spring can integrate with frameworks that are popular in implementing tiles for the objective of the application.

# Apache tiles 3

A common tiles framework that has been proven to give support to Spring is the Apache Tiles 3.x framework. Apache Tiles provides some of the HMS with the common layout design to lessen the time of view implementation. If there are repetitions of view features and components, we create a tile layout where all common components are plotted. Then, this tile layout will be used as a template for all pages that shares common features. This layout consists of different structures of sub-contents. A template or layout will usually contain breadcrumbs, headers, menus and footers.

A version of the index page of the HMS is created using the Tiles framework and this is how the layout design has been derived:

# Configuration

To start using Tiles 3, the
class`org.springframework.web.servlet.view.tiles3.TilesConfigurer` must be
configured to create a tiles container with the definitions in the form of XML files (for
example, `templates.xml` and `definitions.xml`) which will be accessed later by any
valid `TilesView` instance. The instantiation is done through the following `bean`
declaration:

```
<bean id="hmsTilesConfiguration"
  class= "org.springframework.web.servlet
         .view.tiles3.TilesConfigurer">
    <property name="definitions">
      <list>
        <value>/WEB-INF/tiles/tiles.xml</value>
        <value>/WEB-INF/tiles/details.xml</value>
      </list>
    </property>
```

Since the HMS uses `ResourceBundleViewResolver`, all definition files will be mapped to
`org.springframework.web.servlet.view.tiles3.TilesView` in
`views.properties`. Otherwise, we need to create another resolver like
`org.springframework.web.servlet.view.UrlBasedViewResolver` that will view
and read the tiles definitions.

```
<bean id="tilesViewResolver"
  class=   "org.springframework.web.servlet.view.UrlBasedViewResolver">
    <property name="viewClass" value=
"org.springframework.web.servlet.view.tiles2.TilesView" />
    <property name="order" value="0" />
</bean>
```

# Creating the template file

After declaring all the necessary beans objects, a template must be created to design the
base definition of the `tile` configuration or layout which will be the basis of the individual
fragments (tiles) assembly.

The layout of the HMS main page `/hms/index.html` is composed of a header, body, and footer which is depicted as follows:

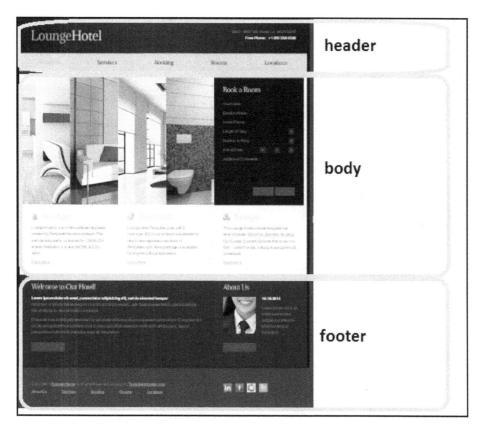

A template file can be implemented using Thymeleaf, JSP or any other view technology. The preceding page uses JSP and it is coded in this manner:

```
<body>
  <div class="main-container">
    <div class="row">
      <div class="col-md-12" id="main-header">
        <tiles:insertAttribute name="myheader" />
      </div>
    </div>
    <div class="row">
      <div id="main-body">
        <tiles:insertAttribute name="mybody" />
      </div>
    </div>
```

```
    <div class="row">
      <div class="col-md-12" id="main-footer" >
        <tiles:insertAttribute name="myfooter" />
  </div></div> </div>
</body>
```

Tiles templates and view components must have a taglib
`<%@ taglib uri="http://tiles.apache.org/tags-tiles" prefix="tiles" %>`
properly declared in each page.

# Creating the definition file

A definition is a composition or the final view page to be rendered on the browser. It is a layout composed inside an XML file which contains layouts of other templates or views through tile attributes. The given home page which is `hms/tilesindex.html`, for instance, uses the following definition file `/WEB-INF/tiles/tiles.xml`:

```
<?xml version="1.0" encoding="UTF-8"?>
<!DOCTYPE tiles-definitions PUBLIC
  "-//Apache Software Foundation//DTD Tiles Configuration
  3.0//EN"
  "http://tiles.apache.org/dtds/tiles-config_3_0.dtd">
<tiles-definitions>
  <definition name="hms.home"
    template="/WEB-INF/tview/tilesmain.jsp">
    <put-attribute name="title"
      value="HMS - Hotel Management System" />
    <put-attribute name="header"
      type="template" value="/WEB-INF/tview/header.jsp" />
    <put-attribute name="body"
      type="template" value="/WEB-INF/tview/tilesbody.jsp" />
    <put-attribute name="footer"
      type="template" value="/WEB-INF/tview/footer.jsp" />
  </definition>
</tiles-definitions>
```

After writing and designing the final draft of the layout, these definition files must be declared inside the `TilesConfigurer` bean. Then, to make it viewable on the browser, these definition files must be mapped with a view name in the `views.properties`:

```
hms.home.(class)=
org.springframework.web.servlet.view.tiles3.TilesView
hms.home.url= hms.home
```

Lastly, just like any typical views, a @Controller must be created to implement a request method that will call our new page.

```
@RequestMapping(value="/hms/tilesindex",
  method=RequestMethod.POST)
  public String indexTilesSubmit(Locale locale,
    Model model, @ModelAttribute HmsFreeBooking freeBookForm) {
      bookingService.reserveBooking(freeBookForm);
      freeBookForm = new HmsFreeBooking();
      model.addAttribute("freeBookForm", freeBookForm);
      return "hms.home";
    }
```

Where it calls the hms.home view name in the views.properties indicated in the preceding code snippet.

## Adaptive layout design in tiles

HMS or any Spring 4.x MVC applications can maintain a number of templates for the entire view pages. This is for the branding and trademark of the website. Some of the view components of a template may vary from one page navigation to another maybe due to the theme requirement while some areas of the template can be fixed throughout like the banners, headers, and footers.

# SiteMesh 3

When it comes to the layout design for a view, another option is SiteMesh. The process of implementing SiteMesh looks similar to Tiles but is much easier to configure and apply to the view layer. SiteMesh does not need any definition file, instead it has a layout that is automatically mapped to some selected views that are filtered by its configuration. The only danger here is when the configuration gets unsystematic and messy which leads to the overlapping of layout distribution in mapping the layout.

## Configuration

To use SiteMesh as the view framework, the HMS needs to register the SiteMesh filter com.opensymphony.sitemesh.webapp.SiteMeshFilter in the web.xml:

```
<filter>
  <filter-name>sitemeshFilter</filter-name>
  <filter-class>org.sitemesh.config.ConfigurableSiteMeshFilter
  </filter-class>
```

```
    </filter>
    <filter-mapping>
      <filter-name>sitemeshFilter</filter-name>
      <url-pattern>/*</url-pattern>
  </filter-mapping>
```

The pages or the templates of SiteMesh must be located inside `/WEB-INF`. To recognize all these templates a `sitemesh.xml` file must be created inside `/WEB-INF` directory. The content of `sitemesh.xml` must look like the following XML:

```
<?xml version="1.0" encoding="UTF-8"?>
<sitemesh>
  <mapping path="/hms/decorate/*"
    decorator="/WEB-INF/decorators/templateDecorator.jsp"/>
    <mapping path="/hms/membership/*"
    decorator="/WEB-INF/decorators/templateLogin.jsp"/>
</sitemesh>
```

The `sitemesh3.xml` configuration above assigns `templateDecorator.jsp` to all views having the URL pattern `/hms/decorate/*`. Whereas the template `templateLogin.jsp` is only mapped to views with the URL pattern `/hms/membership/*`.

# Creating the decorator

Unlike in Tiles, decorators and templates are just typical JSP pages here in the HMS project. The only distinguishing properties of a decorator are the presence of `<sitemesh>` tag libraries:

```
<%@ page language="java" contentType="text/html; charset=UTF-8"
  pageEncoding="ISO-8859-1"%>
<%@ taglib prefix="spring" uri=   "http://www.springframework.org/tags"%>
<%@ taglib prefix="c" uri="http://java.sun.com/jsp/jstl/core"%>
<html>
  <head>
    <title><sitemesh:write property='title'/></title>
      <sitemesh:write property='head'/>
  </head>
  <body>
    <div class="wrapper line1">
      <div class="col3">
      <sitemesh:write property='body'/>
    </div>
  </div>
  </body>
</html>
```

This is mapped to the login view:

```
<%@ taglib prefix="spring"    uri="http://www.springframework.org/tags"%>
<%@ taglib prefix="c" uri="http://java.sun.com/jsp/jstl/core"%>
<%@ taglib prefix="form"
uri="http://www.springframework.org/tags/form"%>

<!DOCTYPE html>
<html lang="en">
<head>
  <title>HMS - Hotel Management System</title>
</head>
<body>
  <form:form commandName="loginForm" method="POST" id="form1">
    <h2><spring:message code="hm_login_title.label" /></h2>
      <fieldset>
        <div class="row">
          <form:input path="username" />
          <spring:message code="hm_username.label" />: </div>
          <div class="row">
            <form:input path="password" />
            <spring:message code="hm_password.label" />: </div>

            <div class="wrapper">
              <a href="#" class="button1">Clear</a>
              <input type="submit" value="Login"
                class="button1">  </div>
      </fieldset>
  </form:form>
</body>
</html>
```

The tag `<sitemesh:write property='title'/>` accesses and loads the SiteMesh template page that gives a default title for the main page. This is overridden if the `<title>` tag of the login page exists.

The next tag is `<sitemesh:write property='head'/>` which accesses and loads the template page which contains elements of the login page's `<head>`.

Then we have the most important `<sitemesh:write property='body'/>` which loads the template that contains the content of the main view page. This template must be evaluated thoroughly since some elements of the `<body>` may have been posted already in the view page.

We then execute the view `hms/membership/login.html`:

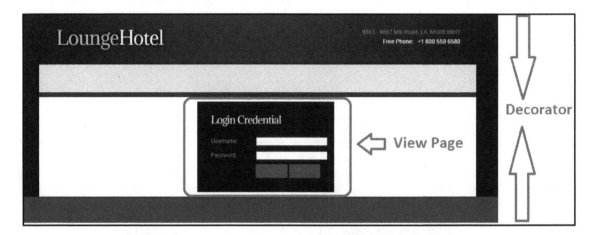

The whole design came from the decorator and only the form component is derived from the `/jsp/decoratorview/login.jsp` page.

## Adaptive layout design in SiteMesh

Some views of the HMS follow some layout created by decorators and some follow Tile templates. SiteMesh must not be used as the sole layout framework in any application because it stores the entire content of your HTML body into memory before it decorates it. If you have many very large pages to layout such as the reports, charts, and graphs in `Chapter 4`, *Human Resource Management System (HRMS)*, it would cause severe memory problems.

Decorators can also employ Kickstrap or Bootstrap frameworks for theming purposes because they have no built-in CSS and JS files to implement client-side user experience.

# Spring's internationalization support

The HMS must have the capability to support many languages which is one of the marketing strategies to promote the business. Spring MVC supports internationalization (i18n) of a web application.

# Configuration

The configuration starts with the declaration of
`org.springframework.web.filter.CharacterEncodingFilter` in the `web.xml`.
Some developers skip this part but for the HMS it is essential to include this class to specify
or enforce character encoding if browsers typically do not set a character encoding by
default. The application prefers to use the encoding setting UTF-8 to achieve the desired
text.

```
<filter>
  <filter-name> encodefilter</filter-name>
  <filter-class>
    org.springframework.web.filter.CharacterEncodingFilter
  </filter-class>
  <init-param>
    <param-name>encoding</param-name>
    <param-value>UTF-8</param-value>
  </init-param>
  <init-param>
    <param-name>forceEncoding</param-name>
    <param-value>true</param-value>
  </init-param>
</filter>
```

Then, declare the object
`org.springframework.web.servlet.i18n.CookieLocaleResolver` which is used to
set a cookie in the client request so that further requests can easily recognize the user's
locale. For example, we can ask the user to select the locale when he launches the web
application for the first time and with the use of a cookie, we can identify the user's locale
and automatically send a locale specific response. The object has some properties to
configure like the default locale, cookie name, and maximum age of the cookie before it gets
expired and deleted by the client browser. The following is a sample bean declaration:

```
<bean id="localeResolver"
  class=
  "org.springframework.web.servlet.i18n.CookieLocaleResolver">
  <property name="defaultLocale" value="en" />
  <property name="cookieName" value="mylocalcookie"></property>
  <property name="cookieMaxAge" value="3600"></property>
</bean>
```

After the resolver, inject the object
`org.springframework.web.servlet.i18n.LocaleChangeInterceptor` used to
intercept the user request and identify the user's locale. The object has a configurable
parameter name used to identify the change in the user's locale.

```
<mvc:interceptors>
  <!-- See the sources -->
  <bean  class="org.springframework.web.servlet
    .i18n.LocaleChangeInterceptor">
    <property name="paramName" value="mylocale" />
  </bean>
</mvc:interceptors>
```

# Creating the resource bundles

Resource bundles are properties files containing all text messages based on the selected
locales. The default resource bundle on the `messages_en.properties` file which contains
some of the text messages used by the HMS for the booking pages is as follows:

```
book_room_title=Book a Room
hms_free_phone=Free Phone
book_room_name=Your name
book_room_email=Email Address
book_room_address=Address

hms_header=PacktHotel
hms_service=Services
hms_about=About Us
hms_booking=Booking
hms_rooms=Rooms
hms_locations=Locations
```

There are French, Spanish, and Filipino equivalents of those text messages and they are
stored in on `messages_fr.properties`, on `messages_es.properties`, and on
`messages_fil.properties`, respectively. The `messages_fil.properties`, for instance,
contains the Filipino equivalent of the above English text.

```
book_room_title=I-reserba ang Silid
hms_free_phone=Libreng Tawag
book_room_name=Pangalan
book_room_email=Liham
book_room_address=Nakatira
book_romm_phone=Telepono
```

If there are special characters we are allowed to use Unicode characters (\uXXXX) so that it gets interpreted properly in the response HTML sent to client requests. Placeholders can also be used if the messages are dynamic and depend on certain arguments like:

```
booking.name=name : {0}, age : {1}, URL : {2}
```

To resolve all the text messages from these properties files, an object `org.springframework.context.support.ResourceBundleMessageSource` must be created. The HMS has this one already injected into the container for its `ResourceBundleViewResolver`; however it only read one file, `views.properties`. To include the resource bundles, the `<property name="basenames">` must be used instead of the `<property name="basename">` to accommodate more properties files. The following is the final version of the bean declaration:

```
<bean id="messageSource"
   class="org.springframework.context.support.
ResourceBundleMessageSource">
      <property name="basenames"><value>config.messages,
i18n.messages</value></property>
</bean>
```

# The Controller

The service of the controller must retrieve the current locale parameter of the view. The locale parameter will be extracted from the query-string of the URL. The values of the parameter are just the name of the locale in the filename `"messages_{locale}.properties`. If the query string is `local=es`, the interceptor will check if there is `messages_es.properties` in the classpath. If it exists, then all the text messages of that language will be used in the entire application.

The HMS home page when called using the
`http://localhost:8080/ch06hms/index.html?locale=en` will show you:

But when I call the home page using the URL
`http://localhost:8080/ch06hms/index.html?locale=fil`, the screen will be:

# The View

All the view pages must use the `<spring:message>` tag from the Spring taglib because this tag displays all the messages inside the properties file. The tag 's code attribute must have the key value defined in the resource bundle.

# Velocity, FreeMarker, and Rhythm

`Velocity` uses references to pass dynamic content into web pages. Macros and variables are a few of these references types used to reference objects defined within the Java code or can receive values inside the web page through a VTL declaration. Setting and using objects uses the # character:

```
#set ($firstName = "Jimmy")
#set ($lastName = "Gimme")
#set ($age = 35)
$firstName $lastName $age
```

**FreeMarker Templating Language (FTL)** can define expressions, functions, and macros within the templates and can use a rich library with predefined directives that give us the possibility to iterate data collections, include other templates, and much more. Setting a variable in FTL uses the # symbol:

```
<#assign firstName = "Jimmy" >
<#assign lastName = "Gimme">
<#assign magazineUrl = 35>
```

In FTL, predefined directives are called by `<#directivename parameters>`, the macros with `<@macro parameters>`, and the expressions using `${expression}`.

`Rythm` is a template engine for Java applications distributed under the Apache License version 2.0 that can process HTML documents, XML documents, SQL scripts, source code, e-mails, and any other kind of formatted text. Rythm was inspired by the .Net Razor project, due to its simple and elegant syntax. Rythm uses the special character @ to introduce all syntax elements:

```
@args String firstName
Hello @firstName!
```

# Advantage and disadvantage of Velocity

Velocity has a well-establish community that supports and contributes to its documentations and bug fixes. Moreover, it has several supporting libraries and sub-projects that make it available to all IDE as plugins. However, Velocity is cumbersome and its templates are quite complicated to create without the use of an effective IDE.

# Advantage and disadvantage of FreeMarker

FreeMarker is already an established templating tool with a remarkable documentation and support groups. The syntax of FreeMarker is very easy to comprehend. The only disadvantage that it gives to developers is its long list of established syntax.

# Advantage and disadvantage of Rythm

Rythm converts templates to Java bytecode which makes its processing time very fast among all the fastest template engines of the Java universe. The only disadvantage is its non-popular and non-extensive documentation which will make it difficult to adapt for newbies.

# Spring mobile

Spring Mobile offers automatic detection of screen devices based on the request transaction. It will filter if the request is coming from a mobile device, tablet, or desktop. With the use of Bootstrap, Kickstrap, and other theming capabilities, we can design beforehand different layouts and templates that will fit per the device. Spring Mobile is Spring's support for web responsiveness.

# Configuration

Initially, the `org.springframework.mobile.device.site.SitePreferenceWebArgumentResolver` and `org.springframework.mobile.device.DeviceWebArgumentResolver` are configured so that site preference and device parameters can be used as arguments to our `@Controller`.

```
<mvc:annotation-driven>
  <mvc:argument-resolvers>
    <bean class="org.springframework.mobile
      .device.site.SitePreferenceWebArgumentResolver" />
    <bean class="org.springframework.mobile
      .device.DeviceWebArgumentResolver" />
  </mvc:argument-resolvers>
</mvc:annotation-driven>
```

# Device detection

Then, we inject three interceptors, namely
`org.springframework.mobile.device.DeviceResolverHandlerInterceptor`,
`org.springframework.mobile.device.site.SitePreferenceHandlerInterceptor`
, and
`org.springframework.mobile.device.switcher.SiteSwitcherHandlerIntercept`
`or`. `DeviceResolverHandlerInterceptor` enables the detection of the device type
parameter called `currentDevice` of `HttpServletRequest` while
`SitePreferenceHandlerInterceptor` enables the `request` parameter
`currentSitePreference` before the request processing. The user's site preference is
stored in the client side as a cookie through the `CookieSitePreferenceRepository`. Its
value will only change after the user chooses another preference.

```
<mvc:interceptors>
  <bean class="org.springframework.mobile
    .device.DeviceResolverHandlerInterceptor" />
  <bean class="org.springframework.mobile
    .device.site.SitePreferenceHandlerInterceptor" />
```

If `/hms/desktop.html` is executed in a mobile browser, the browser is automatically
redirected to `hms/mobile.html` since the application detected that the device is a small
gadget.

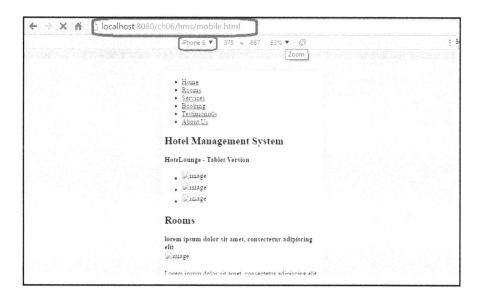

If accidentally the URL is executed in tablet browser, the browser will be redirected to `/hms/tablet.html`.

# URL Mapping

On the other hand, `SiteSwitcherHandlerInterceptor` helps users map the necessary mobile site to execute once a site preference has been chosen. The HMS uses `/hms/mobile` prefix to associate pages for mobile browsers, and `/hms/tablet` for tablet browsers. Once a certain site is opened in a mobile browser, it will automatically redirects the page to the default `/hms/mobile.html` site.

The site switching and redirection is assisted by the device-aware view resolver `org.springframework.mobile.device.view.LiteDeviceDelegatingViewResolver` which manages the mobile views and adjusts the prefix used for resolving devices. This class works with `SiteSwitcherHandlerInterceptor` in defining prefixes or suffixes to map the device to its predefined view without using other URL mapping.

The following is the complete configuration in the `ApplicationContext` container.

```
<bean class="org.springframework.mobile
  .device.switcher.SiteSwitcherHandlerInterceptor"
  factory-method="urlPath">
    <constructor-arg value="/mobile" />
    <constructor-arg value="/tablet" />
```

```
      <constructor-arg value="/ch06" />
  </bean>
  </mvc:interceptors>

  <bean id="liteDeviceDelegatingViewResolver"
    class="org.springframework.mobile
      .device.view.LiteDeviceDelegatingViewResolver">
      <constructor-arg>
        <ref bean="viewResolver"/>
      </constructor-arg>
      <property name="mobilePrefix" value="mobile/" />
      <property name="tabletPrefix" value="tablet/" />
      <property name="enableFallback" value="true" />
      <property name="order" value="3" />
  </bean>
```

# The Controller

All the URL must be recognized by the resolvers and controllers. This is because all this URL will help Spring Mobile in retrieving the SitePreference and Device objects from the incoming request; thus we must declare always these two as local parameters.

```
@RequestMapping(value={"/hms/desktop",
  "/hms/mobile","/hms/tablet"})
public String showAdaptive(SitePreference spf, Device device,
  Model model) {
    switch(spf){
    case MOBILE:
      model.addAttribute("siteType", "Mobile Version");
      return "mobile";
    case NORMAL:
      model.addAttribute("siteType", "Desktop Version");
      return "desktop";
    case TABLET:
      model.addAttribute("siteType", "Tablet Version");
    return "tablet";}
  return "mobile";}
```

# Spring Roo

Spring Roo is a rapid technology technique to create the HMS in a very easy way. It uses an automatic scaffolding of a web tier where models, controllers, and views are created through a series of console commands. There are built-in widgets that can be used easily. The following are some UI files created by the Roo scaffolding process.

HMS has a Roo version and it takes a few Roo commands to create a project:

- To scaffold a Roo project, run the following command in the Roo console:

```
project --topLevelPackage org.packt.hotel.portal
        --projectName Ch06-Roo
```

- To install the JDBC driver:

```
osgi install
--url file:\\\<path>\\mysql-connector-java-5.1.36.jar
```

- To install Hibernate ORM using MySQL datasource, the proper command is:

```
jpa setup --database MYSQL --provider HIBERNATE
          --userName root --password admin
          --hostName localhost --databaseName hms
```

- To generate the entity models with the repository included, the command is:

```
database reverse engineer --schema hms --package ~.jpa.data
                --disableVersionFields --activeRecord true
                --disableGeneratedIdentifiers
```

- To generate controllers:

```
web mvc setup
```

- To create other MVC components:

```
web mvc all --package ~.controller
```

After the series of commands, the following will be the snapshot of the project directory structure of our Roo project:

| Directory | Purpose |
|---|---|
| /styles | style sheets (CSS) |
| /images | graphics |
| /WEB-INF/classes/*.properties | theme configurations |
| /WEB-INF/config/*.xml | Web-related Spring application contexts |
| /WEB-INF/i18n/*.properties | internationalization message files |
| /WEB-INF/layouts/layout.jspx | Tiles definition for master layout |
| /WEB-INF/tags/*.tagx | Tag libraries (pagination, language, etc) |
| /WEB-INF/views/**/* | Tiles and other view artifacts |
| /WEB-INF/web.xml | Web application context |
| /WEB-INF/urlrewrite.xml | URL rewrite filter configuration |

And the final output will contain Roo widgets, themes, and resources:

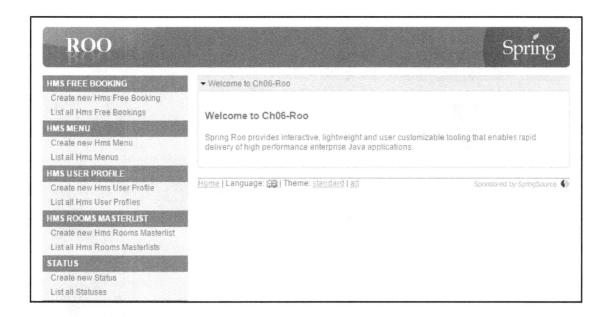

**The Theme**
The theme of this portal was derived from the authors `http://www.temp latemonster.com/`, and `http://webcodebuilder.com`.

# The Hotel Management System (HMS)

The Hotel Management System (HMS) prototype created for this chapter provides different solutions on how to express the main concept of an application through web designs, themes, layouts, and other components that will make a website adaptive and responsive. This study gives us the options on what to use in creating the web concept for our applications in order to provide our users with the appropriate and best user-experience.

Our HMS could be better if we apply user authentication, authorization, security measures, caching, and a little workflow management mechanism which will be discussed in the next chapter.

# Challenge yourself

Create online software for Food Catering and Reservation Services that presents to clients different food menus categorized by occasions. The theme of the application also changes per occasion (for example, Valentine's Day, Christmas Day, New Year's Day), highlighting their seasonal menus and drinks. Aside from the themes and designs, the system must schedule, log, and confirm all reservations.

# Summary

The HMS prototype provides us with different ways on how to translate our web design concept into technical implementation in order to give our users the smartest, most efficient, clever, and intelligent software interfaces. In the case of the HMS and other related applications written in the Spring 4.x framework, this chapter provide us with feasible options to convey the soft-side of our applications to gain more popularity and access.

# 7
# Online Cart System (OCS)

Performance tuning and security are two of the most important criteria to consider before and after software delivery. Performance criteria are drafted at the early stage of software requirement wherein all functional and non-functional requirements are formalized in order for the software to meet. To apply performance tuning measures during and after software development, a team must determine which sections of the software need to be optimized through a software tool called a **profiler**. Profilers measure the behavior of a module or sub-system as it executes, particularly on the collective running-time of all method and function calls. Some of the issues that arise are attributed always to load balancing, data distribution, bottlenecks of workflows and navigations, caching, and code enhancement.

On the other hand, software security is a measure that protects software from its vulnerabilities. It is a solution that helps software respond to different malicious attacks like **session fixation**, **clickjacking**, **cross-site request forgery**, and **denial of service** (**DOS**) attacks. Security must provide b is divided into three maioth authorization and authentication mechanisms to protect user information as well as the software infrastructure. Authentication is a process in which the credentials provided are compared to the database of authorized users' information in a local operating system or within an authentication server. Authorization, on the other hand, is specifying access rights or access policy to resources and information that composes the system. It has always been a challenge for software houses to design unbreakable, solid, and reliable security protocols for software.

This chapter will help us implement and deploy an optimized and secured **Online Cart System** (**OCS**) using the Spring 4.x Framework.

In this chapter, you will learn how to:

- Integrate Spring applications with Activiti BPMN and Spring Web Flow for optimized navigations
- Implement JTA transaction management to data source(s)
- Apply 2nd-level caching to Hibernate transactions
- Apply Spring Cache strategies to DAO
- Implement Spring Portlet MVC for complex software architecture
- Integrate applications with Spring Security
- Use JRebel for intelligent deployment

# Overview of the project

The main objective of this chapter is to create an online shopping system that has a defined and streamlined workflow with a complete security policy. Following is the dashboard design of the online cart system:

- **Login page**: The only difference with this login module compared to the previous login is the existence of a security plan that implements an access control list. Instead of a direct SQL style of authorization and authentication, this page will connect to a third-party plugin that will use an encryption/decryption algorithm to validate authentication credentials and will verify the role(s) of the user to determine its scope of access:

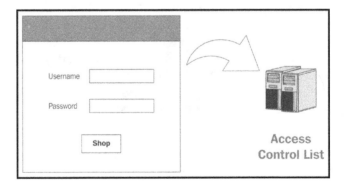

- **Catalog page**: The catalog interface is designed to show the clients all the products each with complete information like its image, name, description, price, availability status, price, and discount. This page is the start of the e-commerce workflow:

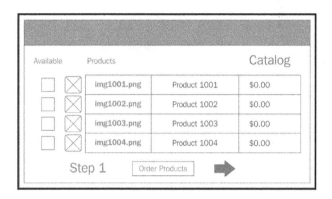

- **Billing address page**: As part of a typical e-commerce portal, this page will ask the buyer to input the complete home, or business, address where the product will be delivered. The assumption is that all products purchased will be delivered to their desired place of delivery. This page will comprise of the second step of the workflow:

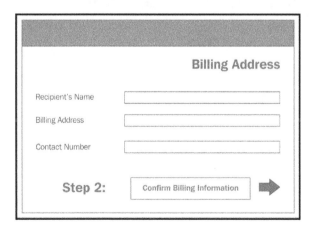

- **Payment details page**: The payment details page will show the summary of all products purchased including the input for the payment type. This page will become the third phase of the workflow:

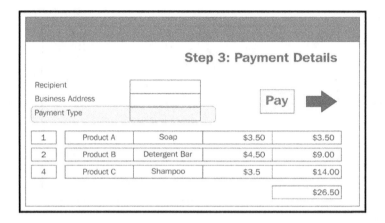

- **Confirmation page**: This page will issue the invoice of the purchase which confirms the payment. This will serve as the end of the workflow:

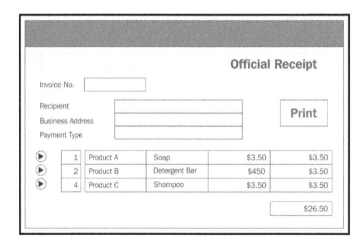

# Technical requirements

To start the implementation, the configuration setup in Chapter 1, *Creating a Personal Web Portal (PWP)*, is still the first step to consider in building the OCS. To enhance the look and feel of the cart system, Spring's solution for responsive and adaptive web design featured in Chapter 6, *Hotel Management System (HMS)*, can be helpful in building the "brand" of the cart system. Invoices and receipt generation can be taken care of by Chapter 4, *Human Resource Management System (HRMS)*, PDF, Word, or Excel rendition techniques.

Following are the add-ons to our usual recipe in building complete and efficient Spring MVC blueprints. These are technologies needed by OCS in order to fortify its features to be one of the most secured and efficient e-commerce software.

# Spring security

Spring Security is a mature, powerful, and highly customizable authentication and access-control framework that can be used to secure not only Spring-based but others like JSF-based applications. It is the de-facto standard for securing Spring-based applications.

Spring Security provides comprehensive security services for J2EE-based enterprise software applications. The implementation can start with simple hardcoded role-based security up to dynamic ACL-based security. The best part of Spring Security is its ability for declarative authentication and authorization which is achieved through storing a list of users and their roles in the database. The database information can then be wired in the security bean configuration setup which does not care much for the table schema of the store.

To integrate this tool to OCS, the POM configuration file must have the following Maven libraries:

- spring-security-web (org.springframework.security)
- spring-security-core (org.springframework.security)
- spring-security-config (org.springframework.security)
- spring-security-acl (org.springframework.security)
- spring-security-crypto (org.springframework.security)
- spring-security-taglibs (org.springframework.security)

# BPMN Activiti

**Activiti** is an Apache-licensed **business process management** (**BPM**) engine which has a core goal of defining processes which comprise of human tasks and service calls executed in a sequence order. It provides APIs to start, manage, and query data about process instances for a process definition. The edge that Activiti has compared to other BPMN providers is that it is a lightweight and highly capable to integration with any Java technology or project.

Activiti complies with BPMN 2.0 standards which are used by any web application driven by the workflow rules such as supply chain, online shopping software, document management systems, and other sequence-based transactions. This tool is a perfect solution for externalizing the user flows/rules of our OCS.

The following are the libraries used to integrate the use of the Activiti plugin:

- `activiti-engine (org.activiti)`
- `activiti-spring (org.activiti)`
- `activiti-rest (org.activiti)`

# Spring Web Flow

**Spring Web Flow** is a framework that allows development of a flow in a web application. The flow guides the user from one element of the application to another. It works on top of Spring MVC and its goal is to design the implementation of stateful navigation contexts and navigation constraints in a web application. The main concept of Spring Web Flow is just like a page flow, drawn as a simple flow chart, where each state in the page flow is either a screen (a view) or the execution of code (an action). Spring Web Flow manages the transition between states, and requires input from the actions, or the views (the user), to determine the next step of the configured execution path of the page flow.

To integrate this plugin to our project, we need the following libraries:

- `spring-webflow (org.springframework.webflow)`
- `spring-js (org.springframework.webflow)`

# Java Transaction API (JTA)

Spring supports MyBatis, Hibernate, and JPA ORM frameworks to manage single or local data sources. Once the application needs multiple data sources, Spring can use Java Transaction API or JTA. It supports XA protocols in order to handle transactions across multiple databases either in a grid or distributed mode.

The existence of JTA in this project is for OCS to manage huge numbers of queries periodically to different data sources without problems. This monitoring feature is common to enterprise commercial applications involving high volume of data access by huge number of users worldwide.

JTA interfaces and classes are already included in the Hibernate 4.x core Maven plugin:

```
<dependency>
  <groupId>org.hibernate</groupId>
  <artifactId>hibernate-core</artifactId>
  <version>${hibernate.version}</version>
</dependency>
```

# Bitronix

Many of the application servers such as **Glassfish**, **Oracle WebLogic**, and **IBM WebSphere AS** have built-in transaction managers that have default support for our OCS's JTA implementation.

Spring's API called
`org.springframework.transaction.jta.JtaTransactionManager` must be found from the vendor-specific container `bitronix.tm.BitronixTransactionManager` in order to implement the JTA transaction successfully.

To use Bitronix interfaces and classes in our project, the Maven plugin below must be present in our OCS POM file:

```
<dependency>
  <groupId>org.codehaus.btm</groupId>
  <artifactId>btm</artifactId>
  <version>2.1.4</version>
  <scope>provided</scope>
</dependency>
```

You have to include `<scope>` provided `</scope>` inside the `<dependency>` tag since we do not include this JAR file in our deployment process.

To configure Bitronix transaction manager in **Tomcat 7**, plugins must be downloaded from `http://olex.openlogic.com/packages/btm`.

# Spring MVC Portlet

**Spring Portlet MVC** is a mirror-image of our Spring MVC container. This MVC framework supports Portlet specification (JSR-168) which highlights unique workflow of portlets. **Portlets** are pluggable, managed, and portal-based web applications that define the user interface look. These can be conceptualized as small applications or sub-systems combined to form a single huge portal view. Portals like servlets handle requests/responses, but in contrast to servlets, portlets support only three request types: action, resource, and render.

This chapter includes Spring MVC portlets as another option or solution in implementing any type of online cart system where all of its flow views are rendered altogether in one portal.

To utilize the interfaces and classes for Spring MVC portlets, the following Maven plugin must be included in our POM file:

```
<dependency>
  <groupId>org.springframework</groupId>
  <artifactId>spring-webmvc-portlet</artifactId>
  <version>${spring.version}</version>
</dependency>
```

# Apache Pluto

JSR-168 has a defined set of APIs used for portal implementation, presentation, security, and personalization. It also has APIs that enable interoperability between portlets and portals. It also needs a JEE application server container that supports its APIs. **Pluto** is the reference implementation of the Java Portlet specification. The current version (2.0) of this specification is known as JSR-286. The previous specification version, JSR-168, covers version 1.0 of the specification. Pluto implements and is fully compliant with both the 1.0 and 2.0 specifications.

Pluto is divided into three main parts, namely:

- **Container**: Which is the core component of the server that provides the portlet specification.
- **Portal**: Which contains all the user interfaces for testing portlets.
- **Portal driver**: Which contains all the libraries needed to execute all portlets code from the applications.

Our OCS portlets will be deployed and executed inside a portlet Pluto container which is also Tomcat-based. This container provides the portlet with the required runtime environment, manages the life cycle of all the portlets, and provides interfaces and classes for portlets to call into. When it comes to user interactions, the container is the one that invokes methods on portlets targeted by an end user interaction given by a selected portal page. The portlet container listens and passes on the user requests transactions from the portal to the hosted portlets. All results will be rendered by the Pluto portal component and not by the container.

To use Apache Pluto without errors, our project needs to first import the `portlet` library that implements JSR-286 standards, which is:

```
<dependency>
    <groupId>javax.portlet</groupId>
    <artifactId>portlet-api</artifactId>
    <version>2.0</version>
    <scope>provided</scope>
</dependency>
```

Then, we need the following Pluto JAR files for the `portlet` libraries:

- `pluto-container` (org.apache.portals.pluto)
- `pluto-portal-driver` (org.apache.portals.pluto)
- `pluto-portal-driver-impl` (org.apache.portals.pluto)

To download the container and find out more about Apache Pluto, visit the site `http://portals.apache.org/pluto/index.html`.

# JRebel

Just to help with our development time, JRebel is a Java Development tool that automatically takes care of our project deployment. This is available in our **STS Eclipse** as a plugin and needs a non-commercial or commercial license to run.

# The OCS database

The OCS schema design, shown in the following diagram, will be implemented in MySQL Server 5.6:

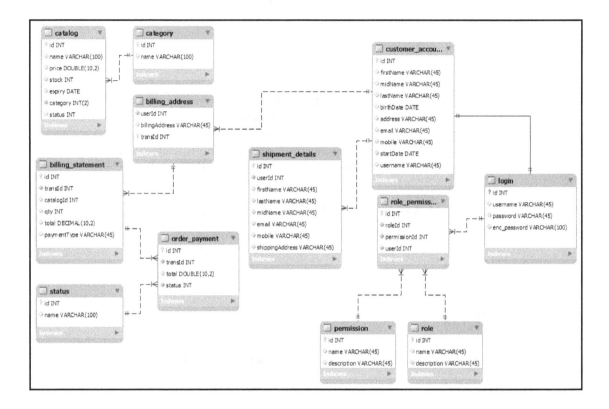

# Data modeling framework

The ORM framework to be used is Hibernate 4.x with JPA to highlight the integration of the JTA transaction manager.

# The software prototypes

This chapter has three Spring MVC project versions namely the Ch07-Activiti, Ch07-WF, and Ch07-Pluto. Project Ch07-Activiti covers Spring Security and Activity BPMN integration with the Spring 4.x Framework. On the other hand, project Ch07-WF discusses the feasibility of Spring Webflow 2.4.x in implementing processes of workflow-based e-commerce applications like OCS. The last one, project `Ch07-Pluto`, provides a portal perspective of implementing OCS wherein there are sets of interconnected portlets which make it convenient for the user to deal with e-commerce systems.

# Spring security implementation

The login authentication of the previous projects was just implemented through using database lookup tables and database validation. The user logs in and asks for their username and password credentials, then controllers call a service that checks if there is a match in the login table or none. No authorization mechanism has been made yet so far at this point.

OCS implementation in project `Ch07-Activiti` uses a third-party plugin for both its authentication and authorization rules. This plugin is called Spring Security which works like this:

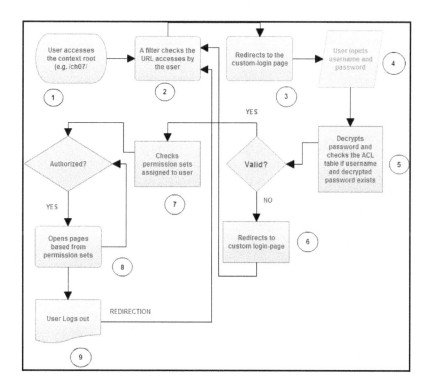

First, the user opens the `/ch07/index.html` URL of OCS. There is a `filter` class that checks the URL accessed by the user. If there is no existing session, the filter will automatically redirect any page to the custom login page `/ch07/ocs/login.html`. It is always the custom login page that becomes the façade of OCS whenever there is no existing valid session. When the user logs in with their username and password credentials, the `filter` class will validate the password or even decrypt it, if it is encrypted. Afterwards, the same filter will check the ACL table (for example, login schema in the **ocs** database) and will verify if the user is authorized to access certain pages. If the user is found to be an invalid user, the filter will redirect the browser to the login page again. Otherwise, the `filter` class will check if the user is authorized to access any pages within the software. Spring Security 4.x has always been an authentication and authorization plugin.

# Configuring the DelegatingFilterProxy

The `filter` class mentioned previously is the API called `org.springframework.web.filter.DelegatingFilterProxy`. The `DelegatingFilterProxy` is a special kind of `filter` class that manages and applies security protocols on all the servlets indicated on its `<url-pattern>` tag. All security protocols are written in beans which are found in Spring Security's `ApplicationContext`. `DelagatingFilterProxy` reads all these beans declared in the container and invokes them.

This `filter` class must be declared in OCS's `web.xml` just like any typical `filter` class declaration:

```
<filter>
  <filter-name>springSecurityFilterChain</filter-name>
  <filter-class>
     org.springframework.web.filter.DelegatingFilterProxy
  </filter-class>
</filter>
<filter-mapping>
  <filter-name>springSecurityFilterChain</filter-name>
  <url-pattern>/*</url-pattern>
</filter-mapping>
```

# Creating the security beans

Aside from the `jdbc.xml`, `dao_services.xml`, and the `ocs-servlet.xml`, another XML file must be created to separate all beans related to the Spring Security plugin—the `ocs-security.xml`. `DelegatingFilterProxy` will read all the beans declared in this file to implement a security policy within the context root.

## The <http> tag

The Spring Security authentication starts with the `<http>` entry. It has two important attributes `use-expressions` and `auto-config`. When `use-expression` is set to `true`, Spring Security then uses Spring EL expressions or regular expressions such as `/ocs/**`, `/css/**`, or `/js/**` rather than enumerating exact URL names in declaring URL names for mapping rules. Now, in Spring 4.x, the `use-expression` property is set to `true` by default. When `auto-config` is set to `true`, Spring Security will use its own `/login` form to implement the entry point of the application. If it is set to `false`, an attribute `entry-point-ref` is used to refer to a custom login page. OCS will have its own custom login page with its own CSS and theme, thus the `<http>` tag is configured as:

```
<security:http auto-config="false" use-expressions="true"
  entry-point-ref="authenticationEntryPoint">

  // See the sources
</security:http>
```

## The custom login page

The custom `/ch07/ocs/login.html` page for Spring Security 4.x has changed a little bit from Spring Security 3.x. Before, the OCS custom login may have been coded like:

```
<form action="/ch07/j_spring_security_check" method="post">
  <label for="j_username">Username</label>
  <input name="j_username" type="text" />

  <label for="j_password">Password</label>
  <input name="j_password" type="password" />

  <input type="submit" value="Submit" />
</form>
```

Where the `j_spring_security_check` is the default URL of the Spring Security `/login` which triggers the authentication process at the POST transaction, `j_username` is the user name parameter of `/login`, and `j_password` is the password parameter.

With the current version, the custom login page can now be written as:

```
<form action="/ch07/login" method="post">
  <input type="text" name="username" />
  <input type="password" name="password"/>
  <input type="submit" value="Submit"
</form>
```

Where `/login` is the default Spring Security URL that calls the authentication process at the POST transaction, the username is the default parameter name for the login name, and password is the default password parameter.

This custom login page must be triggered by the `<http>` tag using the `entry-point-ref` attribute mapped to a `LoginUrlAuthenticationEntryPoint` bean:

```
<beans:bean id="authenticationEntryPoint"
  class="org.springframework.security.web
  .authentication.LoginUrlAuthenticationEntryPoint">
    <beans:constructor-arg value="/ocs/login.html" />
</beans:bean>
```

# Non-Restricted views

All views not part of the security protocol must be under anonymous access using the `<intercept-url>` tag. The custom `/ocs/login.html` file must be under this category. The declaration of these pages must be done inside the `<http>` tag. If the tag's `use-expression` is set to `true`, then the following are valid declaration:

```
<security:http auto-config="false" use-expressions="true"
  entry-point-ref="authenticationEntryPoint">
  <security:intercept-url pattern="/ocs/css/style.css"
    access="permitAll" />
  <security:intercept-url pattern="/ocs/js/*"
    access="permitAll" />
  <security:intercept-url pattern="/ocs/img/*"
    access="permitAll" />
  <security:intercept-url pattern="/ocs/login.html"
    access="permitAll" />
  <security:intercept-url pattern="/ocs/logout.html"
    access="permitAll" />
  // See the sources
```

```
</security:http>
```

Otherwise, the correct syntax must be:

```
<security:http auto-config="false" use-expressions="false"
  entry-point-ref="authenticationEntryPoint">
  <security:intercept-url pattern="/ocs/css/style.css"
    access="ROLE_ANONYMOUS" />
  <security:intercept-url pattern="/ocs/js/*"
    access="ROLE_ANONYMOUS" />
  <security:intercept-url pattern="/ocs/img/*"
    access="ROLE_ANONYMOUS" />
  <security:intercept-url pattern="/ocs/login.html"
    access="ROLE_ANONYMOUS" />
  <security:intercept-url pattern="/ocs/logout.html"
    access="ROLE_ANONYMOUS" />
  // See the sources
</security:http>
```

All static resources like CSS, JavaScript, images, and videos must be declared anonymous to avoid an HTTP 404 status.

The order of the `<intercept-url>` declaration is significant wherein the more specific rules must come first, rather than the more general ones. It is also advisable to include custom login and logout pages under this category.

## Restricted views

All pages that can be accessed only after login must be declared restricted. Using the same `<intercept-url>` tag, we declare views under this category with a valid role, such as:

```
<security:intercept-url pattern="/ocs/**" access="hasRole('USER')" />
```

This indicates that all pages under the URL pattern /ocs/** must be accessed only by an authenticated user with a role USER. User roles and permissions are customized but must be based from the requirement.

# Roles and permissions

A common access control pattern in enterprise applications is the use of role-based access control for authorization. A role represents the high level of abstraction when it comes to user privilege. Permission is a low-level abstraction of user privilege that basically composes a role. A group of roles and permissions create what we call the permission table, or permission set.

To implement role-based authorization, we will create the following tables for roles and permissions:

```
CREATE TABLE `role` (
  `id` int(11) NOT NULL AUTO_INCREMENT,
  `name` varchar(45) NOT NULL,
  `description` varchar(45) NOT NULL,
  PRIMARY KEY (`id`)
) ENGINE=InnoDB AUTO_INCREMENT=5 DEFAULT CHARSET=utf8;
CREATE TABLE `permission` (
  `id` int(11) NOT NULL AUTO_INCREMENT,
  `name` varchar(45) NOT NULL,
  `description` varchar(45) NOT NULL,
  PRIMARY KEY (`id`)
) ENGINE=InnoDB AUTO_INCREMENT=3 DEFAULT CHARSET=utf8;
```

And then one table for the permission sets:

```
CREATE TABLE `role_permission` (
  `id` int(11) NOT NULL AUTO_INCREMENT,
  `roleId` int(11) NOT NULL,
  `permissionId` int(11) NOT NULL,
  `userId` int(11) NOT NULL,
  PRIMARY KEY (`id`),
  FOREIGN KEY (`userId`) REFERENCES `login` (`id`) ON DELETE NO
    ACTION ON UPDATE NO ACTION,
  FOREIGN KEY (`permissionId`) REFERENCES `permission` (`id`) ON
  DELETE NO ACTION ON UPDATE NO ACTION,
  FOREIGN KEY (`roleId`) REFERENCES `role` (`id`) ON DELETE NO
    ACTION ON UPDATE NO ACTION
) ENGINE=InnoDB AUTO_INCREMENT=14 DEFAULT CHARSET=utf8;
```

The `LoginService` is responsible for the retrieval of roles, permissions, and permission sets needed later by the `CustomerUserDetailService` of the authentication manager. All the roles and permissions retrieved by the authentication manager from its `UserDetails` object will be matched by `<intercept-url>` through its attribute access using the `hasAuthority(PERM_ABC)`, `hasAuthority(ROLE_ABC)`, `hasRole(ROLE_USER)`, or `hasRole(ROLE_USER_READ)` expression.

If all the roles and permissions names are prefixed with ROLE_, the hasRole() method must be used. If any generic aliases are used instead then hasAuthority() is preferred.

## Types of web authorization

There are three types of authorization:

- **Full-page**
- **Partial-page**
- **Method-based authorization**

Mapping pages to permission sets using <intercept-url> implements the full-page authorization.

To apply partial-page authorization, any view can import the taglib <%@ taglib prefix="security" uri="http://www.springframework.org/security/tags" %> to restrict users from accessing a portion of the page, based on their permission sets. After the import, use the tag <security:authorize> that uses hasRole() or hasAuthority() expressions to show or hide HTML elements, based on who is currently authenticated when the page is rendered. Following is a sample snippet:

```
<security:authorize access="hasRole('ROLE_ADMIN')">
  <input type="submit" value="Clean Customer Database" />
</security:authorize>
<security:authorize access="hasRole('ROLE_USER')">
  <input type="submit" value="Signup New Customer" />
</security:authorize>
```

Security expressions can be used to secure business functionality at the method level as well, by using annotations such as @PreAuthorize, @PostAuthorize, @PreFilter, and @PostFilter. To enable the use of these annotations inside the service layer, a security configuration must be enabled in the ApplicationContext container:

```
<security:global-method-security pre-post-annotations="enabled" />
```

Then, the annotations mentioned can now be used on any valid services just like:

```
@Service
public class LoginPermissionService {
  @PreAuthorize("hasRole('ROLE_USER')")
  public List<Permission> getAllPermissions() { ... }
  // See the sources
}
```

The authorization process comes after authentication in Spring Security. The whole process will be further explained in this chapter.

# Authentication filter processing

The authentication process starts with applying the `<http>` custom filter determined by the tag:

```
<security:custom-filter ref="authenticationFilter"
  position="FORM_LOGIN_FILTER" />
```

This filter is called `AuthenticationProcessingFilter`. It is so complex that it has several implementations and the one used here in OCS implementation is the `org.springframework.security.web.authentication.UsernamePasswordAuthenticationFilter` since it processes authentication through form submission.

The `FORM_LOGIN_FILTER` is an alias among the Spring-Security filter chain wherein the main filter name is mapped to the login form using the position attribute of `<security:custom-filter>`. If there are other custom filters that need to be added then another filter can be placed either before or after the main filter to form a filter chain.

The filter is injected to the bean through:

```
<beans:bean id="authenticationFilter"
  class="org.springframework.security.web
  .authentication.UsernamePasswordAuthenticationFilter">
  <beans:property name="authenticationManager"
  ref="authenticationManager" />
    <beans:property name="sessionAuthenticationStrategy"
      ref="sas" />
    <beans:property name="authenticationFailureHandler"
      ref="customAuthenticationFailureHandler" />
    <beans:property name="authenticationSuccessHandler"
      ref="customAuthenticationSuccessHandler" />
</beans:bean>
```

The `AuthenticationProcessingFilter` acts like a router and delegates all sub-tasks of authentication to other actors namely the `authenticationManager`, `sessionAuthenticationStrategy`, `authenticationSuccessHandler`, and `authenticationFailureHandler`.

# Authentication manager

Authentication manager attempts to authenticate the `Authentication` object containing the login credential of the user and tries to return a fully populated `Authentication` object (including granted authorities), if successful. Authentication manager is an interface that has a default implementation called **ProviderManager** that has the direct handling of the authentication request. It has a list of `AuthenticationProviders` that it delegates and expects a returning object from.

The simplest `AuthenticationProvider` implemented is `DaoAuthenticationProvider`, it leverages a `UserDetailsService` (as a DAO) in order to retrieve the whole user principal information such as the username, password (encrypted or not), and `GrantedAuthority` from the database. `GrantedAuthority` contains all the roles and permissions retrieved through the `LoginService` methods. This user principal object is called **UserDetails** which is returned to the authentication manager for comparison against the password submitted by `/ocs/login.html` to `UsernamePasswordAuthenticationToken`.

Following is the injection of OCS's authentication manager:

```
<security:authentication-manager alias="authenticationManager">
  <security:authentication-provider
    ref="authenticationProvider"/>
</security:authentication-manager>

<beans:bean id="authenticationProvider"
  class="org.springframework.security
    .authentication.dao.DaoAuthenticationProvider">
  <beans:property name="userDetailsService"
    ref="customerUserDetailsService" />
  <beans:property name="passwordEncoder"
    ref="passwordEncoder" />
</beans:bean>
```

# The UserDetailServiceDao

The object that is returned by the `DaoAuthenticationProvider` is the `UserDetails` object or user principal. OCS has created its class called `CustomerUserDetails` which inherited all necessary elements of `UserDetails`:

```
public class CustomerUserDetails implements UserDetails {

  private String password;
  private final String username;
```

```
private final Set<GrantedAuthority> authorities;
// See the sources

public CustomerUserDetails (String username, String password,
   boolean enabled, boolean accountNonExpired,
   boolean credentialsNonExpired,
boolean accountNonLocked,
   Collection<? extends GrantedAuthority> authorities) {
     if (((username == null) || "".equals(username))
     || (password == null)) {
       throw new IllegalArgumentException(
       "Cannot pass null or empty values to constructor");
     }
   // See the sources
   }

   private static SortedSet<GrantedAuthority> sortAuthorities(
     Collection<? extends GrantedAuthority> authorities) {

       SortedSet<GrantedAuthority> sortedAuthorities =
       new TreeSet<GrantedAuthority>(
         new AuthorityComparator());
       for (GrantedAuthority grantedAuthority : authorities) {
         sortedAuthorities.add(grantedAuthority);
       }
       return sortedAuthorities;
   }

   private static class AuthorityComparator implements
   Comparator<GrantedAuthority>, Serializable {
     private static final long serialVersionUID =
     SpringSecurityCoreVersion.SERIAL_VERSION_UID;

     public int compare(GrantedAuthority g1,
     GrantedAuthority g2) {
       if (g2.getAuthority() == null) { return -1; }
       if (g1.getAuthority() == null) { return 1; }
       return g1.getAuthority().compareTo(g2.getAuthority());
     }
   }
}
```

The `CustomerUserDetails` will be returned as an object by the service called `CustomerUserDetailsService` which is injected into the `setUserDetailService()` property of the `AuthenticationProvider`. Below is a snippet of the highlighted DAO service. The method `loadUserByUsername()` is automatically called by the authentication manager with the username value passed to it. The method `getAuthorities()` mapped all roles and permissions to `GrantedAuthority` entities:

```
@Service
@Transactional(readOnly=true)
public class CustomerUserDetailsServiceImpl implements
CustomerUserDetailsService {

  // See the sources
  @Override
  public UserDetails loadUserByUsername(String username)
    throws UsernameNotFoundException {
      Login user = loginDao.getLogin(username.trim());
      try {
        boolean enabled = true;
        boolean accountNonExpired = true;
        boolean credentialsNonExpired = true;
        boolean accountNonLocked = true;
        return new CustomerUserDetails
        (user.getUsername(),user.getEncPassword(), enabled,
        accountNonExpired,credentialsNonExpired,
        accountNonLocked,getAuthorities(user.getId(),
        loginDao.getUserRoleIds(user.getId()))));
      }
      catch (Exception e) {
        throw new RuntimeException(e);
      }
  }
  // See the sources
  public Collection<? extends GrantedAuthority>
  getAuthorities(int userId,Set<Integer> roles) {
    Set<SimpleGrantedAuthority> authList =
    new TreeSet<SimpleGrantedAuthority>(
      new SimpleGrantedAuthorityComparator());
      authList.add(new  SimpleGrantedAuthority("USER"));
      for (int role : roles) {
        authList.addAll(getGrantedAuthorities(userId,role));
      }
      return authList;
  }
}
```

# Password encoding

Password hashing is one of the key considerations when designing a secure application.

OCS finds it mandatory to encode its customer's password because plaintext or weak hashed passwords can be easily cracked by password guessing, hash injection, brute force attack, or rainbow crack. A hash (or digest) algorithm is a one-way function which produces a piece of fixed-length output data (the hash) from some input data, such as a password.

Spring Security provides the `org.springframework.security.crypto.password.PasswordEncoder` interface, as the password hashing mechanism. Passwords that are encoded by the PasswordEncoder's `encode()` method and the encoded password is verified by its `matches()` method.

Here are some of its implementation classes that became candidates for our OCS's encoding implementation:

- `org.springframework.security.crypto.bcrypt.BCryptPasswordEncoder`: Encoder that performs hashing using the "bcrypt" algorithm.
- `org.springframework.security.crypto.password.StandardPasswordEncoder`: Encoder that performs hashing with the "SHA-256" algorithm + 1024 rounds of stretching.
- `org.springframework.security.crypto.password.NoOpPasswordEncoder`: Encoder that does not perform hashing (for testing).

Spring Security recommends `BCryptPasswordEncoder` when hashing is not required but there is a problem when it comes to its calculation time. When the speed of hashing is the main concern, `StandardPasswordEncoder` should be considered the best option.

But the requirement for hashing sometimes gets complicated to protect the system from infiltrators. Sometimes the SHA-256 of `StandardPasswordEncoder` is not enough so developers need to upgrade to SHA-512 with 1000 stretching. This time, another `PasswordEncoder` will be used but located in a different package: `org.springframework.security.authentication.encoding.PasswordEncoder`. This `PasswordEncoder` implements the `ShaPasswordEncoder` which is used by OCA to encrypt all customer passwords during signup:

```
<beans:bean id="passwordEncoder"
  class="org.springframework.security.authentication
    .encoding.ShaPasswordEncoder">
  <beans:constructor-arg value="512" />
    <beans:property name="iterations" value="1000" />
  <beans:property name="encodeHashAsBase64" value="true" />
```

```
      <beans:property name="saltSource" ref="saltSource" />
</beans:bean>
```

The hashing value of `ShaPasswordEncoder` is adjustable to any value greater than 512 but the adjustment always has an impact to the performance of the generation process.

Sometimes, to make the encryption unpredictable for hackers, "salt" is applied when calculating the hashes. This is an additional string of known data for each user which is combined with the password before calculating the hash:

```
<beans:bean id="saltSource"
  class="org.springframework.security.authentication
    .dao.ReflectionSaltSource">
  <beans:property name="userPropertyToUse" value="username" />
</beans:bean>
```

Encoded passwords must be stored in the database and must not be exposed outside the system. Also, the encrypted password will be `CostumerUserDetailService` to generate the `CostumerUserDetails` object as shown in the following code:

```
@Override
public UserDetails loadUserByUsername(String username)
throws UsernameNotFoundException {
  Login user = loginDao.getLogin(username.trim());
  try {
    boolean enabled = true;
    boolean accountNonExpired = true;
    boolean credentialsNonExpired = true;
    boolean accountNonLocked = true;
    return new CustomerUserDetails
    (user.getUsername(),user.getEncPassword(), enabled,
    accountNonExpired,credentialsNonExpired,
    accountNonLocked,getAuthorities(user.getId(),
    loginDao.getUserRoleIds(user.getId()))));
  }
  catch (Exception e) {
    throw new RuntimeException(e);
  }
}
```

# Authentication failure and success handlers

If the authentication is successful, the `AuthenticationProcessingFilter` coordinates with `org.springframework.security.web.authentication.SimpleUrlAuthentication SuccessHandler` to redirect the control to the main page, which is `/ocs/order.html`. If the authentication is unsuccessful then `org.springframework.security.web.authentication.SimpleUrlAuthentication FailureHandler` is called to redirect the control to an error page or to a custom logout page `/ocs/logout.html`.

# Session management

Depending on the configuration of the `<http>` tag, Spring Security can be managed to always create a session when there is none (`<http create-session="always">`), create one, only if required (`<http create-session="ifRequired">`), never to create a session but only use one that exists (`<http create-session="never">`), or restrict to not create at all `<http create-session="stateless">`. OCS uses the default configuration where it automatically creates one if needed.

On the other hand, our e-commerce portal wants to control users who attempt to open the same account using different browsers. To manage performance, data integrity, and security, a system must allow only one session per user. This feature is called **concurrent session control**. To enable this feature in Spring Security, a listener `org.springframework.security.web.session.HttpSessionEventPublisher` must be declared in `web.xml` to always inform the session registry once a session is destroyed:

```
<listener>
  <listener-class>
    org.springframework.security.web.session
      .HttpSessionEventPublisher
    </listener-class> </listener>
```

Afterwards, a session authentication strategy API named `org.springframework.security.web.authentication.session.CompositeSessio nAuthenticationStrategy` must be injected into the container to manage the session settings in Spring Security:

```
<beans:bean id="sas"
  class="org.springframework.security.web.authentication
    .session.CompositeSessionAuthenticationStrategy">
  <beans:constructor-arg>
    <beans:list>
```

```
    <beans:bean
      class="org.springframework.security.web
      .authentication
  .session.ConcurrentSessionControlAuthenticationStrategy">
  <beans:constructor-arg ref="sessionRegistry" />
    <beans:property name="maximumSessions" value="1" />
  <beans:property name="exceptionIfMaximumExceeded"
    value="true" />
  </beans:bean>
  <beans:bean class="org.springframework.security.web
    .authentication.session.SessionFixationProtectionStrategy">
  <beans:property name="migrateSessionAttributes"
    value="true" />
  </beans:bean>
  beans:bean class="org.springframework.security.web
    .authentication.session.RegisterSessionAuthenticationStrategy">
  <beans:constructor-arg ref="sessionRegistry" />
  </beans:bean>
  </beans:list>
</beans:constructor-arg>
</beans:bean>
```

This bean will be needed by the `<http>` tag to configure its `<session-management>` bean:

```
<security:session-management
  session-authentication-strategy-ref="sas" />
```

Under
`org.springframework.security.web.authentication.session.ConcurrentSessionControlAuthenticationStrategy`, the portal's maximum session per user is set to one, and whenever it is reached, an exception must be returned.

# Session timeout

To manage the session timeout, an `<http>` filter named
`org.springframework.security.web.session.ConcurrentSessionFilter` must be
created in order to redirect the users to a URL when their sessions expire:

```
<security:custom-filter position="CONCURRENT_SESSION_FILTER"
  ref="concurrencyFilter" />
```

The filter two constructor parameters namely the session registry `org.springframework.security.core.session.SessionRegistryImpl` and the URL for session expiry:

```
<beans:bean id="concurrencyFilter" class=
"org.springframework.security.web.session.ConcurrentSessionFilter">
  <beans:constructor-arg ref="sessionRegistry" />
    <beans:constructor-arg value="/session-expired" />
</beans:bean>
```

# URL rewriting

URL rewriting will be applicable only in a secured environment where third-party cookies are disabled in all browsers. To use sessions for managing attributes, we configure our applications to generate **JSESSIONID** in the URL. But exposing session information in the URL is a security risk to applications running on unsecured servers.

Configuring the property `disable-url-rewriting` in the `<http>` tag is one of the best ways to enable or disable URL rewriting.

# Access denied page

To enable the access-denied URL, `<http>` must configure the following bean:

```
<security:access-denied-handler
  error-page="/ocs/access-denied.html"/>
```

The users will be redirected to the URL `/ocs/access-denied.html` whenever they attempt to access pages outside the bound of their permission sets.

# Session fixation protection

Spring Security offers our OCS portal a protection against typical session fixation attacks by configuring a bean that will control the existing session of the user when another authentication process proceeds:

```
<session-management session-fixation-protection="none">
```

By default, the `<session-management>` property session-fixation-protection is set to none, since it cannot be used together with the session authentication `strategy` property. There are three other values that can be used to enable this protection, namely:

- `newSession`: There will be an entire new and clean session to be created when a new authentication is encountered.
- `migrateSession`: A new HTTP Session is created, the old one is invalidated but the attributes from the old session are copied over.
- `changeSessionId`: The old session is retained but with a new session ID.

## Cross-site request forgery

**Cross-site request forgery** (**CSRF**) is a type of attack that happens when a malicious software agent, e-mail, blog, instant message, or program causes a user's web browser to perform an unwanted action on a trusted site for which the user is currently authenticated. Cookie-based transactions and web services are often the target of this kind of attack. Spring Security can solve this kind of problem through enabling a bean in `<http>` configuration:

```
<csrf disabled="true"/>
```

Unfortunately, our OCS must not enable this since all transactions are database-driven and workflow-based, so enabling this bean will cause login authentication problems.

## Custom logout page

To configure the custom logout page, the `<http>` must configure the `<logout>` bean with the following needed properties:

- `invalidate-session`: Allows the session to be set up so that it's not invalidated when logout occurs; set to `true` by default.
- `delete-cookies`: Contains the name of the session cookie to be deleted; usually `JSESSIONID`.
- `logout-success-url`: The URL redirected by Spring Security after a successful logout transaction.
- `logout-url`: The URL of the custom logout page that will trigger the Spring Security predefined `/logout` URL.

The code snippet of the logout view that will trigger the Spring Security logout processing is found as follows:

```
<body>
  <spring:url value="/ocs/logout.html" var="logout" />
  <a class="continue" href="${ logout }">Logout</a>
</body>
```

# Post-login transaction

Given a successful credential, OCS has an interceptor that captures the authenticated user through the `java.security.Principal`. This interface represents the user that Spring Security has allowed to pass through its authentication process. The following interceptor manages the `/ocs/login.html` such that it filters all the request parameters allowed to access the server container:

```
public class UserSessionData extends HandlerInterceptorAdapter {
  @Override
  public void afterCompletion(HttpServletRequest request,
  HttpServletResponse response, Object handler,
  Exception ex) throws Exception {
    Principal username = request.getUserPrincipal();
    HttpSession currentSession = request.getSession();
    currentSession.setAttribute("cartUser",
    username.getName());

  }
}
```

# Transaction management using JTA

The three project versions of this chapter use JTA as the transaction manager, just in case the system gets huge scope implementing more than one data source. Previous chapters highlighted that Spring MVC 4.x uses JDBC as the interface to connect to databases and were also successful in implementing the JPA entity manager that uses `@PersistenceContext` for in-memory collection of entities, which isolates the application from the inner workings of JDBC and database operations. Any CRUD done in the entities automatically updates the tables in the databases.

However, this chapter implements JTA allowing OCS for management of multiple transactions among multiple databases in the future. It is still JPA which will utilize the JDBC connections and SQL-related operations, but with the option, now, of utilizing JTA for delegating distributed transaction management, once databases are added to accommodate numerous records. OCS will only have one data source despite JTA. Chapter 8, *Enterprise Resource Planning (ERP)*, will discuss more about using JTA across multiple data sources.

# JTA manager and JEE servers

By default, the JEE application server provides **Java Transaction API (JTA)** support for **Orion**, **Jonas**, **Oracle WebLogic**, **WebSphere**, and **JBoss**. JTA transactions are more flexible at JDBC transaction handling because we can implement transactional services using one data source or more.

But Tomcat and Jetty does not include a JTA transaction manager, which will cause the following exception once we deploy and execute a JTA project into its container:

```
SEVERE: Exception sending context initialized event to listener instance of
class org.springframework.web.context.ContextLoaderListener
org.springframework.beans.factory.BeanCreationException: Error creating
bean with name 'transactionManager' defined in ServletContext resource
[/WEB-INF/jdbc.xml]: Invocation of init method failed; nested exception is
java.lang.IllegalStateException: No JTA UserTransaction available - specify
either 'userTransaction' or 'userTransactionName' or 'transactionManager'
or 'transactionManagerName' ....
```

# Tomcat and Bitronix configuration

To implement the transaction manager in Tomcat 7, this chapter chose the **Bitronix transaction manager (BTM)** to execute MySQL transactions. First, download the following JAR files from http://olex.openlogic.com/packages/btm:

- btm-2.1.2.jar
- btm-tomcat55-lifecycle-2.1.2.jar
- jta-1.1.jar
- mysql-connector-java-5.1.36.jar
- slf4j-api-1.6.1.jar (Optional)
- slf4j-jdk14-1.6.1.jar (Optional)

Drop all these files inside the <TOMCAT_HOME>/lib folder.

Then, create a configuration properties file for BTM in the `<TOMCAT_HOME>/conf`. The file named as `btm-config.properties` must contain the following basic details:

```
bitronix.tm.serverId=tomcat-btm-node0
bitronix.tm.journal.disk.logPart1Filename=
  ${btm.root}/work/btm1.tlog
bitronix.tm.journal.disk.logPart2Filename=${btm.root}/work/btm2.tlog
bitronix.tm.resource.configuration=
  ${btm.root}/conf/resources.properties
```

Afterwards, create the data source configurations for OCS which can be stored in the configuration in the `resources.properties` file:

```
resource.ds1.className=
  bitronix.tm.resource.jdbc.lrc.LrcXADataSource
resource.ds1.uniqueName=jdbc/ocsDb1
resource.ds1.driverProperties.driverClassName=
  com.mysql.jdbc.Driver
resource.ds1.driverProperties.url=
  jdbc:mysql://localhost:3306/ocs
resource.ds1.driverProperties.user=root
resource.ds1.driverProperties.password=admin
resource.ds1.allowLocalTransactions=true
```

Since OCS wants to have global transaction setup that may span multiple resources, it will be using an XA or Extended Architecture library like `bitronix.tm.resource.jdbc.lrc.LrcXADataSource`, which implements an algorithm called **Two-Phase Commit**. This protocol has two phases, namely Prepare and Commit phases. The first one is the commit-request phase in which the transaction manager coordinates all of the transaction resources to gather votes for the possibility of commit or abort. The second, which is the commit-phase, lets the transaction manager decide whether to commit or abort operations according to the votes of each transaction resource.

After setting the data sources, open the file `<server>/conf/context.xml` and write below `<WatchedResource>WEB-INF/web.xml</WatchedResource>` the tag:

```
<Transaction factory=
"bitronix.tm.BitronixUserTransactionObjectFactory"/>
```

Finally, include `btm-config.properties` in the loading Tomcat environment through adding the following settings in the Tomcat Management Console:

```
-Dbtm.root=C:\<path>\Tomcat7
-Dbitronix.tm.configuration=
  C:\<path>\Tomcat7\conf\btm-config.properties -Xmx1000M  -Xms500M
    -XX:PermSize=256M
```

# JNDI configuration

For centralized and global data sources, it is recommended to have a JNDI setup derived from the data sources configured in Tomcat's BTM transaction managers. JNDI settings must be written inside Tomcat's `context.xml`:

```
<Resource name="jdbc/ocsDb" auth="Container"
  type="javax.sql.DataSource"
  factory="bitronix.tm.resource.ResourceObjectFactory"
  uniqueName="jdbc/ocsDb1" />
```

On the application level, the JNDI resources must be declared in the `web.xml` as:

```
<resource-ref>
  <res-ref-name>jdbc/ocsDb1</res-ref-name>
  <res-type>javax.sql.DataSource</res-type>
  <res-auth>Container</res-auth>
</resource-ref>
```

# Spring and JTA manager configuration

OCS needs JPA to spare its DAO layer from dealing with the complicated queries of MySQL. Implementing JPA starts with creating an entity manager bean for each data source:

```
<bean id="entityManagerFactory1"
class="org.springframework.orm.jpa.LocalContainerEntityManager
FactoryBean">
  <property name="persistenceXmlLocation"
    value="classpath:config/persistence.xml" />
    <property name="dataSource" ref="dataSource1" />
    <property name="jpaVendorAdapter">
    <bean
      class="org.springframework.orm
      .jpa.vendor.HibernateJpaVendorAdapter">
    <property name="showSql" value="true" />
    <property name="databasePlatform"
    value="org.hibernate.dialect
     .MySQLInnoDBDialect" />
    <property name="generateDdl" value="true"/>
    </bean>
  </property>
</bean>
```

The first property of the `LocalContainerEntityManagerFactoryBean` object is `persistenceXmlLocation` which locates the `persistence.xml` file. The other property is the `jpaVendorAdapter` property which gives us the possibility to configure options specific to JPA provider implementation. The last and most important property, is the `dataSource`, which refers to the JNDI bean resources:

```
<bean id="dataSource"
class="org.springframework.jndi.JndiObjectFactoryBean">
  <property name="jndiName"
  value="java:comp/env/jdbc/ocsDb"/>
</bean>
```

# Bitronix transaction manager (BTM) and JTA

Instead of the JPA transaction manager, `org.springframework.transaction.jta.JtaTransactionManager` will be used instead, but Spring must cast `TransactionManager` to `bitronix.tm.BitronixTransactionManager` type since the Tomcat server installed BTM:

```
<bean id="bitronixTransactionManager"
  class="bitronix.tm.BitronixTransactionManager" />

  <bean id="jtaTransactionManager"
    class="org.springframework.transaction
      .jta.JtaTransactionManager">
  <property name="transactionManager"
    ref="bitronixTransactionManager" />
  <property name="userTransaction"
  ref="bitronixTransactionManager" />
</bean>
```

And, to successfully inject entity managers to services to utilize the `@PersistenceContext` object, we need to invoke the following tag:

```
<tx:annotation-driven transaction-manager="jtaTransactionManager" />
```

Another tag as follows, needs to be invoked to activate annotations for JTA and BTM transactions:

```
<context:annotation-config />
```

# The persistence.xml

The `persistence.xml` for our data source must look like this:

```xml
<?xml version="1.0" encoding="UTF-8"?>
<persistence version="2.1"
  xmlns="http://xmlns.jcp.org/xml/ns/persistence"
xmlns:xsi="http://www.w3.org/2001/XMLSchema-instance"
  xsi:schemaLocation="http://xmlns.jcp.org/xml/ns/persistence
http://xmlns.jcp.org/xml/ns/persistence/persistence_2_1.xsd">
    <persistence-unit name="ocsPersistency1"
      transaction-type="JTA">
      <provider>org.hibernate.ejb.HibernatePersistence</provider>
      <jta-data-source>jdbc/ocsDb1</jta-data-source>
      <exclude-unlisted-classes>false</exclude-unlisted-classes>
      <properties>
        <property name="hibernate.dialect"
        value="org.hibernate.dialect.MySQLDialect" />
      <property name="hibernate.show_sql" value="true" />
      <property name="connection.release_mode"
        value="after_transaction" />
      <property name="format_sql" value="true" />
      <property name="cache.use_second_level_cache" value="true" />
      <property name="cache.use_query_cache" value="true" />
      <property name="generate_statistics" value="true" />
      <property name="org.hibernate.cache.ehcache
        .configurationResourceName"
        value="/ehcache.xml" />
      <property name="hibernate.cache.region.factory_class"
        value="org.hibernate.cache.ehcache
          .SingletonEhCacheRegionFactory" />
      <property name="hibernate.transaction.manager_lookup_class"
value="org.hibernate.transaction.BTMTransactionManagerLookup"        />
    </properties>
    </persistence-unit>
</persistence>
```

Where the tag `<exclude-unlisted-classes>false</exclude-unlisted-classes>` means to include all entity classes.

The property `hibernate.transaction.manager_lookup_class` is important and must be present to recognize that the JTA transaction manager is BTM and will be the one to perform all transaction commit and rollback directly into the datasource.

# JTA DAO transactions

OCS uses `javax.transaction.UserTransaction` to persist objects into the table. It is instantiated in order to perform all necessary transaction management. The following code is the JTA way of saving records into the table:

```
@PersistenceContext(unitName="profilePersistency")
EntityManager entityManagerFactory;
// See the sources
@Transactional(readOnly=false, propagation=Propagation.REQUIRED)
  @Override
  public void setCustomerProfile(CustomerAccount account) {
    try {
      UserTransaction utx = (UserTransaction) new
      InitialContext().lookup("java:comp/UserTransaction");
      utx.begin();
      entityManagerFactory.joinTransaction();
      entityManagerFactory.persist(account);
      utx.commit();
    }
    catch (NamingException e) {}
    catch (NotSupportedException e) { }
    // see the sources
  }
```

# Tomcat 7 and BTM integration

To check if the integration is successful, open `<TOMCAT_HOME>/logs/catalina.xxxx-xx-xx.log` and locate the following log:

```
INFO: JVM unique ID: <tomcat-btm-node0>
Nov 14, 2015 3:26:37 PM bitronix.tm.journal.DiskJournal open
Nov 14, 2015 3:26:37 PM bitronix.tm.resource.ResourceLoader init
INFO: reading resources configuration from
C:\MyFiles\Development\Server\Tomcat7/conf/resources.properties
INFO: recovery committed 0 dangling transaction(s) and rolled back 0
aborted transaction(s) on 1 resource(s) [jdbc/ocsDb] (restricted to
serverId 'tomcat-btm-node0')
```

If there is a log that says something like:

```
WARNING: active log file is unclean, did you call
BitronixTransactionManager.shutdown() at the end of the last run?
```

It means you just need to restart the whole Tomcat server or the whole operating system.

# Process and navigation management

OCS is an e-commerce application and, just like any cart or purchasing system, it is really strict on workflow management. Although a simple one, our OCS prototype follows a process starting from the catalog view up to receipt issuance.

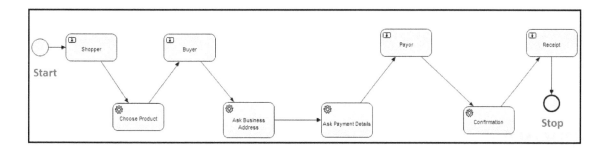

# Managing workflow using Activiti BPMN 2.0

Project Cho7-Activiti shows a version of OCS that implements workflows using Activiti BPMN 2.0. There will be a new ApplicationContext file ocs-activiti.xml that will be created to contain all the needed entities for the Activiti plugin. Although Activiti can help track down the flow process-by-process, its main strength is still logging. Logging is an important means to understand the flow in a complex framework as a process engine.

## Database configuration

Activiti needs a database to log all the process and task information:

```
<bean id="dataSource-activiti"
class="org.apache.commons.dbcp2.BasicDataSource"  destroy-method="close">
  <property name="driverClassName" value="com.mysql.jdbc.Driver"/>
    <property name="url" value=
"jdbc:mysql://localhost:3306/ocs_activiti"/>
    <property name="username" value="root"/>
    <property name="password" value="admin"/>
</bean>
```

# Database transaction manager

A simple transaction manager is implemented to manage the Activiti query transactions to `dataSource-activiti`. The
`org.springframework.jdbc.datasource.DataSourceTransactionManager` is an implementation of `PlatformTransactionManager` which is capable of thread-bound processing of a single database using the `DataSource` factory mechanism:

```
<bean id="transactionManager2"
  class="org.springframework.jdbc.datasource.
DataSourceTransactionManager">
    <property name="dataSource" ref="dataSource-activiti" />
</bean>
```

# BPMN 2.0 process definition

The Activiti plugin supports BPMN 2.0 compliance for workflow transactions. This standard is reflected in a process definition design usually written in an XML file to visualize the workflow processes. BPMN 2.0 has been the language of all process definitions in Activiti to help define and interpret the shapes on the diagram technically and business-wise.

To design a process definition flow visually, as depicted by the previous diagram, install the Activiti Eclipse plugin in STS IDE. The process definition file has an extension of `.bpmn` but Spring supports only its XML counterpart. To change the file to XML format, change the extension to `.bpmn20.xml` just like `cartevents.bpmn` renamed to become `cartevents.bpmn20.xml`. All files must be stored in the `/resources/bpmn/` folder.

# The process engine

The Activiti process engine is responsible for the creation of the Activiti engine needed to generate the entire schema in `dataSource-activiti`, log all process and task events into the system-defined schemas, and manage task activities and process executions based on the process definition file:

```
<!-- <bean id="processEngineConfiguration"
class="org.activiti.engine.impl.cfg. StandaloneProcessEngineConfiguration">
-->
  <bean id="processEngineConfiguration" class=
"org.activiti.spring.SpringProcessEngineConfiguration">
    <property name="dataSource" ref="dataSource-activiti" />
    <property name="databaseSchemaUpdate" value="true" />
    <property name="transactionManager" ref="transactionManager2"/>
```

```
    <property name="jpaHandleTransaction" value="false" />
    <property name="jpaCloseEntityManager" value="false" />
    <property name="jobExecutorActivate" value="false" />
    <property name="deploymentResources"
value="classpath*:/bpmn/cartevents.bpmn20.xml" />
</bean>
<bean id="processEngine" class=
"org.activiti.spring.ProcessEngineFactoryBean">
    <property name="processEngineConfiguration"
ref="processEngineConfiguration" />
</bean>
```

# Built-In Activiti services

After creating the process engine, the `ApplicationContext` must inject the following Activiti objects:

- `RepositioryService` : The object that provides services used to access the repository containing process definitions and deployments.
- `RuntimeService`: The object that provides services used to access the actual runtime information and processes execution details; used for manipulation, update, creation, and removal of components related to process instance, events, and execution variables.
- `TaskService`: The object that provides services used to access the task and form related operations.
- `HistoryService`: The object that provides services used to expose information about ongoing and past process instances only.
- `MnagementService`: The object that provides services used for admin and maintenance operations on the process engine.
- `IdentityService`: The object that provides services used for registering valid users with their roles.

Following are the beans injected by our `ApplicationContext`:

```
<bean id="repositoryService" factory-bean="processEngine"
  factory-method="getRepositoryService" />
<bean id="runtimeService" factory-bean="processEngine"
  factory-method="getRuntimeService" />
<bean id="taskService" factory-bean="processEngine"
  factory-method="getTaskService" />
<bean id="historyService" factory-bean="processEngine"
  factory-method="getHistoryService" />
<bean id="managementService" factory-bean="processEngine"
```

```
factory-method="getManagementService" />
```

# The controllers

All controllers involved in the workflow must utilize all Activiti service beans injected into the container.

The success of the workflow must start from /ocs/signup.html where users are not only registered for access authentication and authorization but also for Activiti user identification. If a user is not found in the dataSource, Activiti's act_id_user table then the workflow will not progress. Thus, the @Controller for the signup view page must include the following snippet:

```
User user = identityService.newUser(username);
user.setPassword(password);
identityService.saveUser(username);
// see the sources
identityService.saveGroup(identityService.newGroup("ROLE_USER"));
identityService.saveGroup(identityService.newGroup("ROLE_BUYER"));
// see the sources
identityService.createMembership(username, "ROLE_USER");
identityService.createMembership(username, "ROLE_BUYER");
```

The workflow start event triggers the ORDER event (/ocs/order.html) which shows the whole master list of products the user will choose from. After the user has chosen its itineraries, the @Controller of the view must generate a new process instance from the repositoryService:

```
ProcessInstance processInstance =
getRuntimeService().startProcessInstanceByKey("shopping");
```

It needs to retrieve the process instance ID to track down the service and user tasks. To tell the process engine that the ORDER phase has been successfully done, it must confirm and complete the taskID=shopper to proceed with the next event. The process engine will log the confirm and complete statuses to establish audit trails.

The succeeding event will do the same confirm and complete with their respective taskIDs given the instance ID except the creation of the process instance:

```
private void confirmAndComplete(String processInstanceId,
String taskID, String username) {
  List<Task> tasks = getTaskService().createTaskQuery()
  .taskCandidateUser(username).list();
  Task task = getTask(tasks, processInstanceId, taskID);
  if (task != null) {
```

```
getTaskService().claim(task.getId(), username);
getTaskService().complete(task.getId());
    }
}
```

The last service task is the RECEIPT event which will officially close the process instance. This eventually will trigger the end event.

# The services

Activiti process flow can utilize Spring @Services, create and pass objects from one task to another, and trigger transactions using the following techniques:

- Methods of typical Spring Services can be invoked by tasks within the process flow found in /bpmn/cartevents.bpmn20.xml:

```
@Service("shopperService")
public class ShopperService {
  public void printData(String var) {
    // See the sources
  }
}
<serviceTask id="chooseProduct" name="Choose Product"
activiti:expression="${shopperService.printData(var)}">
</serviceTask>
```

- A JavaDelegate implementation class can be used to execute a series of service tasks found in /bpmn/cartevents.bpmn20.xml that may involve DAO executions:

```
public class ShopperDelegate implements JavaDelegate {
  private Map<String, Object> variables = new HashMap<>();
@Override
public void execute(DelegateExecution exec)
      throws Exception  {
    variables = exec.getVariables();
    log.info("Executed process with key "
    + "" + exec.getProcessBusinessKey()
    + " with process definition ID: "
    + "" + exec.getProcessDefinitionId()
    + " with process instance ID: "
    + "" + exec.getProcessInstanceId()
    + " with current task name: "
    + "" + exec.getCurrentActivityName()
    + "");
    Log.info(variables.get("project"));
```

```
    }
    }

    <serviceTask id="orderProduct" name="Order Product"
     activiti:class=
    "org.packt.online.cart.portal.activiti.ShopperDelegate">
    </serviceTask>
```

- A listener class can be another solution to execute Spring MVC on the user task level found in /bpmn/cartevents.bpmn20.xml:

```
public class ShopperTaskListener implements TaskListener {
    @Override
    public void notify(DelegateTask task) {
        task.setVariable("var", "Hello");

    }
}

<userTask id="shopper" name="Shopper" >
    <documentation>
    Create order transaction process.
    </documentation>
     <extensionElements>
      <activiti:taskListener
        event="create"
        class="org.packt.online.cart.portal.activiti
        .ShopperTaskListener">
      </activiti:taskListener>
     </extensionElements>
    <potentialOwner>
      <resourceAssignmentExpression>
        <formalExpression>shopper</formalExpression>
      </resourceAssignmentExpression>
    </potentialOwner>
</userTask>
```

# Spring and BPMN layers

Once the user signs up for OCS membership, the SignUpController saves all the user information onto the OCS database. It also creates Activiti's processEngine.getIdentityService() to create a copy of the user credentials at ocs-activiti database which is owned by Activiti.

After creating the user identity, it immediately associates the user to the four groups or stages of the workflows, namely the shopper, buyer, payor, and shipper stages:

```
identityService.saveGroup(identityService.newGroup("payor"));
identityService.saveGroup(identityService.newGroup("shipper"));
identityService.saveGroup(identityService.newGroup("shopper"));
identityService.saveGroup(identityService.newGroup("buyer"));
```

Once the user is registered, they can log on to /ocs/login.html and proceed with CartController which implements the four stages indicated previously. First, the user will view the product catalog under /ocs/order.html which also spawns the workflow instance ID:

```
ProcessInstance processInstance =
  getRuntimeService().startProcessInstanceByKey("shopping");
  processId = processInstance.getId();
```

After choosing the products, the controller will redirect the user to /ocs/billing.html which will tag the user at buyer mode, store all orders into the ocs database, and will generate the payment form. Then, the controller will redirect the user again to /ocs/shipper.html which will ask for the shipping details of the user under shopper mode and store all information in OCS. After asking the details, the controller will ask for the payment details under /ocs/payment.html which tags the user in payor mode. Lastly, the last stage which makes the user in shipper mode will be executed by /ocs/receipt.html. All these four stages will be guided by the workflow in /bmpn/cartevents.bpmn20.xml using the following Activiti task and service event handlers:

```
private void execAndCompleteTask(String processInstanceId,
String cartUser, String taskName) {
  List<Task> tasks = getTaskService().createTaskQuery()
    .taskCandidateUser(cartUser).list();
  Task task = getTask(tasks, processInstanceId, taskName);
  if (task != null) {
    getTaskService().claim(task.getId(), cartUser);
    getTaskService().complete(task.getId());
  }
}
private void execAndCompleteServices(String processInstanceId,
String cartUser, String serviceName) {
  List<Task> tasks = getTaskService().createTaskQuery()
    .taskCandidateUser(cartUser).list();
    Task task = getTask(tasks, processInstanceId, serviceName);
  if (task != null) {
    getTaskService().claim(task.getId(), cartUser);
    Map<String, Object> variables = new HashMap<>();
```

```
        variables.put("project", "ocp");
        getTaskService().complete(task.getId(),variables);
    }
}
private Task getTask(List<Task> tasks,
String processInstanceId, String taskId) {
    for (Task task : tasks) {
        if (task.getProcessInstanceId()
        .equals(processInstanceId) && taskId.equals(taskId)) {
            return task;
        }
    }
    return null;
}
```

All Activiti transactions are logged into the `ocs-activiti` database and one of its important tables is the `acti_hi_actinst` which logs all the four stages of the OCS workflow:

| ID_ | PROC_DEF_ID_ | PROC_INST_ID_ | EXECUTION_ID_ | ACT_ID_ | TASK_ID_ | CALL_PROC_INST_ID_ | ACT_NAME_ |
|---|---|---|---|---|---|---|---|
| 100002 | shopping:6:55004 | 100001 | 100001 | startevent1 | NULL | NULL | Start |
| 100003 | shopping:6:55004 | 100001 | 100001 | shopper | 100004 | NULL | Shopper |
| 100008 | shopping:6:55004 | 100001 | 100001 | chooseProduct | NULL | NULL | Choose Product |
| 100009 | shopping:6:55004 | 100001 | 100001 | buyer | 100010 | NULL | Buyer |
| 100013 | shopping:6:55004 | 100001 | 100001 | orderProduct | NULL | NULL | Order Product |

# Managing workflow using Spring Web Flow

Another prototype of OCS, known as project `Ch07-WF`, uses a technique that allows full representation of the page flows. The implementation of the process flow is clear, straightforward, and detailed on how views and processes are connected. This approach may be simple for simpler applications but it is appreciated more when applications' processes get complex, unlike when we use an Activiti BPMN solution.

## Web flow configuration

First, `FlowExecutor` must be created because this is the `main` class of the process flow and is the facade for the actual flow. It manages the creation of new flows or resumes existing flows. It is an entry into the OCS's web flow system:

```
<webflow-config:flow-executor id="flowExecutor"
```

```
flow-registry="flowRegistry" />
```

Next, a `FlowRegistry` is created to locate and search the flow definition files. It looks within the application's `/WEB-INF/wf/` director, recursively, for any files whose name ends with `flow.xml`:

```
<webflow-config:flow-registry id="flowRegistry"
  flow-builder-services="flowBuilderServices">
  <webflow-config:flow-location
  path="/WEB-INF/wf/cart-order-flow.xml" />
/webflow-config:flow-registry>
```

Then, a handler adapter that serves as the bridge between `DispatcherServlet` and the `FlowExecutor` must be created. This bean, which is called `FlowhandlerAdapter`, delegates requests to a `FlowHandler` manipulating the whole flow based on requests:

```
<!-- Enables FlowHandler URL mapping -->
<bean class= "org.springframework.webflow.mvc.servlet.FlowHandlerAdapter">
  <property name="flowExecutor" ref="flowExecutor" />
</bean>
```

**FlowHandler** handles the requests and execution of the flow, including its outcomes and exceptions. This is a helper class that references the actual flow:

```
<bean class= "org.springframework.webflow.mvc.servlet.FlowHandlerMapping">
  <property name="flowRegistry" ref="flowRegistry"/>
  <property name="order" value="0"/>
</bean>
```

Afterwards, a bean called `MvcViewFactory` creator must be injected to tell the container how the Spring MVC view system is used inside Spring Web Flow. It needs a `viewResolver` such as `InternalResourceViewResolver` or `ResourceBundleViewResolver`:

```
<webflow-config:flow-builder-services id="flowBuilderServices"  view-
factory-creator="mvcViewFactoryCreator"/>

  <bean id="mvcViewFactoryCreator" class=
  "org.springframework.webflow.mvc.builder.MvcViewFactoryCreator">
  <property name="viewResolvers" ref="viewResolver"/>
</bean>
```

# Web flow definition

A web flow definition is an XML file that has its own schema and root element, `<flow>`:

```
<?xml version="1.0" encoding="UTF-8"?>
<flow xmlns="http://www.springframework.org/schema/webflow"
  xmlns:xsi="http://www.w3.org/2001/XMLSchema-instance"
  xsi:schemaLocation="http://www.springframework.org/schema/
  webflow
    http://www.springframework.org/schema/webflow/spring-webflow-
    2.0.xsd">
</flow>
```

All definition files are under the `WEB-INF/wf` folder.

The web flow has three main parts namely the states, transitions, and data objects. States are points on the flow where an action happens, a decision is made, or a view is displayed. The beginning and end of a flow are always states. In some complex implementation, a subset of a flow can be combined together to form a sub-flow and then the sub-flow is a state in the main flow.

Transition, on the other hand, connects two states. A movement of a request from one state to another is called a **transition**. Data is the information that is carried from one state to another. The life span of the data depends on the scope with which it is declared.

# View-states

A view-state defines a step in the flow where a view is rendered to the user. The first defined `<view-state>`, which is sometimes a default state, is considered the start-state of the flow:

```
<view-state id="loginView" view="login">
  <transition on="order" to="orderView" />
</view-state>
<view-state id="orderView" view="order">
  <transition on="billing" to="billingView" />
</view-state>
<view-state id="billingView" view="billing">
  <transition on="shipping" to="shippingView" />
</view-state>
<view-state id="shippingView" view="shipping">
  <transition on="payment" to="paymentView" />
</view-state>
<view-state id="paymentView" view="payment">
  <transition on="confirmation" to="confirmationView" />
```

```
</view-state>
<view-state id="confirmationView" view="receipt">
  <transition on="logout" to="logoutView" />
</view-state>
```

# State transitions

The connection between two states is represented by an XML element <transition>. The transition is often triggered by events, like **Submit** buttons, which carry attributes passed from the previous states.

## End states

The whole workflow will not be considered complete when there is no <end-state>. The end state signifies that a certain flow has finished processing sequences of states and must stop the flow. There can be more than one end state in a workflow.

# Flow actions

Actions are typically inline services that can be executed within flows. These services can be called **scripting**, or **expression languages** like Spring EL. Moreover, these services might be in the form of controller methods, business service layers, DAO transactions, and Plain Old Java Objects or POJOs.

The XML element <evaluate> is the most commonly used kind of action. It simply evaluates the EL expression specified in the attribute expression, or performs the operations specified.

For example, a model object can be mapped to a form view through:

```
<view-state id="loginView" view="login" model="viewScope.loginForm >
  <on-render>
    <evaluate expression="cartController.createLoginForm()"
result="viewScope.loginForm"/>
  </on-render>
  <transition on="order" to="orderView" />
</view-state>
```

Here cartController is the controller bean with a function createLoginForm() having a return value of LoginForm object. If there is no result attribute, then the method does not return anything.

Sometimes service and controller methods can be called during transitions like in the flow as follows:

```
<view-state id="orderView" view="order">
  <evaluate expression=
  "addCartProducts.retrieveProductList(flowScope.cartProducts)" />

  <transition on="billing" to="billingView" />
</view-state>
<view-state id="billingView" view="billing">
  <transition on="shipping" to="shippingView" />
<transition on-exception=
  "org.packt.online.cart.portal.NullCartException"
  to="displayLoginErrorView" />
</view-state>
```

Before the transition from ORDER to BILLING state, a service method retrieveProductList() of the service class addCartProducts validates if a user has purchased any products. If the List<Catalog> is not empty, all records will be stored into the database and will be accessible to the next state. Otherwise, the state will be redirected to an error view state displayLoginErrorView.

# Variable scopes

Spring Web Flow creates variables or objects under scopes. These scopes are just similar to JEE scope components, which determine the time frame of when to access these variables. Under Spring Web Flow, there are five scopes that can be mapped to a newly created object:

- flowScope: Assigns a flow variable; variables under this scope get allocated when a flow starts and destroyed when the flow ends.; any objects stored in flow scope need to be serializable:

  ```
  <evaluate expression= "addCartProducts.retrieveProductList
                        (flowScope.cartProducts)" />
  ```

- conversationScope: Assigns a conversation variable; variables under this scope are used whenever a top-level needs to generate objects to be accessed by its sub-flows; they are destroyed when the top-level flow ends; conversation scope must be serializable.

- viewScope: Assigns a view variable; these are variables that can only be referenced within the <view-state>; these variables get allocated when the <view-state> starts and destroyed when the same <view-state> exits; must be serializable:

```
<on-render>
  <evaluate expression="cartController.createLoginForm()"
                    result="viewScope.loginForm"/>
</on-render>
```

- requestScope: Assigns a request variable; these variables get allocated when a flow is called and destroyed when the flow returns:

```
<set name="requestScope.cartId"
 value="requestParameters.id" type="long" />
```

- flashScope: Assigns a flash variable; these variables get allocated when a flow starts, cleared after every view render, and destroyed when the flow ends; must be serializable:

```
<set name="flashScope.statusMessage" value="Null Cart'" />
```

# Spring MVC portlet

Another implementation showcased in this chapter is project Ch07-Pluto, which is in written in portlets. Some e-commerce portals contain mini portlets running simultaneously and passing data portlet to portlet. A portal is a collection of windowed mini web applications, called portlets, which support features like personalization, content aggregation, and integration into a foreign portal, authentication, and customization.

Portal specification is for complicated supply chains, e-commerce, or workflow-based applications that have complex features other than typical servlet-based transactions. If your project does not need the complexities of portal development then this area of implementation can be skipped.

# OCS as a portal

OCS can be implemented as a portal through the Spring MVC Portlet specification. The idea is depicted in the following screenshot where all phases of the order workflow are represented as portlets running simultaneously on the applications' facade:

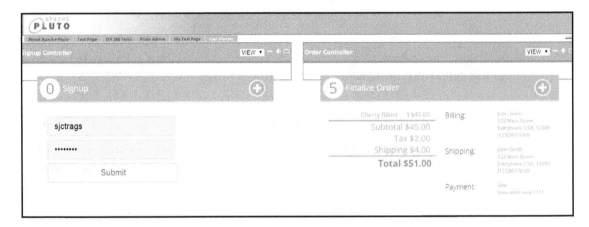

Each portlet can still undergo some Activiti or Web Flow if it has sub-flows to implement. Web services can be generated in order to pass data among portlets.

# Controllers

Each portlet must have only one controller class. The @Controller extends org.springframework.web.portlet.DispatcherPortlet with the following component objects:

- **Portlet Request**: Contains ACTION and VIEW requests; when the request type is ACTION, the Portlet container will call the processAction() method; when the request is of type VIEW, the container will call the render() method defined on the Portlet interface; also contains REQUEST parameters.
- **Render Request**: Represents the request for the render phase; usually contains a GET HTTP request body.
- **Action Request**: Represents the request for the action phase; usually contains a POST HTTP request body.
- **Portlet Response**: Sends response objects back to the portal after every request; contains the portlet frame that will be attached to the **Portal** page.

- **Render Response**: Object used for writing content fragments into the **Portal** page.
- **Action Response**: Used for passing the parameters for the render phase through using `setRenderParamater()`; used to redirect the request into any other resources than letting the normal flow proceed (redirection).

These can be found under the libraries of Java Portlet Specification 2.0 (`javax.portlet`):

```
@Controller
@RequestMapping("VIEW")
public class SignupController {
  @RequestMapping(params = "action=signup")
  public void action(ActionRequest request,
    ActionResponse response,
  LoginForm loginForm, Errors errors,
  SessionStatus sessionStatus) {
    ValidationUtils.rejectIfEmpty(errors,
    "firstName", "firstName.empty",
    "Please, fill in your first name");
    ValidationUtils.rejectIfEmpty(errors,
    "lastName", "lastName.empty",
    "Please, fill in your last name");
    if (!errors.hasErrors()) {
      response.setRenderParameter("action", "login");
    }
  }

  @RequestMapping(params = "action=signup")
  public ModelAndView renderForm(RenderRequest request,
  ModelMap modelMap) {
    return new ModelAndView("signup");
  }

  @RequestMapping(params = "action=login")
  public ModelAndView renderGreeting(RenderRequest request) {
    return new ModelAndView("signup");
  }
  // See the sources
}
```

All method names are developer-defined with an annotation `@RequestMapping` with param attributes like `action=signup` from the above snippet. It means this request method has the key `VIEW` and its value is `signup`. Thus, this method will be called by an `actionURL` with a `VIEW` parameter value `signup`. The same concept is applied to `@ActionMapping` methods.

`@ActionMapping` or `@RequestMapping` without parameters is called once the portlet is loaded into the portal.

# Portlet modes

The Java Portlet Specification 2.0 supports three standard `Portlet` modes:

- **View Mode**: This mode is used to render the view layer of the portlet.
- **Help Mode**: Used to create help screens.
- **Edit Mode**: Used to change the settings of the portlet per user to customize the view.

These modes are already part of the portlet's `@Controller` class.

# Portlet views

View pages must be categorized by a portlet. Specific view resolvers must be in the portlet's `ApplicationContext` container. OCS stores all view pages in this manner:

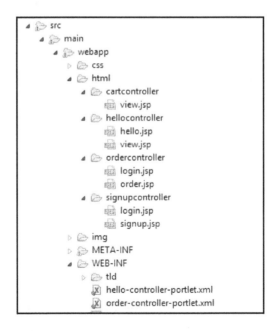

Each portlet view must have an important portlet taglib that generates an `actionURL` or `renderURL` per view needed by the `@Controller` methods. Since OCS uses Apache Pluto as its portlet container, the needed tag library is:

```
<%@ taglib uri="http://portals.apache.org/pluto/portlet-el_2_0"
prefix="portlet"%>
```

To generate the URLs, below is the sample snippet from the project's view:

```
<portlet:renderURL var="clickURL">
  <portlet:param name="action" value="signup"/>
</portlet:renderURL>

<portlet:actionURL var="actionURL">
  <portlet:param name="action" value="signup" />
</portlet:actionURL>
<form action="${ urlAgain }" method="post" class="go-right">
  <!-See the sources -->
</form>
<h1>New member?</h1>
<a href="${ clickURL }">Signup</a>
```

# Application context configuration

Each `@Controller` must be configured in an `ApplicationContext` configuration file. It is just a standard that the name of the configuration file is based on the controller itself. Some of the controllers of OCS are `SignUpController` with its configuration found in `sign-up-controller-portlet.xml` and `OrderController` with its own `order-controller-portlet.xml`. The content is plainly typical Spring 4.x MVC container configurations.

# Portlet configuration

All portlet properties and information must be included in this file. The portal will be looking for this file during deployment:

```
<?xml version="1.0"?>
<portlet-app xmlns="http://java.sun.com/xml/ns/portlet/portlet-app_2_0.xsd"
  xmlns:xsi="http://www.w3.org/2001/XMLSchema-instance"
  xsi:schemaLocation="http://java.sun.com/xml/ns/portlet/   portlet-
app_2_0.xsd http://java.sun.com/xml/ns/portlet/   portlet-app_2_0.xsd"
  version="2.0">
  <portlet>
    <portlet-name>hello-controller</portlet-name>
```

```
      <display-name>Hello Controller</display-name>
        <portlet-class>
          org.springframework.web.portlet.DispatcherPortlet
        </portlet-class>
        <init-param>
          <name>contextConfigLocation</name>
          <value>/WEB-INF/hello-controller-portlet.xml
          </value>
        </init-param>
        <supports>
          <mime-type>text/html</mime-type>
          <portlet-mode>VIEW</portlet-mode>
        </supports>

        <portlet-info>
          <title>Hello Controller</title>
          <short-title>Hello Controller</short-title>
          <keywords></keywords>
        </portlet-info>
        <security-role-ref>
          <role-name>cart-admin</role-name>
          <role-link>pluto</role-link>
        </security-role-ref>
      </portlet>
   <!-Other portlets -->
 </portlet-app>
```

# Defining portlets as portal servlets

A portlet container is built on a servlet container and it has servlet container features for achieving specification. All portlets must be defined in the project's web.xml to be recognized by the Portal container. The URL pattern will be quite different from the normal once since it will be container-specific. OCS portlets must use a PlutoInvoker servlet in order for Pluto to see it, and be able to pass requests to it. The Liferay container has its own way of rendering the portlets:

```
<servlet-mapping>
  <servlet-name>signup-controller</servlet-name>
    <url-pattern>/PlutoInvoker/signup-controller</url-pattern>
  </servlet-mapping>

  <servlet>
    <servlet-name>order-controller</servlet-name>
    <servlet-class>
      org.apache.pluto.container.driver.PortletServlet
```

```
    </servlet-class>
    <init-param>
      <param-name>portlet-name</param-name>
      <param-value>order-controller</param-value>
    </init-param>
    <load-on-startup>1</load-on-startup>
  </servlet>
```

# Apache Pluto deployment

Pluto is a portlet container integrated into an Apache Tomcat server. After deploying the project through Maven or JRebel, run `http://localhost:8080/pluto` and login using your own defined credentials. Click the **Pluto Admin** tab and test your portlets. See the following for a screenshot of the Pluto webpage:

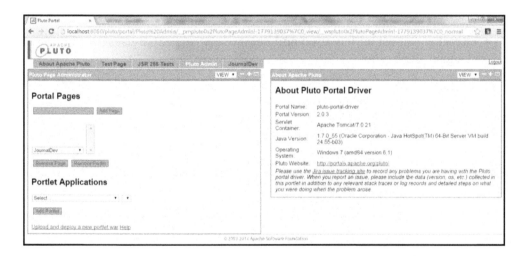

# Spring Cache

Spring Cache applies caching to Java methods, providing the application and environment where results of selective methods are temporarily stored. It is abstracted and is represented through the cache interface. Spring Cache improves the performance of the methods by avoiding multiple executions of the same method giving the same input and result. Note that this type of caching can be applied to the methods which return the same result giving the same input.

# Types of cache

Spring Cache has several implementations and these are:

- **SimpleCacheManager with ConcurrentHashMap (ConcurrentMap-based)**: One of the supported cache managers of Spring MVC 4.x because of its high performance but must not be used in cache eviction:

```
<bean id="cacheManager"
  class="org.springframework.cache.support
      .SimpleCacheManager">
    <property name="caches">
      <set>
        <bean class="org.springframework.cache.concurrent
            .ConcurrentCacheFactoryBean" p:name="default"/>
      </set>
    </property>
</bean>
```

- **Ehcache**: A most widely used and heavy duty cache that uses the Ehcache name to cache all objects:

```
<bean id="cacheManager"
  class="org.springframework.cache.ehcache
      .EhCacheCacheManager" >
    <property name="cacheManager" ref="ehcache"/>
</bean>
<bean id="ehcache"
  class="org.springframework.cache.ehcache
      .EhCacheManagerFactoryBean">
    <property name="configLocation"
      value="classpath:/config/ehcache.xml" />
    <property name="shared" value="true"/>
</bean>
```

- **Gemfire Cache**: Uses efficient caching techniques for storing cached data in the in-memory.
- **Guava Cache**: Uses `LoadingCache` to store all objects into the memory.

OCS project uses Ehcache as its official cache implementation.

# Configure caching

To enable Spring Caching, add the following entity to our `ApplicationContext`:

```
<cache:annotation-driven />
```

Spring provides annotation support for caching. Caching starts by adding the @Cacheable annotation above to the method and parameterizing it with the name of the cache where the results would be stored. The @Cacheable always checks if results exist or not before caching:

```
@Transactional
  @Cacheable("users")
  @Override
  public List<Login> getusers() {
    String qlString = "SELECT l FROM Login l";
    TypedQuery<Login> query = em.createQuery(qlString,
    Login.class);
    List<Login> login = query.getResultList();
    return login;
  }
```

Caches can very quickly grow in volume, and some of the data is not really 100% utilized. @Cacheable cannot properly handle the growing size of the unused cached data. The @CacheEvict annotation is used to indicate the removal of one or more/all values, so that fresh values can be loaded into the cache again:

```
@Transactional
@CacheEvict(value="customers", allEntries=true)
@Override
  public List<CustomerAccount> getAllCustomers() {
    String sql = "SELECT c FROM CustomerAccount c";
    TypedQuery<CustomerAccount> query = em.createQuery(sql,
    CustomerAccount.class);
    return query.getResultList();
  }
```

The parameter allEntries tells the cache manager to empty all records in the cache and prepares the cache for a new set of records.

# Ehcache.xml

All the caches created by Spring Cache are explicitly declared inside the ehcache.xml. Other caches including the Hibernate Cache, are further configured here:

```
<?xml version="1.0"encoding="UTF-8"?>
<ehcache>
  <diskStore path="java.io.tmpdir" />
    <cache name="customers"
```

```
        maxBytesLocalHeap="40M"
        eternal="false"
        timeToIdleSeconds="300"
        overflowToDisk="true"
        maxEntriesLocalDisk="1000"
        diskPersistent="false"
        diskExpiryThreadIntervalSeconds="120"
        memoryStoreEvictionPolicy="LRU"/>
    </ehcache>
```

# Hot deployment using JRebel

JRebel is a tool that instantly adds, changes, and debugs codes and logs these changes automatically without restarting the application server. This tool instantly reloads changes made to a class structure, making a full app redeploy unnecessary. This helps the development of this project since JRebel can be installed in STS Eclipse as a plugin:

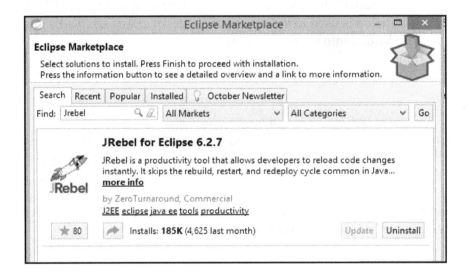

To use JRebel, a license or activation code is needed. Create an account at `https://my.jre bel.com` using your Facebook or Twitter credentials and a free activation code will be given.

Each project must be configured to have `rebel.xml` which is needed for the hot deployment process. JRebel has an administration console where all the needed deployment information is generated per project:

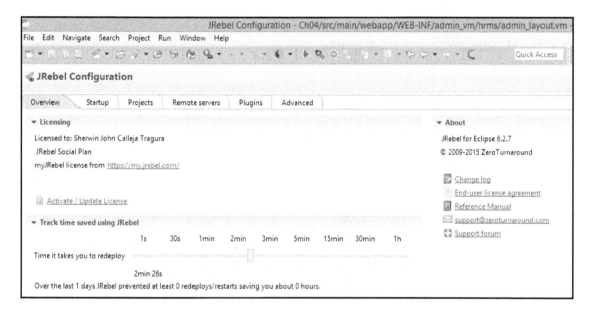

After the configuration, your source codes can now be synchronized to the deployment directory through some commands:

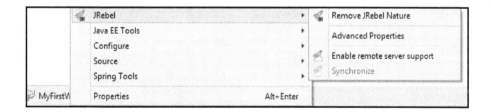

 **Theme design**
The theme of this portal was derived from the templates authored by `http://www.Designscrazed.com/`.

# Online Cart System (OCS)

An application such as OCS will not be complete if it has no authentication and authorization mechanism to protect itself from different web attackers. Spring Security 4.x has been the best solution so far, not only to secure OCS, but also to manage its session-based transactions. To streamline and define the workflow processes, OCS has Activiti BPMN and Spring Web Flow to implement every state and transition of the business flow. Defined and stable workflows can help experts maintain and enhance the processing time of every phase in a flow.

Likewise, Spring Cache can provide applications the most optimal, if not the fastest, way of executing read transactions from the database. With the help of Hibernate's second level caching, Spring Cache can help optimize the number of SQL executions by checking, validating, and returning cache parameters instead of calling the method again.

When it comes to deployment, many existing tools like JRebel can be used to perform hot deployment where any sources codes in the development directories are in sync with the deployed context root. This helps developers from deploying frequently and loading the browser to reflect new updates.

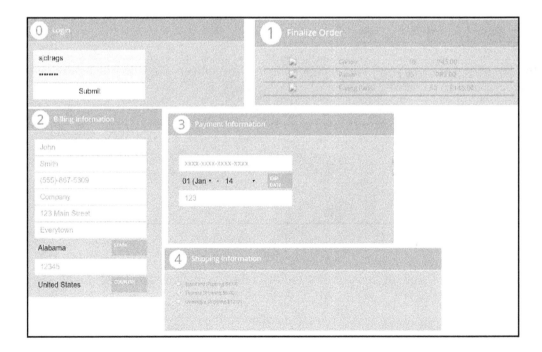

# Challenge yourself

Create a secured workflow based Document Approver Portal with Spring Security 4.x as its security plugin. Use Spring Web Flow 2.4.x to implement the approval processes from one department to another. Choose a company and simulate their business process when it comes to approving memos and memoranda.

# Summary

The use of the Activiti tool, Spring Workflow framework, and portlets saves time in implementing process flows that are needed by so many workflow-based systems. The time spent implementing the flows from the baseline affects the project time, specifically with Spring projects. If the application is so general, then the BPMN 2.0 standard of Activiti can be integrated to Spring 4.x, in order to guide the flow of transactions, without affecting the core features of the system. If the processes are intertwined with the user interfaces, then Spring Webflow 2.4.x would be the best resort. And if the applications provide an independent life cycle per process, with each having its own database and web services, then portlets can be integrated with Spring features. The next chapter will focus on JTA with topics on web services.

# 8
# Enterprise Resource Planning (ERP)

**SOA** or **service-oriented architecture** has been proven popular in creating large-scale systems and integrating legacy systems with new and modern software. The market pushes SOA as one of the most cost-effective ways for building **Enterprise Integration Systems (EIS)** in a heterogeneous computing environment. This will be discussed further in Chapter 10, *Social Task Management System (STMS)*. Interoperability has been the major reason why SOA has been preferred by many businesses in establishing communication between their new and old systems. This capability can help companies save a lot of money in reviving their old systems written in some old languages.

SOA and web services are two different concepts, but web services play a great role in establishing best practices and standards in realizing SOA. This chapter elaborates more on web services and how one can establish ground-up SOA-based applications, clustered or distributed setups, using different solutions provided by the Spring 4.X Framework.

The prototype that will be implemented for this chapter is a customized ERP application for an accounting firm. ERP is business process management software composed of integrated applications or modules that can process and automate operations related to inventory, product planning, deveides interoperability within the Java platform but not outside of ilopment, manufacturing, sales and marketing. To integrate and bridge all these modules together, this chapter has implemented an ERP which has a distributed type of architecture wherein its modules are independent and run applications that communicate together through web services.

This chapter highlights the different web service solutions feasible for integration with the Spring 4.x Framework.

In this chapter, you will learn how to:

- Integrate applications using Spring-WS
- Use JAX-WS and JAX-RS in Spring applications
- Integrate AXIS2, CXF, and XFIRE to expose services and generate clients
- Use Burlap, Hessian, and HttpInvoker remoting techniques to establish interprocess communication among applications
- Establish RMI techniques in invoking processes
- Use JMS and AMQP to implement messaging capability
- Integrate Facebook and Twitter in the application

# Overview of the project

This chapter needs all the essential concepts, installations, and configurations of `Chapter 1`, *Creating a Personal Web Portal*, `Chapter 3`, *Student Management Portal (SMP)*, and Chapter 7, *Online Cart System (OCS)*, to establish a simple but complete ERP solution. The prototype is composed of five modules namely Administration, Sales, Account Receivable, Procurement, and Inventory. The modules are independent sub-applications having their own databases and together they compose the SOA-based ERP in this chapter. Let's explain each of these module applications:

- **Administration module application**: This module manages the users and determines the level of accessibility for the user. It also provides the profile and the authentication information of each user. The following image is the ERP Administration Module:

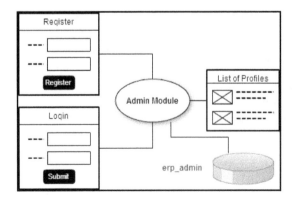

- **Sales module application**: This module highlights the tracking of customers, vendors, and persons by saving information which will be essential in establishing sales leads.
- **Account receivable (AR) module application**: This module helps in tracking all the invoices that are awaiting payment from customers. It also evaluates and manages the payment of each invoice.
- **Procurement module application**: This module highlights the management of the numerous purchase orders in the company and keeps control of purchases either for business process purposes or external projects. The following figures show the different modules:

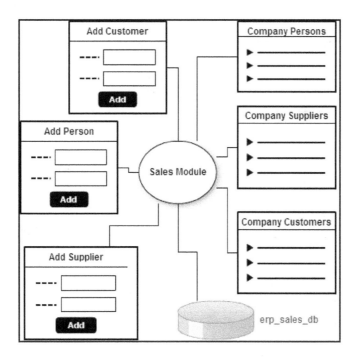

The ERP sales module

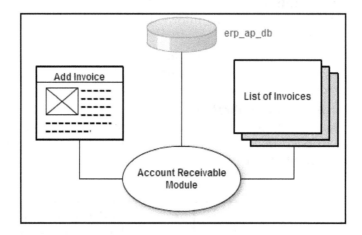

The ERP Account receivable module

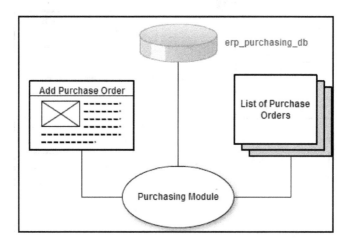

The ERP purchasing module

- **Inventory module application**: This module manages the raw materials inventory in the warehouse or plant, or to your suppliers' warehouses. The following is the ERP Inventory Module:

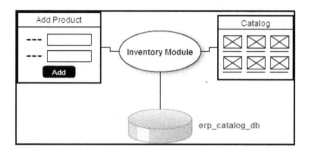

- **The ERP design**: The ERP to be implemented for this chapter runs on top of a customized SOA, where all kinds of web service solutions are used. The objective of the chapter is to produce a comparative analysis among the web service technologies involved in invoking services related to ERP. Each module stores its own specific data in a data center that is shared by the various modules indicated above. All five modules are interconnected using web services to form a unique SOA architecture. The design is depicted in the following diagram:

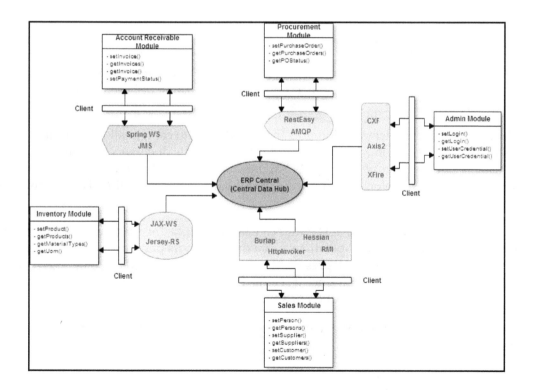

# Technical requirement

The concept of ERP in this chapter examines how web services and remoting can be integrated when the major framework is the current Spring framework. The following are the web services and remote techniques that can still be supported fully by Spring 4.x.

## Spring Web Services

**Spring Web Services** (**Spring-WS**) is a document-driven type of web service solution which is part of the Spring community. Spring-WS is popular when it comes to Contract-First SOAP service development, allowing the generation of WSDL and client objects through XSD files. Since this web service framework is purely Spring in nature, it implements the **Inverse of Control (IoC)** concept on registering its services.

To start implementing Spring-WS, the project POM must contain the following library dependency:

```
org.springframework.ws: spring-ws-core (2.2.4.RELEASE)
```

## JAX-WS integration

JAX-WS is a specification in writing web services that are dependent on XML schemas. There are two popular types of implementation, namely document-based and RPC-based JAX-WS services.

The document-based implementation uses the SOAP body to contain all the parameters. This XML body is written in XML format and is sent as single document information. This style message is loosely coupled and its SOAP messages do not depend on operation names or endpoints for transmission. In some areas of software architecture, this style is known as **message-oriented strategy**.

The RPC-based solution uses the SOAP message body just like the document-based solution but it contains the names of the operations or methods with its parameters instead of an envelope of data. If parameters are present, they are specially defined as valid XSD types. RPC style connotes tight-coupling since it seems the sender's operations are invoked by the recipient in the way methods are called in a typical transaction.

 JAX-RPC is not directly supported by the Spring 4.x Framework.

To use the JAX-WS type of web service solution, copy and paste the following Maven dependency to the POM file:

- `org.jvnet.jax-ws-commons.spring: jaxws-spring` (version 1.9) with some important exclusions
- `com.sun.xml.ws: jaxws-rt` (version 2.2.10)
- `com.sun.xml.bind: jaxb-core` (version 2.2.11)
- `com.sun.xml.bind: jaxb-impl` (version 2.2.11)
- `org.glassfish.ha: ha-api` (version 3.1.9)

All of the mentioned libraries must be compatible with Spring 4.x and must have current versions to avoid lots of conflicts and exceptions.

# JAX-RS integration

RESTful web services are considered resources that can be invoked through **Uniform Resource Identifiers** (**URI**). Developing web applications is easier with RESTful services because all the intricacies and complexities of the software constraints can be taken into consideration by every service. RESTful web service solutions induce loose coupling, scalability, and simplicity.

Results and parameters are easy to deal with because of their flexibility when it comes to MIME-types. REST services are typically used for XML data exchange or **JavaScript Object Notation** (**JSON**) data exchange.

Spring and JAX-RS integration can be implemented using these two popular solutions: Jersey RS and RestEasy RS.

# Jersey RS

Jersey is the reference implementation for the JSR 311 specification, JAX-RS (the Java API for RESTful web services). It provides a set of classes and interfaces to implement RESTful web services in a Java servlet container.

To start with the Jersey RS implementation, POM must have the following libraries:

- `com.sun.jersey.contribs: jersey-spring` (version 1.19) with some important exclusions
- `com.sun.jersey: jersey-servlet` (version 1.19)
- `org.glassfish.jersey.core: jersey-client` (version 2.22.1)

All of the libraries above must be compatible with Spring 4.x and must have current versions to avoid lots of conflicts and exceptions.

# RestEasy RS

RestEasy is a portable and fully certified implementation of JAX-RS which can provide easier RESTful web service implementations. It is part of the JBoss project but can run in any servlet container. It manages a client framework that leverages lots of JAX-RS annotations to make client generation easier. Moreover, RestEasy has a set of providers for XML, JSON, YAML, Multipart, XOP, Atom, and many others. It has an optimized JAXB marshalling into XML, JSON, Jackson, and Atom as well as wrappers for maps, arrays, lists, and sets of JAXB objects.

RestEasy can be used through the following Maven dependencies:

- `org.jboss.resteasy: resteasy-jaxrs (version 3.0.13.Final)`
- `org.jboss.resteasy: resteasy-jaxb-provider (version 3.0.13.Final)`
- `org.jboss.resteasy: jaxrs-api (version 3.0.12.Final)`
- `org.jboss.resteasy: resteasy-spring (version 3.0.13.Final)` with some important exclusions
- `com.fasterxml.jackson.core: jackson-databind (version 2.6.3)`
- `com.fasterxml.jackson.core: jackson-core (versin 2.6.3)`
- `org.jboss.resteasy: resteasy-jackson2-provider (version 3.0.13.Final)`
- `javax.inject: javax.inject (version 1)`

All of the libraries mentioned here must be compatible with Spring 4.x and must have current versions to avoid lots of conflicts and exceptions. Likewise, some of the libraries might be in conflict with the dependencies of JAX-WS, Spring-WS, CXF, and Jersey.

# CXF integration

Apache CXF is a free-licensed web service that supports APIs for JAX-WS and JAX-RS specification. CXF libraries always encounter problems once they are used in collaboration with other web service APIs.

To use CXF, our Maven project must have the following dependencies:

- org.apache.cxf: cxf-rt-frontend-jaxws (version3.1.4)
- org.apache.cxf: cxf-rt-transports-http (version 3.1.4)
- org.apache.cxf: cxf-rt-bindings-soap (version 3.1.4)
- org.apache.cxf: cxf-rt-rs-extension-providers (version 3.1.4)
- org.codehaus.jackson: jackson-jaxrs (version 1.9.13)

All of the mentioned libraries must be compatible with Spring 4.x and must have current versions to avoid lots of conflicts and exceptions. Likewise, some of the libraries might be in conflict with the dependencies of JAX-WS, Spring-WS, CXF, and Jersey.

For more technical documentation on CXF, visit the site: https://cxf.apache.org/.

# Axis2 integration

Apache Axis2 is a SOAP-based web service engine that provides interoperability among applications using interfaces. Axis2 can be published through using a bean-managed Spring container or standalone Axis2 server.

To use the Axis2 platform, the following Maven dependencies are enough to expose some of our services:

- org.apache.axis2: axis2-kernel (version 1.6.3)
- org.apache.axis2: axis2-transport-local (version 1.6.3)
- org.apache.axis2: axis2-transport-http (version 1.6.3)
- org.apache.axis2: axis2-spring (version1.6.3)
- org.apache.axis2: axis2-adb (version 1.6.3)

All of the mentioned libraries must be compatible with Spring 4.x and must have current versions to avoid lots of conflicts and exceptions. Likewise, some of the libraries might be in conflict with the dependencies of JAX-WS, Spring-WS, CXF, and Jersey.

To read more about the features, capabilities, and technical documentation of Axis2, visit: http://axis.apache.org/axis2/java/core/.

# XFire integration

XFire is an open source SOAP-based framework that exposes services using simple and straightforward techniques. Despite its simplicity, XFire provides many advanced features identified in web service specifications that can only be done by its core architecture. For any application, XFire generates web services without adding a single line of extra Java code.

To experience XFire, our application must have the following libraries:

- `org.codehaus.xfire: xfire-core (version 1.2.6)`
- `org.codehaus.xfire: xfire-spring (version 1.2.6)`

# HttpInvoker remoting

Spring HttpInvoker is a Java-to-Java remoting solution that uses a serialization mechanism in exposing services through HTTP and can be thought of as an alternative solution to **Remote Method Invocation** or **RMI**.

Spring supports the HTTP invoker mechanism through its `HttpInvokerProxyFactoryBean` and `HttpInvokerServiceExporter` APIs. The `HttpInvokerServiceExporter` is the API that exports the service beans as HTTP invoker service endpoints, accessible through an HTTP invoker proxy, while `HttpInvokerProxyFactoryBean` is a factory bean for HTTP invoker proxies.

HttpInvoker is popular because of its outstanding performance across firewalls but only with JEE applications.

# Burlap and Hessian remoting

Burlap is an XML-based protocol for web services hosted over HTTP and developed by Caucho. It has `BurlapServiceExporter` that exposes services through a HTTP request handler and `BurlapProxyFactoryBean` that serves as factory beans for clients.

> Although this technology is part of this chapter, Burlap support is inactive and deprecated since Spring 4.0.

On the other hand, Hessian is a binary-based protocol for implementing web services. Its main API, namely `HessianServiceExporter`, exports a service as a servlet-based HTTP request handler. Its `HessianProxyFactoryBean` serves as the factory bean for client applications.

Hessian and Burlap expose services as a Spring bean but they are portable so they can be integrated with other languages such as .NET and PHP.

To use these remoting techniques, include the following dependency in our Maven configuration:

```
com.caucho: hessian (version 4.0.38)
```

# Remote Method Invocation

The JAX-RPC technique of exposing services was directly supported by the previous Spring 2.x through J2EE 1.4 specification. Although RPC-style web services can still be generated through the JAX-WS technique, the current Spring 4.x supports RMI which is considered the Java-based **Remote Procedure Call** (**RPC**). RMI has `RmiServiceExporter` which exports any Spring-managed bean as an RMI service and registers it. It also has `RmiProxyFactoryBean` which is a factory bean used in creating a proxy for an RMI service. This proxy object talks with remote RMI services on behalf of the client.

Through these classes, Spring supports both traditional RMI (that is, `java.rmi.Remote` interfaces and `java.rmi.RemoteException`) and transparent remoting via RMI invokers (any Java interface).

RMI uses the JRMP protocol and not HTTP therefore there might be some firewall issues encountered during client-server communication. Both the callers and the service methods must be running on their respective JVM.

# JMS

**Java Message Service** (**JMS**) is used in generating message production (sending) and message consumption (receiving). Spring has a main class, `JmsTemplate`, which is used for sending and receiving JMS messages synchronously. It requires a reference to `ConnectionFactory` which connects client applications to the JMS provider and contains various configuration parameters, both application-specific and vendor-specific entries.

JMS provides interoperability within the Java platform but not outside of it. Spring application messaging to Ruby or .NET applications is not appropriate for JMS.

This project will use **Apache ActiveMQ** as our JMS provider which will create message queues.

To make use of JMS core packages in Spring, the following dependencies are needed:

`org.springframework: spring-jms (version 4.2.3.RELEASE)`

And to utilize ActiveMQ as the sole message broker, add the following dependency:

`org.apache.activemq: activemq-core (version 5.7.0)` with some required exclusions

# Advanced Message Queuing Protocol

The **Advanced Message Queuing Protocol (AMQP)** is a communication protocol for interoperability between clients and brokers. It is a message protocol that deals with publishers and consumers across different platforms. If JMS can bridge Java-based applications, AMQP can establish interoperability among applications written in different languages with stable AMQP support.

Just like RabbitMQ, AMQP requires a message broker in order for applications to communicate with each other. The architecture requires publishers to generate the messages which can be picked up by the consumers for their own processing. At the middle of this application lies this message broker that ensures that the messages from a publisher go to the right consumers. This broker uses two key components, namely the exchanges and queues which must be configured in the ERP's container.

JMS and AMQP are both used for messaging but the two differ because the former is an API and the latter is a protocol.

Since this chapter will be highlighting RabbitMQ as one of the message brokers, we will need the following dependency for Spring integration:

`org.springframework.amqp: spring-rabbit (version 1.1.1.RELEASE)`

And the following libraries are needed for Spring 4.x to use AMQP for the messaging implementation:

`org.springframework.amqp: spring-amqp (version 1.1.4.RELEASE)`

# ActiveMQ

ActiveMQ is an open source message broker written in Java with a full JMS client that fully supports JMS 1.1. It allows an enterprise setup which permits more than one server and client to communicate as one. It is widely known as one of the most powerful open source messaging and integration patterns servers used in building SOA architecture.

ActiveMQ serves as a JMS persistence provider in communications which allows computer clustering and database integration. It also provides support to virtual memory, cache, and journal persistency. Download ActiveMQ from the following site `http://activemq.apac he.org/`.

# RabbitMQ

RabbitMQ is an open source message broker just like ActiveMQ but it implements AMQP. The literature sometimes describes it as message-oriented, lightweight, reliable, scalable, and portable for messaging. The RabbitMQ server is written in the Erlang programming language and is built on the Open Telecom Platform framework for clustering and failover. Client libraries to interface with the broker are available for all major programming languages.

RabbitMQ is a lightweight, reliable, scalable, and portable message broker which uses a platform-neutral, wire-level protocol called AMQP. It is not a JMS-based broker. Download the tool from the following site `http://www.rabbitmq.com/`.

# Spring Social

Spring Social is a Spring 4.x Framework module which allows applications to connect to a number of social media applications, such as Facebook, Twitter, and LinkedIn for validation, confirmation, or for security purposes. This module uses the **Software-as-a-Service (SaaS)** model for providing web services to clients.

# SoapUI

There are lots of testing tools available to test the effectiveness and correctness of web services. One of the best tools used in this chapter is SoapUI which is an open-source tool used to study performance, test using pre-conditions and post-condition variables, simulate, mock, and perform functional tests on services as well as check the compliance based on the output.

# The ERP databases

Since this project consists of five applications, the following are some of the schema designs of data sources used by the applications:

- The `erp_admin` database:

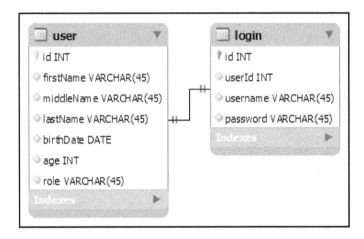

- The `erp_sales` database:

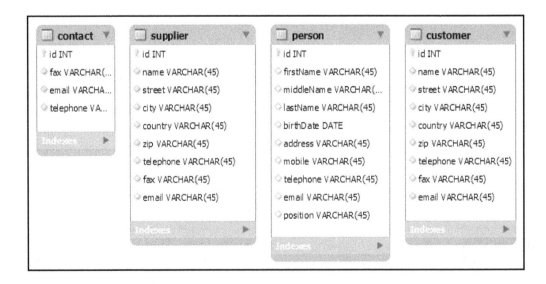

# Data modeling framework

All of the data sources are declared as JNDI resources at the Tomcat level. They are declared as Bitronix data sources managed by BitronixTransactionManager. At the Spring context level, all data access is wrapped by JPA using the Hibernate 4.x Framework. BitronixTransactionManager is auto fetched and injected by Spring as its JTA manager to manage all JPA services for any of the data sources. The following figure shows the JTA and JPA setup with multiple data sources:

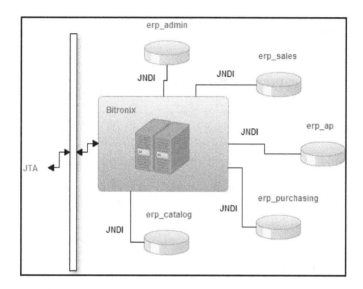

# Multiple JNDI data sources

The `persistence.xml` file contains five persistence units wherein each is configured to fetch its XA-based data source through the JTA transaction manager. Each persistence unit must know that they are all JNDI data sources managed by the Bitronix transaction manager.

Each persistence unit is mapped to their respective EntityManagerFactory, JPA vendor adapter, and JNDI mappings. For more details on JTA-managed data sources, Chapter 7, *Online Cart System (OCS)*, has all the codes and details.

# The concept of web services

The ERP prototype showcased in this chapter provides a profound and detailed pedagogy on how to set up web services given a Spring 4.x platform. The conceptual model is to create an ERP wherein all modules are scattered into different islands of networks or distributed around the network as independent real-time applications that share their results given a set of inputs.

All these applications are designed to communicate with each other through a collection of services. The communication can involve either simple data passing or it could involve two or more services coordinating on some activity.

# Consumer-producer relationship

All five modules are purely client modules meaning there are no repository (DAO) or service layers in each of the applications. The data and service layers are found in a central repository module which is responsible for the generation of web services. The service layer is exposed as a set of web services depending on the technology used.

Each technology has its own way of implementing web services and the client that will consume them. Here are the technologies that are used in this chapter to implement the customized ground-up SOA-based ERP.

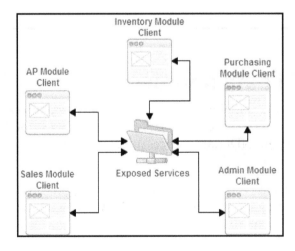

# The Spring REST architecture

Since version 3.0, Spring framework's DispatcherServlet has built-in support for RESTful web service implementation. This feature is still part of the current Spring MVC architecture since it still allows the REST web service implementation using annotations @Controller and @ResponseBody. The annotation @ResponseBody converts the result into JSON or XML depending on the type of data object.

But the Spring 4.x Framework has a new API feature called @RestController which combines both @Controller and @ResponseBody capabilities with improved annotation semantics. The following is a sample @RestController that implements REST services that outputs XML and JSON data:

```
@RestController
public class PaymentAppController {
    @Autowired
    private PaymentApService paymentApService;

    @RequestMapping(value="/erp/paymentmodes.json")
    public List<PaymentAp> showPaymentApJson(){
        return paymentApService.getAllPaymentModes();
    }
    @RequestMapping(value="/erp/paymentmodes.xml")
    public ListPaymentAp showPaymentApXml(){
        ListPaymentAp listPayment = new ListPaymentAp();
        listPayment.setListPaymentAp(paymentApService
            .getAllPaymentModes());
        return listPayment;
    } }
```

The following technologies help to implement web services and remote services.

# The Spring-WS Framework

The Spring-WS Framework is part of the Spring core that focuses on document-driven web service generation using the Contract-First strategy.

## Contract-First versus Contract-Last strategies

Contract-First starts with designing the XSD documents, then, WSDL generation, and lastly, creating the Java interface based upon the schema created. On the other hand, Contract-Last starts first with a set of implemented Java interfaces, then, XSD documents, and lastly the WSDL. On reflection, you'd think that this meant it would create a schema contract, but generally it seems to mean getting hold of some tool that will take a Java interface as an input and deliver a WSDL as an output. Contract-First has been most often the preferred choice due to problems encountered when using Contract-Last:

- Most of the time there are difficulties generating XSDs from objects due to some type mismatch which causes data integrity issues
- Developers can hardly predict what data to expect during data exchange
- It is difficult, even impossible, to reuse generated XSDs because the schema is heavily dependent on the objects
- Since WSDL is dependent on codes rather than XSD files, it makes Contract-Last difficult to use for loosely-coupled implementation

# Web service generation

The account receivable module application accesses the data store from the central data store through Spring-WS. To start, we need to consider our JPA data or entity model as our basis for the first set of our XSD documents. Manually or Eclipse-generated, these XSD file contain all the schema definitions of our JPA entity models and the file must have this format:

```xml
<?xml version="1.0" encoding="UTF-8" standalone="yes"?>
<xs:schema version="1.0" xmlns:xs="http://www.w3.org/2001/XMLSchema"
xmlns="http://invprod.packt.erp.modules.org"
targetNamespace="http://invprod.packt.erp.modules.org"
elementFormDefault="qualified"
attributeFormDefault="unqualified">
   <!-Invoice Entity Model-->
  <xs:complexType name="Invoice">
    <xs:sequence>
      <xs:element name="catId" type="xs:string" minOccurs="0"/>
      // See the sources
      <xs:element name="invoicedProducts"
                    type="InvoicedProducts" minOccurs="0"/>
      <xs:element name="paymentAp"
                    type="PaymentAp" minOccurs="0"/>
    </xs:sequence>
  </xs:complexType>
  <xs:complexType name="InvoicedProducts">
    <xs:sequence>
      // See the sources
    </xs:sequence>
  </xs:complexType>
  <xs:complexType name="PaymentAp">
    <xs:sequence>
```

```
        // See the sources
      </xs:sequence>
   </xs:complexType>
</xs:schema>
```

The entity relationship among data models is considered important in creating the schema definitions to avoid a JAXB parsing problem. The targetNamespace is also an important key in mapping all these schema definitions for the request and response transactions. Next, the following XSD files contain our service request and response needed in the WSDL generation. A sample XSD file looks like this:

```
<?xml version="1.0" encoding="UTF-8" standalone="yes"?>
<xs:schema version="1.0"
xmlns="http://invprod.packt.erp.modules.org/getInvoicedProduct"
xmlns:xs="http://www.w3.org/2001/XMLSchema"
xmlns:invprod="http://invprod.packt.erp.modules.org"
targetNamespace=
   "http://invprod.packt.erp.modules.org/getInvoicedProduct"
   elementFormDefault="qualified">
<xs:import namespace="http://invprod.packt.erp.modules.org"
           schemaLocation="ARDetails.xsd" />
      <xs:element name="InvoiceProductRequest">
          <xs:complexType>
              <xs:sequence>
                  <xs:element name="invoiceId" type="xs:int"/>
              </xs:sequence>
          </xs:complexType>
      </xs:element>
      <xs:element name="InvoiceProductResponse">
          <xs:complexType>
              <xs:sequence>
                  <xs:element name="invoicedProduct"
                    type="invprod:InvoicedProducts"/>
              </xs:sequence>
          </xs:complexType>
      </xs:element>
</xs:schema>
```

In order for the document to be valid, we need to export all the schema definitions from the previous step. The tag `<xs:import>` retrieves and maps all XML entities to the request and response using a valid prefix. Since this file implements the service layer, a valid URI must be mapped to the service which is a requirement for the next step. After creating all the previous XSD files, the object can now be generated from them through the JAXB plugin. Spring has an **Object XML Mapper** (**OXM**) plugin that assists with the mapping between Java objects and XML documents. The module can be integrated with Castor, JAXB, XmlBeans, and XStream support libraries which must also be in our Maven repository.

Objects that were derived from the XSDs above were `ObjectFactory`, `Invoice`, `InvoicedProducts`, `PaymentAp`, `InvoiceProductRequest`, and `InvoiceProductResponse`.

A sample generated blueprint of `InvoiceProductRequest` is shown here:

```
@XmlAccessorType(XmlAccessType.FIELD)
@XmlType(name = "", propOrder = {    "invoiceId" })
@XmlRootElement(name = "InvoiceProductRequest", namespace =
"http://invprod.packt.erp.modules.org/getInvoicedProduct")
public class InvoiceProductRequest {
    @XmlElement(namespace =
        "http://invprod.packt.erp.modules.org/getInvoicedProduct")
    protected int invoiceId;
    public int getInvoiceId() {
        return invoiceId;        }
    public void setInvoiceId(int value) {
        this.invoiceId = value;      }
}
```

Maven has a plugin called `org.jvnet.jaxb2.maven2: maven-jaxb2-plugin` which helps auto generate all the JAXB objects from XSD files. This must be configured in the POM configuration file.

The next step will be the creation of service interfaces and implementation using the JAXB objects created. See the following sample interface code:

```
public interface AccountReceivableService {
    public InvoicedProducts getInvProduct(Integer id);
    public List<InvoicedProducts> getInvProducts();
    public void setInvoicedProduct(InvoicedProducts
            invoicedProduct); }
```

This will have the following implementation:

```
@Service
@Transactional
public class AccountReceivableServiceImpl implements
                AccountReceivableService {
    @Autowired
    AccountReceivableDao accountReceivableDao;

    @Override
    public InvoicedProducts getInvProduct(Integer id) {
            InvoicedProducts invProdWS = new InvoicedProducts();
            Invoice invWS = new Invoice();
            PaymentAp paymentWS = new PaymentAp();
```

```
        invProdWS.setId(accountReceivableDao
            .getInvoicedProduct(id).getId());
        // See the sources
        return invProdWS;           }

    @Override
    public List<InvoicedProducts> getInvProducts() {
        List<InvoicedProducts> lists = new ArrayList<>();
        return lists;       }
    @Override
    public void setInvoicedProduct(InvoicedProducts
            invoicedProduct) {
        // See the sources         }   }
```

Here, Invoice, InvoicedProducts, and PaymentAp are now the generated objects and are *not* from the domain models.

Afterwards, service endpoints must be created to manage the request and response transactions of the previously created services. A service endpoint is the component that deals with processing of web service requests and responses. The Spring servlet intercepts incoming SOAP requests for a defined URL and routes them to an endpoint for processing. An equivalent endpoint for InvoiceProductRequest and InvoiceProductResponse is shown here:

```
@Endpoint
public class AccountReceivableServiceEndpoint {

    private static final String TARGET_NAMESPACE =
      "http://invprod.packt.erp.modules.org/getInvoicedProduct";
    @Autowired
    private AccountReceivableService accountReceivableService;
    @PayloadRoot(localPart = "InvoiceProductRequest",
                namespace = TARGET_NAMESPACE)
    public @ResponsePayload InvoiceProductResponse
        getAccountDetails(
                @RequestPayload InvoiceProductRequest request) {
          InvoiceProductResponse response =
                  new InvoiceProductResponse();
          InvoicedProducts account = accountReceivableService
                  .getInvProduct(request.getInvoiceId());
          response.setInvoicedProduct(account);
          return response;   }
    public void setAccountReceivableService(
          AccountReceivableService accountReceivableService) {
          this.accountReceivableService =
                        accountReceivableService;    }
  }
```

To scrutinize the code, @Endpoint is a specialized annotation of the standard @Component annotation which allows a class to get fetched and registered by the container's component scanning. The TARGET_NAMESPACE is the same URI declared inside the XSD files for the request and response. The @PayloadRoot indicates that the method will intend to process service requests found in the XSD files having the XML root element indicated by the localPart attribute. Finally, the @ResponsePayload annotation indicates the type of the returned value of our SOAP response which can be XML or JSON.

After coding the endpoint, the module is now ready to generate the WSDL. Spring-WS can use the org.springframework.ws.wsdl.wsdl11.DefaultWsdl11Definition object to enable generation of WSDL. Spring uses the schema definitions listed in the schemaCollection property of this API class such as the portType, serviceName, and locationUri to generate a WSDL once requested. Since the generation of WSDL is almost real-time which might affect the performance of the software, the generated WSDL can be stored in a file and can be statically exposed using Spring's <sws:static-wsdl> support. Using the Spring-WS namespace xmlns:sws=http://www.springframework.org/schema/web-services, the following is our Spring 4.x configuration of our InvoicedProducts object's WSDL generation:

```
<sws:annotation-driven />
<bean id="GetInvoicedProductService"
class="org.springframework.ws.wsdl.wsdl11
        .DefaultWsdl11Definition" lazy-init="true">
    <property name="schemaCollection">
      <bean class="org.springframework.xml
          .xsd.commons.CommonsXsdSchemaCollection">
        <property name="inline" value="true" />
        <property name="xsds">
          <list>
            <value>schema/GetInvoicedProduct.xsd</value>
          </list>
        </property>
      </bean>
    </property>
    <property name="portTypeName"
                value="GetInvoicedProductService"/>
    <property name="serviceName"
                value="GetInvoicedProductServices" />
    <property name="locationUri" value="/endpoints"/>
</bean>
```

Lastly, everything would not work well without the Spring servlet that intercepts incoming HTTP requests, namely the
`org.springframework.ws.transport.http.MessageDispatcherServlet`. This class ensures WSDL is context aware and transforms the SOAP address without encoding it. It also auto updates the address when there are changes in the WSDL configuration:

```
<servlet>
     <servlet-name>springws</servlet-name>
     <servlet-class>org.springframework.ws.transport.http
                  .MessageDispatcherServlet</servlet-class>
       <init-param>
              <param-name>transformWsdlLocations</param-name>
              <param-value>true</param-value>
         </init-param>
         <init-param>
              <param-name>contextConfigLocation</param-name>
              <param-value></param-value>
         </init-param>
         <load-on-startup>1</load-on-startup>
     </servlet>
     <servlet-mapping>
         <servlet-name>springws</servlet-name>
         <url-pattern>*.wsdl</url-pattern>
     </servlet-mapping>
     <servlet-mapping>
         <servlet-name>springws</servlet-name>
         <url-pattern>/endpoints/*</url-pattern>
     </servlet-mapping>
```

# Client code generation

To insert and retrieve Account invoices, the AR client module will also access the central data source through Spring-WS. First, it needs to have all the XSD files to generate the same JAXB components because these objects are the ones found in the service implementations. Most importantly, the Spring container of the client must have
`org.springframework.ws.client.core.WebServiceTemplate` which facilitates the access of the web service. This class contains methods for sending and receiving messages and it also uses converters to marshal and unmarshal objects. The Spring container needs assistance from Spring OXM to successfully implement JAXB operations:

```
<oxm:jaxb2-marshaller id="marshaller"
        context-path="org.packt.erp.modules.ws" />
<bean id="webServiceTemplate"
    class="org.springframework.ws.client.core.WebServiceTemplate">
      <property name="marshaller" ref="marshaller" />
```

```
<property name="unmarshaller" ref="marshaller" />
<property name="defaultUri"
    value="http://localhost:8080/ch08/endpoints/
                GetInvoicedProductServiceSoap11" />
</bean>
```

The following is a working invoice form that inputs invoices through Spring-WS web services:

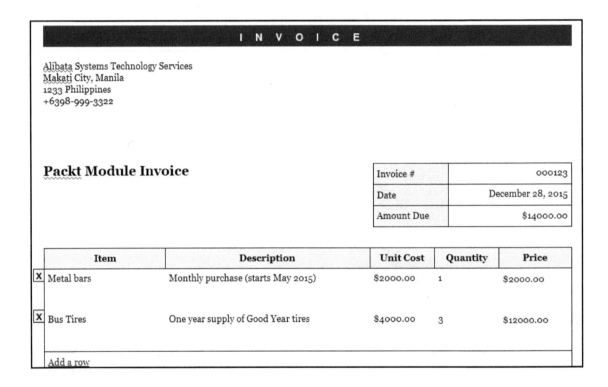

# JAX-WS

The Inventory module of our ERP is designed to access and store data from the central data source through JAX-WS, using both the document-based and RPC-based web services style. Despite all of the disadvantages, the ERP project created the web services for the Inventory module using the Contract-Last strategy, since all the DAO models are already present for mapping to the service layer.

# Web service generation (document-based)

JAX-WS development using the Contract-Last approach starts with creating service interfaces and implementation for the service layer. Part of the inventory form is the list of suppliers which will be coming from another data source, the erp_sales database. To access the list of supplier names, we created a service interface:

```
@WebService
public interface SalesInventoryService {
    public List<Supplier> getAllSuppliers();
    public Contact getContactInfo(Integer id);  }
```

The annotation @WebService is required in an interface that will be implemented as a web service. This annotation on interfaces can have the following attributes:

- name: This attribute specifies the name of the web service which by default is the name of the Java class or interface; during the communication, this attribute is mapped to wsdl:portType
- targetNamespace: This one specifies an XML namespace that represents each service method inside the document which typically is derived from the package containing the web service

To add more attributes, @SoapBinding annotation is attached to specify three attributes for the web service, namely:

- style: This attribute defines the binding type which can be a document or RPC.
- use: This attribute indicates how the data of the SOAP message is mapped, streamed, or validated against the WSDL; LITERAL means that the SOAP body follows an XML schema included already in the WSDL document. If there are some additional XSD rules to be attached to the binding, then ENCODED is more appropriate.
- parameterStyle: This attribute specifies whether all the method parameters will be placed into the message body as a child element of the message root (BARE) or will be wrapped separately into the request and response message body (WRAPPED).

The BARE parameter style is not allowed with RPC style web services.

By default, @WebService is a document style, LITERAL in mapping, and WRAPPED when it comes to the parameter style.

Then, the implementation class will look like this:

```
@WebService
public class SalesInventoryServiceImpl implements SalesInventoryService{
    @Autowired
    SalesInventoryDao salesDao;
    @WebMethod(operationName="getAllSuppliers")
    @Override
    public List<Supplier> getAllSuppliers() {
          return salesDao.getSuppliers();      }

    @WebMethod(operationName="getContactInfo")
    @Override
    public Contact getContactInfo(Integer id) {
          return salesDao.getContact(id);      }
}
```

The @WebService here can optionally have the attributes name and targetNamespace, just like its interface, but it can have three more additional attributes valid only to implementation classes:

- serviceName: This attribute specifies the name of the web service mapped to the wsdl:service of the WSDL; its default value is the name of the Java service class concatenated to the word "Service"
- wsdlLocation: This specifies the location of a pre-defined WSDL; there is no default value if it is not specified which may lead to an incomplete WSDL
- endpointInterface: This specifies the complete name of the service endpoint interface defining the service's interface; there is no default value if it is not specified which will lead to an incomplete WSDL
- portName: This attribute specifies the port name of the web service mapped to wsdl:port of the WSDL; the default value is the @WebService.name attribute value concatenated to the word "Port"

By default, the @WebMethod annotation in the implementation class states that the method will be published as part of the WSDL, otherwise we invoke its attribute exclude=true. The annotations have an attribute operationName="getContactInfo" which explicitly declares the name of the method on the web service. If we omit this attribute, the method of the web service will be named after the method of the class. The service method can optionally use two more annotations, namely @WebResult and @WebParam. The @WebParam annotation customizes the mapping of an individual parameter to a web service message in the WSDL whereas the `@WebResult` annotation is used to map the result of the service to an existing `<wsdl:output>` or to a customized element generated internally.

Now that the web service methods are implemented, we are going to map a JAX-WS URI `/sales-inventory-dao` URL (or any valid servlet URL pattern) to our `SalesInventoryServiceImpl` endpoint. All the require services and data models must also be wired to a separate `ApplicationContext` container. Using the JAX-WS namespace `xmlns:wss=http://jax-ws.dev.java.net/spring/servlet`, here is a complete Spring configuration:

```
<wss:binding url="/sales-inventory-dao">
        <wss:service>
                <ws:service bean="#salesInventoryServiceWS" />
        </wss:service>
    </wss:binding>
    <bean id="salesInventoryServiceWS"
        class="org.packt.erp.modules.service
                    .impl.SalesInventoryServiceImpl"/>
```

Lastly, everything will not be working without the configuration of the `com.sun.xml.ws.transport.http.servlet.WSSpringServlet` which initializes and configures the web service endpoint using `/sales-inventory-dao`. `WSSpringServlet` serves as the service requests using the implementation class. Configure also the `com.sun.xml.ws.transport.http.servlet.WSServletContextListener` class that provides more flexibility in terms of how an application is wired together inside the context container. This listener determines what object to instantiate and inject into the application loaded in the Spring container:

```
<listener>
    <listener-class>
        com.sun.xml.ws.transport.http.servlet
            .WSServletContextListener
    </listener-class>
</listener>
<servlet>
    <servlet-name>jaxws-servlet</servlet-name>
    <servlet-class> com.sun.xml.ws.transport.http.servlet
                WSSpringServlet</servlet-class>
 </servlet>
 <servlet-mapping>
    <servlet-name>jaxws-servlet</servlet-name>
    <url-pattern>/sales-inventory-dao</url-pattern>
 </servlet-mapping>
```

# Client code generation (document-based)

Spring 4.x provides a web service proxy called `JaxWsPortProxyFactoryBean`, a proxy that implements our business service interface. In the following code we have a proxy for `salesInventoryServiceWS`:

```
<bean id="salesDaoClientFactory"
    class="org.springframework.remoting
        .jaxws.JaxWsPortProxyFactoryBean">
        <property name="serviceInterface"
            value="org.packt.erp.modules.service.impl
                .SalesInventoryServiceImpl" />
        <property name="wsdlDocumentUrl"
                value="http://localhost:8080/ch08/
                    sales-inventory-dao?wsdl" />
        <property name="namespaceUri"
          value="http://impl.service.modules.erp.packt.org/" />
        <property name="serviceName"
          value="SalesInventoryServiceImplService" />
        <property name="endpointAddress"
          value="http://localhost:8080/ch08/sales-inventory-dao" />
</bean>
```

Here, `serviceInterface` is the business interface that the clients will access; `wsdlDocumentUrl` is the location of the WSDL; `namespaceUri` corresponds to the `targetNamespace` either indicated in the service endpoint or in the WSDL file; `serviceName` corresponds to the service name found in the WSDL, and `portName` corresponds to the port name.

After the configuration, the library `wsimport` is used to extract JAXB objects from the valid WSDL in order for the client to utilize the web services. The `wsimport` library can be executed at the terminal or through Maven:

```
Command Prompt                                        _ □ ✕

Microsoft Windows [Version 6.3.9600]
(c) 2013 Microsoft Corporation. All rights reserved.

C:\Users\sjctrags>cd..

C:\Users>cd..

C:\>cd jaxws

C:\jaxws>wsimport -keep http://localhost:8080/ch08/sales-inventory-dao?wsdl_
```

# Web service generation (RPC based)

Creating RPC-based web services using JAX-WS is similar to document-based services but with some added processes. Since Spring no longer directly supports RPC, there will be some slight adjustments to the data types returned or passed by the service endpoint.

We start with creating the interface and its implementation. Both must have the RPC web service style, `LITERAL` when it comes to mapping and `WRAPPED` when it comes to parameter style:

```
@WebService(name = "InventoryService")
@SOAPBinding( style = SOAPBinding.Style.RPC, use = SOAPBinding.Use.LITERAL,
parameterStyle = ParameterStyle.WRAPPED)
public interface InventoryService {
    @WebMethod(operationName="getProducts")
    public Catalog[] getProducts();
    @WebMethod(operationName="getProduct")
    public Catalog getProduct(Integer id);
    // See the sources
}
```

At the implementation level, the service methods must directly use `@RequestWrapper` and `@ResponseWrapper` since we will be exposing the service as a direct resource rather than an XML. Both annotations must indicate the `partName` attribute and their respective `targetNamespaces` just like the sample shown here:

```
@WebService(name = "InventoryServiceImpl",
targetNamespace="http://impl.service.modules.erp.packt.org/")
@SOAPBinding( style = SOAPBinding.Style.RPC, use = SOAPBinding.Use.LITERAL,
parameterStyle = ParameterStyle.WRAPPED)
public class InventoryServiceImpl implements InventoryService {
    @Autowired
    InventoryDao inventoryDao;
    @Autowired
    InvoiceAddProduct invoiceAddProductService;

    @WebResult(name="result", partName="result")
    @RequestWrapper(partName="getProducts",
        targetNamespace="http://impl.service.modules
                    .erp.packt.org/GetProductsRequest")
    @ResponseWrapper(partName="getProducts",
        targetNamespace="http://impl.service.modules
                    .erp.packt.org/GetProductsResponse")
    @WebMethod(operationName="getProducts")
    @Override
    public Catalog[] getProducts() {
        List<Catalog> cats = inventoryDao.getProducts();
```

```
        Catalog[] catArray =new Catalog[cats.size()];
        for(int i =0; i < catArray.length; i++){
            catArray[i] = cats.get(i);     }
        return catArray;   }

    @WebResult(name="result", partName="result")
    @RequestWrapper(partName="getProduct",
            targetNamespace="http://impl.service.modules
                .erp.packt.org/GetProductRequest")
    @ResponseWrapper(partName="getProduct",
            targetNamespace="http://impl.service.modules
                .erp.packt.org/GetProductResponse")
    @WebMethod(operationName="getProduct")
    @Override
    public Catalog getProduct(Integer id) {
        Catalog cat = inventoryDao.getProduct(id);
        return cat; }
```

JAX-RPC is selective when it comes to mapping service data types to the WSDL files. RPC only maps and supports the following primitive data: byte, double, float, int, long, and short. For the Java API classes, it recognizes only Boolean, Byte, Double, Float, Integer, Long, Short, String, BigDecimal, BigInteger, URI, Calendar, and Date. It also supports simple and multi-dimensional arrays.

 RPC does not support the Collection framework.

If you look at the previous implementation, all methods store all records of data in an array of objects for transport. For a custom domain object, RPC will only recognize it if it is a valid JAXB element where its exposed instance variables have RPC-supported types. Any data that is not supported or included in the JAXB mapping must be tagged @XmlTransient to avoid a JAXB problem which will give you the following SOAP exception:

```
nested exception is com.sun.xml.ws.streaming.XMLStreamReaderException: XML
reader error: com.ctc.wstx.exc.WstxEOFException: Unexpected EOF; was
expecting a close tag for element <S:Body>
```

A sample domain object and, at the same time, valid JAXB element is shown here with the required annotations:

```
@Entity
@XmlRootElement
@XmlAccessorType(XmlAccessType.FIELD)
@Table(name = "uom", catalog = "erp_catalog")
```

```
public class Uom implements java.io.Serializable {
    private Integer id;
    private String unit;
        @XmlTransient
    private Set<Catalog> catalogs = new HashSet<Catalog>(0);
        // See the sources }
```

From this point onwards, the rest of the configuration is similar to what we did for the JAX-WS document-style.

# Client code generation (RPC based)

A client that accesses RPC-based web services does not have a factory bean dedicated for its service endpoint. The `org.springframework.remoting.jaxrpc.JaxRpcPortProxyFactoryBean` is no longer supported by Spring 4.x, thus, the only requirement is to generate all JAXB elements from the WSL using the same `wsimport` command and directly instantiating the implementations class in order to access the exposed RPC resources:

```
InventoryServiceImplService inv = new
                    InventoryServiceImplService();
InventoryServiceImpl invService =
                    inv.getPort(InventoryServiceImpl.class);
MaterialTypeArray matArray =  invService.getMaterialTypes();
List<MaterialType> productTypes = matArray.getItem();
List<Integer> materialNames = new ArrayList<>();
for(MaterialType mat: productTypes){
    materialNames.add(mat.getId());       }
model.addAttribute("materialNames", materialNames);
UomArray skuArray = invService.getUnitMeasure();
List<Uom> sku = skuArray.getItem();
List<Integer> uomNames = new ArrayList<>();
for(Uom u: sku){
        uomNames.add(u.getId());      }
model.addAttribute("units", uomNames);
```

The following is the finished Inventory module that accesses data resources using JAX-WS, both document-based and RPC-based web services:

## Packt ERP

### Inventory Module

**Add to inventory**

| PRODUCT NAME | | TAGS |
|---|---|---|

| VENDOR | | PRODUCT TYPE | |
|---|---|---|---|
| 2 | ▼ | 1 | ▼ |

PRODUCT DESCRIPTION

| SKU | INITIAL STOCK LEVEL | COST PRICE | WHOLESALE PRICE | RETAIL PRICE |
|---|---|---|---|---|
| 1 ▼ | | | | |

Add Catalog

# JAX-RS (RESTful) web services

Jersey RESTful services were used by the Inventory module to transact with the main data sources. The module enhances the functionality of the RESTful service using Jersey to include **create, read, update, and delete (CRUD)** functionality. The JAX-RS specification is not RPC.

# Web service generation (Jersey)

Jersey is very delicate when it comes to its Maven libraries so before development, be sure to secure all necessary dependencies to avoid JAXB exceptions. Unlike Spring-WS and JAX-WS, creating Jersey RS web services is easy. Under the Inventory module, there are two services written in Jersey that will insert records to catalog the database and retrieve units of measures used by the purchasing order and account receivable invoice forms and these are:

```
@GET
@Path("/getRestUnits")
@Produces(MediaType.APPLICATION_XML)
public Response getUnits() {
```

```
        ArrayList<Uom> list = (ArrayList<Uom>)
                          inventoryDao.getUnitMeasure();
        ListUomAdapter uomAdapter = new ListUomAdapter();
        uomAdapter.setUomList(list);
        return Response.ok(uomAdapter).build();   }
@GET
@Path("/getRestUnits")
@Consumes(MediaType.APPLICATION_XML)
@Produces(MediaType.APPLICATION_XML)
 public Response insertCatalog(Catalog product) {
        inventoryDao.setProduct(product);
        return Response.ok("success").build();   }
```

Each service must identify what type of HTTP request the method will respond to. JAX-RS annotations that indicate a HTTP request type are the following:

- `@POST`: This annotation indicates that the following method will answer to an HTTP `POST` request
- `@GET`: This annotation indicates that the following method will answer to an HTTP `GET` request
- `@PUT`: This annotation indicates that the following method will answer to an HTTP `PUT` request
- `@DELETE`: This annotation indicates that the following method will answer to an HTTP `DELETE` request

The next annotation that is required to be associated with the Jersey RS services is the `@Path` annotation. It sets the URL pattern of the service and attaches it to the context or base URL. `@Consumes` and `@Produces` are two important annotations which determine the type of parameter and return value of a service method, respectively. The `@Produces` defines what MIME type to be delivered by a method annotated with `@GET`, sometimes `@POST`. The MIME type is given by the API `javax.ws.rs.core.MediaType` which is supported by MOXy, Jackson, and Jettison dependencies of Jersey. Some popular media types are `MediaType.TEXT_PLAIN`, `MediaType.APPLICATION_XML`, and `MediaType.APPLICATION_JSON`.

On the other hand, `@Consumes` defines which MIME type is used by a method as parameter(s). Any media types are valid including `MediaType.APPLICATION_FORM_URLENCODED` which indicates form request parameters. It is used as a counterpart to `@FormParam` which maps all form components to the method parameters. These types of services are most of the time `@POST` and are mapped to views like the following Inventory's form transaction:

```
<form action="rest/imventoryrest/unitform" method="POST"
```

```
              enctype="application/x-www-form-urlencoded">
    <input id="unit" type="text" name="unit" />
    <input type="submit" />
</form>
@POST
@Path("/unitform")
@Produces(MediaType.TEXT_PLAIN)
@Consumes(MediaType.APPLICATION_FORM_URLENCODED)
public String setUnitForm(@FormParam("unit") String unit) {
        // See the sources
        return "success";       }
```

Another optional annotation is `@PathParam` which injects values from the URL into a method parameter just like the following example:

```
@GET
@Path("/getCatalog/{id}")
@Consumes(MediaType.APPLICATION_JSON)
@Produces(MediaType.APPLICATION_JSON)
public Response getCatalog(@PathParam("id") Integer id) {
    Catalog cat = inventoryDao.getProduct(id);
    return Response.ok(cat).build();      }
```

When it comes to the specific return value of the method, a service can return a specific object or primitive type just like in `getCatalog()`. But if the service is designed to return both data and metadata like the status of the contract between the producer and the consumer, the `javax.ws.rs.core.Response` can be used. If the contract is successful, the `Response` class can output the status code `200` with the response data. Otherwise, it can give the status code `400`, `401`, or `500` with some desired error message or redirection.

The Jersey RS services will not run if we don't configure the servlet `com.sun.jersey.spi.spring.container.servlet.SpringServlet`. The following initialization parameters must be configured to avoid JAXB exceptions:

- `jersey.config.server.provider.packages`: This parameter determines all the packages where all the Jersey web services are located; multiple packages must be separated by a semicolon
- `com.sun.jersey.config.property.packages`: This parameter determines all the packages of the support libraries of the dependencies needed for JAXB processing; multiple packages must be separated by a semicolon
- `com.sun.jersey.api.json.POJOMappingFeature`: This is a Boolean value that must set to `true` in order to properly map all serialized domain objects with `@XmlRootElement`

# Media type problem

One common exception that will be encountered during Jersey RS development is this:

```
SEVERE: Servlet.service() for servlet [jersey] in context with path [/ch08]
threw exception com.fasterxml.jackson.databind.JsonMappingException:
Infinite recursion (StackOverflowError) (through reference chain:...)
```

To solve this problem always set `com.sun.jersey.api.json.POJOMappingFeature` to `true` in the servlet configuration. Moreover, always use the annotations `@JsonManagedReference` and `@JsonBackReference` to our domain models. These manage the `@JoinColumn` hibernate mapping which is the main JAXB problem. `@JsonManagedReference` is the first part of the referential relationship and the one that gets serialized normally while `@JsonBackReference` is the latter part of the relationship which will be omitted from serialization to ease the JAXB processing.

Another exception is related to returning the `MediaType.APPLICATION_XML` response which says:

```
SEVERE: A message body writer for Java class java.util.ArrayList, and Java
type class java.util.ArrayList, and MIME media type application/xml was not
found.
The registered message body writers compatible with the MIME media type
are:
*/* ->
```

To solve this problem, try to check if you have the latest version of the `jersey-media-moxy` dependency. Also, Jersey *does not* provide `MessageBodyWriter` for all the `Collection` classes so Jersey service methods cannot return `List`, `Set`, `Map`, or `Queue` objects. To combat this problem, there are two options:

- Create a custom `Jersey-style MessageBodyWriter`
- Create a custom adapter for collections

On the side of the adapters and domain models, do not forget to attach `@XmlRootElement` and `@XmlAccessorType(XmlAccessType.FIELD)` on top of the blueprints. Tag all properties that are not important with `@XmlTransient`.

The Inventory module uses adapters to wrap all collections to be transported to the client `@Controller`.

# Web service generation (RestEasy)

Many people are concerned by the exceptions they encounter with Jersey RS development due to dependency and configuration problems. Some resort to RestEasy to create RESTful services rapidly without validating and checking initialization parameters.

In RestEasy, development starts with creating the `javax.ws.rs.core.Application` without any dependency problems. This is a standard JAX-RS class that lists all JAX-RS root resources and providers needed for deployment:

```
@ApplicationPath("/rest/*")
public class PurchasingApplication extends Application {
    private Set<Object> singletons = new HashSet<Object>();
    public PurchasingApplication () {
        singletons.add(new PurchasingService());
        singletons.add(new POPaymentService());
        singletons.add(new PODetailsService());      }
    @Override
    public Set<Object> getSingletons() {
        return singletons;      }   }
```

This application class will be fetched and executed by RestEasy's bootstrap listener configured in the `web.xml` as:

```
<listener>
    <listener-class>org.jboss.resteasy.plugins.server
            .servlet.ResteasyBootstrap    </listener-class>
</listener>
```

It is also responsible for scanning for annotation classes registered in the custom application.

RestEasy web service classes are annotated with `@Named` or `@Component` annotations. Without these annotations, RestEasy will only recognize all injected DAO transactions.

The service method implementation is similar to Jersey since both follow one JAX-RS specification. The annotations `@GET`, `@POST`, `@Path`, `@Consumes`, and `@Produces` are all present defining the services. RestEasy has its own JSON providers that recognize the same media types found in Jersey.

All domain objects must have the necessary JAXB annotations for XML and JSON response type generation. The same policies hold true in declaring `javax.ws.rs.core.Response` or specific objects as return types of the services. But RestEasy can process and return collections of objects without using adapters or a custom `MessageBodyWriter`.

The real challenge lies in the configuration of the servlet
`org.jboss.resteasy.plugins.server.servlet.HttpServletDispatcher`. The
servlet must recognize the custom `PurchasingApplication` for bootstrap. In order for the
servlet to work, we have to customize `ContextLoaderListener` to override the
`customizeContext()` method otherwise all RestEasy service methods will give you status
code 404. The new custom `ContextLoaderListener` will be declared as the new listener of
the application omitting the old one. Since a custom URL pattern will be used instead of the
typical `/*`, the `resteasy.servlet.mapping.prefix` context parameter must also be
configured. The following is the configuration of the `HttpServletDispatcher` servlet:

```
<listener>
    <listener-class>org.packt.erp.modules
            SpringRestEasyContextLoaderListener
    </listener-class>
</listener>
<context-param>
    <param-name>resteasy.servlet.mapping.prefix</param-name>
    <param-value>/rest</param-value>
</context-param>
<servlet>
    <servlet-name>restservlet</servlet-name>
    <servlet-class>org.jboss.resteasy.plugins.server
            .servlet.HttpServletDispatcher
    </servlet-class>
    <init-param>
        <param-name>javax.ws.rs.Application</param-name>
        <param-value>org.packt.erp.modules
                    .PurchasingApplication</param-value>
    </init-param>
</servlet>
```

# Axis2 web service implementation

There are two ways to deploy web services using Axis2. The usual way is to generate the
services in the server and deploy their corresponding `.aar` or Axis Archive files to an
existing Axis2 server. The other one, which is not common, is to deploy the Axis2 web
services within the Spring application wherein all beans will be injected into a Spring
container to fully expose the services. Axis2 libraries cannot be mixed with JAX-WS and
Spring-WS dependencies so a separate Spring container handling its own web service
generation is a good design.

Axis2 caters only for SOAP-based web service implementation.

# Web service generation

All @Service methods must be declared inside an Axis2 service descriptor, which is services.xml. Create a folder path WEB-INF/services/axis2 and drop services.xml inside. The descriptor can contain more than one service and must be written this way:

```xml
<?xml version="1.0" encoding="UTF-8"?>
<serviceGroup>
<service name="loginAxisService">
    <description>Login Service Axis2 version</description>
    <parameter name="ServiceClass" locked="true">
        org.packt.erp.modules.service
            .impl.LoginAxisService</parameter>
    <parameter name="ServiceObjectSupplier">
        org.apache.axis2.extensions
          .spring.receivers.SpringAppContextAwareObjectSupplier
    </parameter>
    <parameter name="SpringBeanName">loginService</parameter>
    <messageReceivers>
        <messageReceiver
            mep="http://www.w3.org/2004/08/wsdl/in-only"
                class="org.apache.axis2.rpc
                    .receivers.RPCInOnlyMessageReceiver" />
        <messageReceiver
            mep="http://www.w3.org/2004/08/wsdl/in-out"
                class="org.apache.axis2.rpc
                    .receivers.RPCMessageReceiver"/>
    </messageReceivers>
</service>
        // See the sources
</serviceGroup>
```

Looking at the preceding XML, all declared services are converted into Spring-aware beans through the SpringAppContextAwareObjectSupplier class. This tells Spring that these objects are valid Spring components even though they are contained outside ApplicationContext. On the other hand, Spring must inject org.apache.axis2.extensions.spring.receivers.ApplicationContextHolder to recognize all these Spring-aware beans inside the service descriptor. This detects and maps all injected services to the SpringBeanName attribute of the services in service.xml. Omitting this bean injection will not recognize any message request and response from the services:

```xml
<bean id="applicationContext"
    class="org.apache.axis2.extensions
        .spring.receivers.ApplicationContextHolder" />
```

All service objects must be declared `locked=true` to stop the object from being overridden by another object with the same parameter name. Exceptions will be thrown if there are discrepancies with parameter names if we locked all parameters.

Message receivers, which are found in the `services.xml`, are special handlers in Axis2. Message receivers must be present in the XML configuration since every operation of the service must have its own appropriate message receiver which may come in different types depending on the purpose of the service.

Lastly, `web.xml` must configure to initialize `org.apache.axis2.transport.http.AxisServlet` which is responsible for reading `services.xml` and exposing it for the client to access. `ContextLoaderListener` must also be declared to scan and read all valid Axis2 objects in the container. It is best practice to derive the URL pattern of the servlet from the path where `service.xml` is located which is `WEB-INF/services/`, thus, AxisServlet will be mapped to `/services/*`.

```
<listener>
        <listener-class>org.springframework.web
            .context.ContextLoaderListener</listener-class>
</listener>
<servlet>
    <servlet-name>AxisServlet</servlet-name>
    <servlet-class>
        org.apache.axis2.transport.http.AxisServlet
    </servlet-class>
    <load-on-startup>1</load-on-startup>
</servlet>
<servlet-mapping>
    <servlet-name>AxisServlet</servlet-name>
    <url-pattern>/services/*</url-pattern>
</servlet-mapping>
```

# Web client generation

The command `Wsdl2Java` is a very important command of Axis2 used to generate client objects, namely the stub and **callback handler**. We can execute `Wsdl2Java` from the terminal, Maven, or through the Eclipse plugin. After the operation, we can use the stub to retrieve all the service methods:

```
LoginAxisServiceStub stub = new LoginAxisServiceStub();
stub._getServiceClient().getOptions().setProperty(
        HTTPConstants.CHUNKED, "false");
LoginAxisServiceStub.GetAllPersons allPersons =
    new LoginAxisServiceStub.GetAllPersons();
```

```
LoginAxisServiceStub.GetAllPersonsResponse response =
    stub.getAllPersons(allPersons);
LoginAxisServiceStub.Person[] persons = response.get_return();
```

# CXF web service implementation

CXF supports JAX-WS document-style, JAX-WS RPC-style, and JAX-RS. The processes in generating CXF web services are similar to that of JAX-WS and Jersey but differ on how these services are injected into the Spring's container.

## Web service generation

First, `ApplicationContext` must declare two XSDs from CXF dependencies and these are `xmlns:jaxws=http://cxf.apache.org/jaxws` and `xmlns:jaxrs=http://cxf.apache.org/jaxrs`. JAX-WS services are declared as service endpoints through `<jaxws:endpoint/>`. The tag assigns a user-defined URL to each endpoint.

```
<bean id="loginService" class="org.packt.erp.modules
        .service.impl.LoginServiceImpl" />
    <jaxws:endpoint id="loginServiceWS"
        implementor="#loginService"
            address="/loginServiceWS">
    </jaxws:endpoint>
```

On the other hand, JAX-RS is declared using the `<jaxrs:server/>` tag. It contains other properties like JSON and XML mapping and parsing providers and media type settings. The complete code is shown here:

```
<bean id="restInventoryService" class="org.packt.erp.modules
                .service.impl.InventoryServiceRestImpl"/>
<jaxrs:server id="restInvService" address="/restInvService">
    <jaxrs:providers>
        <bean class="org.apache.cxf.jaxrs
                .provider.JAXBElementProvider"/>
        <bean class="org.codehaus.jackson
                .jaxrs.JacksonJsonProvider" />
    </jaxrs:providers>
    <jaxrs:serviceBeans>
        <ref bean="restInventoryService" />
    </jaxrs:serviceBeans>
    <jaxrs:extensionMappings>
        <entry key="json" value="application/json" />
        <entry key="xml" value="application/xml" />
```

```
        </jaxrs:extensionMappings>
    </jaxrs:server>
```

In order for our services to work, our `web.xml` must configure a CXF servlet which is responsible for handing CXF web services. Declare also the `ContextLoaderListener` class to further scan and load some necessary beans for web service generation.

# XFire web service implementation

Among some of the old SOAP-based frameworks for web service development is XFire which is surprisingly very easy to be integrated with Spring 4.x. XFire support has been halted but some of the legacy systems still have XFire web services. CXF is the recommended upgrade version of XFire.

## Web service generation

The services are declared inside a separate Spring container. `ApplicationContext` loads two configurations entities, namely the `org/codehaus/xfire/spring/xfire.xml` and the `org.codehaus.xfire.spring.remoting.XFireExporter`, both from the core libraries. These entries are needed to consider the Spring services as XFire components. The following is a sample XFire configuration:

```
<beans>
    <import
      resource="classpath:org/codehaus/xfire/spring/xfire.xml" />
    <bean id="myService" class="org.codehaus.xfire.spring
      .remoting.XFireExporter" lazy-init="false" abstract="true">
        <property name="serviceFactory"
            ref="xfire.serviceFactory" />
        <property name="xfire" ref="xfire" />
    </bean>
    <bean id="loginXFireService"
        class="org.packt.erp.modules
            .service.impl.LoginXfireServiceImpl/>
    <bean id="myClassService" parent="myService">
      <property name="serviceBean" ref="loginXFireService " />
      <property name="serviceClass"
            value="org.packt.erp.modules.LoginXfireService" />
    </bean>
</beans>
```

Lastly, XFire needs `org.codehaus.xfire.spring.XFireSpringServlet` to be configured in `web.xml` together with Spring's `ContextLoaderListener` to load all XFire injections in the `ApplicationContext` container.

 XFire does not support the collections framework so use a single or multidimensional array for returning records of data.

## Web client generation

To access the service methods, we need the interface to create a model XFire's `ObjectServiceFactory`. Then, a proxy factory object will be derived easily using the `xFire` classes and interfaces. Through the proxy factory, the service model, and the service endpoint URL, we get a local proxy for the service:

```
Service serviceModel = new
ObjectServiceFactory().create(LoginXfireService.class);

XFire xfire = XFireFactory.newInstance().getXFire();
XFireProxyFactory factory = new XFireProxyFactory(xfire);

String serviceUrl = "http://localhost:8080/
        ch08-xfire-ws/service/LoginXfireService";
LoginXfireService client = null;
try {
 client = (LoginXfireService) factory.create(serviceModel, serviceUrl);
    } catch (MalformedURLException e) {     }

Login[] login = client.getAllLogin();
```

## HttpInvoker, Burlap, and Hessian remoting

If the applications are communicating are just JEE-based applications and don't necessarily belong to different frameworks, then Spring remoting can be used. Spring 4.x supports the HttpInvoker, Burlap, and Hessian styles of remoting. The Sales module of the ERP uses remoting to access the information of the suppliers, company, and personal customers.

# Remoting through HttpInvoker

First, service interfaces must be created followed by their implementation because these two classes are needed in the configuration:

```
Service
@Transactional
public class PersonServiceInvokerImpl
        implements PersonServiceInvoker{
    @Autowired
    SalesPersonDao personDao;
    @Transactional
    @Override
    public void setPerson(PersonForm person) {
        // See the sources      }

    @Override
    public Person getPerson(Integer id) {
        return personDao.getPerson(id);      }

    @Override
    public List<Person> getPersons() {
        return personDao.getPersons();      }
}
```

To expose it as a remote service, inject the implemented service first as a Spring bean into the dedicated context container and declare and expose it using Spring's `org.springframework.remoting.httpinvoker.HttpInvokerServiceExporter` has the property service that specifies the service class bean-handling, the HTTP request call, and the property `serviceInterface` which specifies the interface to be used by Spring to create proxies for HTTP transaction services.

Below is the complete HttpInvoker remote service configuration:

```
<bean id="personServiceInvoker" class="org.packt.erp.modules
              .service.impl.PersonServiceInvokerImpl"/>
<bean name="/personServiceInvoker.http"
    class="org.springframework.remoting
         .httpinvoker.HttpInvokerServiceExporter">
    <property name="service" ref="personServiceInvoker"/>
    <property name="serviceInterface"
        value="org.packt.erp.modules
                  .service.PersonServiceInvoker"/>
</bean>
```

# Accessing HttpInvoker services

To access the HttpInvoker's remote services, a bean must be injected into the client's Spring container using `HttpInvokerProxyFactoryBean` with the following properties:

- `serviceUrl`: This specifies the URL of the remote service concerned
- `serviceInterface`: This specifies the interface to be used by the client to create proxies for HttpInvoker services

```
<bean id="personServiceInvokerHttp"
    class="org.springframework
        .remoting.httpinvoker.HttpInvokerProxyFactoryBean">
    <property name="serviceUrl"
        value="http://localhost:8080/ch08/
        httpinvoker/personServiceInvoker.http"></property>
    <property name="serviceInterface"
            value="org.packt.erp.modules
            .service.PersonServiceInvoker"/>
</bean>
```

Afterwards, any `@Controller` or Spring components of the module can `@Autowire` the `PersonServiceInvoker` implementation to expose all its transaction methods. Another option is to instantiate the client object in this way:

```
HttpInvokerProxyFactoryBean proxy = new
        HttpInvokerProxyFactoryBean();
proxy.setServiceInterface(PersonServiceInvoker.class);
proxy.setServiceUrl("http://localhost:8080/ch08/
        httpinvoker/personServiceInvoker.http");
proxy.afterPropertiesSet();
PersonServiceInvoker personService =
            (PersonServiceInvoker) proxy.getObject();
```

The method `afterPropertiesSet()` is very important and must be there to perform force initialization with or without exceptions due to configuration problems.

# Remoting through Burlap

This remoting style is deprecated in the Spring 4.x framework but can still be used for some trivial transactions. To generate, we need the service interface and its implementation to define the **org.springframework.remoting.caucho.BurlapServiceExporter** which has the properties to configure, namely the **service** and **serviceInterfaces**. The property **service** determines the service class bean which will be handled by the Burlap service transaction, while the **serviceInterface** determines the interface to be used by Spring as proxies for the

Burlap transaction.

A complete Burlap configuration for SupplierService is as follows:

```
<bean id="supplierService" class="org.packt.erp.modules.service
            .impl.SupplierServiceImpl"/>
<bean name="/supplierService.http"
        class="org.springframework.remoting
                .caucho.BurlapServiceExporter">
        <property name="service" ref="supplierService"/>
        <property name="serviceInterface"
            value="org.packt.erp.modules
                    .service.SupplierService"/>
</bean>
```

# Accessing Burlap services

To access the Burlap service method, a bean must be injected into the client's Spring container using Spring's `BurlapProxyFactoryBean` which has the following properties that need to be configured, namely the `serviceUrl` which specifies the URL of the remote service resource, and `serviceInterface` which specifies the interface used by Spring as proxies for the Burlap service transaction

The following is a complete Burlap client configuration to access the previous supplier remote service:

```
<bean id="supplierServiceHttp" class="org.springframework
        .remoting.caucho.BurlapProxyFactoryBean">
    <property name="serviceUrl"
            value="http://localhost:8080/burlap/
                    supplierService.http"></property>
    <property name="serviceInterface" value="org.packt.erp.modules
            .service.PersonService"/>
</bean>
```

To execute the needed services, Spring components can `@Autowire` the `PersonService` class and its implementation. Likewise, another option to access the service is through instantiating the Burlap client this way:

```
String url = "http://localhost:8080/ch08/
                        burlap/supplierService.http";
BurlapProxyFactory factory = new BurlapProxyFactory();
SupplierService supplierService;
try {
        supplierService = (SupplierService)
            factory.create(SupplierService.class, url);
```

```
        // See the sources
} catch (MalformedURLException e) { // See the sources   }
```

# Remoting through Hessian

Instead of Burlap remoting, Hessian is currently popular for remoting under the Caucho library. Just like HttpInvoker and Burlap, Hessian needs the interface and the counterpart implementation of the services needs to be exposed remotely using a Hessian mechanism. These classes are needed to configure Spring's `HessianServiceExporter` class (see the lines with the properties `service` which specify the service class handling the Hessian call and `serviceInterface`) which specifies and determines the interface used by Spring as proxies for Hessian service transactions.

The following is a complete Hessian configuration for `PersonService` needed to be accessed through remoting:

```xml
<bean id="personService" class="org.packt.erp.modules.service
            .impl.PersonServiceImpl"/>
<bean name="/personService.http"
            class="org.springframework.remoting
                    .caucho.HessianServiceExporter">
    <property name="service" ref="personService"/>
    <property name="serviceInterface"
        value="org.packt.erp.modules.service.PersonService"/>
</bean>
```

# Accessing Hessian services

To access the exposed service, client software must inject Spring's `HessianProxyFactoryBean` class with the property's `serviceUrl` which specifies the URL of the remote service resources and `serviceInterface` which specifies the interface for Spring to use as a proxy for Hessian service transactions.

The following is a Hessian client configuration for the exposed `PersonService` remoting service implementation:

```xml
<bean id="personServiceHttp"   class="org.springframework.remoting
            .caucho.HessianProxyFactoryBean">
    <property name="serviceUrl"
        value="http://localhost:8080/ch08/
            hessian/personService.http"></property>
    <property name="serviceInterface" value="org.packt.erp.modules
            .service.PersonService"></property>
```

```
</bean>
```

If the client object is not found in the container, it can be instantiated like this:

```
String url = "http://localhost:8080/ch08/
      hessian/personService.http";
HessianProxyFactory factory = new HessianProxyFactory();
PersonService personService;
   try {
         personService = (PersonService)
              factory.create(PersonService.class, url);
              // See the sources
            } catch (MalformedURLException e) {            }
```

# Spring containers for remoting

All three remoting strategies can be bundled in one Spring`ApplicationContext` as per our custom ERP. The application creates one `org.springframework.web.servlet.DispatcherServlet` container for all three using only one URL pattern to invoke all the remote services. In some cases, like in our ERP implementation, we have created separate `DispatcherServlet` containers each with different URL patterns (for example, `/hessian/*` for Hessian, `/burlap/*` for Burlap, and `/httpinvoker/*` for HttpInvoker). This is the best practice to avoid confusion when a project's scope gets large.

# Remote Method Invocation

Since JAX-RPC is no longer fully supported by Spring 4.x, **Remote Method Invocation (RMI)** was implemented, which is the easiest and most straightforward strategy for exposing web services in RPC style. In the RMI model, the client sends a message call to the server through a RMI proxy called `RmiProxyFactoryBean`. This RMI proxy handles and converts the call into a remote call procedure through a protocol known as **Java Remote Method Protocol (JRMP)**. Then, a specified RMI service adapter exposed by `RmiServiceExporter` intercepts the remote call over JRMP and forwards the method call to a service.

To expose our `CustomerService` implementation using RMI, the Spring's
`RmiServiceExporter` class must be injected into the server's container with the properties
`serviceName`, `service`, `serviceInterface`, and `registryPort`. The
`serviceName` property indicates the name of the service invoked by the RMI client, the
`service` property specifies the bean class handling the RMI transaction call, the
`serviceInterface` property serves as Spring's proxies for remoting, and the
`registryPort` service is the service port through which the RMI service is exposed.

The following is a complete declaration of our `RmiServiceExporter` for
`CustomerService`:

```
<bean id="customerService" class="org.packt.erp.modules
    .service.impl.CustomerServiceImpl" />
<bean class="org.springframework
    .remoting.rmi.RmiServiceExporter">
    <property name="service"
            ref="customerService"></property>
    <property name="serviceInterface"
        value="org.packt.erp.modules
                    .service.CustomerService"></property>
    <property name="serviceName"
            value="CustomerService"></property>
    <property name="replaceExistingBinding"
            value="true"></property>
    <property name="registryPort" value="1099"></property>
</bean>
```

The `client` module must declare `RmiProxyFactoryBean` with the following properties:
the `serviceUrl` which specifies the URL of the remote service resource and the
`serviceInterface` property which specifies the interface which will be used by Spring as
a proxy for RMI service calls.

The following is an RMI client configuration to access the `CustomerService` transactions:

```
<bean id="customerServiceHttp" class="org.springframework.remoting
            .rmi.RmiProxyFactoryBean">
  <property name="serviceUrl"
      value="rmi://localhost:1099/CustomerService"></property>
  <property name="serviceInterface" value="org.packt.erp.modules
            .service.CustomerService"></property>
</bean>
```

Or, the bean can be instantiated to extract all the resources exposed from the services:

```
RmiProxyFactoryBean factory = new RmiProxyFactoryBean();
factory.setServiceInterface(CustomerService.class);
```

```
factory.setServiceUrl("rmi://localhost:1099/CustomerService");
factory.afterPropertiesSet();
CustomerService bsi = (CustomerService) factory.getObject();
List<Customer> customers = bsi.getCustomers();
```

 The method `afterPropertiesSet()` is very important and must be there to force initialization with or without exceptions due to configuration problems.

# JMS using ApacheMQ

Our custom ERP uses JMS specification to update PO and AR payment status. Spring JMS is part of Spring 4.x that wraps the real JMS service provider such as ActiveMQ or OpenJMS and provides consistent APIs to high-level business processes. Spring JMS can decouple the business logic from the technicalities of the JMS service provider, which in this chapter is ActiveMQ.

Run ActiveMQ and visit its admin console at: `http://localhost:8161/admin/`. Name our queue `packt_queue`. There are always two important classes when writing JMS communication and these are the provider and the sender classes. The provider class is responsible for executing the DAO transactions, e-mail transactions, notifications, and scheduling processes. The sender class asks for parameter(s) from the user, transport parameters to give to providers, and triggers the provider execution. The sender classes are `@Autowired` in the `@Service` or `@Controller` layer of the applications. Sender classes are implemented this way:

```
@Service
public class UpdatePOPayment {
    @Resource(name="jmstemplate")
    private JmsTemplate jmsTemplate;

    public void sendMessage(Integer id){
        final String  msg = id + "";
        jmsTemplate.send(new MessageCreator() {
            @Override
            public Message createMessage(Session session) throws
                             JMSException {
                TextMessage txtMsg = session.createTextMessage(msg);
                return txtMsg;
            }
        });    }
}
```

While the provider class is implemented as a listener class:

```
@Service
public class UpdatePOPaymentListener implements MessageListener {
    @Resource(name="jmstemplate")
    private JmsTemplate jmsTemplate;

    @Autowired
    PurchasingDao purchasingDao;
    @Override
    public void onMessage(final Message message) {
        try {
            message.acknowledge();
            message.getJMSDestination();
              if (message instanceof TextMessage) {
                  TextMessage txtmsg = (TextMessage) message;
                  Int id = Integer.parseInt(txtmsg);
                  purchasingDao.updatePaymentStatus("paid");
              }
        } catch (JMSException e) { }
    } }
```

The `MessageListener` object is used to receive asynchronously delivered messages. A listener assigned to one or more senders of the same session must be designed to entertain only another `onMessage()` execution after the completion of the previous method call.

After creating two classes, a separate `ApplicationContext` container must be created to inject some JMS beans to the container. Two connection factories will be defined, namely the ActiveMQ's connection factory bean which works as an input of Spring's pooled connection factory, and the cached connection factory bean which is necessary in managing the Spring `JmsTemplate` on every send or receive transaction. Next, the destination queue must be defined based on the ActiveMQ configuration. The project uses `packt_queue` as the queue name. Then, the Spring `JmsTemplate` must be created based on the default destination and connection factory's configuration details. Finally, the declaration of all message listeners must be contained inside `org.springframework.jms.listener.SimpleMessageListenerContainer`.

All sender-receiver transactions are recorded in the ActiveMQ server administration console. The ActiveMQ administration console is shown in the following image:

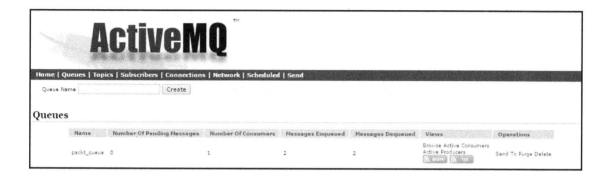

# AMQP using RabbitMQ

Just like JMS, the objective of AMQP is to implement a sender-receiver transaction but without using any JMS-based APIs. AMQP implementation is easier from the point of view of a developer. The ERP project used AMQP to implement payment status updates on several account receivable invoices.

Before we start the development, a RabbitMQ broker must be installed and run. Further configuration can be done on the broker depending on the infrastructure setup of the project, like having a failover component on the server. RabbitMQ has a high-availability policy that needs to be adjusted if AMQP servers are to be clustered. In our project, we used AMQP communication in one RabbitMQ server instance only.

`ApplicationContext` must use `xmlns:rabbit="http://www.springframework.org/schema/rabbit"` to configure the provider and sender classes.

The first step of the development is to create the listener configuration to set up the connection factory, exchange, and queue that will be used by the application. The connection factory basically needs to be configured with the TCP/IP connection parameters in order to locate the RabbitMQ broker using the default port 5672 with the credentials guest/guest for this project. The `<rabbit:admin/>` tag provides this application with the admin rights for creating the queues and exchanges. Afterwards, we create a message queue named `packt_amqp_queue`. The `<rabbit:direct-exchange/>` declares the exchange that will be used by the provider. Its bindings tell the provider to send the message to `packt_amqp_queue`.

Lastly, we create the provider bean, register it in a listener container, and bind it to the connection factory and `packt_amqp_queue`.

```
<rabbit:connection-factory id="connectionFactory"
    host="localhost" username="guest" password="guest" />
<rabbit:admin connection-factory="connectionFactory" />
<rabbit:queue id="packt_amqp_queue" />
<rabbit:topic-exchange id="myExchange" name="ERP-EXCHANGE">
    <rabbit:bindings>
        <rabbit:binding queue="packt_amqp_queue">
    </rabbit:binding>
    </rabbit:bindings>
</rabbit:topic-exchange>
<bean id="aListener"
 class="org.packt.erp.modules.jms.TutorialListener" />
<rabbit:listener-container id="myListenerContainer"
    connection-factory="connectionFactory">
    <rabbit:listener ref="aListener"
    queues="packt_amqp_queue" />
</rabbit:listener-container>
```

The provider class must extend `org.springframework.amqp.core.MessageListener` in order to implement the `onMessage()` method.

On the other hand, we need to create the sender configuration so that the client will transport data to the provider. It needs to first configure the connection factory and the `<rabbit:admin/>` for data exchange properties. Lastly, `AmqpTemplate` must be created for sending and consuming messages. It has support methods such as `convertAndSend()` and `receiveAndConvert()` that start the communication. The `convertAndSend()` method sends any object over the wire in the form of a byte array. The `receiveAndConvert()` method performs synchronous reads on the queue and prints out the string representation of the message. The `AmqpTemplate` will throw `AmqpException` if any problems are encountered during the data exchange:

```
<rabbit:connection-factory id="connectionFactory"
    host="localhost" username="guest" password="guest" />
<rabbit:admin connection-factory="connectionFactory" />
<rabbit:template id="tutorialTemplate"
 connection-factory="connectionFactory" exchange="ERP-EXCHANGE"/>
```

# Spring Social

Another special feature of this ERP application is the use of special registration and authentication through the use of Spring Social. Although Spring Social is best effective with Spring Security in Chapter 7, *Online Cart System (OCS)*, the focus of this chapter is the OAuth protocol which is designed to be used in this project as an authorization mechanism to allow users to access the project.

The `SocialLogin` controller has implemented `/erp/facebooLogin.html` and `/erp/twitterLogin.html` with their respective redirect URL or callbacks. These implementations allow the OAuth protocol to use the REST specification in retrieving the GET requests from the user login parameters and providing POST responses from Facebook and Twitter servers. The handshake will allow users to proceed with accessing the ERP or redirect the users to errors or global pages. This feature shows us the importance of web services not only for data processing but also as the medium for security:

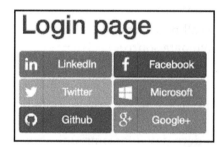

**Theme design**
The themes of this ERP project were derived from the templates which can be found at `http://codepen.io/GeBuOr/pen/mJJmgx`, `http://www.cgiscript.net/scripts.htm`, `http://www.htmlgoodies.com`, `https://css-tricks.com`, and `http://kumailht.com/gridforms`.

# The ERP

The customized ERP shows how extensive the Spring 4.x Framework is when it comes to the implementation of web services and remoting just to coordinate and bundle together different applications given some certain protocols on data sharing. Through this ERP prototype development, it has shown to us the degree of difficulty in creating every solution presented in this chapter. Also this project had laid out the pros and cons of every solution giving us hints on when, where, and how to use them in certain user requirements. The next chapter will guide us through how JavaScript helps Spring in designing portable applicationsâ••applications that can be easily migrated from desktop to mobile or vice versa.

# Challenge yourself

Create an online shopping portal composed of sub-applications `MyPOS`, `MyCatalog`, and `MyInvoice`, which are all full-blown applications interacting and passing records to each other using any of the web service techniques discussed. This time there is no centralized data source. The following are the scopes of each `client` module:

- `MyPOS` creates receipts of all the purchases of the client; it has its own data source `my_pos`
- `MyCatalog` manages all the products the company wants to sell online; it has its own data source `my_catalog`
- `MyInvoice` manages all procurement and payments of products from the vendors; it has its own data source `my_invoice`

# Summary

Web services have been the modern day intercommunication blueprints among huge enterprise applications because they are now the medium for data exchange and many other service-oriented transactions. Lots of technologies support web service implementation in order to cutdown language-specific, platform-dependent, and hardware-branded transactions among islands of enterprise applications. On the other hand, remoting technology has been an old enterprise solution in many cross-platform and distributed architecture scenarios for sharing business logic to enhance software performance.

This chapter has shown us how convenient it is to implement web services and remote transactions in the Spring 4.x Framework due to its lightweight characteristics and its dependency injection principle. Spring has wide support for XML marshaling and JSON mapping which play major parts in data transport for both solutions. Spring can easily work with WSDL generation for SOAP-based web services and REST specification for endpoint web services. Through bean injection, Spring can easily bridge software modules through HttpInvoker, Hessian, and Burlap remote processing. Most of all, Spring can manage messaging through JMS or AMQP to implement service-side events or minor background processing. More topics on service-oriented architecture will be discussed in Chapter 10, *Social Task Management System (STMS)*.

# 9
# Bus Ticketing System (BTS)

Owing to unpredictable and high-bandwidth user access, many of the online reservation and e-commerce systems resort to JavaScript/AJAX to provide their customers with better interactivity and user experience. Aside from its capability to adapt HTML web templates, JavaScript/AJAX scripts do not require pages to be reloaded for every request-response transaction. It can even provide other background processes while the application communicates with the server.

Although there are still considerable disadvantages of AJAX, when it comes to security and performance, owing to its browser-centric model, many architects and engineers invest time in generating new AJAX frameworks that will give clients software, which is less dependent on server-side code, but has a more efficient and enhanced performance. An efficient AJAX-based software design is almost portable to the extent that it will require less effort and budget in migrating software to a new language or platform like re-coding software to run on mobile platforms.

Nowadays, a lot of online software like e-commerce, ticketing, and reservation systems are written mostly in AJAX while the backend is pure PHP or Java frameworks. All these applications cater to the whole nation or world, which explains why, during promo deals, system crashes occur. To minimize system problems, many travel agencies prefer software that is lightweight and easy to tweak once technical problems owing to voluminous access, are encountered.

One application, which is very common to all, is the destination booking system. Whether they are travelers or not, people love to check travel schedules and available tickets online or on their mobile, which means this application is visited by millions of people, at almost the same time, using any platform. This chapter will highlight how to create a Spring 4.x application with a front-end AJAX stack through bus ticketing system (BTS) development.

In this chapter, you will learn how to:

- Write conventional JavaScript AJAX scripts to communicate with Spring
- Develop jQuery-based AJAX scripts to generate data transfer to and from Spring Controllers
- Create `Prototype.js` AJAX scripts to communicate with Spring
- Develop DOM-structured AJAX using Dojo libraries
- Manage tabular data using jQGrid
- Generate visualization with AJAX
- Generate AJAX using DWR
- Use and implement RestEasy JSAPI to generate AJAX transactions
- Implement lightweight messaging using Websocket

# Overview of the project

The Bus Ticketing System (BTS) is a small-scale lightweight application that basically automates purchasing of bus tickets. The software shows a list of destinations containing information and whereabouts of the route. The application can also manage all purchased tickets of the registered users. The following wireframes are expected to appear in the final prototype.

- **Login page**: A typical page that allows the user to access and book tickets. This login page has no other special authentication procedure except through the database validation.

- **Registration page**: The page is used to enroll users to grant booking privileges. The requirement for this page is to enforce users to use an e-mail address as the username.

- **Destination page**: A crucial feature of the application, which shows the list of destinations or routes with details such as the price of the tickets per head, price per ticket, the schedule and the stopover stations. This page also highlights promo deals the company want to impose for a certain period. Below are a few examples of how a destination page would look:
  - The registration page:

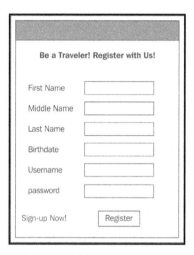

- The destination page:

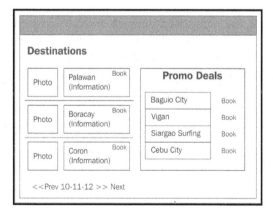

- **Checkout page** – All booked tickets of the users are recorded on this page. Previous and current bookings are managed by the account owner on this part of the application.

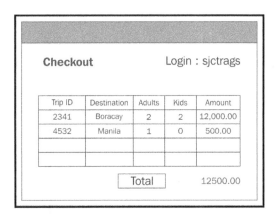

# Technical requirements

Most of the libraries needed in the implementation are JavaScript-based. These scripts can be downloaded or can be directly utilized through HTTP from the vendor's repositories.

# AJAX

AJAX libraries, for instance, are composed of open-source components like HTML, CSS, DOM and JavaScript, which are all accessible in all types of browsers. Asynchronous JavaScript and XML (AJAX) is a technique that allows parts, or all of a web page to be updated asynchronously in the background, during data exchange to the server. With the AJAX engine, the pages still undergo typical servlet request responses, while AJAX transactions do their job simultaneously, without getting the server's attention.

All types of AJAX libraries need Jackson JSON libraries for JSON pre-processing, so POM must include all these dependencies in the project repository.

# jQuery

jQuery is a JavaScript platform that has libraries for extensive CSS and AJAX features. It is a lightweight set of JavaScript libraries, compiled and wrapped as methods that can be called as single lines of code. What is interesting in jQuery is its simplified JavaScript form, which makes AJAX transactions and DOM manipulations easier and simple. This framework can run in any type of browser including Internet Explorer 6.

jQuery libraries can be accessed through:

```
<script src="//ajax.googleapis.com/ajax/libs/jquery/1.11.1/jquery.min.js">
</script>
```

# Prototype framework

Prototype is a JavaScript framework that simplifies client-side web programming. It is implemented as a single file of JavaScript code, namely `prototype.js`. The only difference between jQuery and `prototype.js` is the latter's object-oriented principle behind its libraries and its extensive support on arrays and strings.

Prototype can be accessed through:

```
<script src="//ajax.googleapis.com/ajax/libs/prototype
           /1.7.3.0/prototype.js">
</script>
```

# Dojo

Dojo is another JavaScript library that focuses on DOM parsing rather than on generating libraries for accessing DOM. It loads the whole HTML page, or just part of it, and applies the needed transactions on, or from, it. It can use CSS selectors to access the needed widgets that are part of the client-side process.

To use Dojo, libraries can be accessed through:

```
<script src="//ajax.googleapis.com/ajax/libs/dojo/1.10.4/dojo/dojo.js">
</script>
```

# RestEasy AJAX

In Chapter 8, *Enterprise Resource Planning (ERP)*, we featured how the RestEasy plugin is used as one of the solutions in building JAX-RS web services for Spring 4.x applications. This time, we will be using its AJAX API that provides excellent support for building client-side applications. RestEasy can generate a JavaScript API that uses AJAX calls to invoke JAX-RS services. The JavaScript code, generated for accessing REST APIs, makes the calls to exposed Java objects and methods in a similar way to how they are called in typical Java code.

In order to use RestEasy JSAPI (JavaScript API), the following Maven dependencies must be invoked in the POM file:

- org.jboss.resteasy: resteasy-jsapi (version 3.0.14.Final)
- all the required dependencies of RestEasy used in Chapter 8, *Enterprise Resource Planning (ERP)*

 All of the preceding libraries must be compatible with Spring 4.x and must have current versions to avoid lots of conflicts and exceptions. Likewise, some of the libraries above might be in conflict with the dependencies of JAX-WS, Spring WS, CXF and Jersey.

# DWR

**DWR (Direct Web Remoting)** is an open source project that provides easy AJAX for Java. Besides being the best AJAX framework written and configured in Java, it best integrates with Java frameworks such as Spring 4.x. DWR provides a loosely-coupled way of remotely exposing the Spring-managed beans of any applications to JavaScript. The main goal of DWR is to generate a Java library that can execute both as Java in a JEE server and as a JavaScript in a browser, thus allowing client-side transactions to call server-side objects with ease.

To use DWR, the following Maven dependency is needed:

- org.directwebremoting: dwr (version 3.0.1-RELEASE)

# WebSocket

WebSocket (RFC 6455) is protocol that defines a capability for an application to perform full-duplex communication, typically between a browser (or any valid client) and a webserver. This makes it suitable for highly interactive web applications such as chat, helpdesks, games, and dashboards. A WebSocket client, which is usually JavaScript code, connects to a WebSocket server and a handshake is performed over HTTP. Once the handshake is done, the same connection is used for the TCP-based, bidirectional, and socket-oriented communication. Since the handshake is done over HTTP, firewalls cannot easily block the communications, making it the best alternative for RPC-based transactions.

Spring Framework 4.x includes a new spring-websocket module with comprehensive WebSocket support. It is compatible with the Java WebSocket API standard (JSR-356). To use the API, include the following dependencies in the POM file:

- `org.springframework`: spring-websocket (version 4.1.19.RELEASE)
- `org.springframework`: spring-messaging (version 4.1.19.RELEASE)

# jQGrid

jQGrid is a JavaScript library that uses jQuery to interact with Spring MVC. It uses JSON or XML data, in a client-server data exchange, to provide a tabular representation of data from the server. The library can be downloaded from their website at: `http://www.trirand.com/blog/`.

# The BTS database

The BTS schema design shown in the following figure will be implemented in MySQL Server 5.6.

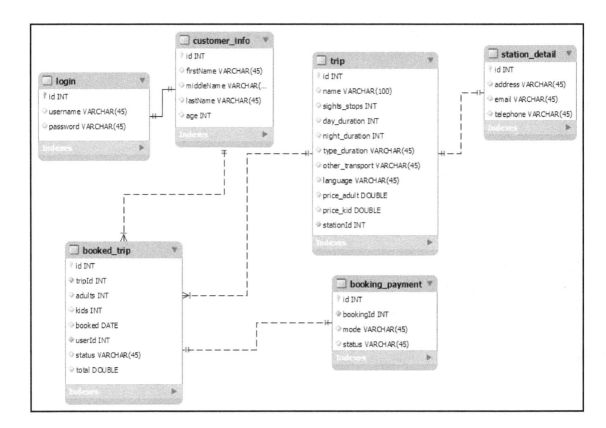

# Data modeling framework

The project used JPA with the Hibernate 4.x framework.

# AJAX and Spring integration

The Spring framework only has one stateless scope, called **prototype**, and the rest of its features are stateless in nature, since it purely uses the HTTP protocol for its request-response transactions. Applications like BTS will be accessed by many users who want to check bus availability, travel perks and other discounts open for a season. To help Spring in responding to several user transactions with one button submission, or to select event, the AJAX model has been adapted to this project.

AJAX uses JavaScript frameworks to simulate multiple request-response transactions at the side of the main HTTP request response. This model utilizes XML or JSON as request and response data. The client generates a data model to be processed by AJAX which will transform that model to an AJAX or XML request parameter. Once the parameter reaches the server, an XML or JSON response will be sent back to the original webpage for rendition. The following figure shows the whole picture of how AJAX behaves during page processing.

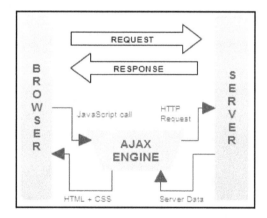

Since Spring 4.x has AJAX support, the framework provides the programming model for defining web services, including services consumed by JavaScript clients. On the client-side, there are many JavaScript libraries and frameworks, that are widely used nowadays, in many web solutions, such as jQuery, Prototype, Dojo and DWR.

# Custom AJAX development

In creating AJAX, we always start with the original means of creating an XMLHttpRequest object to process our transactions. The core of AJAX is always an XMLHttpRequest object, which is available in JavaScript and is free to instantiate. This object must be created to perform an exchange of data between browser and server at the background level. All modern browsers (IE6+, Firefox, Chrome, Safari, and Opera) have a built-in XMLHttpRequest object. For old browsers like IE 5 or IE6, ActiveXObject is used instead of sending AJAX requests.

BTS uses custom AJAX requests in its login mechanism instead of passing username and password as Spring's form request attributes. The /ch09/bts/login.html submits the username and password credentials of the user through a POST HTTP method for database validation on the server's end. The following code describes the whole AJAX transaction.

```
<script type="text/javascript">
  function doAjaxPost() {
   var url = "http://localhost:8080/ch09/bus/testpost.html";
   var username = $('#username').val();
   var password = $('#password').val();
   var params = "username="+username +"&password="+password;
   var xmlhttp;
   if (window.XMLHttpRequest) {
      xmlhttp = new XMLHttpRequest();
   } else {
    xmlhttp = new ActiveXObject("Microsoft.XMLHTTP");    }
   http.open("POST", url, true);
   http.setRequestHeader("Content-type",
           "application/x-www-form-urlencoded");
   http.setRequestHeader("Content-length", params.length);
   http.setRequestHeader("Connection", "close");

   http.onreadystatechange = function() {
        if(http.readyState == 4) {
             alert(http.responseText);    }
   }
   http.send(params);
   // See the sources }
</script>
```

The XMLHttpRequestopen() method will open the request transaction using any of the HTTP methods such as GET or POST, either synchronous or asynchronous type. Asynchronously is preferred because it will allow multiple transactions to be executed in the background together, making the browser responsive to the main client transaction.

The method `setRequestHeader()` provides the needed HTTP headers for the request such as the content-type, content-disposition, or content-encoding. Assuming no errors are found in the request, and all the headers are properly added, the `send()` method must be executed to proceed with the transaction, having the request parameter as its argument if the transaction is `POST`, or null if it is a `GET` transaction. To check if it is a successful handshake between the server and AJAX, the entity `onreadystatechange` must be evaluated and must receive a readyState of 4 or request complete, else an error handler must be triggered. Aside from 4, possible values can be 0 or request not initialized, 1 or server connection established, 2 or request received, 3 or processing request, or 4.

 The `xmlhttp` variable can be re-used many times in a page for sending multiple AJAX transactions because the object XMLHttpRequest is bound only to a one client-server connection per page.

On the server side, the `@Controller` that maps the URL `xmlhttp` is simply written as follows:

```
@Controller
public class LoginFormController {
    @Autowired
    LoginService loginService;
    // See the sources
    @RequestMapping(value="/bts/login", method=RequestMethod.POST)
    public RedirectView submitForm(@RequestBody LoginForm
                                   loginForm) {
      // See the sources
      if(loginService.validateUser(loginForm.getUsername()) == 0){
          return new RedirectView("/ch09/bts/login.html");
      } return new RedirectView("/ch09/bts/index.html"); }
}
```

The `@RequestBody` and `@ResponseBody` found in any controller method are responsible for initiating the XML parsing or JSON marshaling. These two respond to the request header delivered by the AJAX script. XML data is expected if the header is `Accept: application/xml` and JSON if the header `Accept: application/json`.

# jQuery AJAX

Using jQuery can shorten the AJAX scripts to a few lines. It has a robust set of libraries that can handle AJAX requests without writing too many lines of codes with an `XMLHttpRequest` object.

Our application uses jQuery script to retrieve a list of accredited bus destinations and the code is shown as follows:

```
<script type="text/javascript">
  function getServerData(){
      $.getJSON("http://localhost:8080/ch09/bts/stations.json",
              function(response){
                  $("#stationId option").remove();
                  var options = '';
                  $.each(response, function(index, item) {
                      options += '<option value="' + item + '">'
                              + item + '</option>';
                  $("#stationId").html(options);
              });
      });   }

  function setDefaultName() {
      $.get("http://localhost:8080/ch09/bts/name.json",
              function(name){
                  $("#name").val(name);
          });   }
</script>
```

The jQuery functions that play a great role in storing and retrieving data are the following:

- `$.ajax({name:value, ... })`: This method is used to perform an AJAX (asynchronous HTTP) request
- `$.get(url, data, callback, type)`: This method sends a GET request to the server given the URL of the page to load, the map data ( key/value pairs), a callback function to be executed whenever the data is loaded successfully or not, and the type of data to be returned through the callback function which can be XML, HTML, SCRIPT, JSON, JSONP, or TEXT
- `$.post(url, data, callback, type)`: This method sends a POST request to the server given the same as indicated in `jQuery.get()`
- `$.getJSON(url, data, callback)`: This is the function that can be used to make an AJAX call and get the data in JSON format
- `$.serialize()`: This method serializes a set of input elements from a form component into a string of data in preparation for storing or saving data at the server-side; the serialized data is in a standard format that is compatible with almost all server side programming languages and frameworks
- `$.serializeArray()`: This method does the same as `serialize()` except that it creates JSON as a specific output; an alternate method for this is the popular `JSON.stringify()` method

The following is a jQuery that sends FORM components, such as a JSON string, to be stored as a destination detail object after the handshake.

```
<script type="text/javascript">
 $(document).ready(function() {
    $('#submitForm').submit(
        function(event) {
               var frm = $('#submitForm');
               var data = {}
               var Form = this;
         // See the sources
               $.ajax({
                  contentType : 'application/json; charset=utf-8',
                  type: 'POST',
                  url: 'http://localhost:8080/ch09/
bts/add_destination,
                  dataType : 'json',
                  data : JSON.stringify(data),
                  success : function(response) {
                     $('#tripFormResponse').text(response);   },
                  error : function(xhr, status, error) {
                     alert(xhr.responseText);        }
               });
          return false;
       });
     // prevent actual form submit and page reload
      event.preventDefault();});
</script>
```

The controller that maps the URL with the AJAX call above is written as:

```
@Controller
@RequestMapping("/bts/add_destination")
public class TripFormController {
   @Autowired
   TripService tripService;

   @RequestMapping(method=RequestMethod.POST)
   public @ResponseBody String submitForm(TripForm tripForm){
       tripService.addTrip(tripForm);
        // See the sources
       return "Success";   }
```

# Prototype AJAX

The BTS project also promotes the Prototype framework for solutions that need fewer, but more robust libraries. Its core global AJAX object is `Ajax.Request()` which serves as a factory of all the necessary methods for handling AJAX transactions. To instantiate this object, two details are needed; the request URL and the HTTP method:

```
new Ajax.Request('http://localhost:8080/ch09/bts/bookingproto.html,
    { method:'GET' });
```

By default, Prototype implements asynchronous transactions with the needed callback handlers.

BTS uses Prototype in saving destination data and is written as:

```
<script type="text/javascript">
function submitTripData() {
 new Ajax.Request(
    'http://localhost:8080/ch09/bts/bookingproto.html',
    {
     method: 'POST',
     parameters: $('submitForm').serialize(true),
     onComplete: function(transport)    {
         alert(transport.responseText);
     }
     onFailure: function(){ alert('Error in form data!') }
 }); }
</script>
```

Prototype is object-oriented in nature, and there are other objects that can be instantiated to implement other AJAX features, like JSON marshaling and un-marshaling. Compared to jQuery, codes are compacted with less function calls but with more callback handling.

Aside from `onComplete` and `onFailure`, other callbacks that can be filtered and used are `onUninitialized`, `onLoading`, `onLoaded`, `onInteractive`, `onComplete` and `onException`. On the server side, the controller that maps the URL must have methods that return `@ResponseBody` using any type of response. The following code interacts with the Prototype script above with a `plain/text` response:

```
@Controller
public class BookingController {
@RequestMapping(value="/bts/bookingproto",
                method = RequestMethod.POST)
    public @ResponseBody String bookTripProtoSubmit(
             BookingForm bookingForm){
        // See the sources
```

```
                return "success";     }   }
```

# Dojo AJAX

Dojo contains some modules that need to be imported before coding the AJAX script. Some of the popular modules like `dojo/dom`, `dojo/query`, `dojo/on`, `dojo/domReady` are defined first, before acquiring needed functions.

BTS uses Dojo in many of its search pages one of which is its search destination page, which has the following Dojo script:

```
<script type="text/javascript">
define(["dojo/request/xhr","dojo/dom","dojo/on","dojo/domReady!"],
        function(xhr,dom,on){
            var tripId = $('#tripid').val();
            var param = '{ id: tripId }';
            function listDestinations(){
              xhr('http://localhost:8080/ch09/bts/searchtrip.html',
                  { method:"post",
                    data:param, preventCache:true}).then(
                    function(data){
                     dom.byId("searchResults").innerHTML=data;
                    },
                    function(err){
                        alert(error);       },
                    function(evt){      }
              );
            }
            on(dom.byId("custSearchBtn"),
                   "click",callAjaxListing);     } );
</script>
```

Dojo codes starts with loading modules using the function `define`. This function can automatically load dependencies for any module indicated as its parameters. The dependency list is passed to the function before the exact modules are registered.

The most important module, that needs to be loaded first, is the `dojo/domReady` because it simply triggers the start of all DOM transactions when the DOM has loaded properly and is ready for processing. The core DOM module is the `dojo/dom` which has a method `byId()` which return a pointer or reference to a particular node indicated by its component ID. The method is essential for retrieving or passing data to the component.

The AJAX support of Dojo is found in the `dojo/request/xhr` module which provides an asynchronous way of sending and receiving information in a browser based-platform. This module is implemented in a cross-browser fashion, so that the end developer doesn't need to be aware of the differences between different browsers in order to use the functionality. The `xhr()` method returns a response with the handled data, errors and progress data if the browser supports XHR2 progress events. All these responses are handled by functions as shown in the above example.

The last Dojo module used in this project was `dojo/on` which is a general-purpose event-handler module for DOM nodes and other event-emitting objects, providing normalized event-listening and event-dispatching functionality. This module is designed to be lightweight and fast, based on modern browsers' event model. The `on()` calls the function `listDestinations()` once the button named `custSearchBtn` is clicked.

Through the years, Dojo has always been tagged as Spring-friendly because it does not require the server side to return XML or JSON. It only requires service methods to return typical request attributes just like in our controller below:

```
@Controller
public class TripController {
@RequestMapping(value="/bts/searchtrip",
             method = RequestMethod.POST)
    public List<Trip> retrieveTrips(Integer tripId){
        // See the sources
        return "tripService.getTrips();     } }
```

# RestEasy JSAPI

Unlike Dojo, RestEasy AJAX is very particular about the type of request data that it transports, and response data that it receives, from the server. RESTEasy can generate a JavaScript API that uses AJAX calls to invoke JAX-RS operations. Chapter 8, *Enterprise Resource Planning (ERP)* gives the details on how to set up and develop RestEasy RESTful web services. One of BTS's RESTful services, which saves all ticket bookings of a valid user, is found below:

```
@Path("/rest")
public class BookServiceImpl implements BookService {
    @Autowired
    BookingDao bookingDao;

    @Path("/reserveSeat")
    @POST
    @Consumes("application/json")
```

```
@Produces("text/plain")
@Override
public Response reserveSeat(BookingForm bookForm) {
    // See the sources
    try { bookingDao.setBooking(bookedTrip);
        return Response.ok().entity("Booked.").build();
    }catch(Exception e){
        return Response.ok().entity("Failed.").build();
    }    }
```

After developing and testing all RestEasy web services, generate the AJAX script by declaring the JSAPI servlet in the web.xml.

```
<servlet>
    <servlet-name>RESTEasy-JSAPI</servlet-name>
    <servlet-class>
        org.jboss.resteasy.jsapi.JSAPIServlet</servlet-class>
    <load-on-startup>2</load-on-startup>
</servlet>
<servlet-mapping>
    <servlet-name>RESTEasy-JSAPI</servlet-name>
    <url-pattern>/bus/js/rest-api.js</url-pattern>
</servlet-mapping>
```

Any URL pattern can be mapped to the servlet, but it is recommended to have a URL pattern with the .js extension since a JavaScript is expected to be generated by the JSAPIServlet. To ensure correctness, always register listener ResteasyBootstrap to scan resource and provider classes, and declare context parameter resteasy.scan with the value true to auto-detect existing RestEasy JAX-RS services.

If the following exception is encountered,

```
Java.lang.NullPointerException
org.jboss.resteasy.jsapi.ServiceRegistry.scanRegistry(ServiceRegistry.java:69)
org.jboss.resteasy.jsapi.ServiceRegistry.<init>(ServiceRegistry.java:63)
org.jboss.resteasy.jsapi.JSAPIServlet.scanResources(JSAPIServlet.java:75)
org.jboss.resteasy.jsapi.JSAPIServlet.init(JSAPIServlet.java:37)...
```

do not forget to load the HttpServletDispatcher servlet first, followed by JSAPIServlet through the use of the <load-on-startup> tag:

```
<servlet>
<servlet-name>RESTEasy</servlet-name>
<servlet-class>
  org.jboss.resteasy.plugins.server.servlet
            .HttpServletDispatcher</servlet-class>
```

```
    // See the sources
  <load-on-startup>1</load-on-startup>
   </servlet>
// See the sources
   <servlet>
   <servlet-name>RESTEasy-JSAPI</servlet-name>
   <servlet-class>
      org.jboss.resteasy.jsapi.JSAPIServlet</servlet-class>
   <load-on-startup>2</load-on-startup>
   </servlet>
// See the sources
```

To use the AJAX, import `/bus/js/rest-api.js` through the `<script>` tag, and access all
the service classes and methods, the way they are accessed in JVM is as follows:

```
<script language="javascript"
            src="../bus/js/rest-api.js"></script>
<script language="javascript">
    function addBookingForm()  {
        var idTxt = document.getElementById("id").value;
        var userIdTxt = document.getElementById("userId").value;
        // See the sources

        var data = {$entity: { id: idTxt,  userId: userIdTxt,
         tripId: tripIdTxt,  adults: adultsTxt, kids: kidsTxt,
         booked: bookedTxt, total: totalTxt, status: statusTxt }};
        var message = BookServiceImpl.reserveSeat(data);   }
    </script>
```

# Direct web remoting

In the same way as RestEasy, DWR exposes all services and methods remotely as AJAX
utilities that can be accessed in the same way that they are accessed as Java APIs. Between
the two, DWR is the easiest to use, because it directly exposes all service components as
JavaScript utilities, without dealing with request and response types.

DWR configuration starts with writing its services. All DWR services are `@Transactional`
since we are using the JPA framework with Hibernate 4.x. They are also `@RemoteProxy`
which means these are services to be exposed remotely by DWR. The methods of the service
classes are all `@RemoteMethod` which means they will all be exposed remotely by DWR as
AJAX functions. BTS uses DWR services to store all new users in the database.

The following is the code of the service class.

```
@RemoteProxy
@Transactional
@Service
public class RegisterServiceImpl implements RegisterService {
    @Autowired
    private RegisterDao registerDao;

    @Transactional
    @RemoteMethod
    @Override
    public void registerUser(RegisterForm registerForm) {
        CustomerInfo customerInfo = new CustomerInfo();
        // See the sources
        registerDao.setLogin(login);
    } }
```

Then, all the data and form models to be used by DWR must be exposed remotely. All beans classes that will be accessed remotely must be declared @DataTransferObject. If these bean classes are Hibernate domain classes, DWR will marshal and unmarshal this object using a certain converter, like converter=H3BeanConverter.class, with attributes type="hibernate4". If bean classes are typical ones, like form models, these must be declared as type="bean" which have a remote name like javascript="registerForm". Each property of these **Data Transfer Objects (DTO)** must also be exposed using the annotation @RemoteProperty. A sample DWR DTO is shown as follows:

```
@DataTransferObject(type="bean", javascript="registerForm")
public class RegisterForm {
    @RemoteProperty
    private String firstName;
    @RemoteProperty
    private String middleName;
    @RemoteProperty
    private String lastName;
    // See the sources  }
```

Afterwards, we declare org.directwebremoting.spring.DwrSpringServlet in the web.xml and configure its ApplicationContext container, dwr.xml. This container must have the DWR namespace xmlns:dwr="http://www.directwebremoting.org/schema/spring-dwr to access all the tag libraries. Using the tag libraries, let DWR scan all the @Remoteproxy services and @DataTransferObject beans by declaring the <dwr:annotation-scan/>:

```
<spring-dwr:annotation-scan base-package="org.packt.bus.portal"
    scanDataTransferObject="true" scanRemoteProxy="true"/>
```

The attribute `scanRemoteProxy` scans all the `@RemoteProxy` classes within the base package, when set to true, whereas the `scanRemoteProxy` scans all the DTO objects for the view page. Then, add the tag `<dwr:configuration />` which is left empty since BTS uses annotations instead of tag libraries like `<dwr:convert/>`. Another tag that needs to be present is the `<dwr:annotation-config />` which basically tells Spring that all DWR components are configured using annotations.

After deployment, first check the `/dwr/index.html` to validate if all services and methods are recognized and exposed remotely by the DWR servlet. Once all DWR components are ready for use, the AJAX script must be written in this manner:

```
<script type="text/javascript"
     src="${ contextPath }/dwr/engine.js"></script>
<script type="text/javascript"
     src="${ contextPath }/dwr/interface/RegisterServiceImpl.js">
</script>
<script type="text/javascript"
     src="${ contextPath }/dwr/util.js"></script>
<script type="text/javascript">
   function saveUser(){
       var registerForm = {
       firstName: document.getElementById("firstName").value,
       // See the sources
       };
       RegisterServiceImpl.registerUser(registerForm,{
               callback:function(registerForm){       }
   });    }
</script>
```

In order to fully utilize DWR, the following base JavaScript libraries must be imported:

- `/dwr/engine.js`: These are mandatory functions since they are used to marshal calls from the dynamically generated JavaScript interfaces to the server; it is vital to DWR object processing
- `/dwr/util.js`: Recommended since it contains a number of utility functions to help you update your web pages with JavaScript data

# WebSocket

AJAX has also been useful in establishing small-scale chat rooms, message boards or helplines for customers in many lines of business. For instance, in this application, BTS creates a customer service page that accepts complaints or commendations from users for certain issues. This feature uses WebSocket protocol to automate the helpdesk, which can be upgraded to chat rooms for more interactivity.

First, we create a socket handler and endpoint mapping to establish a handshake. A sample handler is shown as follows:

```
@ServerEndpoint(value="/chat/feedback")
public class CustomerHandler extends TextWebSocketHandler {
    @OnMessage
    public void onMessage(String message, Session session)
    throws IOException, InterruptedException {
        session.getBasicRemote().sendText("Your complaint: "
            + message
            + " is being taken into consideration. Thank you!"); }
    @OnOpen
    public void onOpen() {
        // Logs open connection }
    @OnClose
    public void onClose() {
        // Logs close connection with or without errors    } }
```

And the AJAX that transports all comments from the client page to the server must access the endpoint URL, above, through jQuery's WebSocket object. The script used by the customer service page is shown as follows:

```
<script src="//ajax.googleapis.com/ajax/libs/
            jquery/1.11.1/jquery.min.js"></script>
<script type="text/javascript">
  var ws = new WebSocket('ws://localhost:8080/ch09/helpdesk');
  ws.onopen = function() {
  $('#console').append('websocket opened' + '<br>');
  };
  ws.onmessage = function(message) {
  $('#console').append('receive message : '
      + message.data + '<br>');    };
  ws.onclose = function(event) {
  $('#console').append('websocket closed : '
      + event.reason + ' code: ' + event.code);   };
  function messageSend() {
  ws.send($('#message').val()); }
</script>
```

The AJAX above creates a new connection attempt through instantiating `WebSocket('ws://localhost:8080/ch09/chat/feedback')`. During the attempt, the client is looking for a handshake status with the server. If the handshake is successful, and a connection is established, the `socket.onopen()` event handler is executed. The client is notified through the `socket.onmessage()` after the server recognizes the handshake. The client will send a message to the server using the `socket.send()` function. All these client-side services communicate with their corresponding methods in the `CustomHandler` above.

BTS is made ready for SockJS and STOMP implementation.

# jQGrid

JQGrid (**JQuery Grid**) provides solutions for representing and manipulating tabular data on the web. This AJAX solution converts local array data into XML or JSON type. First, we create a controller that will retrieve all records of trips objects:

```
@RequestMapping(value="/bts/trips", method=RequestMethod.GET,
    headers="Accept=application/json")
public @ResponseBody List<Trip> getTrips(){
    return tripService.getTrips();      }
```

Then, jQuery receives the list of objects in JSON format:

```
$.when($.getJSON('http://localhost:8080/ch09/bts/trips.json'))
    .then(function (data) { ... }
```

If the jQuery transaction has no errors, the JSON will be used to populate jQGrid, eventually creating the data set:

```
$(document).ready(function() {
$.when($.getJSON('http://localhost:8080/ch09/bts/trips.json'))
    .then(function (data) { $("#trips").jqGrid({
        datatype: "local",    height: 250,    width: 700,
        colNames: ['TRIP ID', 'NAME', 'SIGHTS', 'DAY', 'NIGHT',
            'TYPE', 'OTHER', 'LANG', 'ADULT', 'KID'],
          colModel: [{  name: 'id', index: 'id', width: 10,
                    sorttype: "int"}, ......],
});
 var names = ['id', 'name', 'sightsStops', 'dayDuration', 'nightDuration',
'typeDuration', 'otherTransport', 'language', 'priceAdult', 'priceKid'];
    var tripsData = [];

    for (var i = 0; i < data.length; i++) {
        tripsData[i] = {}; tripsData[i][names[0]] = data[i].id;
```

```
                   // See the sources  }
      for (var i = 0; i <= tripsData.length; i++) {
        $("#trips").jqGrid('addRowData', i + 1, tripsData[i]); }
    });
  });
```

Although Chapter 6, *Hotel Management System (HMS)* provides other solutions in generating tabular data using ExtJS, AngularJS and Thymeleaf, many developers prefer jQGrid because it is simple to implement and the syntax is near to jQuery scripts.

# Google Chart visualization

The HRMS prototype in Chapter 4, *Human Resource Management System (HRMS)* has proved to us that Spring 4.x can help solve data modeling problems using visualization tools and plugins. As well as the server-side transactions, Spring can use AJAX to generate charts, graphs and other advance plots using JavaScript objects like those found in Google Chart APIs.

The GoogleAjaxController has a service/bts/trips/year which provides JSON data to a view, and produces a line graph using JavaScript code:

```
<script type="text/javascript"
   src="https://www.gstatic.com/charts/loader.js"></script>
 <script type="text/javascript"
src="//ajax.googleapis.com/ajax/libs/jquery/1.10.2/jquery.min.js"></script>
<script type="text/javascript">
    google.charts.load('current', {
        packages : [ 'corechart' ]    });
    google.charts.setOnLoadCallback(drawLines);
    function drawLines() {
      var jsonData = $.ajax({
            url: "http://localhost:8080/ch09/bts/trips/year",
            dataType: "json",
            async: false
      }).responseText;
  var data = new google.visualization.DataTable();
    data.addColumn('number', 'Month');
    data.addColumn('number', 'Trip Frequency');
    var json = $.parseJSON(jsonData);
    for (var i=0;i<json.length;++i){
          alert(json[i].month);
          data.addRows([
                      [json[i].month, json[i].numTrips]
          ]);       }
      var chart = new google.visualization.LineChart(
```

```
                        document.getElementById('chart_div'));
        chart.draw(data, {
            title: 'Year 2016 Trip Abalysis',
            curveType: 'function',
            legend: { position: 'bottom' }
        });    }
    </script>
```

To load the APIs, the view page must call `/charts/loader.js` which contains all the functions for creating charts. For line and other core graphs, the JavaScript code must execute `google.charts.load("current", {packages: ["corechart"]})` initially. Then, the loader must recognize a callback method that will implement the simulation through the `google.charts.setOnLoadCallback()` method. Afterwards, JQuery will retrieve the JSON data from the `@Controller` and will convert the JSON object to a `DataTable` for plotting. The `google.visualization.LineChart` JavaScript object will be instantiated to generate the line graph from the generated DataTable.

 **Theme design**
The theme design of the application is derived from: `http://themeforest.net/item/gofar-multipurpose-travel-booking-template`.

# The Bus Ticketing System (BTS)

The Bus Ticketing System (BTS) gave us solutions on how to integrate AJAX into Spring 4.x specification, in order to establish client-server processing. Despite vulnerabilities and risks on client-based solutions, Spring Security, Spring Social's Oath authentication service, or Captcha, can provide security for our AJAX transactions. BTS or any client-centric application can easily be integrated into ExtJS, AngularJS and CSS for user experience and responsiveness.

In general, anything made up of AJAX is manageable and flexible because all of its major processes are decoupled from its server specification.

# Challenge yourself

Create a **movie ticketing system** that is a hybrid of Spring and AJAX wherein all major input and output transactions and validations will be done by any AJAX solutions above. Study how to validate using JavaScript and how to build pop-up error messages using jQuery UI.

# Summary

This chapter has given us a clear picture of the Spring framework which relies heavily on browser-based transactions. Spring's flexibility and robustness gave us an architecture where the bulk of processing is done on the client-side, whether it is a simple data presentation, or a complicated socket-driven chat messaging feature. Because of its high-adaptability to JavaScript APIs, Spring can make browser-centric applications which are easier to design, test and deploy.

# 10
# Social Task Management System (STMS)

Recently, the massive number of people joining social networking sites has triggered a social media boom that has given people a clearer vision and goal of how to face their everyday endeavors. Social media applications provide users with workflow models, in order to perform their daily tasks efficiently and effectively. At business level, social software gives employees a smarter outlook, in order to finish their jobs at a specified time with the deserving team effort.

**Social Task Management** (**STM**) is one of the social technologies that helps preserve and enrich interpersonal communication and relationships in the workplace. Existing enterprise applications, both intranet and Internet, have existing forums, message boards, chat rooms, and other customer- and sales-related modules to establish feedback systems, not only between customers and clients, but also among people in the company. The **Social Task Management System** (**STMS**) adds color, human emotion, analytics, and meaning to these existing features, to create a suggestive and reactive model of the workplace. This type of application gives the employee a more corporate reality setup, which can help them understand and absorb the causes and effects of their everyday tasks.

Technically, the system involves continuous interaction between the constituents within and outside the company, which leads to an abrupt increase of posts, tweets, and comments. Unlike in typical software, social media applications always need data warehouses and data management because of the high bandwidth of incoming and outgoing messaging as usage time increases.

This chapter will provide some ways to create STM applications using the Spring 4.x libraries and plugins appropriate for applications that can handle big data management.

In this chapter, we will cover the following topics:

- Utilizing the Spring Data JPA framework to manage data sources
- Integrating Spring MVC with MongoDB as an alternative data management platform
- Creating domain models and efficient data searching using the SOLR framework
- Implementing graph searching using the Neo4j framework
- Establishing enterprise channels and workflows using the Spring Integration framework

# Overview of the project

This chapter will only focus on the messaging side of the portal, where employees can post anything related to their job for others to see and comment on. Technically, the scope revolves around posting messages regarding task issues, project deliverables, professional comments, suggestions, or labor issues concerning employees in a certain project in the company. The mechanism is quite similar to Chapter 5, *Customer Feedback System (CFS)*'s, but this time it has the capability to generate data analysis showing which posts trigger happiness, sadness, amusement, inspiration, frustration, and fear. Aside from mood analysis, STMS can also find out the number of posts belonging to each office's department, rank, or position.

The prototype consists of the following basic core modules:

- **Message area**: This dashboard-like feature lets any employee post anything about their experiences and situations. Since this prototype is designed to run as an intranet application in a company or department, there will be no user authentication to establish open communication.

- **Data analytics**: This feature identifies the mood of the day, the trending keyword of the day, and some other necessary statistics that are helpful when settling issues among workers and employers.

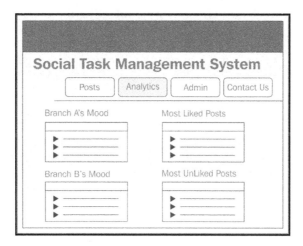

- **Administration page**: The purpose of this page is to manage the posts, such as deleting or updating some keywords that might be too personal or offensive against a particular party.

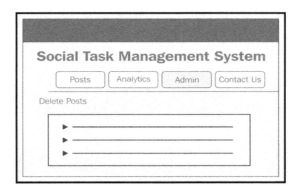

# Technical requirements

Currently, the major challenge in developing social media applications is creating an efficient design of different repositories that can be unified to handle the abrupt increase in data generated by high volumes of user interactivity. Given the complexities of data stores, many are looking for an optimized solution of data mining and query techniques that can save a lot of project time, cost, and effort without affecting the performance of the system.

Aside from the data management part, social media applications, nowadays, would be profitable and powerful if they could be easily integrated with some existing legacy and enterprise applications, such as ERP. Again, there are lots of SOA or web service solutions, discussed in Chapter 8, *Enterprise Resource Planning (ERP)* that could be the best solution to the problem, but what systems need, nowadays, is a solution that can save project resources.

This chapter introduces lightweight Spring modules, namely and **Spring Integration**Spring Data and Spring Integration. Spring Data was developed to unify and simplify the access to different kinds of persistence store, both relational database systems and NoSQL data stores, while Spring Integration is a module responsible for establishing **Enterprise Application Integration (EAI)**.

# Spring Data JPA

Spring Data JPA is one of the popular Spring projects that can simplify a data access layer of the project by entirely removing the DAO implementation. This chapter will introduce the creation of Spring 4.x applications that only require interfaces to define the query transactions. Instead of the complicated and cumbersome configuration of the Hibernate JPA framework, done in the previous chapters, the STMS prototype in this chapter uses Spring Data JPA to reduce the effort of generating queries, auditing transactions, and creating data tables with pagination to be rendered by views.

To start Spring Data JPA implementation, the following Maven dependencies must be part of the project libraries:

- `org.springframework.data: spring-data-jpa` (version `1.9.2.RELEASE`) with some required exclusions
- Other dependencies, such as Hibernate 4 Framework core APIs

Spring Data JPA is for applications that use relational databases as their data storage.

# Spring Data MongoDB

Another prototype of the STMS application uses MongoDB as the data storage. MongoDB is a NoSQL database management system composed of sets of documents, where one document is a combination of different key/value properties. Spring Data MongoDB is the module of Spring that has support for all APIs for both functional and annotated query configuration. Its configuration is flexible and straightforward, and follows Spring's data-centric approach.

To use this module, the following Maven dependencies must be included in the POM file:

`org.springframework.data: spring-data-mongodb` (version `1.7.2.RELEASE`)

# Spring Data REST

To let two or more STMSes share their data, Spring Data Rest is employed to expose entities directly, without having to implement DTOs or DAOs. Spring Data Rest is another Spring module that is a lightweight implementation of RESTful web service endpoints. It helps developers to focus on CRUD or query services, rather than configuring the platform.

To utilize Spring Data Rest, include the following dependencies in the project's POM:

`org.springframework.data: spring-data-rest-webmvc (version 2.4.2.RELEASE)`

# Spring Data Solr

In order to query big data, Apache Solr provides any application an efficient basic, advanced, or full-text, search feature for any views. To protect the performance of the system from search overhead, many applications transfer the search processing task to an external server such as Solr, especially when data becomes too large.

Some ORM frameworks, such as Hibernate, have built-in Solr server support to provide not only search optimization techniques, but also data caching, pagination, and full-text search implementation using dynamic queries.

The Spring 4.x has a straightforward Spring Data Solr, which simplifies Apache Solr integration into any Spring application. To use this module, the following libraries must be included in the Maven repository:

`org.springframework.data: spring-data-solr (version 1.5.2.RELEASE)`

# Neo4J

Spring Data Neo4J If the amount of users and data exchanges runs into the millions, then a graph search server is recommended to search for uncountable tags, vocabulary, contexts, and keywords from the data store. Out of the many alternatives of graph search server, Neo4j is the most optimal, accessible, and available NoSQL data store for persisting graph data.

A graph is a data structure with finite sets of vertices connected by edges. Visually, graphs depict the relationship between nodes, domains, or entities through the edges that connect them. A graph search is not a typical query transaction because it uses the connectivity or relationship among domain objects in the database. Once the search criteria have been submitted, graph search only filters all the data related to the specific domain, unlike in a typical query where it looks for the criteria in all possible domains of the database. Correlation of data is important in a graph search; thus, the degree of association among records, and the frequency of record access, are more highly regarded than the correctness of the context search.

To integrate Spring 4.x applications with the Neo4j server, the following dependencies must be in the POM file:

- `org.springframework.data: spring-data-neo4j` (version `3.4.2.RELEASE`)
- `org.springframework.data: spring-data-neo4j-rest` (version `3.4.2.RELEASE`)
- `com.fasterxml.jackson.core: jackson-databind` (version 2.6.3)
- `com.fasterxml.jackson.core: jackson-core` (version 2.6.3)

 The given Maven API classes and interfaces used by this chapter only support transactions under Neo4J server 2.2.0 to 2.2.10.

# Spring integration

To consolidate different enterprise systems, such as legacy or modern software applications, experts always resort to **Enterprise Application Integration** (**EAI**) middleware because of their popularity and availability in commercial or open-source portals. There are many ways to create an EIA solution, such as using different web service technologies bundled together, or using the complex (**ESB**Enterprise Service Bus (ESB) (for example, Mule ESB) to bridge systems by deploying them into its container. Given a scarce resource for a project, an architect must seek or design middleware that can be implemented within schedule and cost.

For easy configuration, and fast implementation, Spring Integration must be the first among all the options, because it does not require many external APIs or servers, and the solution can be deployed within the project's `ApplicationContext` container. It supports both XML and annotated configuration, and it can be used to bridge any JEE applications without lots of cumbersome configuration.

To use Spring Integration, the following Maven dependencies must be found in the POM file:

- `org.springframework.integration: spring-integration-core` (version `4.1.4.RELEASE`) with some necessary exclusions
- `com.fasterxml.jackson.core: jackson-databind` (version 2.6.3)
- `com.fasterxml.jackson.core: jackson-core` (version 2.6.3)

# Collaborative data analysis concept

The STMS simply aims to provide a survey, in order to find out the everyday motivation and mood of a sample population of employees from two companies, namely company *A* and company *B*. Each company will have its own STMS, with similar features presented in the preceding wireframe requirement. Each company will have to gather the tasks, deliverables, work issues, and accomplishments of their employees through the social software and later analyze and derive reports summarizing certain factors that affect the workplace. Although it will take more time to create a full-blown STSM portal, the scope of this chapter only covers the messaging and posting of tasks and issues where the moods and motivation can be derived:

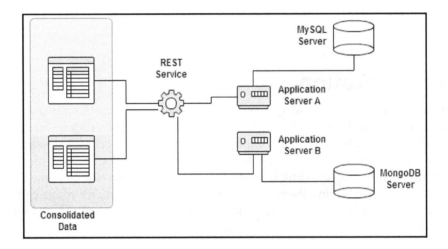

The preceding architecture design describes the setup of the two STMSes, where each has its own application server and database management system. Company *A* uses MySQL as its database server, while company *B* has MongoDB to store its data. With their respective STMSes, both companies store and retrieve data, but each has the capability to consolidate their data together using REST endpoints. This type of solution can be regarded as collaborative data mining, where different surveys are conducted in different sub groups or strata and are collected to test different hypotheses. Each SMTS can employ different supervised, or unsupervised, learning algorithms, but what is important, now, is how different numbers of queries can be implemented to access huge amounts of data without causing performance problems.

# Database configuration

Since the architecture needs to configure two different data repositories within a schedule, Spring Data will be the ultimate solution to assist the setup of the project.

## Spring Data JPA configuration

To implement JPA persistency in the project's data model, we declare interfaces that will handle repository transactions or queries. These interfaces can be any of the following types:

- `org.springframework.data.jpa.repository.JpaRepository<E,ID>`: The interface containing generic JPA abstract methods
- `org.springframework.data.repository.CrudRepository< E,ID >`: The interface containing CRUD abstract methods associated with a domain's specific attribute types
- `org.springframework.data.repository.PagingAndSortingRepository< E,ID >`: An extension of the `CrudRepository` interface with sorting and pagination abstract methods

`<E, ID>` is a generics entity with *E* as the specific domain model and ID as the domain's serialized `@ID` property type. An example of a custom-defined JPA repository is `PostRepository`:

```
@Repository
public interface PostRepository extends
                              JpaRepository<Post, Long> {
    public List<Post> findAll();
    public List<Post> findByStoryContainingIgnoreCase(
                              String story);
    // See the sources
    public List<Post> findByPosition(String position);
    @Query("select p from Post p where p.id = :id")
    public List<Post> findByIdIs(@Param("id") Integer id); }
```

`PostRepository` has a `@Repository` annotation to register its corresponding auto-generated implementation as a Spring repository.

All the preceding abstract methods, except `findByIds`, are automatically generated, mapped to domain properties, and overridden by the module after compilation. Therefore, misspelled or undefined methods will result in compiler error.

```
40    public List<Post> findMsg();
41
42  }                  ⊗ Invalid derived query! No property findMsg found for type Post!

    <                                                        Press 'F2' for focus
```

All custom-made abstract methods, such as `findByIds`, to be implemented by the module, must use the `@Query` annotation that contains the custom JPA query statement. To create dynamic queries, we use the `@Param` annotation to bind the query parameter to the service method parameter.

Then, all these defined interfaces must be injected and recognized by Spring Data JPA. The Spring Data JPA is utilized by Spring through its namespace, `xmlns:jpa=http://www.springframework.org/schema/data/jpa`, and its corresponding XSD file. To bootstrap all repository interfaces, the module must recognize all these classes through `<jpa:repositories base-package="org.packt.analytics.portal.repository" />`. It is also mandatory to have `<context:annotation-config />` and `<context:component-scan base-package="org.packt.analytics.portal" />` tags present in the container configuration since Spring Data is all driven by annotations. The rest of the configurations are the usual `DataSource` and `EntityManagerFactory` registration discussed in the previous chapters.

## Spring Data MongoDB configuration

Since company *B* is expected to store more data than company *A*, owing to its size, MongoDB was configured to cater for reading and writing the data. Although MongoDB does not require relational schema design, the ERD shown in the company *A* project figure will still be the basis for its collection and documents. **Collections** are the database counterpart in MongoDB that contains dynamic schemas that store JSON-like documents or records. There is no definite structured schema design in MongoDB.

To start the configuration, all domain models must have `@Document` annotation to specify the collection where the data is to be persisted. Omitting this annotation will save the data in a collection that has the same name as the domain class.

Another requirement is for the domain object to have a primary key @Id, which is sometimes preferred to be a String type. A domain object is mapped to a document in MongoDB with an auto-generated primary key _id, which is mapped to the @Id property of the model bean. All domain objects are required to have an @Id property.

Other annotations that could be present are @DBRef and @PersistenceConstructor. The former establishes an entity relationship between domain objects if there are foreign key constraints, while the latter marks the constructor that is to be used to create entities when fetching data from the Mongo Server.

Sample MongoDB domain models of this project are as follows:

```
@Document(collection="post")
public class Post {
    @Id
    private Integer id;
    // See the sources
    @DBRef("likes")
    private Set<Likes> likeses = new HashSet<Likes>(0);

    @DBRef("unlikes")
    private Set<Unlikes> unlikeses = new HashSet<Unlikes>(0);

    @DBRef("comments")
    private Set<Comments> commentses = new HashSet<Comments>(0)    }

@Document(collection="likes")
public class Likes {
    @Id
    private Integer id;
    // See the sources    }

@Document(collection="unlikes")
public class Unlikes {
    @Id
    private Integer id;
    // See the sources    }

@Document(collection="comments")
public class Comments {
    @Id
    private Integer id;
    // See the sources    }
```

After all domain objects are set for use, we define the interfaces that will generate our transaction services. These classes can extend any of the Spring Data JPA repository APIs mentioned previously, or use the MongoDB-specific service method generator, which is `org.springframework.data.mongodb.repository.MongoRepository<E,ID>`.

In order to inject all domains and services, we need to load the Spring Data MongoDB into the container using the namespace `xmlns:mongo=http://www.springframework.org/schema/data/mongo` and its XSD. After loading the module, the container must recognize the Mongo server configuration details:

```
<mongo:mongo id="mongo" host="localhost" port="27017"/>.
```

To auto-implement all the abstract methods in the custom repository interfaces, the container must register `org.springframework.data.mongodb.core.MongoTemplate` given the name of the collection, STMS, and the server configuration:

```
<bean id="mongoTemplate"
class="org.springframework.data.mongodb.core.MongoTemplate">
    <constructor-arg ref="mongo"/>
    <constructor-arg name="databaseName" value="stms"/>
  </bean>
```

To recognize all repository annotations, we declare `<mongo:repositories base-package="org.packt.analytics.portal.repository"/>`. For other Spring-based annotations, `<context:annotation-config />` and `<context:component-scan base-package="org.packt.analytics.portal" />` tags must also be included in the container.

# Database search techniques

Small applications may not easily include search engines in their functionality, because most of them do not have many database read/write operations. But for applications that involve data analysis and mining, wherein data ranges from medium to huge size, search optimizations must be planned well.

Some of the factors that can affect query plans are the type of database system to be used, the number of join operations each query needs, and the complexity of the query syntax to be implemented. Most query plans cost a lot of time and effort, thus delaying the project or adding overheads to the overall system performance.

Integrating Spring 4.x applications with Solr and Graph search servers give immediate but optimal solutions to search problems. Unlike planning based on data integrity, consistency, and referential integrity, which needs lots of attention, Solr and Graph search solutions do not require too many SQL intricacies.

# Document-based and full-text search

Apache Solr indexes all words found in a document and builds a hash table of indexed entries and the corresponding frequencies of the occurrences of each entry. Since all data in Solr is in JSON format, the term **document** refers to a record, while a **field** is synonymous with a column in the relational database context.

Solr retrieves documents simply by creating a search query with a simple /select statement (`qt`) with a filter (`fw`) limited to the field name (`fl`), and with a corresponding response writer (`wt`) that will encode the query response (that is, JSON, XML, and Python). The Solr server, `http://localhost:8983/solr`, allows us to search all records from its database instance.

## Configuring the Solr server

The Solr server can be installed as an embedded Solr using `Solr.war` or as an external HTTP Solr server. The former requires Spring to compile its components with the classes found in the WAR file, making it easier for `ApplicationContext` to directly initialize a Solr core, add documents to the index, and execute queries. Meanwhile, installing the Solr server separately requires the Spring container to access Solr through the HTTP protocol. This chapter prefers installing Solr as a separate server because, aside from it separating the Spring implementation from the server, it also promotes loosely-coupled infrastructure design.

After the installation, it is necessary to install a Solr core index where all field data will be indexed. A Solr core index can be created either through the Web using the Solr Core Admin page, or through the terminal command `solr create -c <core name>`. Other commands, such as `solr start`, are essential in booting up the server, while `solr stop`â☺☺all shuts down all instances of Solr.

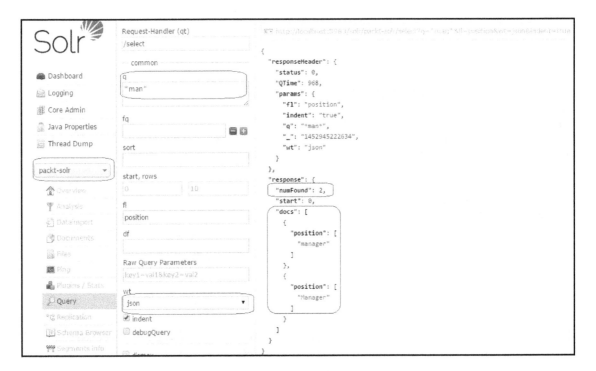

Every core index in Solr has two main configuration files that need to be checked and updated before starting the development. The configuration files, which are found in our `\solr-5.4.0\server\solr\packt-solr\conf`, are as follows:

- `schema.xml`: This file defines the types and fields of the documents to be indexed and managed by the `solrconfig.xml` file; It must contain all POJO elements needed to be indexed and searched otherwise the Spring Data Solr queries will return empty records
- `solrconfig.xml`: This file contains advanced components such as request handlers, scanners, and query parsers

# The Spring-Solr integration

To load the bean methods into the container, we declare the namespace `xmlns:solr=http://www.springframework.org/schema/data/solr` and its XSD to utilize the tags needed for container injection. Then, we convert some JPA domain models or create an independent set of models to become Solr search documents through an `@SolrDocument` annotation, mapping all its domain data to the Solr core. Its data must be tagged with the `@Field` annotation to successfully create the links with all the mappings inside `schema.xml`. Optionally, a domain data can use a separate Solr field name indicated in `schema.xml` through `@Field` annotation as well (for example, `@Field("likes_mul")` ). By convention, the `@Field` annotation can be applied either to a field or setter method.

The Solr document fields must be declared inside Solr core's `schema.xml`. For instance, the domain model post is as follows:

```
@Entity
@Table(name = "post", catalog = "stms")
@SolrDocument(solrCoreName = "packt-solr")
public class Post implements java.io.Serializable {

    @Field
    private Integer id;
    @Field
    private String subject;
    // See the sources
    @Field("likes_mul")
    private Set<Likes> likes = new HashSet<Likes>(0);
    @Field("unlikes_mul")
    private Set<Unlikes> unlikes = new HashSet<Unlikes>(0);
    @Field("comments_mul")
    private Set<Comments> comments = new HashSet<Comments>(0);
    // See the sources
}
```

It must have `id` and `subject` declared in `schema.xml` as follows:

```
<field name="id" type="string" indexed="true" stored="true"
    required="true" multiValued="false" />
<field name="subject" type="string" indexed="true"
    multiValued="false"  stored="true"/>
```

 Each record in Solr can only be recognized by a unique string type ID.

However, fields such as `likes`, `unlikes`, and `comments`, which are special multivalued elements, must be declared through creating custom dynamic fields as follows:

```
<dynamicField name="*_mul" type="text_general" indexed="true"
    stored="true" multiValued="true"/>.
```

 Fields that are `text_general` are multivalued string entries.

After setting the POJOs, the `@Repository` classes are the next component to be defined in the container. These repository interfaces must extend the base Spring Data Solr API, which is `org.springframework.data.solr.repository.SolrCrudRepository` for the auto-generation of all Solr search methods. Moreover, we can create custom query transactions through `@Query`, which may apply pagination using `Page` and `Pageable` APIs. The custom Solr `@Query` follows the Lucene query syntax, which consists of the field name followed by a colon "`:`" and then an expression of wildcards and the parameters of the query:

```
public interface PostSolrRepository extends
        SolrCrudRepository<PostSolr, String>{
    List<PostSolr> findByStory(String story);

    @Query("subject:*?0*")
    List<PostSolr> findBySubject(String subject);
```

The `PostSolrRepository` is one of the STMS repository classes that implements all *out-of-the-box* Solr query methods. These repository classes must be configured in the Solr server `<solr:solr-server id="solrServer" url="http://localhost:8983/solr" />`.

From its configuration, `SolrTemplate` must be instantiated in order to implement all interface methods of `SolrCrudRepository`:

```
<bean id="solrTemplate"
      class="org.springframework.data.solr.core.SolrTemplate">
        <constructor-arg index="0" ref="solrServer"/> </bean>
```

In order for Spring to recognize all Solr repository annotations, we need to inject
`<solr:repositories base-`
`package="org.packt.analytics.portal.solr.repository" multicore-`
`support="true"/>`, where `multicore-support` is set to `true`, allowing indexing to
more than one Solr core index. Spring-based configuration tags such as
`<context:component-scan base-package="org.packt.analytics.portal" />`
and `<mvc:annotation-driven />` must also be found in the container's configuration to
load all Spring-aware annotations.

# The Spring-Neo4J integration

Another way of searching data with an emphasis on performance and security is through
graph search. To construct a graph search query or cypher, graph database engines need to
be installed to store records as nodes connected together internally, just like graphs. One
popular graph database system is Neo4J, which is used by our STMS application.

Relational databases use the concepts of schema, records, and fields to represent data. The
interrelationship of these concepts lies in the foreign key integrity of the schemas involved.
**Entity-relationship diagrams** (**ERDs**) are often the basis of database design and provide a
general picture of how data is interconnected through foreign key constraints. In graph
search database design, join operations are auto-constructed using the concept of
relationships.

In a graph database engine, nodes are used to represent data, wherein each node is
equivalent to a record or entity. These nodes are connected through a special kind of
relationship that could be called foreign keys or map-reduce. The model basically depicts a
huge graph data structure consisting of nodes, vertices, and connectivity. Aside from its
fine-grained and flexible design, the main goal of this data model is to leverage the
execution of heavy query transactions such as `JOIN` operations. When running JOIN
queries, the graph database will just return a fixed list of connected nodes instead,
eliminating much of the overhead of query parsing.

The following figure shows the data connectivity of the `Post`, `Comments`, and `Likes` domain inside a Neo4J database:

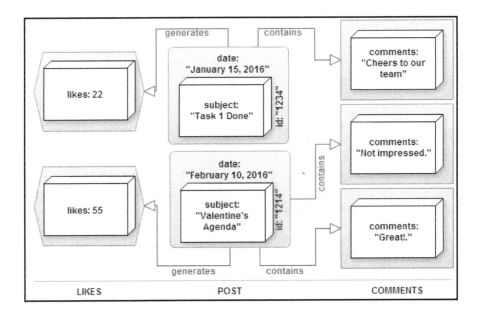

## Configuring the Neo4J graph search server

Neo4J version 2.2.10 can be installed on any operating system platform. After a successful installation, Neo4j needs a location where it can create its database. It has the main launcher panel to assist the user in choosing the desired database location. Once the location is set, enable data store upgrade in the `neo4j.properties` file by uncommenting this line:

```
allow_store_upgrade=true
```

Aside from upgrading, the configuration file is also used to fine tune the JVM size and properties that will fit to the projected data of the STMS application. For database server authentication settings, the other file, `neo4j-server.properties`, must be configured to prevent the user from directly accessing the nodes and their relationships. To manage the server startup and shutdown, the launcher has the corresponding buttons to be clicked to load or unload database files. Finally, the Neo4J web admin console will be available for access through the default URL `http://localhost:7474`.

The Neo4J administrative application is the only channel for developers to directly manipulate the database instance using cypher, the declarative graph query language. A cypher is a Neo4J statement that has both SQL and graph-specific functionality used to retrieve and update graph structures concisely and graphically. A cypher that saves a particular `Post` node is written as follows:

```
CREATE (post:Post {id:12345, subject:"Valentine's Agenda",...,...})
RETURN post
```

A cypher that retrieves a `Post` node, given a constraint, is as follows:

```
MATCH (post:Post {id:12345 }).
```

## Spring-Neo4J integration

Just like Solr, Neo4J core can be integrated into the Spring container to directly store and access the graph database without using any URL invocation. But project deployment and code management will be easier if we separate the server from the application codes. The Spring Data Neo4J module handles Neo4J integration robustly with annotated mappings and transaction management.

The first requirement is to convert the domain model, or create another set of POJO to be used as `@NodeEntity`. Then, we choose the primary key of the node and declare them using `@GraphId`. This tells Spring Data Neo4J that this is an identifier that we can use for lookups. Afterwards, we choose some of the node properties that need to be indexed into the graph server using the `@Indexed` annotation. One of the node entities of the project is written as follows:

```
@Entity
@Table(name = "post", catalog = "stms")
@NodeEntity
public class Post implements java.io.Serializable {

    @GraphId
    private Integer id;
    @Indexed(indexType = IndexType.FULLTEXT,
            indexName = "searchBySubject")
    private String subject;

    @Indexed
    private String mood;

    @RelatedTo(type = "REPORTS_TO", direction=Direction.INCOMING)
    private Set<Likes> likess = new HashSet<Likes>(0);
    // See the sources  }
```

Relationships are essential to establishing the graph schema. There are two types of relationship that can be used to link nodes: `simple` and `complex`. A simple relationship only involves incoming and outgoing connectivity between two nodes, like our `Post` and `Likes` domains shown in the preceding code snippet with the use of `@RelatedTo` annotations. On the other hand, complex relationships require the creation of relationship entities that consider behavior other than connectivity. These custom entities also decide which nodes will be the `@StartNode` and `@EndNode` in the relationship.

Next to be created are the repository classes. Just like any other custom repository layer under Spring Data, the module only requires interfaces to be defined with `org.springframework.data.neo4j.repository.GraphRepository<E>` as its superclass, where `E` is the generic placeholder referring to the node entity. This interface API contains the predefined abstract methods that can be auto-generated by the module, and also allows the creation of custom cyphers using the `@Query` annotation.

Lastly, the Spring Data Neo4J module must instantiate the `Neo4JTemplate` to implement all interface methods needed for graph server transactions in either embedded or separate server installation strategy; Neo4J does not currently support the XML-based configuration. STMS has a JavaBean configuration for its Neo4J transactions which is as follows:

```
@Configuration
@EnableNeo4jRepositories(basePackages = {
"org.packt.analytics.portal.graph.repository" })
@EnableTransactionManagement
@ComponentScan(basePackages = { "org.packt.analytics.portal" })
public class Neo4JRepositoryConfiguration extends Neo4jConfiguration {

    public static final String uri = "http://localhost:7474/db/data/";
    public static final String user = "neo4j";
    public static final String pass = "packt";

    Neo4JRepositoryConfiguration() {
      setBasePackage("org.packt.analytics.portal.model.data");   }

    @Bean
    GraphDatabaseService graphDatabaseService() {
      return new SpringCypherRestGraphDatabase(uri, user, pass);   }
}
```

## Integration pitfalls

If the Neo4J database version is not supported by the Spring data module version, then the following compilation error will be encountered:

```
Caused by:
```

```
org.neo4j.kernel.impl.storemigration.StoreUpgrader$UpgradingStoreVersionNot
FoundException: 'neostore.nodestore.db' does not contain a store version,
please ensure that the original database was shut down in a clean state.
```

# Codeless REST implementation

Repositories created by Spring Data modules can be exposed directly as REST web services without creating the DTO and DAO layers. Since the two STMS portals will be exchanging data for data analysis, we will be exposing some of the repositories as REST endpoints.

Before implementing any repository, a specialized servlet, `org.springframework.data.rest.webmvc.RepositoryRestDispatcherServlet`, must be declared in the `web.xml` file to recognize the module's service exporter APIs. All repository classes must be exposed using the URL pattern associated with the servlet. Assuming that the URL pattern is `/api/*`, the following repository class can retrieve all the records in JSON format through the URL `http://localhost:8080/ch10A/api/posts`, where `posts` is the service endpoint derived from the name of the repository's domain or entity:

```
public interface PostRestRepository
    extends JpaRepository<Post, Integer> { // See the sources }
```

To assign another endpoint name to the repository, the annotation `@RepositoryRestResource` is used, which consists of two attributes: `rel` and `name`. The `path` attribute is the path segment to which the resource is to be exported, while `rel` is the relative value needed to access the resource. The default value of these two attributes is the repository name.

The following snippet shows how to change the `PostRestRepository` interface's endpoint to `/posts`:

```
@RepositoryRestResource(path="posts", rel="posts")
public interface PostRestRepository
    extends JpaRepository<Post, Integer> { // See the sources }
```

To expose the individual method of the repository, the annotation `@RestResource` is applied to each service method.

All REST endpoints generated by Spring Data REST can be validated through the URL `http://localhost:8080/ch10A/api/`, which will list all exposed resources used by the project.

To avoid JSON mapping errors during compilation, it is advisable to implement @RepositoryRestResource for all domain models.

# Enterprise integration architecture

This chapter aims to build two STMS portals that will gather data from separate locations, but in the end will evaluate, analyse, and synthesize all the data gathered by the portals. The communication process between the two must be composed of data passing, computations, remoting, and notifications rolled into one big transaction. Instead of writing a series of complicated web services to simulate the data extraction and exchange workflow, the Spring Integration module is used to pass objects wrapped inside a message, and then tunnels the message from one end to the other. The implementation procedure is decoupled from the main core logic of the applications since Spring Integration follows sets of enterprise integration design patterns that have built-in and ready-to-use endpoint standards such as transformers, filters, splitters, gateways, aggregators, service activators, and adapters. STMS implemented its message banning and violation escalation through channels, gateways, and service activators:

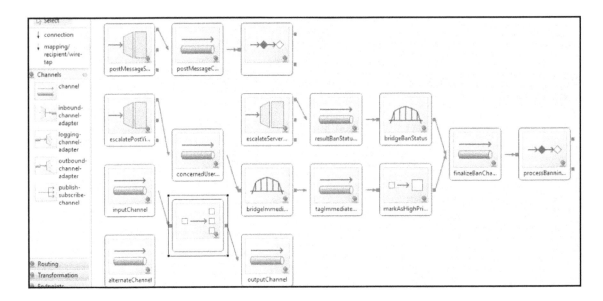

After loading and registering the Spring Integration namespaces, namely
`xmlns:int=http://www.springframework.org/schema/integration` and
`xmlns:int-ws="http://www.springframework.org/schema/integration/ws"`, into
the container, all types of endpoint implementation can be easily accessed to build either
the endpoint-to-endpoint or publisher-subscriber model of communication among
applications.

**Theme design**
The theme design of the application came from the web designers of `http
s://templated.co/`.

# Social task management system

The Spring 4.x Framework has given us excellent solutions for building various applications
with different requirements, from a simple personal portal with fewer data read/write
transactions up to big data applications producing data analysis and reports. Either simple
or complex, this chapter introduced the Spring Data project, in order to provide less
boilerplate code, by building grid-like or clustered social media software interchanging
data, queried by some optimized data search mechanisms:

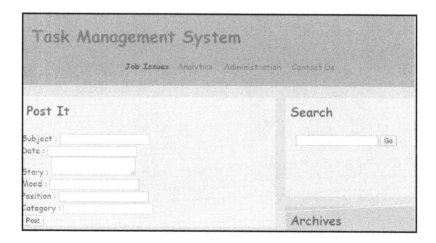

# Challenge yourself

Study how `https://www.surveymonkey.com/` works. Create a custom survey system that gathers data regarding some issues or current events. Make five instances of this portal, deploy them in separate locations, and let them interchange data for data mining.

# Summary

This chapter gives us a clear picture that Spring can deal with all the core concepts discussed in this book through its Spring data modules alone. It has a centralized infrastructure of accessing the data layer with different specific repository support, giving us the abstraction to implement easier query transactions. Spring data saves software development a lot of time from mapping domain objects, to its persistence layer, up to exposing all those records as web services. Moreover, it breaks the misconception that Spring is bulky when it comes to libraries, and complex when we talk about configuration.

# Index

# D